BIRDS OF IRELAND
FACTS, FOLKLORE
& HISTORY

BIRDS OF IRELAND
FACTS, FOLKLORE
❧ & HISTORY ❧

GLYNN ANDERSON

The Collins Press

Published in 2008 by
The Collins Press
West Link Park
Doughcloyne
Wilton
Cork

British Library Cataloguing in Publication Data

Anderson, Glynn
Birds of Ireland : facts, folklore & history
1. Birds - Ireland - Folklore 2. Birds - Ireland -
    Miscellanea
    I. Title
    398.3'698'09415
    ISBN-13: 9781905172726

Design and typesetting by Burns Design
Typeset in Adobe Garamond and Trade Gothic Condensed
Printed in Malta by Gutenberg Press Ltd

Mixed Sources
Product group from well-managed
forests, and other controlled sources
www.fsc.org Cert no. TT-CoC-002424
© 1996 Forest Stewardship Council

The paper used for this book is FSC-certified and
totally chlorine-free. FSC (the Forest Stewardship
Council) is an international network to promote
responsible management of the world's forests.

In memory of
Roy & Anne
to whom I owe everything,

and to Lucy,
my love.

Contents

Facing page: Crane (Grus grus) with stone to stay awake, by Ulisse Aldrovandi (16th Century).
(Courtesy of the University of Bologna Library).

65

THIS BOOK WAS written to complement traditional bird identification guides. It developed from my desire to know more about man's perception of and interaction with birds. Such interaction is in the realm of custom and tradition and is handed down in folklore, myth and belief. While we share some common interaction with birds worldwide, tradition and folklore are very localised. So this book is about the birds of Ireland, where I grew up and reside. For the most part, the information related is Irish lore, except in noted cases where a very interesting story or name from another part of the world begs to be included. The bulk of the book is a species-by-species account of Irish birds. Only the rarest birds are excluded. Our most familiar birds have left the most lore behind and their sections tend to be bigger. Each account describes the species in question and its associated history, myths, traditions, beliefs, culinary aspects, related place names, and alternative English, Irish, Ulster Scots and scientific names. Interesting facts and figures, not normally found in traditional identification guides, complete each account. I hope it brings as much joy to you in reading it as it did to me in researching it.

Readers are encouraged to send Irish bird folklore, alternative names and place names, etc, to folklore@irishbirds.net.

GLYNN ANDERSON

Many people have contributed personal recollections of stories, remembered poems and old bird names. To all of you, I am very grateful. I would particularly like to thank the following: Bert Ahern (Cork), Ann Brennan, Eunice Black, Judith Flynn, Joe Fox, Stephen Hewitt, Mary Higgins, Bríd Kennedy, Gerry Kennedy, Professor Josepha Lanters (University of Wisconsin-Milwaukee), Tom Lynch, Mgr Joseph Maguire, Liz McCarthy, Felix McKillop, Brendan McSherry, Jim Millar, Treasa Ní Ghearraigh, Séamus Ó Coileáin, Professor John O'Halloran (University College Cork), Michael O'Meara, Stephen O'Sullivan, Edward Parker. Thanks to Francis Duggan in Australia for permission to use his poems 'Libby' and 'Gabhairin Reo'. Thanks to Colm Ó Caomhánaigh for use of his online dictionary of bird names in Irish, an excellent resource, and to Ciarán Ó Duibhín for use of his online Ulster Gaelic resource, also excellent (see 'Useful Websites' section for links to both).

Thanks to the Natural History Museum, London, for the use of images from the works of John Gould, forming the bulk of the images used throughout this book.

Thanks to the following individuals and organisations for permission to use copyrighted material in this book: the staff of BirdWatch Ireland, BirdLife International and A&C Black (Poyser) for use of bird population numbers; the authors of *Birds in Europe* (2004) and *Seabird Populations of Britain and Ireland* (2004) (Mitchell, P.I., Newton, S.F., Ratcliffe, N. and Dunn, T.E.,) for results of the *Seabird 2000 Census*; the European Union for Bird Ringing for use of bird longevity records; The Board of Trinity College Dublin for use of an image from the Book of Kells; the Library of the University of Bologna for the use of two images from the works of Ulisse Aldrovandi (su concessione della Biblioteca Universitaria di Bologna); the Pepys Library of Magadalen College, Cambridge, for an image depicting the 'Battle of the Birds' in Cork from a Samuel Pepys madrigal; A. P. Watt Ltd, on behalf of Gráinne Yeats, for excerpts from the poetry of William Butler Yeats; A. M. Heath & Co. Ltd for a portion of *At Swim-Two-Birds* by Flann O'Brien (© Flann O'Brien); R Dardis Clarke, 17 Oscar Square, Dublin 8, for use of *The Blackbird of Derrycairn* by Austin Clarke; Faber and Faber Ltd for use of 'Goatsucker' from *Collected Poems* by Sylvia Plath, © the estate of Sylvia Plath, and portions of 'Serenades' from *Wintering Out* and 'The Yellow Bittern' from *The School Bag*, both by Seamus Heaney, © Seamus Heaney.

Thanks to the staff of the National Botanic Gardens, Dublin, and to my family, Lucy and Lucy Senior, and my brothers for all their advice, support and understanding.

Finally, thanks to the staff of The Collins Press and associated designers, proofreaders and others who worked diligently to bring this book to print.

Cormorant.

1. How to use this Book

The book is written on a species-by-species basis, laid out, in many ways, like a bird identification guide. Wild birds are listed in broadly traditional taxonomic order, with divers and grebes first and passerines (songbirds) last. Following the wild birds is a section on domestic birds, a group very rich in folklore and tradition. Finally, there is a section on birds that were formerly more common in Ireland and that may now be greatly reduced or extinct here.

1.1 SPECIES LAYOUT

Each entry begins with the species' name in English, Irish (e.g. Magpie – Snag breac) and 'scientific' or 'Latinised' (e.g. *Pica pica*). Where known, the subspecies most likely to be seen in Ireland is listed (e.g. *Pica pica pica*). An image of the bird follows. The images provided are of the genre of historical art, and are not recommended for identification purposes. The narrative introduction to the bird starts with a brief description. The description should not be used for identification. The author recommends the use of a good field guide to Irish birds for identification purposes. *The Complete Guide to Ireland's Birds* by Dempsey and O'Clery (Dublin, 2002) is ideal. Any special abilities, unusual attributes or quirks of the bird are listed next. Where interesting, the meaning of the species' name in all three 'languages' is explained. There follows a number of paragraphs regarding history, beliefs, myths, traditions and customs, and weather lore regarding the bird, where these exist. The word 'beliefs' is used rather than 'superstitions', which is somewhat pejorative and in any case, many of the beliefs have at least an echo of truth to them and still pertain today.

Most birds that can be seen in Ireland are included, with only those least encountered by humans excluded. Lore and tradition is about familiarity. So, the more common the bird, the more interaction it has had with humans and the more lore has built up around it. Consequently, some of the birds have entries many pages long, while some may only have a single paragraph. Interesting poems or quotes about the bird may appear next, especially where written by an Irish poet. A number of optional sections may then follow. These include 'Culinary', describing if and how the bird was eaten, 'Place Names', listing some of the places around the country named after the bird in Irish and English. Such place names are from towns, villages and townlands around the country and are by no means exhaustive.

It is hoped that the explanation of the names in Irish will stimulate the reader to look for bird-related place names in his or her own locale. 'Names' lists the alternative names of the species in Irish, English, Ulster Scots and scientific, where available. Names in the English language either were in widespread use in the English-speaking world, including Ireland, or were local to Ireland only. Locally common names from other countries are excluded, with some exceptions. The multiplicity of local names is recorded in the following riddle from Northern Ireland, where each bird is mentioned twice:

> *The cuckoo and the gowk,*
> *The laverock and the lark,*
> *The heather bleat and mire snipe,*
> *How many birds is that?*

Each bird's entry includes a section on 'Facts & Figures'. These are chosen from those that may not be found in conventional bird guide books. For example, the species' population numbers in the Republic of Ireland and their longevity[1] are listed, where known. Population figures are useful in giving a feel for numbers of a species of bird relative to another species. If you are not sure if the sparrow in your garden is a House Sparrow or Tree Sparrow, it helps to know that there are about a million pairs of breeding House Sparrows here but only two to three thousand breeding Tree Sparrows. Any other interesting information regarding the bird is listed here.

Bird population numbers are taken from BirdLife International's (2007) species factsheets, downloaded from www.birdlife.org. For the most part, breeding bird numbers in the Republic of Ireland are shown. In a few places, wintering numbers in Ireland are shown, where these are available. In each case, the period during which the original bird count was made is documented, e.g. Great Northern Diver: 1,400 wintering birds (94–00). Note that some figures are for the total number of birds and some are for pairs, as noted. The breeding numbers derive originally from national surveys, published in a number of atlases of breeding and wintering birds, starting back in 1968. Specifically, the sources used by BirdLife International include *The New Atlas of Breeding Birds in Britain and Ireland* (1988–1991), Poyser 1993; *The Atlas of Wintering Birds in Britain and Ireland*, Poyser, Carlton, 1986; I-WeBS data from BirdWatch Ireland and the Seabird 2000 census (1998–2002).

1.2 IMAGES

Images used in this book are taken from ornithological books printed mostly in the nineteenth century. A number of sources are used. Over half of the images are from books written by the English ornithologist John Gould (1804–1881). These images are courtesy of the Natural History Museum, London. Most are taken from lithographs from *Birds of Europe* (1837, five volumes) and *The Birds of Great Britain* (1862–73). The images are by Gould himself, his wife Elizabeth and by others including the poet Edward Lear, Henry Constantine Richter, Joseph Wolf, William Hart and Gabriel Bayfield.

A number of images have been taken from the work of the von Wright brothers, Wilhelm (1810–1887) and Magnus (1805–1868). Their most noted work was *Svenska Fåglar* (Swedish Birds) published in 1838.

A number of images are from the works of Rev Francis Orpen Morris (1810–1893). Morris was born in Cork and spent much of his early life in Kerry. His family moved to England when he was fourteen. Most of Morris' books were written by him but illustrated by Alexander Lydon. Woodblock colour printing was used. Some were coloured by hand. Morris' images in this book are taken from *A Natural History of British Birds* (six vols, 1850–1857). Compared to Gould's images, Morris' are somewhat plain and academic but they have a special beauty of their own.

The remaining images are taken from the works of Archibald Thorburn Charles D'Orbigny, Henrick Grönvold, Sir William Jardine, John Gerrard Keulemans, Henry Leonard Meyer, Johann Friedrich Naumann, Prideaux John Selby, Edouard Travies and Harrison Weir.

1.3 CONVENTIONS

Most 'beliefs' are referred to in the past, even though in some cases the belief may still pertain today. For the most part, each species of bird is referred to in the plural. This is a move away from the traditional way of referring to a species as a single bird. Thus, wherever possible, for example, 'the Starling' is referred to as 'Starlings' or 'a Starling'.

1.4 ABBREVIATIONS USED IN 'NAMES' SECTIONS

Ach.	Achill Island		LN.	Lough Neagh
Ant.	County Antrim		Lou.	County Louth
Arm.	County Armagh		Ltm.	County Leitrim
Aran.	Aran Islands		mal.	male
AS.	Anglo-Saxon		May.	County Mayo
Bel.	Belfast		Mea.	County Meath
BL.	Belfast Lough		Mona.	County Monaghan
c.	coast		Mun.	Munster
Car.	County Carlow		NA.	North America
Cav.	County Cavan		ne.	northeast
CI.	Clare Island, County Mayo		nw.	northwest
Cla.	County Clare		Off.	County Offaly
Conn.	Connacht		Omt.	Omeath
Conm.	Connemara		per.	perhaps
Cck.	Carrickfergus		poe.	poetic
Crk.	County Cork		Ros.	County Roscommon
Der.	County Derry		Scan.	Scandinavia
Din.	Dingle, County Kerry		Sco.	Scotland
Don.	County Donegal		Sha.	Shannon River
Dow.	County Down		Skl.	Skelligs
Drg.	Drogheda		SL.	Strangford Lough
Dub.	County Dublin		Sli.	County Sligo
Eng.	England		stan.	standardised
Eur.	Europe		UK	United Kingdom
fem.	female		Uls.	Ulster
Fer.	County Fermanagh		US	United States
Gal.	County Galway		Tipp.	County Tipperary
HH.	Horn Head		Tory.	Tory Island
inc.	incorrect		Tra.	Tralee
Insh.	Inishowen, County Donegal		Tyr.	County Tyrone
inl.	inland		Wal.	Wales
Kilk.	County Kilkenny		Wat.	County Waterford
Kry.	County Kerry		Wex.	County Wexford
Lar.	Larne, County Antrim		Wic.	County Wicklow
Lim.	County Limerick		Wth.	County Westmeath
LI.	Lambay Island		yng.	young

2. An Overview of the History & Folklore of Irish Birds

2.1 A BRIEF HISTORY OF BIRDS IN IRELAND

The Ice Age

A review of the history of birds in Ireland must start before they were here. With the onset of the last Ice Age, around 30,000 BC, anything that was living here was completely eradicated. Until about 12,000 BC, Ireland was almost entirely covered with a sheet of ice. Life must have been minimal but perhaps some Arctic birds made their homes here. The Ice Age ended with a slow withdrawal of ice from south to north. We can imagine that some seabirds, with their ability to fly, were the first animals to re-colonise and take advantage of the warming conditions. Sea levels were low because of the amount of frozen water, and animals and small birds must have crossed on a land bridge between Ireland and Europe. When all the ice had melted, Ireland became an island again and small sedentary bird species no longer colonised the country. Today we are left with an avifauna of considerably fewer species than Britain, which in turn has fewer species than continental Europe. As an isolated island on the edge of Europe, we are simply too far away, too hard to access and have too few distinct habitats.

The Stone Age

With the ice gone, rugged grasses began to grow again, followed by trees. Birds, and animals such as Giant Deer that had made it across the land bridge, would have had the island to themselves, untroubled by man. The first humans in Ireland were hunter-gatherers who arrived probably around 8000–7000 BC from Britain, and initially made their settlements close to water. Most of the island would have been covered with forest and was impenetrable at this time. The settlers hunted birds and other animals with bows, spears and harpoons made from flint. With the arrival of the New Stone Age (Neolithic) in about 4000 BC, farming began to develop. Yet birds were still hunted and bird domestication probably came much later. This status quo continued right through the Bronze Age (2000 BC –500 BC) and the arrival of the Iron Age (500 BC) and the Celts.

Middens

The history of human interaction with birds in Ireland starts with the bone evidence of birds found in caves and later in kitchen midden deposits. Middens were dumps of domestic waste, which yet yield evidence of what our ancestors were eating. They date from the time of early hunter-gatherers (several thousand years BC) right through to the Middle Ages. In such dumps, we find evidence of a lot of the common birds we see today in Ireland and of some birds that are no longer here. For a review of these lost birds, see Section 5.

The Celts

The Celts and their religion probably survived until about AD 400, when Christianity came to Ireland. In the meantime, the Romans conquered Britain around AD 43 but never invaded Ireland. The Celts and their druids placed enormous importance on the augury of birds. A first-century bowl or cup from Keshcarrigan, County Leitrim has an elongated bird as a handle. Birds were believed to be other-worldly and messengers of the gods. The Celts watched them carefully and predicted the future by how they flew, how they called and when they appeared and disappeared. The prejudice against eating goose flesh in parts of Ireland may date from the time of the Celts who held geese and other domestic fowl sacred. In Greece, at this time, first Aristotle (fourth century BC) and then Pliny the Elder[1] (AD 23– AD 79), a few hundred years later, were writing down the first observations, descriptions and classifications of birds.

The Domestication of Birds

It was probably not until the first few hundred years AD, that domesticated geese and chickens came to Ireland, probably through Celtic trade with the Romans. Some suggest domestic chickens did not arrive here until the Vikings brought them. Before domestication, birds would have been hunted with bows, spears and with traps. Some birds would have been kept in sacred enclosures for religious purposes. It was an easy progression to keep them for food. It is likely that Ireland teemed with wildlife right up to the end of the Middle Ages in the sixteenth century. Bird populations were probably quite large, feeding on an unexploited cornucopia of fish, insects and wild plants.

Facing page: Folio from the Book of Kells with St John depicted as an eagle in the bottom right corner. (Courtesy of the Manuscripts Department of Trinity College Library, Dublin).

The Coming of Christianity

The arrival of Christianity by AD 400, brought many changes. As was the case in many countries, Christianity took many of the extant religious traditions and adopted and adapted them to its own use. The druidic feast days, Imbolg, Bealtaine, Lughnasa and Samhain were adapted to Christian festivals and stories and legends about birds became stories and legends about Christianity and birds. Many stories of birds attending to Christ and the saints can be found throughout this book. Irish Christian monks of the early Middle Ages wrote about Christianity and about nature. Their poetry is still fresh and descriptive of the birds and other animals around them. From the period of the seventh to the ninth centuries, their most important graphic work survives in works such as the Book of Kells and Book of Durrow. These books are brilliantly decorated often with birds and other animal symbols.

Other Irish artefacts were depicted with birds. Herons appear on the Ardagh Chalice (ninth century). Many high crosses are adorned with birds. A tiny sixth/seventh century gold filigree bird, probably a Wren, was found during Michael J. O'Kelly's excavation of a ringfort in Garryduff, County Cork in 1946.

The Vikings & the Normans

The next major change for Ireland was the coming of the Vikings towards the end of the first millennium. They brought their Raven gods with them, often displayed on flags and banners. They also brought domesticated chickens in large numbers. Not long after the Vikings came the Normans. They brought domesticated ducks, semi-domesticated Mute Swans and peacocks and, perhaps, Pheasants. They also brought something new for the Irish nobility: falconry. Falconry had been introduced to England by the Saxons, at least by the eighth century. With the sport of falconry came a certain managed protection for birds of prey that was to last to the end of the seventeenth century. Falconry did not really take off in this country to the extent it did in others, but Irish birds of prey were highly valued and were exported to Europe and given away as high-value gifts.

Gerald of Wales

The Normans also brought with them Giraldus Cambrensis aka Gerald de Barry aka Gerald of Wales. Gerald was a Norman monk and something of an explorer and author. He could also be called, perhaps, the first birdwatcher in Ireland. Gerald wrote about his travels here, particularly in his *Topographia Hiberniae*, part of which might be described as the first Irish birdbook. While he was something of a dreamer and was not too complimentary to the contemporary Irish, his work includes a fascinating description of many Irish birds and their habits. It is available today in English translation and is referred to in many places in this book.

The Renaissance

Not much happened in Ireland, from an ornithological point of view, for the next few hundred years. The very beginnings of modern ornithology were seen during the Renaissance (fifteenth to seventeenth centuries) but it was not until the eighteenth century that it really took off, and developed yet further in the nineteenth century. During the Renaissance, a new breed of naturalists returned to the ancient practices of direct observation of plants and animals. This early interest focussed on nomenclature and classification. A few writers in the sixteenth century, Pierre Belon, Konrad Gesner, Guillaume Rondelet, Francis Willughby and John Ray, wrote considerable works on birds. The Italian naturalist, Ulisse Aldrovandi (Aldrovandus) (1522–1605) whom Linnaeus called 'the father of natural history', collected 7,000 natural history specimens and wrote several important works on 'Ornithologiae'. The English naturalist William Turner (1508–1568) is sometimes called the 'father of English botany' and was perhaps the first 'modern' ornithologist. He is remembered for, amongst other things, writing the first printed book entirely about birds.[2] Willughby (1635–1672) and Ray (1627–1705) worked together on one of the first major classification systems. Their work *Ornithologiae libri tres* (1676) is regarded as one of the most important early works of scientific ornithology. Ray has become known as the 'father of English natural history'. Dutch-born Gerard Boate (1604–1650) wrote *Ireland's Naturall History*, published in 1652. Though a wonderful historic work, it was filled with myth and hearsay and was far from scientific, and bore a dedication to Cromwell! Philip O'Sullivan Beare (1590–1634/1660) wrote his *Zoilomastix*,[3] a defence of Irish culture, around 1626, in Latin and with bird names written in Irish. An Englishman, Fynes Moryson (1566–1630) travelled through Ireland and wrote about what he saw, including our birds, in one volume of *An Itinerary*. This was later republished as a *History of Ireland* (1599–1603) in 1735.[4]

Up to this period, birds of all kinds were referred to as 'fowl'. The word 'bird' itself was only used for the smallest songbirds and for young birds.

Barnacle Geese 'hatching' from a Barnacle Tree, Ulisse Aldrovandi 16th Century. (Courtesy of the University of Bologna Library).

Guns

Towards the end of the seventeenth and beginning of the eighteenth centuries two important things began to happen. Interest in falconry began to wane while the keeping of game for shooting began to increase, in parallel with the development of better muskets and ultimately, a type of shotgun known as a 'fowling piece'. Birds of prey rapidly changed from heroes to villains. Soon, birds of all kinds were being shot in massive numbers and shotguns became bigger and bigger. By the nineteenth century, punt guns had been invented. These large-bore guns (over two inches) fired over half a kilo of shot at a time. They were mounted directly on punt boats and were aimed by pointing the whole boat, though accuracy was unnecessary. One particular gun, 'Irish Tom' was fourteen feet long, weighed three hundred pounds, had a bore of over two inches and fired three pounds (1.4 kg) of shot at a time. It was used up to the 1930s in Ireland. Unbelievable numbers of wildfowl were 'harvested' for commercial operations and just for 'sport'. Hundreds could be killed with just one shot. Though banned in the US in the nineteenth century, bores of up to 1.75 inches are still legal in the UK today. Sir Ralph Payne-Gallwey (1848–1916) was a major advocate of the 'sport' of fowling and wrote an important work, *The Fowler in Ireland,* in 1882. Despite being a manual for killing birds in every way, the book provides a valuable account of our birds and their provincial names. His record of thousands of birds killed every year by the sporting gun leaves us in no doubt as to why our feathered friends are shy of human company.

The Eighteenth Century

By the eighteenth century, scientific ornithology had really begun to take off. A whole book could be and indeed has been written on the Swedish naturalist Carl Linnaeus (1707–1778) aka Carolus Linnaeus aka Carl von Linné. Although he worked primarily with plants, he identified and renamed a large number of our familiar birds. His development and establishment of the binomial system of naming (*e.g. Genus species*) revolutionised the study of the natural world and is still used today. Around this time, the picture becomes clouded by the huge number of people who became interested in natural history and ornithology. In Britain, the naturalist George Edwards (1694–1773) wrote a number of important works on the history of birds and became known as the 'father of British ornithology'. Others who made considerable contributions to ornithology during this period included Mark Catesby (1683–1749), Georges de Buffon (1707–1788), Gilbert White (1720–1793), Mathurin Brisson (1723–1806), Thomas Pennant (1726–1798), Morten Thrane Brunnich (1737–1827), John Latham (1740–1837), William Lewin (1747–1795), Johann Gmelin (1748 –1804), Louis Pierre Vieillot (1748–

1831), George Montagu (1752–1815), Thomas Bewick (1753–1828) and Coenraad Jacob Temminck (1778–1858). There are many more but space and legibility preclude inclusion. The only Irish naturalist of note, active at the time, was Belfast man John Templeton (1766–1825). Templeton is often referred to as the 'father of Irish Botany' and was also a keen ornithologist.

The Nineteenth Century

The flurry of activity of the eighteenth century was nothing compared to that which came with the dawn of the nineteenth century. In the developed world, ornithology in the modern sense became established. It became a hobby of the well-to-do with free time on their hands. The clergy in particular were heavily involved. The hobby of birdwatching developed hand-in-hand with the science of ornithology and both expanded greatly into the twentieth and twenty-first centuries. The availability of binoculars and cameras towards the end of the nineteenth century made birdwatching more interesting and eventually brought it to a wider audience. Birdwatchers could now look at birds up close without shooting them, although many still did.

A scientific approach to nature took centre stage. The British Ornithologist's Union (BOU) was formed in 1858 and the Royal Society for the Protection of Birds (RSPB) in 1889. Explorers, travelling to the far corners of the world and bringing home exotic species, encouraged a new interest in birds and natural history. In Ireland too, for the first time perhaps since Gerald of Wales, several works appeared about Irish birds. As already mentioned, the development of the gun led people to shoot and collect birds in large numbers. Eggs were also collected for study purposes. Many new species were described and named. The variations and similarities of birds across the world were noted and many explanations appeared. By the very end the nineteenth century, the first bird ringing had taken place in Denmark and Germany.

Perhaps the only naturalist who can be said to have had more of an influence than Linnaeus was Charles Darwin (1809–1882). Darwin changed the world with his theory of natural selection and evolution, described in his book of 1859, *The Origin of Species*. His work was influenced in part by the observation of the finches and their bills in the Galápagos archipelago. Several other influential bird books appeared in the Victorian period. In the US, the Scottish–American Alexander Wilson (1766–1813) made a name for himself with *American Ornithology* published at the end of his life. He has a number of birds named after him including Wilson's Petrel and Wilson's Phalarope. He became known eventually as the 'father of American ornithology'. To some extent, Wilson paved the way for John James

Audubon (1785–1851), the most famous American ornithologist. As was the way at the time, Audubon shot thousands of birds as subjects for his illustrations. His *Birds of America* was first published between 1827 and 1838.

The English naturalist William Yarrell (1784–1856) wrote a number of books including *The History of British Birds* (1843) which became the standard reference work of the day. The White Wagtail (*Motacilla alba yarrellii*) is named after him. The English ornithologist and artist Prideaux John Selby (1788–1867) produced a number of illustrated bird books as did the Scottish naturalist Sir William Jardine (1800–1874). Another Scottish naturalist, William MacGillivray (1796–1852), wrote an number of important books on birds and advised Audubon. The English ornithologist John Gould (1804–1881), who assisted Darwin in his studies, produced a number of beautifully illustrated and lithographed books. These included the *Birds of Europe* (1837) and *The Birds of Australia* (1848). The illustrations from some of these books are reproduced in this book. Gould's illustrations were created by a series of artists including the poet Edward Lear (1812–1888), Henry Richter (1821–1902), Joseph Wolf (1820–1899) and Gould's wife, Elizabeth. Another ornithologist, Rev Francis Orpen Morris (1810–1893), was born in Cork and lived most of his young life in Ireland. He wrote a number of books on birds, including *A History of British Birds* (1850), which were illustrated by Alexander Lydon (1836–1917). Some of his illustrations also appear in this book. The Scottish ornithological artist, Archibald Thorburn (1860–1935), studied with Joseph Wolf and illustrated numerous bird books of the day including *Coloured Figures of the Birds of the British Isles*, by Thomas Powys (Lord Lilford, 1833–1896).

Irish Ornithology in Modern Times

'He does not know a Hawk from a Handsaw.'[5]

In Ireland, Belfast man William Thompson (1805–1852) wrote extensively for nature periodicals of the day and produced the *Natural History of Ireland* in three volumes between 1849 and 1851. Thompson, a member of the Belfast Natural History Society founded in 1821, produced perhaps the first comprehensive list of Irish birds. He was followed by John Watters, who produced the *Natural History of Birds of Ireland* in 1853. The Rev Charles William Benson (1836–1919), one-time headmaster of Rathmines School, Dublin, and rector of Balbriggan, produced the delightful *Our Irish Song Birds* in 1886. An Englishman, Alexander Goodman More (1830–1895), who later became Keeper of Natural History at the National Museum, produced lists of Irish birds in 1885 and 1890, as well as important botanical publications.

In 1900, a number of important works were produced in Ireland. Irish naturalists Richard John Ussher (1841–1913) and Robert Warren (1829–1915) produced *Birds of Ireland* while Richard Manliffe Barrington (1849–1915) produced *Migration of Birds as Observed at Irish Lighthouses and Lightships*. Ussher and Warren's *Birds of Ireland* was originally planned to be penned in association with More and Barrington but More fell ill and Barrington chose to work on his own book. In 1904, Ussher helped to found the Irish Society for the Protection of Birds (ISPB), which later helped to introduce the Wild Birds (Protection) Act of 1930 and later still became part of the Irish Wildbird Conservancy. Barrington's work was particularly interesting. He organised bird migration watches at fifty-eight lighthouses and lightships around Ireland from 1881 to 1897. The movements of tens of thousands of individual birds were reported by light keepers, interpreted by himself and published in 1900.

The most famous Irish naturalist of the twentieth century was undoubtedly Robert Lloyd Praeger (1865–1953). Praeger was a true naturalist in the wide sense of the word. He co-founded *The Irish Naturalist* and produced a number of works on Irish natural history including the narrative *The Way that I Went* in 1937 and a *Natural History of Ireland* in 1950. He was the first president of *An Taisce* (the National Trust for Ireland). Praeger passed the baton to a number of Irish naturalists including Father P. G. Kennedy, Major Robert (Robin) Francis Ruttledge (1899–2002) and Lt. Col. Charles F. Scroope. Between them, they produced a number of important works but are remembered mostly for the *Birds of Ireland*, published in 1954. Ruttledge also started the *Irish Bird Report* in 1953 and published *Ireland's Birds* in 1966, which became the standard reference book of its time. He set up the first bird observatory on the Saltee Islands and helped with the acquisition and creation of the Wexford Slobs. Ruttledge helped to found the Irish Wildbird Conservancy (IWC) in 1968 and was its first president. The IWC was formed from the amalgamation of the Irish Society for the Protection of Birds (ISPB), the Irish Ornithologists' Club (founded 1950) and the Irish Wildfowl Committee.[6] Today, the IWC trades as BirdWatch Ireland. In Northern Ireland, the interests of birds are looked after by the Northern Ireland Ornithologists' Club, set up in 1965, the RSPB Northern Ireland and the Ulster Wildlife Trust. C. Douglas Deane wrote the *Handbook of the Birds of Northern Ireland*, published in Belfast in 1954.

In 'modern' times, a number of Irish authors have produced excellent guide books to Irish birds. These include David Cabot, Don Conroy, Gordon D'Arcy, Eric Dempsey, Clive Hutchinson, Oscar Merne, Killian Mullarney, Michael O'Clery, Oran O'Sullivan and Jim Wilson. In the 1960s, 1970s and 1980s, nature shows on RTÉ, such as Éamon de Buitléar's *Amuigh Faoin Spéir* and Gerrit van Gelderen's *To the Waters and the Wild*, kept Irish people in touch with nature. The RTÉ radio show,

Mooney Goes Wild, has helped to open up nature to a wider audience. Recreational ornithology continues to become more popular in Ireland and BirdWatch Ireland has a number of affiliated local branches around the country. Many who are involved in recreational bird watching today are becoming more and more involved in bird and habitat conservation and in lobbying government from local to European level. Such lobbying led to the introduction of the Wildlife Acts of 1976 and 2000 in the Republic of Ireland and the Wildlife (Northern Ireland) Order 1985 (Amended 1995).

For the scientifically minded, ornithology courses are available. Professor John O'Halloran of University College Cork, leads the largest ornithological research group in Ireland. As well as bird modules in Zoology and Ecology, Professor O'Halloran's group runs PhD research programmes on a number of species including Barn Owls, Choughs, Corncrakes, Crows, Dippers, Song Thrushes, Stonechats, Mute and Whooper Swans, and woodland birds, farmland birds and bird population trends. Ornithology modules of one kind or another are available from most of the other universities in Ireland under the guise of zoology or ecology.

Irish birds face an uncertain future. On the negative side, human development is seriously threatening their existence. Many birds, once common, are critically reduced in numbers and some face extinction. On the positive side, more and more people are becoming interested in birds and the natural world as a whole. More people are lobbying on behalf of birds and the environment and there is a greater awareness of the global threat from climate change and the need for all of us to make changes, to save our natural world and, ultimately, our planet and ourselves. Perhaps we can avoid the sort of Ireland inadvertently foreseen by Lane in *Caoine Cill Cháis* (Lament for Kilcash) written in the eighteenth century:

Ní chluinim fuaim lachan ná gé ann,
ná fiolar ag éamh cois cuain,
ná fiú na mbeacha chun saothair
thabharfadh mil agus céir don tslua.
Níl ceol binn milis na n-éan ann
le hamharc an lae ag dul uainn,
náan chuaichín i mbarra na ngéag ann,
ós í chuirfeadh an saol chun suain.

Ducks' voices nor geese do I hear there,
nor the eagle's cry over the bay,
nor even the bees at their labour
bringing honey and wax to us all.
No birdsong there, sweet and delightful,
as we watch the sun go down,
nor cuckoo on the top of the branches
settling the world to rest.

Pepys – Battle of the Birds – Cork, 1621 (Courtesy of the Pepys Library, Magdalene College, Cambridge).

2.2 BIRDS AS PREDICTORS OF THE FUTURE

'No one knows better than a bird of the air where treasures are concealed.'[1]

What the Greeks called ornithomancy, the Romans called augury: the ability to predict the future from watching birds. Roman priests, called Augurs, interpreted the will of the gods by analysing the flight of birds. Such signs from the gods were called auspices.[2] A favourable auspice was *auspicious* and an unfavourable one *inauspicious* and these terms still pertain today. Augurs were *inaugurated* and this term still pertains to the setting up in office of a new official. The expansion of the Roman Empire helped to push the Celts to the western fringes of Europe and Ireland. The Celts and their druids brought bird divination with them but it is not clear if they learnt it from Greco-Roman civilisation or vice versa. While we may still predict the weather from the flight and song of birds, all aspects of the future were once predicted by birds. In some cases birds were thought to bring specific messages from the gods. In Ireland, Blackbirds, Ravens, Wrens and Starlings were among the birds used for divination. Indeed the Starling's Irish name *druid* may be very ancient. Most of these birds were dark if not black. All black birds were associated with the 'Other World' beyond the lives of mortal beings. Later, with the arrival of Christianity, they were associated with the devil. In an Irish text dated c. AD 900–1200, twenty-eight different prognostications are given which could be deduced from a Raven's behaviour while nine different Raven calls are related and their significance pointed out.[3]

15

As in other countries, when Christianity arrived in Ireland, instead of completely wiping out the aboriginal Celtic beliefs, many of them were adapted and adopted into Christian lore. Thus the feast of St Brigid (1 February) may be a Christian version of the feast of the Celtic goddess Brigit (*Imbolg*). Michaelmas (29 September), celebrating the Archangel Michael, may be a continuation of the Celtic celebration of the autumnal equinox (*Lá Leathach an Fhómhair*) and Martinmas (the feast of St Martin of Tours, 11 November) when the blood of a goose or cock was spilt and spread around the house, may reflect an ancient Celtic ritual.

Divination from birds remains in Irish culture to the present day. Though our lives no longer revolve around the flight of birds, we still believe, to some extent, in bird-divined weather lore and our old belief systems are still preserved in our rich use of proverbs in both the Irish and English languages.

2.3 BIRDS IN IRISH MYTHOLOGY

Before the era of modern birdwatching, man's interaction with birds was a much more mystical practice. Birds were literally beyond our grasp. From prehistory we have seen birds as messengers from the 'other side', as pests, as objects of beauty and of course as food. Their ability, beyond ours, to fly has imbued them with an other-worldly magic. In pre-Christian times, many birds were associated with gods and heroic figures. Crows were associated with war and death and the gods Badhbh, Macha and the Morrigan. It was a crow of some kind which landed on the shoulder of Cúchulainn to show that he was finally dead. Ravens were also associated with Cúchulainn's father Lugh. Herons (and/or Cranes), Cormorants and sometimes owls were associated with both the Cailleach witch and the sea god Manannán Mac Lir. Manannán's father, Lear himself, was associated with wild swans through the story of the Children of Lir. Aengus of the Tuatha Dé Danann, sometimes regarded as the god of love, was said to have four birds, symbolising kisses, above his head. Clíona, the Irish goddess of love and beauty and banshee queen of the Munster fairies had three brightly coloured birds who ate apples from an other-worldly tree and whose song could induce sleep and heal the sick. In the historical cycle of Irish mythology, the story of Buile Shuibhne tells the story of Sweeney, an Irish king who is turned into a half-man, half-bird creature by St Ronan before eventually being killed with a spear.

2.4 BIRDS AS FOOD

If we were not using birds to divine the future, we were eating them. We have probably eaten birds and their eggs for as long as we have lived side by side. Archaeologists use the term 'midden' for an old domestic waste dump. Bones of numerous species of bird have been found in middens at several sites in Ireland. With the exception of a few poisonous birds from New Guinea, all birds are edible. However, their degree of edibility can vary greatly. Many fish-eating birds were regarded as close to inedible because of their diet. In times of want, though, everything was 'fair game'. If you could catch it you could eat it. Catching animals that can fly has never been easy. Stones, spears, arrows and later guns and nets have been used to catch and kill flying birds and some birds could be caught on the ground with traps and by stealth. If you had the time, the easiest way to source an avian meal was to raid a nest and raise the chicks. This was the beginning of the domestication of birds.

Since at least the time of the Normans, the hunting and consumption of 'game' birds has been regulated and largely kept as the reserve of the nobility. Exotic birds like peacocks and Mute Swans were introduced by the Normans and kept semi-domestically and eaten on special occasions. The ownership of a Mute Swan was stamped on its bill. The poor had to do with whatever they could catch legally or poach. In the time of the Great Famine, bird numbers dropped greatly and did not recover for many years. Now in the twenty-first century most non-vegetarians eat a small number of farmed birds in huge numbers; chickens, turkeys, ducks and geese are the most common with some domesticated quail and birds new to farming like Ostrich and guineafowl. A small percentage of the population still eat semi-domesticated game birds like Pheasant, grouse, Woodcock and partridge.

Today's domestic chickens are descendents of wild Asian Jungle Fowl (*Gallus gallus*) brought to Ireland initially by trade with the Romans and later, in big numbers, by the Vikings. Domestic geese are descended from wild Greylag Geese (*Anser anser*) and were probably introduced to Ireland in the first few centuries AD. Domestic ducks came later with the Normans and domestic turkeys may not have arrived until the eighteenth century. Pigeons were reared in dovecotes since the time of the Romans and are now served in high-end restaurants as squab. Geese were particular favourites for all who could get their hands on them and they were often eaten on special days like St Michael's Day (Michaelmas, 29 September, *Fómhar na nGéanna*) and St Martin's Day (Martinmas, 11 November). It was said that if you ate a goose on Michaelmas Day, you would not want not for money for the rest of the year. No part of a goose was spared: goose feathers were used for pillows, quilts and mattresses, quills were used for writing and fishing floats, the eggs for baking, grease (*úsc gé*) for baking and polishing, the wings for dusting and the blood for soup and 'goose pudding'. Goose grease or 'goose-seam/goosame' rubbed into the chest was also regarded as good for any pulmonary ailment and was used for general muscle pains.[1] It became the woman's job to husband the poultry. Women would often barter fowl and their eggs at fairs and gained some financial independence in this way.

Every wild bird in Ireland has been eaten at one time or another, especially in times of want. Eggs were also eaten but those of the bigger birds were favoured. Some birds were particularly favoured and some were particularly disliked.

Of the smaller birds, Blackcaps, Yellowhammers, Snow Buntings and Wheatears were considered especially good to eat. Sand Martins were also eaten. Thrushes of all kinds were always caught and eaten.

Of the bigger birds it was generally regarded as being best to eat younger birds as the old were tough and stringy. This was true of Rooks, swans, geese, Gannets and Storm Petrels (which were known as 'mutton birds'). Most water birds were eaten. Some, whose diet consisted entirely of fish or other marine creatures, were regarded as close to inedible because of their fishy texture. These included divers, grebes, Shelduck, scoter, mergansers, Cormorants and Shags. Most favoured water birds were the swans, geese, ducks and herons. Brent Geese were regarded as the finest geese to eat and Pintails were regarded as the finest ducks to eat. Pochard, Shoveler, Goldeneye, Tufted Duck, Scaup, Teal, Gadwall, Wigeon, Eider, Coot, Moorhen and Water Rails were also eaten and the unfortunate Corncrakes, now a rarity, were considered a delicacy. Shearwaters, Fulmars and, in olden days, Bitterns were also eaten. Tough old birds, particularly Bean and White-fronted Geese were used to make giblet soup.

Of the waders, Lapwings were eaten extensively in Ireland, usually roasted or in pies.[2] Their eggs (*uibheacha Pilibín*) were considered a delicacy, as were those of Oystercatchers. The rare Dotterels were eaten and considered a delicacy. Their unwillingness to flee has probably led to their rarity. Probably the most highly regarded waders for the table were the Golden Plovers, regarded as having a more delicate flavour than their cousins, the Grey Plovers.[3] Knot were the most highly regarded of the small waders.[4] Godwits were eaten and their name may derive from 'good-to-eat'. Redshank were thought of as close to inedible. Snipe and Jack Snipe, while wild, are regarded as game birds. Both were highly prized for the table. All parts of a Snipe were eaten except the gizzard. Even Snipes' long bills were eaten roasted. Their larger cousins, Woodcock, were especially regarded and are still hunted. Most of the innards were eaten and the brain regarded as a particular delicacy.

Most gulls and terns were eaten in times of want but were avoided at other times because it was believed they carried the souls of dead sailors. Black-headed Gull eggs were eaten in large numbers which led to a decline in the species. Similarly

Sandwich Tern eggs were eaten. Most auks and their eggs were eaten. People living along the Atlantic coast often undertook perilous missions to seasonally hunt auks and other seabirds and their highly nutritious eggs from near-inaccessible cliff ledges. Men would lower themselves down sheer cliffs on ropes. At Carrick-a-Rede near the Giant's Causeway, County Antrim, men lowered themselves in cradles from ropes flung across to the sea stack. On nearby Rathlin Island strips of cliffs and slopes were apportioned to individual collectors. Similar seasonal hunts occurred on the Aran Islands off Galway and the Blaskets off Kerry. Many seabirds were salted to be eaten later or sold on the mainland. Guillemots and Puffins were more favoured than Razorbills. Puffins were particularly favoured in soups in Ireland and were regarded as a delicacy despite their fishy taste. Younger birds were favoured. They were barbecued on tongs with a piece of burning turf or cinder to absorb the excess fat.

The Christian Bible was clear about what birds could and could not be eaten. In Leviticus 11 we read:

And these are they which ye shall have in abomination among the fowls;
they shall not be eaten, they are an abomination: the eagle, and the ossifrage,
and the ospray,
And the vulture, and the kite after his kind;
Every raven after his kind;
And the owl, and the night hawk, and the cuckoo, and the hawk after his kind,
And the little owl, and the cormorant, and the great owl,
And the swan, and the pelican, and the gier eagle,
And the stork, the heron after her kind, and the lapwing, and the bat.

This chapter and the culinary entries for each species in this book record the historical practice of eating wild birds but are in no way an endorsement of the practice. The hunting and disturbance of wild birds and their young and nests is now outlawed on the island of Ireland by the Wildlife Acts of 1976 and 2000[5] in the Republic of Ireland and the Wildlife (Northern Ireland) Order 1985 (Amended 1995). Almost all of our wild birds are now protected by these acts save for some which are classified as game or pest birds and some for which special permission is required for hunting seasonally.

2.5 BIRD FOLKLORE THEMES

Through researching bird folklore and beliefs, a number of recurring themes and trends becomes evident. These may be categorised as: weather lore, beliefs about migration, birds bearing warnings, birds as signs of good and bad luck, birds used for food, health and cures and other general beliefs. These themes are described in detail here with the exception of birds as food (see Section 2.4). In addition, Ireland's rich language has preserved many proverbs and similes and these are listed too.

2.5.1 GENERAL BELIEFS

'Ná creid feannóg is ná creid fiach.'[1]

Beliefs about birds have changed through time. In prehistory, birds were seen as messengers from the 'Other World' and played an important role in society. Now, in an increasingly urban world, birds are being more and more marginalised. In the interim, beliefs have been changing. Birds of the night like owls and Nightjars and black birds like crows and swifts were at best mistrusted or else regarded as downright evil. Owls were messengers to the 'Other World' but could guide us to it and through it. To counter the evil influence of an owl, people put irons in their fires or threw salt, hot peppers or vinegar into the fire. In doing so, the owl would get a sore tongue, hoot no more, and no one close would be in trouble.[2]

Swallows and martins were regarded as supernatural beings, yet were generally well loved and not associated with the devil like Swifts or wagtails. If a Swallow or its nest were disturbed, the cows' milk would turn to blood.[3] Similarly, in County Wexford, it was believed that if a martin's nest was destroyed, the cows' milk would be tainted with blood.[4] It was also considered bad manners to destroy a martin's nest while it was migrating abroad[5] but in any case, a martin would never build its nest on a house where there was strife.[6] If a Swallow nested in your barn it would not be hit by lightning as long as the nest was there. It was also believed that a cat would not kill a Swallow.[7] While on the subject of nests, by tradition, Rooks were supposed to start building their nests on 1 May, but if this fell on a Sunday they would wait until the following day.[8]

Crows generated their fair share of beliefs, mostly of the dark kind. It was said that a baby would die if a Raven's eggs were stolen. It was also said that if Jackdaws did not frequent a ruined castle or tower, then it was surely haunted.

In England, it was believed to kill a Raven or Chough was to harm the spirit of King Arthur who visited the world in this form. Choughs are protected in Cornwall, for this reason.[9]

Wagtails, the gypsy birds, were also regarded as birds of the devil. Their eggs were never touched. The constant bobbing of the birds' tails and their somewhat 'upright' attitude was regarded as impure and gained them the reputation of being the devil's minions and the name 'Devil's Bird'.[10] It was believed the birds had three drops of the devil's blood on their tails which they could not stop from bobbing.[11] This is evident in the old Irish rhyme:

Wee Mister Wagtail, hopping on a rock,
Daddy says your pretty tail is like a Goblin's clock
Wee Willie Wagtail, how I love to see,
Wee Willie Wagtail, wag his tail at me.
Wee Mister Wagtail, running by a pond,
Daddy says your pretty tail is like a Goblin's wand.

Anon

Religious bird lore was very important probably even before the advent of Christianity. When Christianity arrived, many birds' special features were explained in relation to Christian allegory. Both Robins and Swallows were believed to have had their throats and breasts burned red from bringing fire to earth from the heavens. The red patches on the faces of Goldfinches were said to be the blood of Christ left when a Goldfinch tried to remove the crown of thorns.[12] It was also believed that a Crossbill tried to pull the thorns from the head of Christ on the cross and was given the crossed bill as a reward.[13] A variation of this says a Crossbill was trying to pull the nails from Christ's limbs and twisted its bill in the process. The male Crossbill's red colour was also attributed to the blood of Christ. It was believed that if a Yellowhammer began to sing at three in the afternoon, it was a summons to prayer for souls in purgatory. Oystercatchers are marked with a faint cross on the breast, which was believed to be the symbol of Christ.[14] This is explained by a northern Irish folktale that when Christ was hiding by the Sea of Galilee, an Oystercatcher covered him with seaweed so that he could not be found and was rewarded with the cross on its breast.[15] An alternative legend has it that St Bride was fleeing from her persecutors and collapsed at the seashore. Seeing her distress, Oystercatchers covered her with seaweed and hid her. In thanks she blessed the birds and gave them the sign of the cross. From this the birds are also known as St Bride's or St Brigid's birds.

Many birds were believed to carry dead souls or were dead people incarnate. The belief of transmigration of human souls into birds goes back to ancient times. Often these bird-souls would come back with a message or warning. The best-known story worldwide refers to ocean-going albatrosses.[16] Albatrosses were believed to carry the souls of dead seamen and it was very bad luck to kill one. It was also believed that Mother Carey's Chickens, the Storm Petrels, contained the souls of dead seamen who came to warn their brethren of approaching storms. Gulls in general were often regarded as repositories of souls and were not harmed if it could be avoided. Back on land, when Sedge Warblers sang at night, and particularly at midnight, their voices were believed to be those of dead babies who chose to return temporarily from the 'other side' to sing, to soothe the hearts and minds of their poor grieving mothers. Magpies were regarded as the repositories of the souls of evil-minded or gossiping women.[17] Yet swans contained the souls of virtuous women and they had the capability of turning back into human form.[18] It was believed that the voice of a Linnet was that of an unhappy soul trapped in the 'Other World'. Even humble sparrows were thought to carry the souls of the dead and it was unlucky to kill them.[19]

Perhaps our most haunting legend is that of the 'Seven Whistlers', widespread across Europe in many variations. The legend tells of seven ghostly birds, usually Curlews, Whimbrels and plovers (though sometimes geese or swans), which are heard or seen flying overhead at night. Their haunting call presages death or disaster. One variation suggests the birds carry the grief-stricken souls of unbaptised babies condemned to roam the skies forever, or the souls of drowned seamen come to warn others at sea (See Section 3.8 for a full description). Another legend widespread across Europe is that of the Gabriel Hounds: a spectral pack of hounds which trails across the sky at night often led by a ghostly hunter. In Ireland, we have similar stories of the 'Lough Gur Hunt' in County Limerick. The hunt is a group of ethereal hounds that fly across the sky at night barking and howling. They presage death in the house of whosoever should hear them. These stories are most likely derived from hearing flocks of geese (Barnacle or Canada Geese) flying overhead at night, which can make a sort of barking call.

The existence of fairies, pookas and the like was a mixed blessing and it was best to keep them at bay wherever possible. Roosters crowing were believed to keep spirits away at night. Egg shells were regarded as being the dwelling places of fairies so they were always crushed when the egg was eaten.[20] In some places in Ireland, to prevent kites from taking chickens, the shells in which they were hatched were hung up in the roof of the house.[21] Similarly, a Dunnock's blue-green eggs were regarded as charms against witches' spells when strung out along the hob. They were regarded as especially good for keeping witches and spirits from coming down the chimney!

2.5.1.1 Forewarning

'a little bird told me . . .'

Birds were particularly good at warning us about what the future held in store. Alas nearly all warnings were bad news, particularly pertaining to imminent death, and were usually given by black birds.

A bird flying into a house, foretold an important message, usually a death in the family. This was particularly so if the bird was a Robin. The same was said for birds pecking at the window and again Robins particularly so.[22] The exceptions were Swallows whose appearance in the house was a good omen.

Any kind of crow, but particularly a Raven, flying directly over a home or a group of people walking was an omen of death.[23] If a Hooded Crow rested on a house it meant death or great misfortune to a member of the household: '*A crow on the thatch, soon death lifts the latch.*' Similarly a flight of Rooks over an army spelt imminent defeat.[24] More particularly, a Jackdaw falling down the chimney was a portent of bad luck or death.[25] Nonetheless if a Blackbird built its nest on or near your house, it was actually a good omen. Of course it was widely considered an ill omen to meet a single Magpie (a type of crow) on the road, from which we get the rhyme 'One for sorrow, two for joy . . .'

It was believed that if a Raven hovered near a herd of cattle or sheep, the animals would be found to be diseased. It was also said that if Starlings did not follow grazing cattle, then some witch's spell had been put upon them.[26] Three seagulls flying together, directly overhead, were taken as a warning of death soon to come.

Birds calling were also portents of death. If a cock crowed at midnight someone close was dead or dying. In England, it was a death omen if a cock crowed three times between sunset and midnight. Crowing at other times was often a warning against misfortune. The boom of a Bittern (now very rare in Ireland) was regarded as a warning from the spirit world and this might be one possible explanation for the wailing of the banshee. In Pomeroy, County Tyrone, it was said that 'a blackbird or thrush which sings before Candlemas[27] will be sure to mourn many days afterwards'.[28] If you heard a Cuckoo before your breakfast, you would be hungry for the year.[29] If you happened to be stooping when a Cuckoo made his first call, there would be a death in the family; similarly if you heard a Cuckoo in a graveyard.[30] The place where you heard a Cuckoo for the first time would be the place where you would spend the rest of your life.[31]

Blackbirds were said to impart mystical messages and it was believed that they could freely pass into the 'Other World'. They were associated with witches and druids and the Welsh goddess Rhiannon. The birds could put a person into a trance through singing and could give access to the 'Other World'.

Hens roosting in the morning were said to be foretelling a death, usually that of the farmer or someone in his household. If a rooster crowed near the threshold or entered the house it was an omen that visitors would arrive.[32]

Only a few of these warnings were good news. A wish made upon seeing the first Robin in spring would come true, but only if the wish was completed before the Robin flew away. On St Valentine's Day, the first bird a girl would see would give a clue as to the man she would marry. If it was a woodpecker, she would not marry at all. If it was a Robin, he would be a sailor, if a Blackbird, a clergyman, if a sparrow, he would be poor man (though they would be happy) or a farmer, if a Crossbill, an argumentative man, if a dove, a good man, and if it was a Goldfinch, he would be a millionaire. Hearing the Cuckoo's first song in spring was another way to learn to whom you would be married. After hearing the Cuckoo, you must look under your right foot where you will see a white hair. Take the hair, keep it with you and the first name you hear thereafter will be that of your future spouse.[33] Variations suggest the colour of the hair will be that of your spouse's hair.[34] Hearing a Black-backed Gull at night was taken as a good sign as there were fish to be had.[35]

2.5.1.2 Luck

Beyond warning, some birds could bestow luck on a person. Of course, luck could be good or bad and it seems you took your life in your hands when you ventured out with the chance of meeting birds.

It was considered unlucky to have pigeons visit your haggard or farmyard, unless you kept pigeons yourself.[36] It was particularly unlucky if a lone pigeon flew into your farmyard.[37] Even hearing the hoot of an owl was associated with bad luck. However, if you hear an owl, all is not lost: you must immediately take off your clothes, turn them inside out and put them back on.[38] Luckily, most owls appear at night! If an owl entered your house it was necessary to kill it at once, for if it flew out again it would take the luck of the house with it.[39] It was also bad luck to see an owl in the sunlight. Even an owl flying across your path was bad luck.

While of course it was unlucky to see a single Magpie, the ill-effects could be mitigated or altogether avoided by taking off your hat and bowing to the bird.[40] In Dublin, to mitigate the bad luck, children were encouraged to say '*Hello Mr Magpie, how do you do? How is your wife and your children too?*'

It was very unlucky to kill a Robin or disturb its nest or eggs. Similarly, it was very unlucky to interfere with a lark's nest. Skylarks were purported to have three spots on their tongues. Each spot represented a curse and if you ate a Skylark, you would bring the three curses down upon you. While Wrens were very much mistrusted, it was considered very bad luck to kill a Wren or destroy its nest on any day other than

St Stephen's Day. Such an act would result in a death in the family. While it was thought bad luck to kill a heron, people seemed to get over this fear in times of need when herons were eaten in big numbers. It was thought very bad luck to kill a Cuckoo or destroy its eggs[41] and it was believed to be very unlucky to bring a Corncrake into the house, dead or alive.

So much for the bad luck; there was some good luck to be had too. It was universally regarded as good luck to have bird droppings land on your head. It was also lucky to be awakened by birds singing on the morning of your wedding. If a lark was heard on the morning of St Brigid's Day,[42] the day would be sunny and those who heard it would enjoy great fortune throughout the year.[43]

Generally speaking, Swallows and martins were associated with good luck. Swifts, appearing black, were associated with the devil and bad luck. It was especially lucky if a Swallow or martin built its nest in your house and even more so if the bird returned the following year. Consequently, it was considered very unlucky to kill a Swallow or disturb its nest in any way. It was very lucky for a Swallow to fly into your home.[44] If a Blackbird built its nest on or near your house, it was a good omen. The building of a new rookery near a house was regarded as good fortune. Consequently, if a rookery near your home was suddenly abandoned, it was a sign that some misfortune was to fall upon your home.[45]

On Tory Island, it was regarded as good luck to have a Cuckoo's nest on your land. If you heard a Cuckoo with your right ear, you would have luck all summer long[46] but if you heard it with your left ear, the summer would not be fun for you.[47] It was also lucky to hear the Cuckoo on the morning of your wedding. If you heard it from inside a building, it was bad luck.[48]

Finding a dead crow on the road was good luck but crows in a churchyard were bad luck.

A white rooster was considered very lucky, and should not be killed as it protects the farm on which it lives. Black cocks, however, were more ill-omened, being often associated with sacrifice.

2.5.1.3 Odd Beliefs

There follows a review of somewhat unique beliefs that do not suggest easy categorisation.

Gerald of Wales[49] on a tour of Ireland in the twelfth century recorded the belief that dead bodies of Kingfishers would not rot and recommended keeping them between clothes in order to keep moths away and give a pleasant perfume. He also believed that if they were hung by the bill (when dead), they would get a new set of feathers every year.

It was believed that banshees used Waxwings as torches to guide them through the night. It was also said that no man has ever found a Waxwing's nest. We now know that Waxwings breed in Scandinavia so their nests are indeed never seen in Ireland. It was similarly believed that Curlews did not build nests because they could not be found. St Patrick had blessed a Curlew on the Isle of Man so that men would never be allowed to find their nests.

Cranes were perhaps once common in Ireland (see Section 5.1.2) but they were confused with herons. There is much lore about them. It was believed that migrating Cranes swallowed a stone before they departed. The stone acted as ballast, keeping the Cranes on course even in heavy winds. Aristotle tells us the regurgitated stone was a touchstone (tester) for gold. Gerald of Wales believed the Crane's liver was so powerful it could digest iron.[50] It was believed that one of the wonders of Ireland was a Crane to be found on Inishkea Island[51] (*Inis Gé*, goose island), off County Mayo, where it had lived since the beginning of the world and would continue to live there until the end of the world.

Gerald of Wales also mentions the presence of Ospreys in Ireland in the twelfth century. He relates an erroneous belief that an Osprey's left and right feet were distinctly talented. It was believed that one of the Osprey's feet was equipped with talons to catch fish and that the other was more webbed and used for swimming. Today we know that both feet have talons. It was also believed that Ospreys had the power to put fish under a spell and that they were covered in an oily substance which was irresistible to fish.[52]

For anglers, dipping the bait into water in which a *corr-iasc* (heron) had been cooked would give it the heron's power of catching fish. To catch a heron itself, all you had to do was sneak up behind and shout 'lie down' and the bird would fall in fright.

It was believed that a swan could put a person under a spell with her beautiful singing voice. While under the spell, time passed more quickly for the person and they could awake to find the world a changed place. Swans pairing for life was a sign of fidelity. As such, a swan's (or hen's) feather, sewn into a husband's pillow would ensure his fidelity.[53]

It was believed that Gannets were incapable of landing or taking off from any rock except marble. As a result, it was thought they lived at sea all the time and even laid floating eggs on the waves and hatched them between wing and body.[54]

2.5.1.4 Health & Cures

Some birds were particularly good at preventing or curing ill health but a few caused health problems. It is not clear how old these beliefs are but they should certainly not be taken as sound medical advice!

The Anglo-Saxons believed that the bones and body fat of sea eagles possessed curative properties.[55] It was also believed that a Kingfisher in full plumage was an antidote to certain diseases.

Swallows seemed to be particularly useful against illness. In Roman times, it was believed that Swallows could cure all problems of the eyes. To quote Marcellus of Bordeaux: '*When you hear or see the first Swallow, go, without speaking, to the first well or fountain and there wash your eyes and pray God that that year they may not be dimmed, and so the Swallows will carry away all trouble from them.*' A Swallow was also believed to have a special stone in its stomach. If this stone was taken at the August full-moon, it would cure epilepsy, blindness and stammering.[56] A recipe from 1692 promising a cure for 'falling sickness' and 'sudden fits' (epilepsy) calls for fifty Swallows to be ground up with mortar and pestle and added to an ounce of caster sugar and white wine vinegar.[57] Swallows could also cure toothache . . . (from Marcellus): '*when you see a Swallow, hold your tongue and go to "pure shining water" and dip your middle finger of the right hand in and say: "I say to thee, O swallow, as this will never be in thy beak, so may my teeth pain me no more for a year."*'

On the negative side, if you had your hair cut, it was risky to leave the cuttings around for if a Swallow lined its nest with them, you would have headaches all summer long.[58]

It was believed that if a person with jaundice could fix his gaze on a Yellowhammer, the patient would be cured but the bird would die.[59]

Ailments of the mouth could be cured by bringing a live goose and placing its bill in the patient's mouth for five minutes for nine successive mornings.[60]

On Valentia Island, County Kerry in the late nineteenth century it was believed that the first egg laid by a little black hen, eaten the very first thing in the morning, would keep you from fever for a year.[61]

To create an ointment for burns, the body of a Crane (or heron) should be buried for a month in a suitable container in a manure heap. At the end of the month, the greasy oil that has collected at the bottom of the container can be applied to burns.[62]

Owl soup was a cure for whooping cough.

It was believed that a sick person lying on a pillow of pigeon (or hen) feathers could not die but instead would be terribly agonised and tormented. Consequently, it was often the practice to remove a pillow from under the head of the dying if it was felt they could not pass on.[63]

Eating the joints of the Redshank was a cure for Bright's disease of the kidneys.[64]

2.5.2 WEATHER LORE

Predicting the weather was useful in an agrarian and sea-going culture. It was often a matter of life and death whether this year's crops were harvested successfully or not. As a result, a rich history of bird-related and other weather lore has been passed down in Ireland perhaps for thousands of years. What makes weather lore particularly interesting is that at least some of it is grounded in fact based on observation. Today we know gulls do come inland when bad weather is approaching so there is truth in the entreating rhyme: '*Seagull, seagull sit on the strand, there's an end to fair weather when you come to land.*' Swallows often fly lower to catch insects which have in turn moved lower when rain and windy weather are approaching. Consequently Swallows flying high were a sign of sunshine to come: '*When the Swallows fly high, the weather will be dry.*' A low-flying 'V' formation of geese was a sign of imminent rain. In practice this may also be true as the birds fly beneath low rain-bearing cloud.

Singing birds predict the weather too. A wild pigeon cooing in a tree was an indication of mild weather[65] whereas the whistle of the Blackbird warned that rain was on the way. If a lark was heard on the morning of St Brigid's Day,[66] the day would be sunny.[67] If a cock crowed while perched on a gate or at nightfall, the next day would be rainy. Hearing a Corncrake at dusk meant fine weather was on the way.[68] A Lapwing seen screaming in wheeling flight in the evening was a sure sign of a dirty night[69] with particular emphasis on frost.[70] When Curlews made a double whistle, this was a sign of coming rain.[71] A single long clear call from a Whimbrel meant fine weather was on the way while a quivery repeated call meant rain was coming.[72]

From the time of the Roman augurs, the flight of a bird was important. A heron flying south was a sign of good weather.[73] Other birds' habits could be observed too. Rooks feeding in a village or close to their nests in the morning meant bad weather was coming. Moreover, Rooks flying far from their nests meant good weather was to come. Lapwings coming down off the mountain presaged bad weather. A congregation of Starlings foretold frost[74] as did the sudden appearance of a wild swan at an unusual location.[75]

In some parts of the country, early bad weather in May is referred to as *gairbhín* or *garbhshíon na gcuach*,[76] the little rough patch that comes with the Cuckoo. In other parts, Cuckoos were believed to bring fine weather.[77]

Sparrows hopping on the road were an indication of bad weather[78] and if a Scaup (or Pochard or Goldeneye) was seen sleeping on a calm day, it was taken as a sure sign that a storm was coming.[79]

Kingfishers have much lore attached to them. A somewhat odd belief informs us that when stuffed and suspended by a thread a Kingfisher's bill points in the direction of the prevailing wind.[80]

At sea, Storm Petrels were regarded as the directors of weather. If the appearance of a Storm Petrel was a bad omen for sailors,[81] one coming aboard a boat was sure to cause great consternation. It was believed that they lived in the midst of hurricanes.[82] Their appearance presaged bad weather. Yet in some places, they were regarded as the sailors' friends coming to warn them of an approaching storm. As such, it was considered very unlucky to kill them. Each bird was said to contain the soul of a dead seaman.

2.5.3 MIGRATION BELIEFS

'The stork in the heavens knoweth her appointed times; and the crane, and the turtle dove, and the swallow observe the time of their coming.' Jeremiah 8:7.

Today, we have a comprehensive understanding of migration. Many birds come to us in Ireland in summertime. Others come in winter, and many of our resident birds are joined by foreign birds of the same species in winter. Some stop here while on their way elsewhere. Some travel from high ground to low ground or from inland to coastal regions. Some spend almost all their lives at sea and only come to Irish shores to breed.

Some of our summer birds come from Africa and some from Europe. They come mostly to breed. When the newly-hatched have learned to fly and have somewhat fattened up, they depart, usually with their parents, to fly thousands of miles to warmer climates, and to escape our winter. Spare a thought for the poor juvenile Cuckoos. Once raised and fattened by their surrogate parents, they must fly thousands of miles on their own, to their winter homes in Africa; a journey never undertaken before, to a place they have never been. Spare a thought too for our Arctic Terns. The most-travelled birds in the world journey here to breed, from the Antarctic, a round-trip journey of about 30,000 kilometres.

Our winter visitors come to capitalise on the rich and bountiful food available here. They only leave to breed on their traditional breeding grounds. Mostly water birds come in winter. They come from Greenland, Iceland, Canada, Northern Europe and even Siberia, to escape the extreme winter conditions there.

Before the era of scientific ornithology, migration was poorly understood, if at all. Few people left their own neighbourhood let alone their own country, so a bird's long-distance movements were never tracked. People were, of course, aware that some birds seemed to appear in the summer and then disappear again in the winter and others appeared in the winter and disappeared in the summer. Some of these birds were important food sources that just disappeared from time to time. Explanations were needed and some of them are fascinating.

In 350 BC, Aristotle in his *Historia Animalium* demonstrated his awareness, to some degree, of bird migration but he got some things terribly wrong. He believed, for instance, that Swallows hibernated for the winter and this belief persisted to at least the nineteenth century. Swallows come to us in Ireland in spring/summer from Africa. When the Swallows disappeared in late summer/autumn it was believed that they went to hibernate at the bottoms of ponds for the winter. There are even written reports of fishermen bringing up such hibernating Swallows in their nets.[83] Who knows what they really had? The summer-visiting Wheatears generated similar beliefs. Such beliefs may have come about from young birds, hatched late in summer, being abandoned in their nests by the parents.

The Seven Sleepers

The bat, the bee, the butterfly,
The cuckoo, and the swallow,
The heather-bleet and corncraik
Sleep all in a little hollow.

Anon (Scottish, Manx and many variations)

If Swallows and Wheatears hibernated, then what Cuckoos and Corncrakes did was even more amazing. Both species also travel to us from Africa in the summer. When Cuckoos disappeared at summer's end it was believed that they changed into hawks for the winter and then back into Cuckoos again in spring/summer. This belief was probably fuelled by a Cuckoo's broadly similar appearance to a hawk. Furthermore, it was believed that Corncrakes turned into Moorhens in winter and back into Corncrakes in spring/summer.[84] It was also widely believed that Corncrakes could not fly at all so migration was out of the question.[85] Some people believed Cuckoos laid up over winter in hollow tree trunks.[86]

'Bird transmutation' was a phrase coined by Aristotle to describe the changing of one bird species into another. It was prompted by his observation of the movement of redstarts and Robins. Redstarts migrated south from Greece in winter and Robins migrated south, into Greece, from further north. The disappearance of redstarts and simultaneous appearance of Robins led Aristotle to deduce that one transmuted into the other.

Perhaps the oddest belief regarding migration is that of the Woodcock's winter movements. Woodcock have an uncanny ability to 'predict' the weather and their migratory cycles are always in tune with the waxing and waning moon. Non-resident Woodcock come to Ireland from Scandinavia in November, usually arriving on the first full moon of that month (the Woodcock moon). People put two and two together and concluded that Woodcock must live on the moon, only returning to

Earth and Ireland to breed, before returning to the moon in spring. This belief was popular at least as late as the early nineteenth century.[87] Swallows, Nightingales, Cuckoos, Fieldfares and Redwings were also believed to spend at least some time on the moon.

> *But whether upward to the moon they go,*
> *Or dream the winter out in caves below,*
> *Or hawk at flies elsewhere, concerns us not to know.*

John Dryden, from *The Hind and the Panther*, 1687

It was not until the beginning of the nineteenth century and the introduction of banding and ringing, that bird migration became a scientifically accepted principal.

2.5.4 FISHY BIRDS

Barnacle Geese may not have been suspected of living on the moon but their origins were certainly under question. They breed in Greenland and when winter proves too cold, they come to a warmer western Europe and Ireland to feed and sit it out. No one had ever been to Greenland to see a Barnacle Goose's nest so an interesting theory arose to describe their lifecycle. Gerald of Wales tells us in the twelfth century that Barnacle Geese are hatched from eggs that cling to woody flotsam and jetsam on the sea. He describes how they grow while hanging from these timbers by their beaks. Eventually when fully grown they detach from the timber and live out their adult lives. From this alleged watery origin came the belief that Barnacle Geese were more fish than fowl and as such, religious permission was given to eat them in times of fasting.

Many other water birds were considered more fish than fowl and permission was given by the Catholic Church to eat them during Lent and other times of fasting. Brent Geese, scoter ducks, Cormorants, shearwaters, Great Auks and perhaps more were appointed so. The practice of eating such 'fishy birds' became so widespread that, in 1215, at the General Lateran Council, Pope Innocent III formally forbade the practice.[88]

2.5.5 FOLKLORE IN LANGUAGE

'A proverb is shorter than a bird's beak.'[89]

Where folklore is not preserved in fable it is often preserved in language, passed down as proverbs. This chapter lists some of the bird-related proverbs still living in the Irish and English languages today. Some are in English and some in Irish, translated where possible to preserve the meaning of the proverb. The English proverbs are a mix of those originally in the Irish language and those which have perhaps always been in English.

2.5.5.1 Proverbs

IRISH

An fhaid a bheidh naosc ar mhóin is gob uirthi.
As long as there will be a snipe on the bog and a beak on her
for ever and ever.

Blas an seachtú crosáin.
The taste of the seventh razorbill
the feeling of having eaten to excess.

Cé gur beag díol dreoilín caithfidh sé a sholáthar.
Little as a wren needs, it must gather it
you can't take anything for granted.

Chonálfadh sé na corra.
It would freeze the herons
it is bitterly cold.

Codladh an traona chugat!
May you have the sleep of the corncrake
(Dingle, Kerry[90]) This may be a good wish or a curse, as corncrakes could often be heard calling all through the night.

Cuireadh an ghealbhán chun arbhair na gcomharsain.
The sparrow's invitation to its neighbour's corn
somebody generous with something that does not belong to them

Dealbh an dreoilín.
the size of the wren
(Monaghan[91]) tiny or nothing.

Drochubh, drochéan.
Bad egg, bad bird
You can't change nature.

Éirí le giolcadh an ghealbhain.
To rise with the sparrows' chirping
to get up early.

Is é seoladh (tionlacan) an philibín óna nead aige é.
'He has the lapwing's guidance/escort from the nest'
he is evading the issue.

Ní féidir leis an ghobadán an dá thrá a fhreastal *or* **Ní thagann an dá thrá leis an ngobadán.**
The sandpiper cannot attend to two beaches at the same time
do one thing at a time.

Is garbh mí na gcuach.
The month of the cuckoo is severe [April/May].

Is geal leis an bhfiach dubh a ghearrcach féin.
The raven thinks its own nestling fair
'a face only a mother could love'.

Is leor don dreoilín a nead.
A wren only has need for its nest
don't covet what you don't need.

Nuair a chanann an chuach ar chrann gan duilliúr, díol do bhó is ceannaigh arbhar.
When a cuckoo sings on a leafless tree, sell your cow and buy corn.
This proverb is sometimes written as '**Má labhríonn an chuach ar chrann gan duilliúr, díol do bhó agus ceannaigh arbhar.**' *If the cuckoo calls from a tree without leaves, sell your cow and buy corn.* Or sometimes: '**An tráth a ghaireann an chuach ar an sceach lom, díol do bhó agus ceannaigh arbhar.** When the cuckoo cries on the bare thorn bush, sell your cow and buy corn.*

Scata ban no scata géanna.
A group of women or a flock of geese
similarly noisy.

Sparáil na circe fraoigh ar an bhfraoch.
The grouse sparing the heather
unnecessary frugality.

ENGLISH

A bird with one wing cannot fly.[92]
Said to a person to make him take a second drink.

'A crow on the thatch, soon death lifts the latch.'

A goose/turkey never voted for an early Christmas.

A wild goose never reared a tame gosling . . .
Like father like son.

A wren in the hand is better than a crane to be caught.
Be thankful for what you have.

Do not send a goose with a message to the fox's den . . . or
Do not leave the fox minding the geese . . .

Every bird as it is reared and the lark for the bog.
The innate nature of things.

Every part of a goose is used except the honk.

'He is in the book of the raven.'
He is not to be trusted.

It's as hard to see a woman crying as it is to see a barefooted duck.
Women tend to cry.

It's a long way from home that the plover cries.[93]

May you never be sent to the gander paddock.
May you never be in your wife's bad graces.[94]

Small goslings make fine geese.
To encourage patience.

There'll be white blackbirds before an unwilling woman ties
the knot . . .[95]

The robin and the wren are God's two holy men.

Time enough lost the ducks.
Procrastination . . . don't delay, secure the ducks.

What's good/sauce for the goose is good/sauce for the gander . . .

When the fox is the preacher, let the goose not listen to his
sermon . . .[96]

When the sky falls we'll all catch larks.
(Said to mock someone with grandiose or impossible plans.)

'You'll follow the crows for it.'
(You'll miss it after it's gone.)

There is an old saying, **'up with the lark'**, referring to those of us who rise early in the morning . . . it was one of the first birds to sing in the morning.

2.5.5.2 Curses

When bad language was frowned upon to describe one's dislike for something, a curse could usually do just as well. A few bird-related curses remain in Irish and English:

IRISH

Nar fheice tú an chuach ná an traonach arís.
May you not live to see the cuckoo or corncrake again.

ENGLISH

If you wanted to give someone a fairly mild curse, something like 'a **magpie on your wheat field gate'**[97] might suffice. A little stronger might be '**six eggs to you and half of them rotten'**.[98] A medium strength curse goes like '**the curse of the crows (or ravens) on you'**[99] or '**the curse of the goose that lost the quill that wrote the Ten Commandments on you'**.[100] If you were really ticked off with someone you might say '**may you ride Rogan's gander to the dickens'**[101] or '**with all your money, airs and graces, may you be left where the crows don't shite'**.[102] If you really wanted to pull out the big guns, you might say '**may your hens take the disorder, your cows the crippen**[103] **and your calves the white scour! May yourself go stone-blind so that you will not know your wife from a hay-stack!'**[104] Finally, the succinct '**the fate of Ned's cock to you!'**

2.5.5.3 Similes

The Irish language is particularly rich with similes. There seems to be one for every occasion. A few remain in the English language too.

IRISH

Chomh bán le faoileog.	As white as a seagull.
Chomh beag le dreoilín.	As small as a wren.
Chomh binn le ceol na n-éan.	As sweet as the birds singing.
Chomh binn leis an fhuiseog.	As sweet as the skylark.
Chomh binn le smóilín.	As sweet as a little thrush.
Chomh breabhsánta le glasóg.	As spruce/sprightly as a wagtail.
Chomh dubh le cleite an fhéich.	As black as a raven's feather.
Chomh dubh le préachán.	As black as a crow.
Chomh dubh leis an bhfiach.	As black as the raven.
Chomh dúr doicheallach le colúr céileachais a mbeadh cochall air le ceann dá threibh.	As dour and churlish as a mating pigeon with the hackles up at one of his own.
Chomh fial leis an éan fionn.	As generous as a kite. (i.e. not generous!)
Chomh geal leis an eala.	As white or as pure as the swan.
Chomh géarradharcach le gainéad.	As sharp-eyed as a gannet.
Chomh h-anásta le gé a bheadh ag siúl ar rópa.	As clumsy as a goose on a rope.
Chomh haerach le druid.	As chirpy as a starling.
Chomh haibí le spideog.	As frisky as a robin.
Chomh hard leis an iolar.	As high as an eagle.
Chomh héadrom le gealbhan, Chomh héasca le gealbhan.	As light as a sparrow.

Chomh héadrom le lon ar sceach.	As light as a blackbird on a bramble.
Chomh lag le héan gé.	As weak as a gosling.
Chomh leitheadach leis na cuacha.	As conceited as the cuckoo.
Chomh leochaileach leis an éan turcaí.	As tender as a young turkey.
Chomh liath leis an iolar.	As grey as an eagle.
Chomh lom le gé bhearrtha.	As naked as a plucked goose.
Chomh meabhrach breabhsach le seabhac aille.	As intelligent and sprightly as a sparrowhawk.
Chomh meidhreach le dreoilín teaspaigh.	As gay as an exuberant wren.
Chomh ríméadach leis na cuacha.	As jubilant/proud as the cuckoo.
Chomh sona le cuach i nead a comharsan.	As happy as a cuckoo in it's neighbour nest.
Chomh tuartha le gé ghoir.	As 'washy' as a brooding goose.

ENGLISH

As bald as a coot.	As crazy as a loon.
As happy as a lark.	As queer as a coot.
As thin as a rail.	As wise as an owl.

2.6 BIRD NAMES

'I am friend to the pilibeen, the red necked chough, the parsnip landrail, the pilibeen mona, the bottletailed tit, the common marshcoot, the speckletoed guillemot, the pilibeen sleibhe, the Mohar gannet, the peregrine ploughgull, the long eared bushowl, the Wicklow smallfowl, the bevil beaked chough, the hooded tit, the pilibeen uisce, the common corby, the fishtailed mudpiper, the cruiskeen lawn, the carrion seacock, the green ridded parakeet, the brown bogmartin, the maritime wren, the dovetailed wheatcrake, the beaded daw, the Galway hillbantam and the pilibeen cathrach.'

from *At Swim-Two-Birds*, Flann O'Brien.[1]

Bird names have many origins. Some are very ancient and some have come to us from the pens of ornithological writers from the seventeenth, eighteenth and nineteenth centuries. Up until at least the seventeenth century, the language of natural science and philosophy was Latin. What standardisation there was, of bird names, dated from the time of Aristotle. When the first bird books came out in the English language, from the seventeenth century onwards, many names were translated from Latin to English and these names then became the de facto standard. In Ireland, we share standard bird names, in the English language, with the UK, but we have our own local names. A visitor from Yorkshire, for example, might be at a loss to understand the local names for birds in County Kerry, and vice versa. The same could be said for a visitor from Ulster. Of course, we have local and old names in the Irish language too. Some of these may be quite ancient but some have been adopted and adapted from English and indeed Latin, in the last few hundred years. Local names in Irish vary by local dialect too. In Ulster, we have a third language, Ulster Scots, with a rich vocabulary of bird names, many borrowed from Scotland.

We have become very much used to our standard bird names, even if we may not be sure of their origins. Having a list of alternative names tells us a little more about the birds and how people perceived them in the past. Many of our familiar birds had completely different names a century ago. The Windhovers, Woodquests, Throstles, Ruddocks, Ouzels, and Titlarks, of yesterday are the Kestrels, Woodpigeons, Song Thrushes, Robins, Blackbirds and pipits of today. In Ulster Scots, the names Whaup, Gowk and Laverock were as common as Curlew, Cuckoo and Skylark. In Irish, names were not standardised until the twentieth century. Before that, a multitude of colourful regional names abounded. Some birds were given familiar personal names and a list of these can be found in Section 2.6.1.

Here is a pick of some of the more colourful names to be found in this book. Some were quite gritty. Grebes were called 'Arsefoot' because of the odd rear placing of their feet. The Wheatear's name 'White-Arse' derives from its white rear end.

Skuas had a reputation for eating the droppings of other birds and this is reflected in their names in all languages. In Ireland, they were called, amongst other things, Shitehawks or Dirtbirds. In Irish they were *Faoileán an chaca* (the shite gull) or *Tomáisín chac na bhfaoileán* (little Tommy gull-shite) in Kerry. In Ulster, they were given the wonderful name 'gabshite'. Some Irish names were more pleasant: Gannets were labelled *Amhasán*, the hooligan bird; the Nightjar was called *Púicín gaoithe*, the little wind pooka; and the Jack Snipe was the *Mini-gabhair* (mini-goat) or *Meannán aeir* (little goat of the air), from its goat-like bleating. Spare a thought for the poor Dotterel, a rare summer visitor to upland regions. Its naive tolerance of people allowed it to be approached and killed easily. From this behaviour, the poor bird was named *Amadán móinteach*, the 'bog idiot'. The 'Foolish Guillemot' was named for similar reasons. Herons were named after girls with long necks: *Cáití fhada* (long Katy), *Síle na bportach* (Julie of the Bog). Stonechats and Reed Buntings were *Donnchadh an chaipín* (male, Denis with the cap) and *Máirín an triubhais/triúis* (female, little Mary of the trousers). The Dunnock was either *Bráthair an dreoilín* (the Wren's brother) or *Máthair chéile* (the Mother-in-law). The Long-eared Owl is still called *Ceann cait*, the cat's head. The English language yields some weird and wonderful names too. In Galway, the Little Tern was called the 'Fairy Bird'. Storm Petrels were known as Mother Carey's Chickens or Mutton-Birds and Bitterns were 'butter' or 'bitter-bums'. From Waterford, we have the charming 'Tittery Hay Bird' (Meadow Pipit). From Ulster, we have the delightfully named Corn Dumpling (Corn Bunting), Snowflake (Snow Bunting) and the Guttersnipe (Snipe). White-fronted Geese were Laughing Geese while Herring Gulls were Laughing Gulls. Quail were called 'Wet-my-feet' after their call. The Curlew was the 'rainbird' while the Red-throated Loon was the 'rain goose'. 'Elk' were wild swans, 'Alp' were Bullfinches and 'Cowboys' were Ring Ouzels from Tipperary.

On the more sinister side, Barn Owls were called 'ghost owl' in English and *Scréachóg reilige* (graveyard screecher) in Irish. Nightjars were 'goat-suckers' and had a sinister reputation. Swifts, wagtails and Yellowhammers were the 'Devil's Bird'. However, the church had its own birds too. Teal were St Colman's Bird while Eider were St Cuthbert's Duck and Oystercatchers were St Bride's or St Brigid's Bird. Goldfinch were *Coinnleoir Muire* (Mary's candle bearer) and Robins were *Spideog Mhuire* (the Virgin Mary's Robin) in Kerry.

2.6.1 FAMILIAR BIRD NAMES

Birds have always had familiar names. During the Middle Ages, birds were given familiar names, almost as if they were members of the family. This is true in both the Irish and English languages. Many of these names persist in one form or another. We are very familiar with Robin Redbreasts but we also have Tom Tits, Jenny Wrens and Willie Wagtails. Some names still persist in a different form. Magpies may once have been called Maggie Pies and Jackdaws were Jack Daws. Birds were personified as if there was just one of each species. If you had seen a Jackdaw you might have said 'I saw Jack in the tree'. The same was true in Irish. A heron might have been called *Síle na bportach* (Julie of the Bog). A Blue Tit was *Diarmaidín* (little Dermot). A selection of the more familiar names in both Irish and English follows:

English

Blue/Great Tit:	Tom
Heron:	Julie the Bogs, Joaneen the Bogs, Molly the Bog, Sheila Crane, Narry the Bogs, Long Tall Sally
Jackdaw:	Jack
Lapwing:	Phillipene (little Phillip)
Magpie:	Mag, Maggie
Raven:	Bran, Brendan, Brion
Robin:	Robin Redbreast
Snipe:	Jill Snipe (corresponding to the Jack Snipe)
Song Thrush:	Mavis
Storm Petrel:	Laura of the Ocean
Wagtail:	Willie
Whitethroat:	Polly Whitethroat, Peggy Chaw
Wren:	Jenny, Sally

Irish

Blackcap: Donnchadh/Donncha an chaipín (Denis with the Cap), Máirín an triúis (little Mary with the trousers)

Blue Tit: Diarmaid beag (little Dermot)

Dove/Pigeon: Colm

Dunnock: Máthair chéile (Mother-in-law), Bráthair an dreoilín (Wren's brother)

Goldcrest: Diairmín, Diarmín riabhach (little streaked/striped Dermot/Jerry)

Heron: Cáití fhada (Long Katie), Máire fhada (Long Mary), Nóra na bportach (Nora of the Bog), Síle na bportach (Julie of the Bog), Siobhán na bportach (Joan of the Bog, Jónaí an scrogaill, Joan of the long thin neck).

Jack Snipe: Seáinín dírúach

Lapwing: Pilibín (little Philip)

Meadow Pipit: Seánín na lathaí (Johnny of the mud)

Raven: Bran, Dónall dubh (black Donal)

Reed Bunting: Brian na giolcaí (Brian of the reeds)

Skua: Tomáisín chac na bhfaoileán (little Tommy gull-shite)

Sparrow: Seán an chaipín (John with the cap)

Storm Petrel: Peadairín na stoirme (little Peter of the storms)

Stonechat: Donncha an chaipín (Dennis with the cap), Máirín an triúis (little Mary of the trousers)

Wagtail: Suibháinín an bhóthair (little Joan of the street), Siobhán ghlas an charn aoiligh (grey Joan of the dung-hill)

Yellowhammer: Siobháinín bhuí (little yellow Joan)

2.6.2 STANDARDISATION OF BIRD NAMES

This book presents bird names in English, scientific (Latinised), Irish and to some extent, Ulster Scots. That each bird should have different names in several languages is confusing enough. That each language should have several names for each bird, is potentially bewildering. In the scientific world, scientific names have always been used to identify any bird uniquely, or indeed any species of living thing, anywhere in the world; at least in theory. Thus we know that the North American 'Common Loon' and the European 'Great Northern Diver' are one and the same bird, *Gavia immer*.

Despite the common Latin, efforts have been made in several languages to standardise the official name of every bird, to further reduce confusion. The aim is not to eradicate other national or local names but to have one name that all can identify with. In the English language, the International Ornithological Congress has made an initiative to standardise bird names. There have been a number of initiatives to list standard English names. Some of the most common are: Howard & Moore, Gill & Wright, Sibley & Monroe, Clements and the American Ornithologists' Union (AOU). In 2006, Gill and Wright published a list, *Birds of the World: Recommended English Names*,[2] following fifteen years of research. This list of over ten thousand names can be seen at **www.worldbirdnames.org**. While by no means universally supported, it may prove to be the most widely accepted standardised list worldwide. The list has been endorsed by the International Ornithological Congress. Names from this list are used as the title names for each species in this book.

A similar initiative was taken with the Irish language. The Terminology Committee (*An Coiste Téarmaíochta*), working originally to the Irish Department of Education, and, since 1999, to *Foras na Gaeilge*, has produced a standardised list of names, later published by the Irish Wild Birds Committee. These names can also be found in the government publication *Ainmneacha Plandaí agus Ainmhithe*[3] (plant and animal names). Names from this list are also used as the title names for each species in this book.

To finish this section on standardisation, the reader should be aware, that although scientific names are supposed to be unique, several archaic synonyms crop up from time to time. Indeed 'standard' scientific names are increasingly being changed as DNA evidence shines new light on some species' taxonomic positioning. Scientific synonyms are listed under each species' alternative names, where present.

3. Wild Birds – Éin Fhiáine

3.1 LOONS (DIVERS) – LÓMAÍ

Loons are large shy water birds, famed for their haunting cry. Powerful birds built for pursuing fish underwater, they are at home in all sea conditions. A loon's plumage changes radically from summer to winter making winter identification difficult. The sexes are alike. Loons are heavy, with solid bones unlike other birds and need a long take-off on water. They are called divers in Europe and loons in North America although the word 'loon' is of European origin, coming from the Shetland Island word *loom* (meaning 'lame') which in turn was inherited from Scandinavia. It is reflected in the Irish name *Lóma* and the birds' almost total inability to walk on land. Loon has become the standard name of the International Ornithological Congress although Irish ornithologists will refer to these birds as 'divers'. Arguably, the word 'loon' is much more evocative. The birds are truly other-worldly.

The haunting cry differs among the three species found in Ireland but is somewhat suggestive of manic laughing. A loon's call is wild and piercing and utterly unforgettable. They are most likely to be heard in the summer months. Loon nests are made from floating vegetation and have a sort of slipway into the water, which the chicks utilise when leaving the nest.[1] Chicks often ride on the parents' backs.

They are skilled divers and have valves on their nostrils that they can close underwater.[2] They also have the ability to alter their buoyancy and can float at the surface with just the head out of the water.

The generic name *Gavia* comes from Latin (and Italian) meaning 'gull'. In Irish, many of the words for loons are also used for grebes, as the birds were confused. Though broadly similar, loons and grebes are not closely related and are good examples of convergent evolution. Loons, once considered very primitive birds from an evolutionary point of view, are now considered more recent than the ducks, geese and swans.

Of the five species of loon worldwide, three[3] can be seen in Ireland: Great Northern Loons, Black-throated Loons and Red-throated Loons. A fourth species, the Yellow-billed Loons (*Gavia adamsii, Lóma Gobgheal*) are very rare visitors from the Arctic.

Proverbs & Similes:
As crazy as a loon.

CULINARY
Divers were regarded as inedible due to their fish diet and the stringy nature of the meat.

3.1.1 The Great Northern Loon[4]

Lóma mór | *Gavia immer immer*

The largest and best known of the loon family, Great Northern Loons are famous for their haunting call as sometimes heard in American wilderness movies. This tremolo call is sometimes called 'loon laughter' and is quite other-worldly.

Like all loons in Irish waters, they are unlikely to be seen in their fabulous summer colours. They are largely black and white with a black head and striped neck. The rest of the body is mottled black and white. In winter, the birds are dull brown-black on the head with white face and throat with a mottled brown-black and white body.

The specific *immer* is probably from the Latin to dive or immerse so *Gavia immer* translates literally as 'diving gull'. It may be from the Scandinavian *emmer* meaning 'ash-coloured'. The Irish *Lóma Mór* translates directly as 'big loon'.

NAMES

English: Allan Hawk, Arran Hawk (ne.), Common Loon, Ducker, Ember goose, Great Northern Diver, Gunner, Holland Auk, Hollands Hawk, Imber (Diver), Ring-necked Loon (Crk.), Sea Loon, Speckled Diver

Irish: Éan glas na scadán[5] (green herring-bird, Kry.), Faocha mhór, Gairg, Lóma mhór, Lúma (Din., Wat.), Lúnadán, Tumaire

Scientific: Colymbus glacialis, Colymbus imber, Colymbus immer, Colymbus maximus, Colymbus torquatus, Gavia torquata, Urinator imber

FACTS & FIGURES

Winter visitors. Fish eaters. Seen off all coasts in winter. About 1,400 wintering birds (94–00). Live max twenty-five years. Collective name: a raft of loons. The national bird of Canada and the states of Ontario, Canada, and Minnesota, USA. About five species of *Gavia* worldwide. Order: *Gaviiformes*; Family: *Gaviidae*.

45

3.1.2 The Black-throated Loon[6]

Lóma Artach | *Gavia arctica arctica*

As they are winter visitors to Ireland, we are generally deprived of the Black-throated Loons' stunning summer colours. In winter, the birds are generally dark on top with white chin and throat and dirty white beneath. In summer, they show a stunning grey head, red eye and black throat with side stripes and body generally streaked black and white. Like most loons, they are ungainly on land and have an eerie wailing call. About the size of Herring Gulls, they are slightly larger than the Red-throated Loons and have broader bills. They can spend up to two minutes underwater. The Irish and Latin names *artach* and *arctica* respectively, are self-explanatory.

NAMES

English: Arctic Loon, Black-throated Diver, Lesser Imber

Scientific: Colymbus arcticus, Eudytes arcticus, Eudytes balticus

FACTS & FIGURES

Rare winter visitors from Continent. Fish eaters. One pair bred recently in Donegal. Weigh up to 2.5 kg. Live max twenty-seven years. Amber list. About five species of *Gavia* worldwide. Order: *Gaviiformes*; Family: *Gaviidae*.

3.1.3 The Red-throated Loon[7]

Lóma rua | *Gavia stellata*

CULINARY

Loons were generally considered as poor to eat but Watters described the flesh of a Red-throated Loon as 'extremely well flavoured'.[8]

NAMES

English: Allan Hawk (BL.), Burrian (Uls.), Ducker, Galrush (rain goose, Dub.), Holland Auk, Hollands Hawk, Lune (Crk., Wex.), Red-throated Diver, Sea Loon, 'Second Speckled Diver' (sic), Speckled Diver

Irish: Faocha rua, Foitheach rua (red grebe)

Scientific: Colymbus lumme, Colymbus septentrionalis, Colymbus stellatus, Colymbus striatus, Eudytes septentrionalis, Gavia lumme, Urinator septentrionalis

Red-throated Loons differ from the other loons in a number of ways. They are the smallest and the only species of loon that can take off directly from land. They can also take off vertically from water, unlike the other loons, although they are unable to fly for several weeks at the end of the breeding season during the moult. While uncomfortable on land, they can travel large distances when necessary.

'Red-throats' are capable of varying their buoyancy, thus 'hiding' almost totally underwater with just bill and eyes showing, crocodile-style. Like Cormorants, they have a reputation for gluttony and have been known to suffocate from attempting to swallow large fish. They have relatively small breeding territories and will tolerate other breeding pairs nearby. They are highly susceptible to marine oil pollution.

The generic name *stellata* is from the Latin for stars and refers to the spangled pattern on their backs in winter. The Irish *Lóma rua* means 'red loon'.

FACTS & FIGURES

Rare but widespread winter visitors. Fish eaters. Up to six breeding pairs in summer, all in Donegal, and decreasing (97–02). Up to 1,100 wintering birds (94–00). Live max twenty-three years. Amber list. About five species of Gavia worldwide. Order: *Gaviiformes*; Family: *Gaviidae*.

3.2 GREBES – FOITHIGH

Of the twenty or so species in the grebe family worldwide, five can be seen in Ireland. They are fantastic water birds of lake and coastal waters and are more common than loons. They tend to be solitary birds marked by a dramatic change in plumage from summer to winter. In Ireland, we have two resident species, the fabulous Little Grebes and the regal Great Crested Grebes. In winter, we are visited by three other species, Horned Grebes,[1] Black-necked Grebes and Red-necked Grebes, the latter being particularly uncommon. Because of their solitary and uncommon nature, grebes do not figure strongly in Irish folklore and tradition. Great Crested Grebes, while nearly hunted to extinction in the nineteenth century for their crest and down feathers, were previously numerous, but has never fully recovered. As with most birds, they were eaten during hard times and provided a generous meal.

Grebes are known to consume their own feathers in large numbers. It is presumed that this is to line the stomach and slow digestion, to help with the number of fish consumed and the digestion of their bones.

3.2.1 The Great Crested Grebe

Foitheach mór | *Podiceps cristatus cristatus*

Great Crested Grebes are magnificent, double-crested birds. In summer, adults are resplendent with their chestnut lion's mane, side-burns and crest. These bright colours are lost in winter. Apart from their striking appearance in summer, Great Crested Grebes are known for their incredible courting dance. These excellent swimmers usually spend the winter at sea but come inland, in spring, to their favoured ponds. To begin the dance, a pair of grebes (the sexes are alike) approach head on. They shake their heads and rise out of the water face-to-face while uttering a rough cackling call. The birds then dive to the bottom and resurface to offer each other weed in a symbolic gesture of support and provision. Horned Grebes (*Podiceps auritus*) have a similar dance.

Like most grebes and divers, the feet are placed well back on the body for strong swimming, thus making them slow and clumsy on land and gaining them the name shared with Dabchicks, 'Arsefoot'. As they do not want to walk far, their nest is usually a floating raft of reeds at the edge of the water. When the striped chicks arrive, they are often ferried around on the parents' backs, which afford protection from the likes of scavenging Pike (*Esox lucius*).

The name 'grebe' probably comes from medieval French. The generic *podiceps* is from Latin meaning 'rump-footed' while the specific *cristatus* means 'crested'.

History: The soft head and crest feathers were called tippet feathers or grebe fur. These became very fashionable in the nineteenth century and thus in great demand for the millinery trade. As a result, the birds were nearly hunted to extinction in the UK. Luckily, the idea of bird conservation was gaining momentum at the time and the British government brought in new legislation to protect these beautiful birds. An organisation known as the 'Fur, Fin and Feather Folk' was formed by a group of women to protect these birds. This was the precursor to the Royal Society for the Protection of Birds (RSPB).

CULINARY

Though regarded as unpalatable, they were taken and eaten in hard times. They were also taken for their fur, crest feathers and skins.

NAMES

English: Crested Grebe, Greater Loon (west), Horn Ouzel (Uls.), Tippet Grebe (Don.), Tossel Head (Uls.)

Irish: Faoithean, Foithióch, Lúnadán, Spágaire (clumsy walker)

Uls. Scots: Molrooken (LN.)

Scientific: Colymbus cristatus

FACTS & FIGURES

Resident but scarce carnivores. Absent from many counties. Migrate internally within Ireland. Up to 2,500 breeding pairs in summer (88–91). Live max nineteen years. Amber list. About nine species of *Podiceps* worldwide. Order: *Podicipediformes*; Family: *Podicipedidae*.

3.2.2 Horned Grebe

Foitheach cluasach | *Podiceps auritus auritus*

& Black-necked Grebe

Foitheach píbdhubh | *Podiceps nigricollis nigricollis*

Horned and Black-necked Grebes are similar uncommon winter visitors, the Black-necked being far the less common. In winter, the birds are hard to tell apart, with black cap, dark upperparts, dirty white lower parts and conspicuous red eye. The Black-necked has a noticeable upturned-bill. In summer, the birds show striking plumage. Both have rusty red flanks, and dark upperparts with a red eye and yellow swept-back ear plumes but they are more easily told apart in summer. The Horned Grebe has much bigger yellow plumes on the head and has the general appearance of a small Great Crested Grebe. The 'Black-necked' does have a distinctive black neck with black head and breast.

Most sightings of the Black-necked in Ireland are in winter in the Wexford or Cork areas though some may still stay to breed in summer. Black-necked grebes were noticed breeding here in 1915. A colony of up to 300 pairs was discovered in Roscommon in 1929 before their lake was drained.

The Horned is much more likely to be seen in coastal bays and inlets all around the country. The name has been standardised to Horned Grebe. Irish ornithologists will be familiar with the birds as Slavonian Grebes.

NAMES

HORNED

English: Dusky Grebe, Sclavonian Grebe, Slavonian Grebe (Eur.)

Scientific: Podiceps cornutus

BLACK-NECKED

Scientific: Columbus auritus, Columbus cornutus

FACTS & FIGURES

Horned: Uncommon winter visitors from Northern Europe. Carnivorous. Live max seven years.

Black-necked: Uncommon winter visitors from Continent. Some breeding but numbers dropping. Carnivorous. Live max seven years. Red list. About nine species of *Podiceps* worldwide. Order: *Podicipediformes*; Family: *Podicipedidae*.

Horned Grebe

Black-necked Grebe

3.2.3 The Little Grebe

Spágaire tonn | *Tachybaptus ruficollis ruficollis*

Little Grebes or Dabchicks are amiable water birds found on quiet lakes and, sometimes, urban ponds. By their small size, they could be mistaken for the young of a larger species. Quite private birds, they spend a great deal of time underwater where, like many water birds, they seek refuge when threatened. They can remain underwater for some time but will often resurface at the lake's edge, out of sight, under reeds or overhanging foliage. Like some of the divers, they have the ability to sit semi-submerged in the water like a submarine or alligator with just the bill and eyes showing.

Like many water birds, their winter plumage is a pale reflection of their brilliant summer colours. In summer, they show a beautiful horse-like chestnut-red about the face and neck with a yellow spot at the base of the bill and a white powder-puff of feathers at the rear end.

Dabchicks build floating nests at the edge of a pond. The young are beautifully striped and are often ferried about on the adults' backs. Even with young on board, the adults will dive but the young bob to the surface like buoyant balls of fluff. At breeding time, Dabchicks have a call reminiscent of a horse whinnying.

Dabchicks, along with Coot, Moorhen and other species that nest at the water's edge have suffered greatly from the introduction of American Mink (*Neovison vison*), many of which escaped from mink farms.

The name Dabchick, or Dopchick as it used to be, probably comes from the old English 'dop' to dive. For those who like words, Dabchick is one of the very few words in the English language with the letters 'abc' together.

The Irish name *spágaire* probably comes from *spágach* meaning 'flat-footed' or 'clumsy' as these birds are very ungainly on land. *Tonn* means 'wave' which is a possible translation but it's likely that the word was originally *donn* meaning 'brown', thus *Spágaire tonn* translates as 'brown clumsy-bird'. An old name for the Dabchick in the UK is 'arsefoot'[2] probably because the feet are set so far back, like the loons. My mother called them 'ducky-divers' but then Cormorants or anything else that disappeared under the water was likely to be similarly labelled.

NAMES

English: Arsefoot, Bantam Grebe (Uls.), Black-chin Grebe, Dabchick, Diddiper (Wat.), Dipper, Drink-a-penny[3] (SL.), Penny Bird (Cck., Uls.), Puffin (inland), Tom Puddin' (Ant.), Willie Hawkie (Ant.)

Irish: Ducaire, Gabhlán uisce (water martin), Lapairín/Laparán locha, Laipirín, Lúnadán beag (Conn.), Tumaire/Tomaire beag (little diver)

Uls. Scots: Tam Whinney, Wee Diver, Whitterick

Scientific: Colymbus fluviatilis, Colymbus minor, Colymbus nigricans, Colymbus ruficollis, Podiseps fluviatilis, Podiceps/Podiseps minor, Podiseps minutus, Podiseps ruficollis, Sylbeocyclus minor

FACTS & FIGURES

Common resident carnivores with seasonal migration within Ireland. Up to 2,500 breeding pairs (88–91) with numbers increased in winter and overall numbers declining. Live max thirteen years. About five species of *Tachybaptus* worldwide. Order: *Podicipediformes*; Family: *Podicipedidae*.

Poetry: from*: 'Libby'*

Their great love for nature was their common bond
And on spring evenings they often walked to gray gum pond
Just to watch the little Dabchick dive for prey
Such happy memories never fade away.

Francis Duggan

3.3 HERONS & EGRETS – CORRA 'S ÉIGRITÍ

Only one species of the heron family *Ardeidae* is common in Ireland, the Grey Heron (*Ardea cinerea*) and its ubiquity here has generated a great deal of lore. Of the sixty or so other species in the family, worldwide only a handful are seen in Ireland, and rarely at that. Little Egret (*Egretta garzetta*) numbers are increasing and they are now locally common and breeding along the east and south coasts.

There is no significant biological difference between herons and egrets. White species tend to be called egrets. Bitterns (*Botaurus stellaris*), once more common in Ireland, make some rare appearances from Britain (see Section 5.1.1). Purple Herons (*Ardea purpurea*), Night Herons (*Nycticorax nycticorax*), Little Bitterns (*Ixobrychus minutus*) and Cattle Egrets (*Bubulcus ibis*) make very rare appearances.

Herons, egrets and Bitterns fly with their necks retracted, unlike the similarly large cranes, storks and spoonbills.

Grey Herons

3.3.1 The Little Egret

Éigrit bheag | *Egretta garzetta garzetta*

Little Egrets may once have been plentiful in Ireland. While they were absent from our shores for many years they have recently been making something of a comeback, probably due to our warming climate. The species bred for the first time in 1997 in Cork. They are beautiful snow-white birds looking something like dwarf albino herons, with pristine yellow feet. Despite being targeted in the past for the pot, and by the fashion industry for their feathers, their numbers are continually increasing in Ireland. Egrets get their name from the French word *aigrette* meaning a 'little heron'. The word has now also come to mean the long ornamental plume such as seen on an egret or heron. In the past, egrets suffered greatly for their plumes, with large numbers being taken to decorate ladies' hats. The Irish name *Éigrit bheag* translates directly as 'little egret'. The specific garzetta is the Italian word for the bird.

Our warming climate may yet attract significant numbers of the Little Egret's cousin, the Cattle Egret (*Bubulcus ibis, Éigrit eallaigh*) and single birds are now being seen, from time to time, arriving from continental Europe.

CULINARY

Egret was recorded in the bill of fare for the famous feast served to George Neville, at his enthronement as Archbishop of York, in 1466, in which one thousand birds were served up![1]

NAMES

Scientific: Ardea garzetta, Herodias garzette.

FACTS & FIGURES

Uncommon resident carnivores. Up to fifty-five breeding pairs (97–01) with numbers increasing. Live max twenty-two years. Amber list. About fourteen species of *egretta* herons/egrets worldwide. Order: *Ciconiiformes*; Family: *Ardeidae*.

3.3.2 The (Grey) Heron

Corr réisc | *Ardea cinerea cinerea*

Ireland's tallest birds, Grey Herons are striking water birds of river, lake and coast. The sexes are similar. The adults are largely grey with a grey-white neck and yellow bill, a black eye-stripe and black plumes when breeding.

When hunting, herons are solitary birds, fishing by the water's edge or searching for frogs in damp fields. With hunting over, they can often be seen congregating in the evening or at any time at good fishing grounds. They nest in tall trees in sometimes huge communal heronries. Nests are often reused year after year and can become quite large.

All herons have small serrations like the teeth of a comb on the side of their middle claw. These are used for preening in places where the heron cannot reach with its bill. Herons also have special feathers that slowly crumble into 'powder down', a cleansing powder. These are rubbed in with the claw and the powder assists in waterproofing. This powder, beneath the breast feathers, may be responsible for some reports of luminescence in herons, similar to that reported in Barn Owls.[2]

When displaying, Grey Herons perform 'bill-clappering', a ritualistic clapping together of the bills. The sound can carry great distances. After displaying, the male heron holds out a symbolic branch in his bill. The female takes it and uses it to start her nest.

Like many fishing birds, herons were persecuted in the past, as it was believed they were a danger to fish stocks. Today they suffer from toxins in the food chain, cold winters and collisions with overhead wires. They cannot fly in heavy wind and are particularly affected by storms.[3] When flushed they seem to ascend directly upwards.

The name heron was probably only adopted in the late seventeenth century, the birds previously being known as hernshaws or henshaws. The generic *Ardea* is the Latin for heron and the specific *cinerea* means 'ashy-coloured'. The Irish *corr* means 'heron' or 'Crane' and *réisc* means 'bog' or 'marsh'. Alternatively, the name could once have been *cor éisc* meaning 'fish-crane'.

Ireland's largest heronry (*garrán corr*) can be found in a 400-year-old weathered oak grove on Inishfendra Island near Newtownbutler, County Fermanagh.

History: The coat of arms of the Irish Ahern(e) family shows three standing herons.

Beliefs & Traditions: Herons are still commonly called cranes in Ireland. They should not be confused with the real Cranes (*Grus grus*) which were once more common here (see Section 5.1.2). The confusing of names makes historical references difficult to resolve.

Herons were hunted with Peregrines by royalty and nobility. Henry VIII brought in legislation to protect them – from everybody but royalty and nobility.

Herons (and/or cranes) were associated with both the Cailleach and the sea god Manannán Mac Lir. They represented the logical mind, as well as patience while healing. They were birds of the moon, magic, shamanic travel, secrets, and deep mysteries as well as symbols of contemplation, vigilance, divine wisdom and inner quietness. They were also symbols of the eternal struggle between good and evil. As a result, it was thought bad luck to kill a heron[4] (even though they were eaten when times were bad).

For anglers, dipping bait into water in which a *corr-iasc* had been cooked would give it the heron's power of catching fish. To catch a heron itself, all you had to do was sneak up behind and shout 'lie down' and the bird would fall in fright.

The (Grey) Heron continued

Hunters were careful however to avoid the large pointed bill with which it was believed the heron would poke out an eye. It was also believed here that small eels could pass safely through the digestive system of a heron, only perhaps to be eaten again.[5]

Keating, in the seventeenth century tells us of a queen and her handmaid who were turned into two herons at the word of St Colmcille[6] (sixth century).

Cures: In Ulster, it was believed that the fat of a heron, killed on a full moon, was believed to be an excellent remedy for rheumatism.

Weather: A heron flying south was a sign of good weather.[7]

Proverbs & Similes:

Chonálfadh sé na corra. ('*It would freeze the herons.*' [It is bitterly cold])

CULINARY

Herons were royal game birds and were reserved for the royal hunt. Heron was a highly regarded dish 'as much esteemed as Pheasants and Peacocks'.[8] They were often hunted with falcons.

PLACE NAMES

Heronstown: Dollymount, just north of Dublin city was formerly called Heronstown.
Corlough: Co. Cavan,
Co. Fermanagh, Co. Leitrim,
(Corloch, heron lake).
Heronstown: Co. Meath.
Inishnagor: Co. Donegal,
Co. Sligo (Inis na gCorr, crane or heron island).

NAMES

English: Blue Heron (Uls.), Crane, Fencock, Hernshaw, Joaneen the Bogs (Crk.), Johnny-the-Bog, Julie the Bogs, Long Tall Sally, Long-necked Heron, Molly the Bog (Crk.), Narry the Bogs (Kry.), Sheila Crane (Crk.), Stork (Kry.)

Irish: Cáití/Cáitigh fhada (long Katie, Conn.), Corr éisc (fish crane), Corr ghlas (grey crane), Corr ghrian (sun crane), Corrghlaise, Corrghréine, Corr iasc, Corr m(h)ona(dh)/Corr mhóna (bog crane, Tyr.), Corr riasc, Fiadh-chuirre, Jónaí[9] an scrogaill (Joan of the long thin neck, Din.), Máire fhada (long Mary, Conn.), Nóra an ragaidh (rough Nora), Nóra na bportach (Nora of the bog), Síle an phortaigh, Síle an ragaidh (rough Julie), Síle na bportach (Julie of the bog), Síle (fhada) na bportaigh ([long] Julie of the bogs), Síle na bportaithe (Din.), Síle raga, Siobhán na bportach (Joan of the bog, Crk.), Siobháinín an phuirt (Crk.), Siobháinín na cuaiche (Crk.)

Uls. Scots: Cran, Hern, Long-necked Hern

Scientific: Ardea major

FACTS & FIGURES

Common resident carnivores. Almost one metre tall. Wingspan almost two metres. Live max thirty-five years. Up to 10,000 breeding pairs (88–91) with numbers inflated in winter. Collective name: a siege of herons. About fourteen species of *ardea* herons/egrets worldwide. Order: *Ciconiiformes*; Family: *Ardeidae*.

3.4 DUCKS, GEESE & SWANS – LACHAIN, GÉANNA'S EALAÍ

There are nearly 150 species of ducks, geese and swans worldwide. Over thirty of these can be seen in Ireland and these are mostly ducks. These birds have evolved to live on water, both inland and at sea, with the ability to swim and float, with webbed feet and flattened bills. Many can produce water-resistant oil with which to clean and insulate their feathers. Comprising the family *Anatidae*, swans tend to be the largest, geese are medium-sized and ducks are the smallest. Some big ducks are larger than small geese, for example, Eider ducks or even Mallards can be bigger than Brent Geese. Ducks that can be seen in Ireland can be divided further into diving ducks (e.g. Tufted Duck), dabbling ducks (e.g. Wigeon), fish-eating sawbills (e.g. mergansers), sea ducks (e.g. Eider) and Shelduck. Geese tend to be divided into grey geese (e.g. Greylag), black geese (e.g. Brent Goose) and white geese (e.g. Snow Goose). Swan and geese sexes are alike but ducks are often very different. Swans and geese mate for life but ducks can be more promiscuous.

Nearly all ducks, geese and swans have been used for food and many such as Eider ducks and most geese have been harvested for their soft feathers. Geese have been used through time as 'watch-geese' because of their loud honking and territorial instinct. Many geese and swans have been domesticated for thousands of years. For Mallard and Greylag Geese and domesticated birds, please see Section 4.

Anser is the Latin for goose. *Anas* is Latin for duck. 'Goose' comes from the Anglo-Saxon *gos*. 'Swan' comes from the Anglo-Saxon *Swanne*. 'Duck' comes from the Anglo-Saxon *duce* to dive.

Collective name: a ballet of swans, a bank of swans, a bevy of swans, a dopping of ducks, a flush of ducks, a herd of swans, a lamentation of swans, a paddling of ducks, a plump of waterfowl, a raft of ducks, a sownder of swans, a team of ducks, a wedge of swans, a whiteness of swans.

Beliefs & Traditions: There is a prejudice against eating geese in some parts of Ireland that may date back to the time of the Celts who held them as sacred. St Martin's Day (Martinmas) falls on 11 November and is especially celebrated in Germany and Scandinavia. In the fourth century, St Martin (of Tours) was betrayed by the honking of a flock of geese[1] when he tried to hide in a flock before being appointed bishop. He got his revenge by cooking one for dinner!

Another version suggests that St Martin was lecturing the people of a village one day about their wicked ways and a goose started honking so loudly that it interfered with his speech. Not to be outdone he ordered the goose slaughtered, and then finished his sermon. Afterward the goose was cooked and served to him. In this version however, St Martin choked to death while eating the goose.

On Ireland's western islands, Connacht, north Munster, and south Leinster a tradition grew whereby on every St Martin's Eve (10 November), a goose or black cock or white hen was killed and the blood was sprinkled on the floor and threshold and sometimes in the four corners of each room of the house.[2] In some places, every member of the household was sprinkled in blood, often with the sign of the cross on the forehead. It was thought very unlucky not to do so. In other parts of the country, the blood was sprinkled on the doorposts and windows of the house, on the corners of the house, and in the stable and barn to keep out bad spirits. The flesh of the animal was cooked and eaten the next day, St Martin's Day.[3] Geese were also eaten on St Michael's Day (*Fómhar na ngéanna*, Geese Harvest or Michaelmas), 29 September in both Ireland and Britain, a tradition which dates back to a time when tenants included a goose in the rent payment to the landlord. Lady Wilde tells us that the son of a king choked on a goose bone but was restored by St Patrick. So the king ordered a goose to be sacrificed every year on the anniversary of that day and in honour of St Michael.[4] It was said, that if you ate goose on Michaelmas Day you would not want for money for the rest of the year. It was also a tradition on this day for farmers to give a gift of a goose to the poor and to sell the down and feathers for pillows and mattresses.

No part of the goose was spared: goose feathers were used for pillows and quilts, quills were used for writing, the eggs and fat for baking, the wing was used for dusting and the blood for soup. It was said all parts of the goose were used, except the honk!

Weather: A low-flying 'V' formation of geese was a sign of imminent rain. In practice, this may be true, as the birds fly beneath low rain-bearing cloud.

Proverbs & Similes:

A goose never voted for an early Christmas . . .

A wild goose never reared a tame gosling . . .[5]

Don't send a goose with a message to the fox's den . . .[6]

Don't leave the fox minding the geese . . .

Scata ban no scata géanna. (A group of women and a flock of geese are similar [noisy])

Small goslings make fine geese.[7] (To encourage patience.)

What's good/sauce for the goose is good/sauce for the gander . . .

When the fox is the preacher, let the goose not listen to his sermon . . .[8]

3.4.1 The Mute Swan

Eala bhalbh | *Cygnus olor*

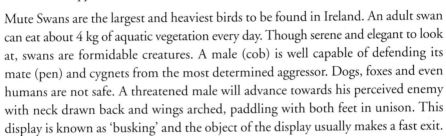

'*The silver swan, who, living had no note,*
When death approached unlocked her silent throat.' [9]

Mute Swans are the largest and heaviest birds to be found in Ireland. An adult swan can eat about 4 kg of aquatic vegetation every day. Though serene and elegant to look at, swans are formidable creatures. A male (cob) is well capable of defending its mate (pen) and cygnets from the most determined aggressor. Dogs, foxes and even humans are not safe. A threatened male will advance towards his perceived enemy with neck drawn back and wings arched, paddling with both feet in unison. This display is known as 'busking' and the object of the display usually makes a fast exit.

The Mute is one of three swan species found in Ireland today. With their conspicuous red bills, Mutes are by far the most common. The much rarer Bewick's (*Eala Bewick*) and Whooper Swans (*Eala ghlórach*) have yellow and black bills. Mute Swans do not sing, hence the name, but they do make a number of noises including the formidable warning hiss and a selection of low grunts for communication. A cob with its wings in the classic upright position is giving a clear message to keep away. However, the flat back of a swan provides an excellent platform on which to carry young cygnets. Mute Swans are the only swans capable of holding their neck in a curve. Their 'clamorous wings',[10] as Yeats put it, make a very distinctive, almost musical sound when flying.

Typically, swans pair, build their nest and raise their young away from other swans. In winter though, they often gather in large groups on open stretches of water. Nests may be reused year after year. Swans have a reputation for mating for life but this is not always true. While a pair may stay together for many seasons, they can split up. In fact, it is said that this 'divorce' rate among swans is lower in Ireland than the UK.

While swans are well loved in Ireland, they do get a hard time from litter and discarded fishing equipment. There is a high mortality rate from ingesting lead weights and fishing line and hooks and from collision with overhead power lines.

Both the generic name *cygnus* and the specific name *olor* are Latin for swan, so the *Cygnus olor* is the 'swan swan'. The word 'swan' was originally *swanne* and may be from the Latin *sonus* meaning 'sound'.

History: It is believed that the Normans, and possibly Richard I himself, introduced Mute Swans into Britain and Ireland from Cyprus at the close of the twelfth century. A Mute Swan phase where young birds are mostly white instead of grey and have pink or grey feet instead of black is today identified as a form of leucism but was once regarded as a separate species, the Polish swan (*Cygnus immutabilis*).

The Mute Swan continued

Beliefs & Traditions: Most myths and legends including the legend of the 'Children of Lir' refer to the native winter swans. See Section 3.4.2.

Swans' pairing for life was a sign of fidelity. As such, a swan's feather, sewn into a husband's pillow, would ensure fidelity.[11] It was bad luck to kill a swan[12] or even to interfere with the body of a dead swan[13] as it was believed that they held the souls of virtuous maidens.

It was believed (incorrectly) that Mute Swans only sang at the moment before death, hence the phrase 'swansong'.

Proverbs & Similes:

Chomh geal leis an eala.

(As white or as pure as the swan.)

Poetry: The serenity and beauty of the swan is well known and has moved many a poet. Yeats wrote a number of poems featuring swans, from the deeply beautiful 'Wild Swans at Coole' to the disturbing 'Leda and the Swan' of 1928. The latter recants the Greek tale. Leda was a beautiful woman living in Sparta. She caught the eye of Tyndareus, the King of Sparta, and they were married. She had several children as his queen, including the famous Helen of Troy. However, Helen was not in fact Tyndareus' child, but a child of the god who came to earth disguised as a huge swan. Captivated by Leda's beauty, he seduced her and, still in his swan form, made love to her. She then produced an egg from which Helen was born.

from: 'The Wild Swans at Coole'

> The trees are in their autumn beauty,
> The woodland paths are dry,
> Under the October twilight the water
> Mirrors a still sky;
> Upon the brimming water among the stones
> Are nine and fifty swans.

William Butler Yeats, 1919, from *The Collected Poems of W. B. Yeats* (Macmillan, 1993)

CULINARY

Swans were initially owned by the rich and powerful and kept semi-domestically as decorative objects in private gardens. They were known as 'royal birds' and were highly prized for the table but were saved for special occasions. Some carried ownership marks on the bill or feet. Payne-Gallwey recommended only young birds as fit for the table. They are now a protected species.

NAMES

English: cob (male), cygnet (yng.), pen (fem.), tame swan

Irish: Cráin eala (fem. breeding swan), Gall, gandal (eala) (male), Geis/Géis (Kry.), Searfán (Kry.)

Scientific: Anas olor

FACTS & FIGURES

Common resident omnivores. Widespread in all counties but locally scarce. Up to 10,000 breeding pairs (88–91). Can weight up to 13 kg, reach a metre and a half in length, have a two- to three-metre wing span and can live max twenty-eight years in the wild or up to fifty years in captivity. The national bird of Denmark. About six species of *cygnus* swans worldwide. Order: *Anseriformes*; Family: *Anatidae*.

3.4.2 The Whooper Swan

Eala ghlórach | *Cygnus cygnus cygnus*

& Bewick's Swan

Eala Bewick | *Cygnus columbianus bewickii*

Whooper Swan

While Mute Swans are our common resident swans with which most Irish people are familiar, there are two other migratory swans that visit our shores every year; Whooper Swans and Bewick's Swans. While superficially similar to 'Mutes', both Whooper's and Bewick's have bright yellow bills contrasting with the Mutes' red/orange. The yellow on the bill of Bewick's Swans is less extensive than that of the Whooper's and all Bewick's have a unique pattern by which they can be identified as individuals. A flock of Bewick's flying overhead is easily identified, sounding somewhat like a war-tribe on the move.

Visiting Whooper Swans generally come from their breeding grounds in Iceland. Bewick's breed in the Arctic tundra of Russia and the western population there visits us in winter. Five per cent of the world's Whooper Swans spend the winter on Lough Erne. Whooper Swans are very close relatives of the North American Trumpeter Swans (*Cygnus buccinator*) while Bewick's Swans are a sub-species of

The Whooper Swan & Bewick's Swan continued

Bewick's Swan

Tundra Swan and are close relatives of the North American Whistling Swans (*Cygnus columbianus columbianus*). Bewick's Swans were named after the British naturalist Thomas Bewick (1753–1828) who wrote the celebrated *A History of British Birds* at the end of the eighteenth century. The first person to describe Bewick's Swan, distinguishing it from the Whooper Swan, was William Yarrell (1784–1856), in 1830. Whooper Swans are named after their whooping call. The Latin *colombianus* refers to the Columbia River in the western US after which the American Whistling Swan was named. Quite oddly, Whooper Swans were called 'elk' in parts of England and Northern Ireland.

History: As Mute Swans did not arrive in Ireland until around the twelfth century, Whooper and Bewick's Swans can be said to be our original native swans and are likely to be the 'wild swans' referred to in Irish legend. These swans are collectively called winter swans or just wild swans. Gerald of Wales mentions the presence of a large number of swans in the north of the country in the twelfth century and these are likely to be Whooper or Bewick's. Robert Payne in the sixteenth century mentions a *'great store of wild swannes . . . much more plentiful than in England'*.[14]

Beliefs & Traditions: Swans were birds of mystery and magic, held sacred in Ireland in antiquity. It was widely believed that the souls of people were embodied in swans and that angels could appear as swans and so killing a swan was totally forbidden. It was believed that a swan could put a person under her spell with her beautiful singing voice. While under the spell, time passed more quickly for the person and they could awake to find the world a changed place.

Swans are most famous in Irish lore for their role in the legend, originally from the Glens of Antrim, of the Children of Lir[15] (*Oidheadh Chlainne Lir*). Lear, the Irish god of the sea, took Aoife as his third wife. He had four children by his previous wife: Fionnuala, Aed, and the twins Fiachra and Conn. Aoife was barren and became jealous of the children. She took them to Lake Derryvaragh in Westmeath. Aoife ordered her servants to kill the children but they refused, so she used her magic to change them into swans. She cursed them to live as nomadic swans for nine hundred years. Only if a southern woman married a northern man would the spell be broken. Aoife's servants told her father, Bodb, what she had done and he turned her into a wind spirit. Bodb and Lear then went to Lake Derryvaragh to keep the children company. Lear made a law that no swans could be killed in Ireland, and in a sense this law is still in force today as swans are protected. After nine hundred years, the swans returned home but all traces of their father were gone. The elusive wedding between the southern woman and northern man took place and the swans turned back into humans but died immediately because of their age. Today a winter swan still appears on the coat of arms of County Westmeath and the shape of Lake Derryvaragh is said to look like a swan from the air.

The 'Wooing of Etáin' (*Tochmarc Étaine*) legend tells of the Irish King Midir of the Tuatha Dé Danann and his obsession with the beautiful Etáin of Ulster. In short, Midir ends up playing an ancient chess-like game with Eochaid, the High

The Whooper Swan & Bewick's Swan continued

King and husband of Etáin, at Tara. In one game he plays for a kiss or embrace from Etáin and wins. When Midir appears before Etáin to claim his prize, the pair change into swans and fly away through a hole in the roof.

In Mayo, it was believed that swans contained the souls of maidens who had died virtuous and that they had the capability of turning back into women. Anyone who interfered with a wild swan would die by the end of the year.[16] Echoes of this belief are found in swan-maiden legends all over Europe. A typical version tells a man who finds a beautiful maiden swimming in a lake wearing nothing but a cloak. The man takes the cloak, marries the woman and they settle down and have children. From that point on, the man does not let the woman have the cloak back. Inevitably, spurred by a great urge, the woman finds the cloak, puts it on, turns into a swan and flies away.

A folk tale from County Clare tells of the O'Quins of Inchiquin in the fifteenth century. One day, a young chief of the O'Quins was walking on the west shore of Lough Inchiquin when he saw some wild swans. He caught one and brought it home whereupon it turned into a beautiful woman. She agreed to marry him on three conditions: the marriage should be a secret, he should never ask an O'Brien to his house and he should avoid all games of chance. One day, after several happy years and two children, O'Quin went to the races. After the races, he asked some O'Briens back to his house to play cards whereupon his wife burst into tears, turned back into a swan and disappeared into the lake with her two cygnets. A belief endured in the area that if a swan were killed on the lough, one of the villagers would die.[17] This type of 'swan-maiden' legend endures right across Europe.

PLACE NAMES

Carravinally, Co. Antrim. (Ceathramh na n-ealaí (the swan's quarterland)
Swan Island, Larne Lough, Co. Antrim. Swan Island, Strangford Lough, Co. Down. Tullynally Castle, Co. Westmeath, Tullach an allach (the swan's hill)

NAMES

WHOOPER

English: Elk (Ant, Dow.), (Great) Wild Swan, Hooper, Hooping Swan, Whistling Swan[19]
Irish: Ela, Gall, Géis
Scientific: Anas cygnus, Cygnus ferus, Cygnus musicus

BEWICK'S

English: Tundra Swan (US), Wild Swan
Irish: Eala Bhewick, Gall, Géis
Scientific: Anas colombianus, Cygnus bewicki/bewickii, Cygnus islandicus, Cygnus minor, Olor bewickii, Olor colombianus

FACTS & FIGURES

WHOOPER

Herbivorous winter visitors. A handful breeds here, nesting in Donegal. Up to 9,000 birds in winter (94–00). Live max twenty-six years. Amber list. The national bird of Finland.

BEWICK'S

Herbivorous winter visitors. Up to 1,000 birds in winter (94–00) but declining. Live max twenty-three years. Amber list.
About six species of cygnus swans worldwide. Order: *Anseriformes*; Family: *Anatidae*.

The concept of a 'swan song' dates, at least, from the time of Aristotle. It is derived from the belief that a swan will sing a song the moment before it dies. As this is unlikely to be a Mute Swan, we may presume that it is the Whooper or Bewick's swan which is referred to. Indeed it is said that a Whooper Swan on being shot will expel air involuntarily thus making a song-like sound. Gerald of Wales mentions this in the twelfth century. Orlando Gibbons' madrigal of 1612 mentions the swan song:

'*The Silver Swan*' (madrigal)

> *The silver swan, who, living had no note,*
> *When death approached unlocked her silent throat.*
> *Leaning her breast upon the reedy shore,*
> *Thus sang her first and last, and sang no more:*
> *'Farewell, all joys! O Death, come close mine eyes!*
> *More Geese than Swans now live, more Fools*
> *than Wise.'*

Orlando Gibbons, 1612

Weather: A sudden appearance of a wild swan at an unusual location is a sure sign of severe frost to come.[18]

Poetry:

from '*The Wings of Love*'

> *From the lake and the sky and the rings of the jumping fish;*
> *Till our ears are filled from the reeds with a sudden swish,*
> *And a sound like the beating of flails in the time of corn.*
> *We shall hold our breath while a wonderful thing is born*
> *From the songs that were chanted by bards in the days gone by;*
> *For a wild white swan shall be leaving the lake for the sky,*
> *With the curve of her neck stretched out in a silver spear.*
> *Oh! Then when the creak of her wings shall have brought her near,*

James Henry Cousins (1873–1956)

3.4.3 The Brent Goose[20]

Cadhan | *Branta bernicla hrota* (white-bellied race)
Branta bernicla bernicla (dark-bellied race)

Any Dubliner living along the coast will be very familiar with the huge flocks of Brent Geese that arrive every winter to graze on any piece of open grass. They are most likely to be the geese arriving in long v-shaped skeins. They have become quite used to heavy traffic passing by and go busily about their business. They are constantly calling, with their own special 'cronking' call. They are small, generally grey-black with varying white to dark underbellies and a dull dirty-white neck ring.

Of the black geese group, Brent Geese come in a number of varieties (races). The ones we are most familiar with in Ireland are the Pale-bellied Brent that visit from Greenland and Canada. Ireland provides the only wintering ground for this race of goose in Europe. Dark-bellied Brent (*B.b.bernicla*) are much rarer visitors from Siberia and, the American Black Brant (*B.b.nigricans*) are rarer still.

The word 'brant' probably comes from the Norse 'brand' meaning 'burnt'. The generic *bernicla* means 'barnacle' as this bird has always been confused with the Barnacle Goose. The Irish *cadhan* is a name meaning 'brent' or 'barnacle' goose and is a diminutive of *cadhnóg*. Jeff Greenhalgh[21] suggests the birds may be named after St Brendan, the sixth century Irish saint who travelled extensively and may have been familiar with the birds. In the sixteenth century at least, the birds were referred to as *Anser brendinus*.

History: Watters tells us, in the mid-nineteenth century, that Brent Geese visited Dublin Bay in huge numbers and, '. . . an island opposite Clontarf we have seen at times almost black with numbers of these birds'.[22]

CULINARY

Brent were generally regarded as the finest geese to eat.[23] Boate[24] in the eighteenth century thought them 'rank' but he may have been referring to Barnacle Geese and he notes that the taste varies greatly depending on their diet. Watters tells us that markets in Liverpool, Manchester and Edinburgh were supplied with Brent Geese obtained in Ireland.[25]

PLACE NAMES

Gortnagoyne: Co. Galway, Co. Roscommon (Gort na gCadhan, Brent Goose field)

NAMES

English: Barnacle (Uls.), Black Goose, Sea Goose, Wexford Barnacle

Irish: Cadhnóg, Gé dhubh (dark-breasted form)

Uls. Scots: Bernicle (Uls.), Black Bernicle, Sea Bernicle

Scientific: Anas bernicla, Anas brenta, Anser bernicla, Anser brendinus, Anser brenta, Anser ferus, Anser scoticus, Anser torquata, Anser torquatus, Bernicla brenta

FACTS & FIGURES

Common winter visitors. Herbivorous. Found in most coastal areas. Up to 14,000 wintering birds (94–00). Live max twenty-eight years. Amber list. About six species of *Branta* geese worldwide. Order: *Anseriformes*; Family: *Anatidae*.

3.4.4 The Barnacle Goose

Gé ghiúrainn | *Branta leucopsis*

Barnacle Geese are beautiful black, white and grey birds that visit Ireland in winter, almost exclusively from Greenland. They are close relatives of the more common Brent Geese, which are also winter visitors. Small geese, the 'barnacles' can be seen in many locations around the Irish coast, particularly favouring islands. The Latin *leucopsis* means 'white-faced'. The Irish *giúrann* means 'barnacle'.

Beliefs & Traditions: It was believed that Barnacle Geese were a type of fish or shellfish and were born on old timber (particularly fir-tree wood) on the bottom of the sea. In his *Topographia Hibernica* of 1186, Gerald of Wales wrote:

'*They [Barnacle Geese] are produced from timber tossed along the sea and are at first like gum. Afterwards, they hang down by their beaks as if they were seaweed attached to the timber and are surrounded by shells in order to grow more freely. Having thus in the process of time been clothed with a strong coat of feathers, they either fall into the water or fly freely away into the air. They derive their food and growth from the sap of the wood or from the sea by a secret and most wonderful process of alimentation. I have frequently seen with my own eyes more than a thousand of these birds hanging down on the seashore from one piece of timber enclosed in their shells and already formed. They do not breed and lay eggs like other birds nor do they ever hatch any eggs, nor*

CULINARY

According to Audubon, the flesh of a Barnacle Goose is sweet and tender, and highly esteemed for the table.[28] However, Payne-Gallwey did not rate them at all. This apparent difference, whilst perhaps a matter of taste is more likely a matter of misidentification as Brent Geese were often incorrectly referred to as 'barnacles' in Ireland. Barnacle geese could be eaten during Lent as they were regarded as fish.

PLACE NAMES

Inishkea Islands, Co. Mayo
(*Inis Gé*, goose island)

NAMES

English: Clakis, (Land) Bernicle/ Bernacle, Northern Bernicle, Norway Barnacle/Bernicle, (White-faced) Bernacle, White-faced Barnacle, White-fronted Bernicle

Irish: Éan giúghrainn (barnacle bird), Gé giúghrainn, Gearán, Gighring (Don.), Giodhraing, Giodhrán, Giodhrann (Don.), Giúghraing, Giúghrann, Giughrannach/Giuirneach (Aran.), Giuirlín

Scientific: Anser bernicla, Anas erythropus, Anser leucopsis, Bernicla leucopsis

69

The Barnacle Goose continued

do they seem to build nests in any corner of the earth. Hence bishops and religious men in some parts of Ireland do not scruple to dine off birds at the time of fasting because they are not flesh nor born of flesh.'[26]

While Gerald seems to have been gravely misled, there is a simple explanation of this misunderstanding. The shellfish *Lepas anatifera* is known in English as the Goose Barnacle. A cursory glance at a photo of a colony of these shellfish shows that they look something similar to the necks, heads and beaks of Barnacle Geese. Thus, the goose was named. This ties in with the Barnacle Goose being migratory, breeding in Greenland, and the nests never being found in Ireland. This belief pertained in Donegal until the early part of the twentieth century.

In any case, Barnacle Geese were regarded by the church as a type of fish and could be eaten as fish during Lent[27] and other times when meat eating was forbidden for religious reasons.

Poetry: '*A Marbáin, a díthruhaig*'

Tellin cíarainn
cerdán cruinne,
cróán séim;
gigrainn, cadain,
gair ré samain,
seinm ngaorb céor.

Bees, beetles,
Humming of the world,
Gentle crooning
Barnacle Geese, Brent Geese
Winter clamours
Music of a dark torrent.

Anon (ninth century)

FACTS & FIGURES

Winter visitors. Herbivorous. Some feral breeding in Strangford Lough. Up to 9,000 wintering birds (94–00). Live max twenty-four years. Weigh almost 2 kg. About six species of *Branta* geese worldwide. Order: *Anseriformes*; Family: *Anatidae.*

3.4.5 The (Greater) White-fronted Goose

Gé bhánéadanach |

Anser albifrons flavirostris (Greenland White-fronted Goose)
Anser albifrons albifrons (Russian White-fronted Goose (rare))

CULINARY

White-fronts were eaten. Payne-Gallwey regarded them as good eating, behind the Brent and young Bean Goose. Both the Bean (rare) and White-front were used in giblet soup in Ireland.[29]

NAMES

English: Barred Goose, Bog Goose,[30] Great Harrow Goose, Greater White-fronted Goose, Laughing Goose (Don.), Tortoise-shell Goose, White-faced Goose

Irish: Gandal (male), Gé (bheag) fionn ([little] white goose), Gé ghlas[31] (grey goose)

Scientific: Anas albifrons, Anas erythropus, Branta albifrons

FACTS & FIGURES

Locally common winter visitors. Herbivorous. Present locally in the west, northwest and Wexford. Up to 12,000 wintering birds (94–00). Live max twenty-five years. Amber list. About eight species of *Anser* worldwide. Order: *Anseriformes*; Family: *Anatidae*.

Traditionally known in Ireland as Bog Geese, White-fronted Geese look very much like Greylags on first inspection. Actually, the 'white-fronted' in the name refers to the white ring around the base of the bill which distinguishes it from all other 'grey' geese, except for Lesser White-fronted Geese (*Anser erythropus*), very rare vagrants from northern Europe. The Greenland *flavirostris* race has a distinctly orange bill compared to the pink of other races, which explains the scientific name. Adult 'white-fronts' also have distinctive black bars across the belly. Sexes are alike. The majority of Ireland's 'white-fronts' are of the *flavirostris* race which come to us from western Greenland via Iceland. In fact, half to three-quarters of the world's 'Greenland' race winter in Ireland. A few vagrants of the Siberian race *albifrons* stray to Ireland in winter. The birds tend to be nervous and take flight at the slightest sign of danger. Flying in groups, they adopt the typical goose 'V' formation. The Irish name *Gé Bhánéadanach* literally means 'white-faced goose'. The Latin *albifrons* means 'white-browed'.

The (Common) Shelduck

3.4.6 The (Common) Shelduck

Seil-lacha | *Tadorna tadorna*

The largest ducks in Ireland, Shelduck are exotically coloured goose-like ducks. Males (sheldrake) and females (shelduck) are broadly alike, being generally black and white with a broad chestnut band across the chest, a dark green, almost black head and bright red bill. Males have a large red knob on their bills. Females tend to quack in true duck fashion while the males honk and whistle.

Shelduck nest in old rabbit burrows and holes in trees and the like. Females have the ability to carry their young on their backs. Both male and female can be quite aggressive during the mating season. The nest burrows can sometimes be quite a distance from the sea but, as soon as the chicks emerge, they are led to the sea by the parents, in line, sometimes a distance of several miles. The young from different families sometimes group together forming 'nursery schools' or crèches. After breeding, most of the adults depart in mid-summer to Britain and Germany on a sort of summer vacation, and form huge moulting flocks, only to return to Ireland in autumn/winter. A few 'baby-sitter' adults stay behind and mind the young birds in their crèches.

In New England and other parts of the US, the Red-breasted Merganser and Goosander are often called Shel-Duck or Shel-Drake. The word derives from the Middle-English *scheld* (meaning 'variegated'). The term is often used, locally, for other ducks. The *seil* in the Irish *Seil-lacha* is probably just an expression of the English shel, with *lacha* meaning 'duck'. The scientific *tadorna* is from the French *tadorne* and is perhaps originally Celtic with the meaning 'pied duck'.

CULINARY

Shelduck are generally regarded as inedible. Payne-Gallwey described them as 'vile'.[32] Watters tells us that they did appear in the markets.[33]

NAMES

English: Bar Duck/Barduck[34] (Uls.), Bardrake, Burrow Duck (Don.), Mussel Duck, Sand Goose, Scale-Drake (SL.), Shell-Goose, Shelldrake, Shellduck

Irish: Lacha bhreac/Lacha bhreach (mottled duck), Lacha chriosrua (red-banded duck)

Uls. Scots: Sheildrake

Scientific: Anas cornuta, Anas tadorna, Tadorna cornuta, Tadorna vulpanser, Vulpanser tadorna

FACTS & FIGURES

Common resident carnivores. Up to 1,000 breeding pairs (88–91). Live max twenty-four years. Weigh up to 1.5 kg. Amber list. About six species of *Tadorna* worldwide. Order: *Anseriformes*; Family: *Anatidae*.

3.4.7 The (Northern) Shoveler

Spadalach | *Anas clypeata*

Shoveler are beautiful dabbling ducks with fat shovel-like bills. With their green heads, the drakes can be confused with Mallard but the beautiful chestnut belly and spoon-shaped bill is distinctive. Locally common in winter where they arrive from Scandinavia and Russia, they breed in small numbers at a few Irish locations in summer. Their broad shovel-bills are adapted for water filtering and have developed comb-like teeth, which enable them to strain food, as would a whale or indeed a flamingo. Shoveler will sometimes swim in tight circles to cause a whirlpool, forcing food particles to the surface. The Irish *spadalach* translates roughly as 'spoon or spatula duck'. The specific *clypeata* is from Latin meaning 'shield-shaped' (referring to the bill).

CULINARY

Shoveler were traditionally shot by hunters and while highly regarded for the table were regarded as inferior to Mallard. In the US, they were often referred to as 'neighbour's Mallards' because some hunters give them to their neighbours, keeping the tastier Mallards for themselves. On the other hand, Payne-Gallwey regarded fresh-water Shoveler as second only to Pintail.[35] Watters also regarded them highly.[36]

NAMES

English: Blue-winged Shoveller, Flapper (yng. Don.), Maiden Duck (Wex.), Scupper-bill, Sheldrake/Shelldrake (Wat.), Shovel-bill, Spoonbill (Uls., Wat.), Whinyard[37] (Wat.)

Irish: Slapaire (slovenly creature), Spadalghob (spatula-bill)

Scientific: Clypeata macrorhynchos, Rhynchaspis clypeata, Spathulea clypeata, Spatula clypeata

FACTS & FIGURES

Resident omnivores. Up to 100 breeding pairs (88–91). Perhaps 8,000 in winter. Live max twenty years. Weigh up to 1 kg. About fifty species of *Anas* ducks worldwide. Order: *Anseriformes*; Family: *Anatidae*.

The (Common) Goldeneye

3.4.8

Órshúileach | *Bucephala clangula clangula*

Goldeneye are beautiful ducks, locally common in Ireland in winter. Males and females vary considerably in colour to the extent that they were thought of as separate species in the nineteenth century, the females and young birds being known as Morillons. Males are generally white, with tiger-like black markings on the back, dark green domed heads (looking black from a distance), white face patches and the conspicuous bright yellow eyes from which they get their names. Females on the other hand, are generally dull-grey with chestnut/chocolate domed heads and the same conspicuous yellow eyes. Males have a dramatic whistling courtship display, regarded by some as the most dramatic of all ducks. Fast fliers, their wing-beats make a very distinctive whistling sound. The scientific name *Bucephala* is from the Greek word *boukephalos* meaning 'ox-' or 'buffalo-headed' while *clangula* refers to the whistling sound of the bird's wings. The Irish *órshúileach* translates directly as 'golden-eyed' and is the only Irish word for this bird. American Goldeneye are of the same species but different race: *Bucephala clangula americana*.

CULINARY

Goldeneye were eaten but were not considered good, with a very strong taste.[38] They were sold in Dublin markets in the nineteenth century.[39]

NAMES

English: Curre (LN.), Fresh-water Wigeon (SL.), Golden-eye Diver, Golden-eye Duck, Golden-eye Garrot, Magpie Diver, Magpie Wigeon, Morillon (yng. & fem.), Painted Duck, Popping Wigeon (Drg.), Whistle-Wing, Whistler (Uls.)

Scientific: Anas clangula, Anas glaucion, Clangula glaucion, Clangula vulgaris, Fuligula clangula, Glaucion clangula, Glaucionetta clangula

FACTS & FIGURES

Locally common winter visitors with a few stragglers staying for summer. Omnivorous. Males weigh up to 1 kg. Live max sixteen years. Amber list. Three species of *Bucephala* worldwide. Order: *Anseriformes*; Family: *Anatidae*.

The Tufted Duck

The (Greater) Scaup

3.4.9 The Tufted Duck

Lacha bhadánach | *Aythya fuligula*

& the (Greater) Scaup

Lacha iascán | *Aythya marila marila*

Affectionately known as 'tufties', Tufted Ducks are small but charming black and white diving ducks with a tuft on the head, often found on local ponds. The Irish *badánach* means 'tufted'. The alternative *tonnóg* may mean 'wave-bird' or 'dark-bird' (*dunnóg*). The specific *fuligula* is from Latin, meaning 'sooty-throated'.

Close relations, Scaup are much less commonly seen, but sometimes a few can be found in a local 'tuftie' flock. Scaup and 'tufties' look very similar, with bright yellow eyes and dark head and chest. Scaup can be identified by their lack of tuft and grey rather than black backs. The Irish *lacha iascán* means 'fish' or 'mussel duck'. *Aythia* is from Greek, meaning 'gull' or 'diving bird'. The specific *marila* is from Greek, meaning 'charcoal'. The name 'scaup' (originally Scaup duck) means 'mussel-bed' reflecting the birds' alleged favourite meal.

Weather: If a Scaup (or Pochard or Goldeneye) was seen sleeping on a calm day, it was taken as a sure sign that a storm was coming.[40]

CULINARY

Scaup were eaten but were regarded as third-rate because of their oily taste.[41] Tufted Duck, on the other hand, were regarded as excellent.[42] Both were sold in Dublin markets.

NAMES

TUFTED

English: Crested Diver, Gold-eye Duck (Wex.), Little Black Diver, Tufted Pochard, Tuftie (sl.), Tufty (sl.), White-sided Diver (Arm.), White-sided Duck (Arm.)

Irish: Lacha dhubh (black duck), Tonnóg bhadánach (tufted wave-bird) (Ant.)

Scientific: Anas fuligula, Fuligula cristata, Fuligula fuligula, Nyroca fuligula

SCAUP

English: Black Diver, Black-headed Diver, Black Wigeon[43] (Uls), Blue-Bill, Blue-Billed Wigeon, Bridle Duck (fem., Dub.), Diving Wigeon, Green-headed Diver (male, Bel.), Mule (Wex.), Mussel Duck, Norway Duck (Bel.), Scaup Pochard, Spoonbill, White-faced Duck

Irish: Lacha scápach (mussel duck)

Scientific: Anas marila, Fuligula marila, Fuligula marila/marilla, Nyroca marila

FACTS & FIGURES

TUFTED: Common resident. Live max twenty years. Up to 2,500 breeding pairs (88–91). Up to 25,000 birds in winter. Amber list.

SCAUP: Winter visitors. Up to 3,000 birds in winter (94–00) but dropping. Live max fourteen years. Amber list. About twelve species of *Aythya* worldwide. Order: *Anseriformes*; Family: *Anatidae*.

3.4.10 The (Common) Pochard

Póiseard | *Aythya ferina*

CULINARY

Frequently hunted, Pochard were among the most highly regarded ducks for the table. Payne-Gallwey thought freshwater Pochard to be the best of the diving ducks.[46] They were very common in Dublin markets in the nineteenth century.[47]

NAMES

English: Bog Wigeon, Bull-headed Wigeon (Uls.), Diving Wigeon, Dun Bird, Freshwater Wigeon (Uls.), Gold Head (Uls.), Poker, Poker-Head, Red-head (Uls.), Red-headed Diver, Redheaded Pochard, Red-headed Wigeon, Whinyard (Wex.), Winnard,[48] Wigeon-Diver (Crk.)

Irish: Cromlacha (Kry.), Lacha mhásach (big-bottomed/big-thighed duck), Pislacha (Kry.)

Scientific: Anas ferina, Fuligula ferina, Nyroca ferina

FACTS & FIGURES

Omnivorous. Up to fifty breeding pairs (88–91) with perhaps 30,000 in winter. Live max twenty-three years. Amber list. About twelve species of *Aythya* worldwide. Order: *Anseriformes*; Family: *Anatidae*.

Pochard are diving ducks, somewhat similar to Tufted Ducks and Scaup, with which they can hybridise. Male Pochard have distinctive chestnut-red heads, which make them quite easy to identify in Ireland. The body is grey and white with black rump and breast. The females are a largely grey-brown with a brown head and breast. Their heads are somewhat triangular in shape. *Aythya* is from Greek, meaning 'seabird'. The specific *ferina* is from Latin, meaning 'game'. The name 'Pochard' derives from poker and poacher, which means to poke around, i.e. looking for food.[44]

Beliefs & Traditions: If a Pochard (or Scaup or Goldeneye) was seen sleeping on a calm day, it was a sure sign that a storm was coming.[45]

3.4.11 The (Eurasian) Teal

Praslacha | *Anas crecca crecca*

Teal are Ireland's smallest ducks. What these dabbling ducks lack in size, they make up for in exotic colouring. Males have beautiful chestnut heads with a patch of iridescent green swirling down from the eye. The rest of the body is largely grey with a telltale cream/yellow rear. Females are an overall dull greyish brown. Males make a whistle-like piping sound, something like that of a Golden Plover, while females make a Mallard-like quack.

A group of Teal is known as a 'spring' from their habit of rising almost directly into the air when disturbed. They are also reported as being the only duck known to scratch while in flight. They are also the only duck that will knowingly land on ice. The feet of captured Teal have been found to be completely frozen solid. Another subspecies of Teal, the American or Green-winged Teal (*Anas crecca carolinensis*) is a very rare vagrant visitor to Ireland.

The (Eurasian) Teal continued

The specific *crecca* may be of Scandinavian origin, meaning 'duck' or from Greek, meaning 'a harsh sound'. The Irish *praslacha* means 'fast duck', as Teal are amongst the fastest flying birds in the world. The name Teal itself is a very ancient name for the bird.

Beliefs & Traditions: Teal were a symbol of earnestness and quickness of action. Gerald of Wales relates a story about St Colman and Teal ducks.[49] He says there is a lake in Leinster, favoured by Teal, which are, since St Colman's time, extremely tame and tolerant of man, taking food from the hand. Once, a young person was drawing water from the lake and by chance scooped up one of the Teal with the water. Later, while cooking meat in the water, he noticed the meat would not cook. He found the Teal in the water and immediately returned it to the lake. When he returned, his meat was cooked. It was believed these Teal could never be killed or injured.

Later, the Norman Robert Fitzstephen was travelling past the same spot with Dermot, King of Leinster, when one of his archers hit one of the Teal with an arrow. He placed it to be boiled in a pot with other meat. He burned three pots without cooking the bird. The meat was still raw. When his host noticed the Teal in the pot, he exclaimed in tears, 'Alas for me that this misfortune should ever have happened in my house. That was one of the birds of St Colman.' Then the meat was cooked in a pot on its own and, not long after, the archer died.

CULINARY

Teal were eaten frequently in Ireland and highly regarded for the table, with a 'gamey' taste. Payne-Gallwey regarded them as third in line for taste after Pintail and Shoveler.[50]

NAMES

English: Common Teal, Green-winged Teal[51] (US), Little Wigeon, St Colman's Bird

Irish: Crannlacha,[52] Praslacha ghlaseiteach (green-winged teal), Prisleacha,[53] Siolta[54]

Scientific: Netta crecca, Querquedula crecca

FACTS & FIGURES

Resident omnivorous dabbling ducks. Up to 1,000 breeding pairs (88–91) with numbers declining. Numbers hugely inflated in winter with birds visiting from Britain and the Continent. Collective name: a spring of Teal or a diving of Teal. Live max twenty-one years. Amber list. About fifty species of Anas ducks worldwide. Order: *Anseriformes*; Family: *Anatidae*.

3.4.12 The Garganey

Praslacha shamhraidh | *Anas querquedula*

Garganey are rare visitors from Africa and are the only ducks that migrate to the south and southeast coasts of Ireland in summer. They are beautiful chestnut-headed dabbling ducks with a distinctive white head-stripe. In Irish, Garganey are known as *Praslacha shamhraidh*, 'summer Teal'. The name 'garganey' may derive from the Italian *gargarismo* 'to call'. The specific *querquedula* may share the same root as the Irish *cearc*, coming from the Indo-European *qerqo* 'to make a sound'. The names may derive from the drakes' very odd insect-like calls.

NAMES

English: Summer Teal, Easterling (Kilk.), Lady-fowl (Kilk.), Diver (Kilk.), Wigeon (Kilk.), Cricket Teal (UK)

Scientific: Anas circia, Cyanopterus circia, Pterocyanea circia, Querquedula circia, Querquedula glaucopterus

FACTS & FIGURES

Rare summer visitors. Omnivorous. Perhaps two pairs breeding (88–91). Live max fourteen years. Amber list. About fifty species of *Anas* ducks worldwide. Order: *Anseriformes*; Family: *Anatidae*.

3.4.13 The Gadwall

Gadual | *Anas strepera*

Gadwall are neither very common dabbling ducks, nor are they very striking, looking a little like female Mallards. Males are largely grey, females a dull brown. They have distinctive chestnut and white panels on the wings usually only seen when flying. Many may be descended from introduced or escaped birds from Britain. They tend to be very shy, yet often associate with Coots, from which they steal food. They favour fresh water, and in Ireland they breed in small numbers at Lough Neagh and south Wexford, having been first discovered breeding in Ireland some seventy years ago. The specific *strepera* may derive from the Latin *strepo*, meaning 'a rattling call'. The Irish *gadual* and the English 'Gadwall' may derive from the Latin *quedul*, 'to quack', also found in the specific name of the Garganey (*Anas querquedula*).

CULINARY

Gadwall were regarded as good to eat.

NAMES

English: Brown Duck, Grey Duck

Scientific: Chauelasmus strepera, Chaulelasmus streperus, Dafila strepera, Mareca strepera, Maroca strepera

FACTS & FIGURES

Resident but uncommon, mostly vegetarian, dabbling ducks. Up to 100 breeding pairs (90). Locally common in winter with numbers increased by foreign birds. Live max twenty-two years. Amber list. About fifty species of *Anas* ducks worldwide. Order: *Anseriformes*; Family: *Anatidae*.

3.4.14 The (Eurasian) Wigeon

Rualacha | *Anas penelope*

Wigeon are large, brilliantly coloured dabbling ducks that winter in Ireland, often in the company of Teal. While females are a dull grey-brown colour, males show a melange of colours, looking somewhat like exotic ice creams. Males have largely chestnut heads from which we probably get the Irish name *rualacha* meaning 'red duck'. The forehead is cream/yellow, looking something like a receding hairline. The breast is a delicate pink. The rest of the body is largely grey, separated from the black rear by a vertical white line. Males make a whistling sound, while females seem to purr. The specific *penelope* is from Greek, meaning 'duck', after *Penelope*, daughter of Icarius, who was cast into the sea as a child by her father, only to be rescued by seabirds called 'penelopes'.

CULINARY

Wigeon were frequently eaten in Ireland but are reputed to lack the 'gamey' taste of other ducks. Payne-Gallwey regarded them as fifth in line for taste after Pintails, Shoveler, Teal and Mallard.[55] Wigeon from fresh water were preferred.

NAMES

English: Black Wigeon (fem., yng., Lou.), Golden-crested Wigeon, Golden Head (male, north Lou.), (Golden-headed) Widgeon, Grass Wigeon/Duck, Whistler, Yellow Head, Yellow Poll (male)

Irish: Glaslacha (Kry.), Lacha cheann-ruadh (red-headed duck), Lacha rua (red duck), Lacha ruadh (red duck), Praslacha[56] (Kry.)

Uls. Scots: Wudgeon (Ant.)

Scientific: Mareca penelope

FACTS & FIGURES

Common winter visitors, mostly vegetarian. A handful breeds. 80,000 birds wintering (94–00). Live max thirty-four years. Collective name: a coil of Wigeon. Amber list. About fifty species of *Anas* ducks worldwide. Order: *Anseriformes*; Family: *Anatidae*.

3.4.15 The (Northern) Pintail

Biorearrach | *Anas acuta acuta*

Pintail are among Ireland's most exotic ducks. Locally widespread in winter, these elegant and graceful dabbling ducks breed in small numbers at a few locations in summer. The drake has a magnificent dark chocolate-brown head, a yellow/cream patch at the rear and, of course, a fabulous needle-like 'pin' tail. They are easily identified by their up-ended dabbling, with their pin tails pointing straight up. The Irish *biorearrach* means 'pin tail'. The specific *acuta* is from Latin, meaning 'pointed'.

CULINARY

Pintail were highly regarded for the table, with a 'gamey' taste. Payne-Gallwey rated them number one of all ducks.[57] Watters tells us they were sold in Dublin markets.[58]

NAMES

English: Harlan (Wex.), Lady Bird/Duck (Dub.), Sea Pheasant, Spear Wigeon

Irish: Gruagach, Lacha stiúrach (rudder duck)

Uls. Scots: Cran Wigeon

Scientific: Dafila acuta

FACTS & FIGURES

Resident. Mostly vegetarian, but will eat invertebrates. Maybe two breeding pairs (88–91). Up to 7,000 birds wintering. Weigh up to 1.5 kg. Live max twenty-seven years. Amber list. About fifty species of *Anas* ducks worldwide. Order: *Anseriformes*; Family: *Anatidae*.

3.4.16 The Black Scoter

Scótar | *Melanitta nigra nigra*

Scoters are large black sea ducks that spend almost all their time at sea. As a result, they are relatively unknown to most. They have a wild, primeval aspect, and will not be seen on the local pond. Of the three species of scoter that can be seen in Irish waters, by far the most common are the aptly named Black Scoters.[59] These birds can be seen on some of the big lakes in the west of Ireland in summer. A Black Scoter is a blocky, totally black duck with a small knob and yellow patch on the bill. The species are very hard to tell apart from all but close up, and do not help by mixing in large flocks.

The other two scoters, the Velvet (*Melanitta fusca fusca*, *Sceadach*) and Surf Scoters (*Melanitta perspicillata*, *Scótar toinne*) are seen in Irish waters in winter, and then rarely.

The name 'scoter' is probably related to the word 'coot' and refers to the bird's sooty colour. The generic *melanitta* is from Greek, meaning 'shining black'. The specific *nigra* is from Latin, meaning 'black'.

CULINARY

Scoters were eaten but were noted for their fishy flavour. There was dispensation to eat them during Lent[60] as, with the Barnacle Goose, it was uncertain whether they were meat or fish. They appeared uncommonly in the Dublin markets but, Watters tells us, were highly esteemed in France in the nineteenth century.[61]

NAMES

English: Black Diver (east c.), Black Duck (Dub.), Black Scoter, Black Wigeon[62] (Uls.), Common Scoter

Irish: Lacha scótarach

Scientific: Anas nigra, Melanitta nigrifes, Oedemia negra, Oidemia nigra

FACTS & FIGURES

Uncommon resident omnivores. Up to 100 breeding pairs (95–99) and decreasing, but up to 20,000 birds wintering. Live max sixteen years. Red list. Five species of *Melanitta* worldwide. Order: *Anseriformes*; Family: *Anatidae*.

3.4.17 The (Common) Eider

Éadar | *Somateria mollissima mollissima*

Large, beautifully coloured sea ducks, Eiders are renowned for providing soft feathers for our quilts and duvets (Eider downs). About the size of a Brent Goose, the male is largely white with a black cap, rear and wings and delicate green on the back of the neck and base of the large bill. The breast can have a pink tint depending on the bird's diet. Females are dull brown. Both sexes have a dramatic streamlined head with the bill merging seamlessly into the forehead. Male Eiders have a delightful call, sounding something like an 'ooo' expression of surprise. A flock of ooo-ing Eiders sounds something like a throng of gossiping old women. Although uncommon in Ireland, they are probably the most abundant sea ducks in the world. Eider females often crèche their ducklings together in large floating flocks as protection from predators. These crèches tend to stay together until the ducklings are reared. First breeding in Ireland was in Donegal in 1912.

The generic *somateria* is from Greek meaning 'body'. The specific *molissima* is from Latin meaning 'soft', referring the down feathers.

CULINARY

Eiders were eaten in Ireland where they could be found.

NAMES

English: Cuddy Duck, St Cuthbert's Duck (Sco.)

Irish: Colc (quilt), Lacha Lochlannach[63] (Norse duck)

Scientific: Anas mollissima

FACTS & FIGURES

Locally common resident carnivores. Common along the north coast from Sligo to Antrim. Very rare elsewhere in the country. Up to 1,000 breeding pairs (88–91) with numbers increasing. Live max thirty-seven years. Three species of *Somateria* duck worldwide. Amber list. Order: *Anseriformes*; Family: *Anatidae*.

3.4.18 The Long-tailed Duck

Lacha earrfhada | *Clangula hyemalis*

These exotic winter-visiting sea ducks are rarely seen in Ireland. Males are largely black and white in winter, with a distinctive black breast, pinkish face patch and rosy-coloured tip to the bill. Females are dull brown-grey with white highlights. The birds congregate in large 'rafts' at sea. They are robust ducks, capable of diving to great depths and remaining underwater for minutes. Only the males have the long black pin-like tails. The Irish *Lacha earrfhada* means 'long-tailed duck'. The generic *clangula* refers to the call and the whistle of the wings. The specific *hyemalis* is from Latin meaning 'winter'.

CULINARY

Watters, in the nineteenth century, describes the flesh as 'disagreeable and tough'.[64]

NAMES

English: Long-tailed Sheldrake, Northern Hareld, Oldsquaw (NA.)

Irish: Lacha bhinn

Scientific: Anas glacialis, Anas hyemalis, Harelda glacialis, Harelda hiemalis

FACTS & FIGURES

Scarce winter visitors. Over 200 birds (94–00). Carnivorous. Live max twenty-two years. Only species of *Clangula* in the world. Order: *Anseriformes*; Family: *Anatidae*.

3.4.19 The Mergansers

Síoltaí

Red-breasted Merganser	Síolta rua	*Mergus serrator*
Goosander[65]	Síolta mhór	*Mergus merganser merganser*
Smew	Síolta gheal	*Mergellus albellus*

Red-breasted Merganser

Goosander

Smew

NAMES

MERGANSER

English: Bardrake (Dow.), Barduck[69] (Uls.), Comber (Uls.), Crested Diver, Fishing Duck, Herring Scale (Uls.), Land Harlan (Wex.), Popping Wigeon (Lou.), Sand Harlin, Saw-Bill (Gal.), Sawbill Widgeon/Wigeon (Gal.), Scale(r) duck (SL.), Scamler (Uls.), Shelduck (inl.), Spear Wigeon (Uls.)

Irish: Crannlacha[70] (tree duck, Kry.), Gairg (Gal.),[71] Tumaire rua (red diver, Kry.)

Scientific: Merganser serrator

GOOSANDER

English: Common Merganser (US), Diving Goose, Dun Diver, Fishing Goose, Land Cormorant (Dub.), Shell Duck (Sha.), Spear Wigeon (Crk., Kry.)

Irish: Sioltaidhe

Scientific: Merganser castor, Mergus castor

SMEW

English: Easterling, Lady Fowl, Magpie Diver, Weasel Wigeon, White Merganser, White Nun, White Wigeon

Irish: Smiú

Scientific: Mergus albellus

Red-breasted Mergansers and Goosanders are large ducks belonging to the fish-eating sawbill family. They are striking birds with shimmering green heads and red bills. Both have bills with serrated edges for holding fish. Red-breasted Mergansers are further endowed with a punk-rock style crest on the head. Goosanders, the larger of the two, are rare visitors to our island but Mergansers are locally common, year-round residents found in isolated pockets around the country. Mergansers migrate to the coasts in winter. Goosander numbers are slowly increasing in Ireland, which scientists attribute to our warming climate. In countries where they are common, Goosanders are disliked and sometimes persecuted by anglers for their fish-eating ways.

A third and much smaller species of sawbill, Smew are very rare winter visitors to Lough Neagh and the Wexford Slobs though Watters, in the mid-nineteenth century, tells us that they were the most common of the Mergansers on the east coast.[66] They are very striking birds showing all over white with distinct black lines, giving a 'cracked ice' appearance. Lady Fowl was an alternative Irish name for Smew from the association of the birds' white plumage with the Virgin Mary.[67] The alternative 'Easterling' refers to the birds coming to Ireland from the east.[68]

The generic *mergus* is Latin for a diving bird. The specific *merganser* derives from the same.

CULINARY

The merganser family were generally regarded as inedible on account of their fish-eating diet. Nonetheless they were sold in the markets.

FACTS & FIGURES

MERGANSER

Common fish eaters. Up to 2,500 breeding pairs (88–91) and nearly 3,000 birds wintering. Live max twenty-one years. Amber list.

GOOSANDER

Goosander: Rare visitors from the Continent. Up to fifty breeding pairs (88–91). Live max fourteen years. Amber list.

SMEW

Very rare winter visitors from the continent. Live max ten years. Six species of sawbill worldwide including four species of *Mergus* and one species of *Mergellus*. Order: *Anseriformes*; Family: *Anatidae*.

3.5 OTHER WATER BIRDS

3.5.1 The (Northern) Gannet

Gainéad | *Morus bassanus*

Ireland's largest seabirds, Gannets, are related to pelicans. They are distinctive birds with their white plumage and yellow heads. Tens of thousands of pairs breed every year on Little Skellig Island off County Kerry. Gannets dive, in a classic 'W' shape, from a height of up to 30 metres, hitting the water at nearly one hundred kilometres per hour and plunging to a depth of up to four metres. As the birds can grow up to a metre long and weigh nearly 4 kg, it is wise not to get in the way. They have air sacs under their skin to cushion the blow and have no nostrils. Fish up to one metre long are taken and are usually knocked out by the impacting Gannet, which then scoops up the stunned fish on its way back to the surface.

Gannets lack brood patches (featherless skin) on the belly so the single egg is kept warm beneath their webbed feet, which have numerous blood vessels. When the chick starts hatching, the egg is moved to the top of the feet to avoid it being crushed. Gannet breeding sites are colossally crowded hives of activity. Each breeding pair has a tiny, well-defined patch of ground on which to rear their young. The parents take turns incubating the eggs with the 'off-duty' bird spending the entire day fishing at sea. The young eat regurgitated fish from the returning birds. Gannets must be careful to land exactly on their own territory as disputes can be deadly. Once down, the Gannet can only take off from well-defined and well-used 'runways'. These runways are kept clear at the edges of the colonies and each Gannet must walk the gauntlet through other territories to reach them. The departing birds signal their non-aggressive intention by walking with their bills pointing directly to the sky as a swordsman would hold up his sword. Birds behaving so are granted passage but the ritual must be strictly adhered to.

Fishermen follow Gannets to find fish and the Gannets will eat fish detritus discarded from trawlers. Modern fishing nets are a threat to the bird as they easily get entangled, but numbers are increasing.

The name 'Gannet' comes from the Anglo-Saxon *ganot* meaning 'goose'. The Latin *Morus bassanus* translates roughly as 'Foolish Bird from Bass Rock' (in Scotland). The birds are also called Solan Geese in Northern Ireland and Scotland from the rock Sula Sgeir (Gannet skerry) or Solan Rock some forty miles off the northern Scottish coast.

Beliefs & Traditions: It was believed that Gannets were incapable of landing or taking off from any rock except marble. As a result it was thought they lived at sea all the time and even laid floating eggs on the waves and hatched them between wing and body.[1]

Proverbs & Similes:
Chomh géarradharcach le gainéad
(As sharp-eyed as a gannet).

PLACE NAMES

Poll an Ghainnéid (Gannet's hole, Dingle, Co. Kerry)

CULINARY

Young birds, called guga, were a favourite and are still, controversially, collected and eaten in parts of Scotland. As well as for food, the birds were used for medicine and William Turner in 1544 wrote that they were 'most valuable for many a disease'. Gannets were collected from Little Skellig off Kerry and in the nineteenth century the whole island was rented out to allow young Gannets to be taken. At that time a whole Gannet could be sold for between two and three shillings, big money at that time.

NAMES

English: Chandel Goose (Eng.), Gant (Uls.), Gentleman (Eng.), Solan Goose (Uls., Don., Kry.), Swift-flying Goose (west)

Irish: Amhasán (hooligan-bird, Ant.), Amhlóg (Lou., Arm.), Corr (yng., Din.), Gainnéad, Gainnéan (Don.), Gainnéid, Guga (yng.), Ogastún (Kry., Conn.), Scaladóir[2] (from its sudden dive, Don.), Sealadóir (Don.), Seoladóir (sailor), Súlaire (per. 'sharp eye', Kry.), Ugasdún

Scientific: Anser bassinus, Sula alba, Sula bassana (bass rock Gannet), Pelecanus bassanus

FACTS & FIGURES

Resident fish eaters. Up to 33,000 breeding pairs (99–02). Britain and Ireland have 70–80 per cent of the European population. Can reach almost one metre long and weigh 3.5 kg. Live max thirty-seven years. Amber list. Ten species of *Sulidae* (Gannets & Boobies) including three *Morus* worldwide. Order: *Pelecaniformes*; Family: *Sulidae*.

3.5.2 The (Northern) Fulmar

Fulmaire | *Fulmarus glacialis auduboni, Fulmarus glacialis glacialis*

Fulmars are wild pelagic (sea-going) water birds from the petrel family looking very much like a cross between a gull and an albatross. Fulmars are relatively new to Ireland although the English name probably comes from the Gaelic *fulmaire*, which in turn probably comes from Scandinavia. They arrived in Ireland and Britain around the beginning of the twentieth century, probably originating in Iceland. This recent arrival is reflected in the Ulster name 'new gull'. A few bred for the first time in Mayo in 1911 and they have been increasing in numbers ever since. The huge increase likely arises from their adaptation to eating fish waste from trawlers. They come to land only to breed and it seems that they tolerate land only when necessary, confining themselves to remote cliffs. They are almost unable to walk. While incubating, they can be approached quite closely, without stirring. They give a short warning 'bark' and ornithologists know to take this quite seriously. When they consider their personal space sufficiently invaded, they project an evil-smelling stream of liquid and regurgitated fish known as 'fulmar oil' at their perceived attacker. Both adult and chick can produce this avian projectile vomit and they tend to be accurate. While unpleasant to humans, it can matt the feathers of a predatory bird leading to its death. Living almost entirely at sea, they are able to drink seawater. The excess salt in their blood is then excreted and filtered through tubes on the tops of their bills from where they get their family name, 'tubenoses'.

While normally looking broadly white like a gull, a few all-grey birds, known as Blue Fulmars, stray into Irish waters from the Arctic. Huge numbers are lost to long line fishing.

Beliefs & Traditions: Seeing a Fulmar at sea meant bad weather was on the way.

CULINARY

As a relative newcomer to Ireland, they have little culinary history here. In Scotland, and particularly the island of St Kilda, they have been a very important food source. Catching Fulmars was a dangerous and smelly occupation. When prepared for the pot, it was important to remove the evil-smelling oil first. This was sometimes used as fuel for lamps and for medicinal purposes.

NAMES

English: Fulmar Petrel, Molly Mawk, New Gull (Uls.)

Irish: Cánóg bhán (white puffin, Din.), Cánóg liath (grey puffin)

Scientific: Procellaria cinerea, Procellaria glacialis

FACTS & FIGURES

Common resident fish eaters. Migrate around the coasts of Ireland and out to sea and back. 33,000 breeding pairs (99–02) and increasing. Live max forty-three years. Weigh 0.75 kg. Two species of *Fulmarus* worldwide. Order: *Procellariiformes*; Family: *Procellariidae*.

3.5.3 The Manx Shearwater

Cánóg dhubh | *Puffinus puffinus puffinus*

Shearwaters are dark, broadly gull-like seabirds that visit Irish waters in the summer and are very rarely seen inland. Of the six[3] species that can be encountered in Irish waters, the Manx is by far the most common. The birds are black on top and white below with long pointed wings.

The birds spend their winters far out to sea and come to the coast in the summer to breed. They nest in colonies of burrows on islands and remote headlands. During the breeding season, they tend to spend their days fishing at sea only returning to their burrows at night. There they can be heard, from above ground, uttering a variety of weird and wonderful cackling calls. From this, they get their Skelligs name 'night bird'. The call is interpreted in Irish as *ná déin é, ná déin é* (don't do it, don't do it). The name 'shearwater' comes from their habit of gliding just above the waves, wingtips caressing the water. The scientific *puffinus* comes from old English meaning 'puffed-out' or fat. The birds were called 'mackerel cocks' in Ireland because they preceded the appearance of mackerel along the east coast.[4]

CULINARY

The birds and their eggs were eaten in Ireland. The Catholic Church permitted these birds to be eaten during Lent.[5]

NAMES

English: Hagdown (Great Shearwater, Wat.), Herring Hawk (Uls.), Mackerel Cock (Ll.), Night Bird (Skl.), Wind Fairy

Irish: Cánóg dhubh/dubh (Din.), Fothaíoch (yng., Din.), Púicín gaoithe (little wind pooka)

Scientific: Procellaria anglorum, Procellaria puffinus, Puffinus anglorum

FACTS & FIGURES

Summer visitors. Fish eaters. 33,000 breeding pairs in (99–02). Live max forty-nine years. Amber list. Over twenty species of *Puffinus* worldwide. Order: *Procellariiformes*; Family: *Procellariidae*.

3.5.4 The (European) Storm Petrel

Guairdeall | *Hydrobates pelagicus*

Storm Petrels are common sea-going birds, about the size of sparrows, which most Irish people will only encounter from the deck of a car ferry. Yet Ireland has the world's largest breeding population. They are the most common petrels to be seen in Irish waters, the other two rare visitors being Leach's Petrel (*Guairdeall gabhlach, Oceanodrama leucorhoa leucorhoa*) and Wilson's Petrel[6] (*Guairdeall Wilson, Oceanites oceanicus exasperatus*). All petrels, shearwaters, prions and fulmars are called 'tubenoses' as they have two long tube-nostrils running along the tops of their bills. They can drink seawater and the excess salt in their blood is then excreted and filtered through these tubes. Like shearwaters, Storm Petrels nest in burrows and are very ungainly on land. They lay huge eggs relative to their size. Chicks are well fed and, when hatched, may be left to fend for themselves. Like Fulmars, both adults and chicks can defend themselves on land by ejecting a foul-smelling fishy substance, projectile-vomit style, at a would-be attacker.

Scott Weidensaul[7] describes Storm Petrels as seabirds that look as though they had been 'dipped entirely in dark chocolate, save for a white thumbprint left on their rumps'.

CULINARY

The young were raided from their nesting burrows and were highly valued as food. They became known as 'mutton-birds'.[11] Because of their small size, they were probably swallowed whole.

PLACE NAMES

Chicken Rock Lighthouse, a lighthouse to the south of the Isle of Man, is named after Mother Carey's Chickens. Though not Irish, it is well known to Irish sailors.

Known in folklore as Mother Carey's Chickens,[8] or Sea Swallows (see Arctic Tern), the birds are known to become much more active before a storm and to warn sailors accordingly as they commonly follow boats eating any discarded fish offal. The name Mother Carey probably comes from a sailor's prayer (*Mater Cara* or *Madre Cara* meaning 'dear mother')

The name 'petrel' itself is derived from St Peter. The birds have a habit of hovering just above the waves and 'scratching' at the water, thus earning themselves the belief that they could walk on water. The generic name *Hydrobates* comes from the Latin *hydros* and *batein* meaning 'water' and 'tread' respectively. The Irish name *Guairdeall* translates as 'hoverer' probably as a result of the birds' hovering water-dance. The 'storm' part of the name comes from the appearance of these birds inland having been blown in on a storm.

Beliefs & Traditions: If the appearance of a Storm Petrel was a bad omen for sailors,[9] one coming aboard a boat was sure to cause great consternation. It was believed that they lived in the midst of hurricanes, directing bad weather.[10] Their appearance presaged bad weather. Yet in some places they were regarded as the sailors' friends 'come to warn them of an approaching storm' and it was most unlucky to kill them. The belief was that each bird contained the soul of a dead seaman.

Poetry: from '*Ode to Mother Carey's Chicken*'

Yea, lift thine eyes, my own can bear them now:
Thou 'rt free! thou 'rt free. Ah, surely a bird can smile!
Dost know me, petrel? Dost remember how
I fed thee in the wake for many a mile,
Whilst thou wouldst pat the waves, then, rising, take
The morsel up and wheel about the wake?
Thou 'rt free, thou 'rt free, but for thine own dear sake
I keep thee caged awhile.

Theodore Watts-Dunton (1832–1914)

NAMES

English: Gourder (Kry.), Laura of the Ocean, Martin-oil (Gal.), Mother Carey's Chicken,[12] Mutton-bird (yng.), Sea Swallow, Stormie (sl.), Stormy Petrel, Witch (Kry.)

Irish: Áinleog mhara (sea swallow), Bríochtóg na mara (sea witch, Kry.), Ceann biorach na stoirme (Kry.), Clamprán (quarreller), Éan an anró (rough weather bird), Éan úisc (grease/oil bird, Antrim), Gearr/Géarr róid (little storm bird, Insh., Don.), Gearr/Géarr úisc (small oil bird, Tory., Don.), Guardal (wanderer, whirler, Din.), Máirtíneach (na hola) (martin oil), Peadairín na stoirme (little Peter of the storms), Súipín (per. unkempt, Din.), Urdhubhán (dark creature, May.)

Scientific: Procellaria pelagica, Thalassidroma pelagica

FACTS & FIGURES

Summer fish-eating visitors. Can be seen off any coast but have specific breeding sites. 100,000 breeding pairs (99–02) in about twenty-eight burrow colonies. Collective name: a wisp of petrels. Live max thirty-two years. Amber list. Over twenty species in the family *Hydrobatidae*, including one *Hydrobates* worldwide. Order: *Procellariiformes*; Family: *Hydrobatidae*.

3.5.5 The (Great) Cormorant

Broigheall | *Phalacrocorax carbo carbo/sinensis*

& (European) Shag

Seaga | *Phalacrocorax aristotelis aristotelis/desmarestii*

Cormorant   Shag

Cormorants are large black-green water birds often seen fishing on coasts and inlets around Ireland. Their close cousins, the Shags (or Green Cormorants), are very similar and it can be hard to tell them apart from a distance. Shags are greener and smaller than cormorants and have a small crest and yellow mouth line in the summer breeding season. In summer, Cormorants are easily identified by their bright white markings on the face and flanks. They can also be told apart by the way that they dive for fish. Cormorants are more likely to be seen on inland waterways than shags and fly higher above the water.

Like Gannets, Cormorants and Shags have no brood patches and keep their eggs warm with their warm-blood-enriched flipper-feet.

Viewing a fishing Cormorant or Shag can be a frustrating endeavour as they constantly dive for fish and return to the surface only briefly. Cormorants and Shags give much better views when resting up after a fishing session. They can often be seen sitting up on an island or buoy with wings outstretched. This is normally described as the Cormorant drying its wings but may be a means of spacing out the roosting birds.

Like other creatures, Shags are poisoned by the 'red tide'. This is a periodic population explosion of the tiny dinoflagellates (unicellular algae) which causes the sea to turn a pinkish colour and is also the scourge of fish-farmers. The red tide produces toxins which are poisonous to those who eat it, right up the food chain to man.

Cormorants previously suffered greatly at the hands of fisherman but were protected by law in Ireland in 1976 and 2000. Of the forty species of cormorant and shag worldwide, there is no significant physiological difference between them and the names are often interchangeable.

The word 'cormorant' probably comes from the Latin words *corvus* and *marinus* meaning 'sea crow' and indeed one of its Irish names, *Fiach mara*, means 'sea raven'. The genus name *phalacrocorax* is from the Greek meaning 'bald raven'. The word 'shag' probably comes from the Icelandic *skegg* meaning 'beard'. In Northern Ireland, the Shag is called 'skart' in English and *scarbh* in Irish and both words probably come from the old Norse word *skarfr*, describing the call. One of the Irish alternatives, *Cailleach dhubh* was used extensively for both Cormorant and Shag and translates as sea hag or sea witch. In Synge's play *Riders to the Sea*, Cathleen says of the boy that has drowned: '*Ah Nora, isn't it a bitter thing to think of him floating that way to the far north, and no one to keen him but the black hags that do be flying on the sea.*'

CULINARY

Cormorants and Shags were eaten in Ireland but were not favoured for their 'fishy' taste. Kevin Danaher[14] notes that fishermen near the mouth of the Shannon did trap and eat Cormorants but that they were as tough as old boots and tasted of every fish they had eaten.

FACTS & FIGURES

CORMORANT

Common resident fish eaters. Widespread along the coast and common inland in winter. Nearly one metre in length. 4,500 breeding pairs (99–02) and increasing. Live max twenty-three years. Weigh up to 3 kg. Collective name: a flight of Cormorants. Amber list.

SHAG

Common resident fish-eater. Widespread along the coast but absent from the east coast in summer. Weigh 2 kg. 3,400 breeding pairs and decreasing (99–02). Live max thirty years.

Nearly forty species in the *Phalacrocoracidae* family (cormorants and shags), including about seventeen species of *Phalacrocorax* worldwide. Order: *Pelecaniformes*; Family: *Phalacrocoracidae*.

The (Great) Cormorant & (European) Shag continued

Beliefs & Traditions: Irish sailors were vary wary of Cormorants and Shags. Just seeing a group of Cormorants at sea was considered bad luck. Stories of mermaids with webbed feet around our coasts may be linked to Cormorants and Shags. Indeed one Irish name for the Cormorant, *Murúchaill* means 'mermaid'.

Thompson tells us that people around Lough Neagh believed that Cormorants must visit seawater every day and that they would die if they did not get a drink of salt water every twenty-four hours.[13]

PLACE NAMES

Carraig na Seagaí	Co. Waterford	(Shags' Rock)
Carraig na Siogaí	Carbery, Co. Cork.	(Shags' Rock[15])
Cuas a' tSeaga	Co. Kerry	(Shag's Cove)
Gabhlín a' tSeaga	Co. Waterford	(Shag's Inlet)
Lackanscarry	Co. Limerick	(Leaca na Scairbhe, cormorant's slope)
Poinnte an tSeaga	Co. Waterford	(Shag's Point)
Ruenascarrive	Co. Antrim	(Rubha na Scarbh, cormorant's point)

Any place with 'cailleach' or 'cally' in the name may refer to a hag/witch, or to an owl, or perhaps, on the coast, to a cormorant.

CORMORANT NAMES

English:
Billydiver
Black Diver[16] (Uls.)
Corporal (Uls.)
Ducky Diver (Wat.)

Irish:
Cabhail scréachóg (screeching old hag Aran.)
Cailleach dhubh (black witch/hag)
Calliach (hag)
Claimhfhiach (mange-Raven, Kry.)
Colliagh dhubh (black hag)
Dubhéan ballaire (Kry.)
Duibhéan (black-bird, Don.)
Fiach farraige (sea Raven, Kry.)
Fiach mara (sea Raven, Dingle, Kry.)
Gairfhiach (Kry.)
Gairg
Muir-bhran (sea crow)

Murúchaill (merman, mermaid)
Scarbh (Ulster Irish, Ant.)
Seaga (Mun.)
Seagadh

Uls. Scots:
(Black) Scart
Karbie
Skarf (Ant.)
Willie Dooker
Wool-Cottar

Scientific:
Carbo carbo
Carbo cormoranus
Pelecanus carbo

SHAG NAMES

English:
Black Hag (Uls.)
Black Paddy (Uls.)
Crested Cormorant
Green Cormorant
Green Diver (Uls.)

Irish:
Cailleach dhubh (black witch)
Cailleach mhara (sea witch)
Scarbh (Ant.)
Seagadh
Sioga

Uls. Scots:
(Green) Skart/Scart

Scientific:
Leucocarbo aristotelis
Pelecanus aristotelis
Pelecanus graculus
Phalacrocorax cristatus
Phalacrocorax graculus

3.5.6 The Corncrake

Traonach | *Crex crex*

& the Water Rail

Ralóg uisce | *Rallus aquaticus aquaticus*

Corncrakes (or Land Rails) are among the most extraordinary birds in Ireland. Summer visitors from Africa, Corncrakes were well loved and locally common birds in Ireland until modern farming methods, including machine mowing of hay, began to clash with their nesting habits. They are birds of wet meadowland and are still found along the Shannon. Corncrakes have been declining in numbers across Europe but are beginning to make a small comeback in Ireland. Farmers have been encouraged to change their habits and, in some cases, are paid to do so and now Ireland is becoming one of their last refuges. Corncrakes make a very distinctive call, not unlike the sound of a clock being wound, from which they get their onomatopoeic scientific name *Crex crex*. Many people who are familiar with the Corncrakes' call have never seen one, as they are very secretive birds keeping low in the long meadow grass. They can be heard both day and night and when present in larger numbers in the past, had a reputation for keeping people awake at night. They behave like game birds, taking to the air as a very last resort when pursued. Corncrake chicks are sweetness personified. On hatching, these small balls of fluff immediately follow their mother everywhere in a determined line. Corncrakes spend their winters in south-eastern Africa, in Madagascar, Mozambique, Tanzania and Zambia.

The Corncrake & the Water Rail continued

Water Rails are cousins of the Corncrakes and although present in much greater numbers, are perhaps even more elusive. They make strange animal-like noises known as 'sharming' from deep within the reeds which sound a little like the squeals of a pig. Indeed they get their name 'rail' from the French *raille*, to rattle, which is somewhat indicative of their call. They also make various grunts and barks and a sound not unlike the passing of wind. They are very thin birds, which helps them to creep between the reeds without revealing their presence. Like Corncrakes, Water Rails rarely fly, preferring to elude potential predators by running, which they do expertly across mud or pond vegetation with their specially adapted feet. From this, they get their Ulster Scots name 'segan-runner'. The Water Rail's chicks are little balls of black fluff.

The name 'Corn Crake' has recently been recommended by the International Ornithological Congress as the standard name for 'Corncrake'.

Beliefs & Traditions: How Corncrakes made their amazing 'crex' sound was a matter of some debate. Some believed that they lay on their backs and rubbed their legs together thinking that they were holding up the sky,[17] others that they pushed their bills into the ground while some believe that they plucked at their wings with a leg, like a fiddle.[18]

Because Corncrakes are migratory birds and are only seen in Ireland in summer, it was believed that in the winter months the birds changed into a different species, the Moorhen[19] or Water Rail.[20] Others believed that Corncrakes could not fly at all.[21] It was also believed to be very unlucky to bring a live or dead Corncrake into the house.

Weather: Hearing a Corncrake at dusk meant fine weather was on the way.[22]

Proverbs & Similes: As thin as a rail.

Curses:

Nar fheice tú an chuach ná an traonach arís.
(May you not live to see the cuckoo or corncrake again)

Codladh an traona chughat.
(May you have the sleep of the corncrake [may you be up all night], Dingle, Kerry)

Poetry: from '*Lullaby of London*' (As I Walked Down by the Riverside)

> *Though there is no lonesome Corncrake's cry*
> *Of sorrow and delight*
> *You can hear the cars*
> *And the shouts from bars*
> *and the laughter and the fights*

The Pogues

CULINARY

Unfortunately, both Corncrakes and Water Rails were taken for the table. Both were highly regarded, Corncrakes especially so.[23] Corncrakes sometimes showed up in markets.

PLACE NAMES

Carrowntryla, Co. Galway, Co. Roscommon (Corncrake quarter land)
Carrowtreila, Co. Mayo (Corncrake quarter land)
Coolatreane, Co. Fermanagh (Corncrake meadow)
Lugatryna, Co. Wicklow (Corncrake hollow)

NAMES

CORNCRAKE

English: Land Drake (Uls.), Land Rail, Land Rake (Uls.)

Irish: Gearr goirt/Geárr guirt[24] (small field bird), Gortéan (field bird, Kry.), Sicín tradhain (Wat.), Spide traghain/tradhain (little crake, Mea.), Tradhlach (west & nw.), Tradhna (Kry.), Tradhnach, Traghan, Traghnach, Traona (Din.), Tréanach, Troghan[25]

Uls. Scots: Crek (Ant.)

Scientific: Crex pratens(is), Gallinula crex, Ortygometra crex, Rallus crex

WATER RAIL

Irish: Caidhlín (Conn.), Rallóg/Rálóg Uisce (Water Rail), Traona/Traonach Uisce (Water Rail)

Uls. Scots: Segan-runner, Wee Water Hen

FACTS & FIGURES

CORNCRAKE

Summer visitors. Omnivores. About 157 breeding pairs (98–02). Red list.

WATER RAIL

Resident omnivores. Present in all counties but scarce. Up to 2,500 breeding pairs (88–91). Live max eight years. Amber list.

About 130 species in the *Rallidae* family, including two species of *Crex* and ten species of *Rallus* worldwide. Order: *Gruiformes*; Family: *Rallidae*.

3.5.7 The (Eurasian) Coot

Cearc cheannann | *Fulica atra atra*

& the (Common) Moorhen

Cearc uisce | *Gallinula chloropus chloropus*

Coot

Moorhen

Members of the rail family, Coots and Moorhen are very common throughout Ireland. Being relatively tolerant of human presence, they are found in lakes, parks, and almost any area of open water. From the distance, they can look similar. Coots are slightly larger, with a black and white face and bill while Moorhens are dark blue-black with a conspicuous red bill. Coots are more likely to take bread in town parks. Both birds swim with a distinctive pigeon-like bobbing motion that is more accentuated in Moorhen.

A Coot's call sounds a little like its name: a shrill horn-like 'coot' from the reeds. Their feet, while not exactly webbed, have beautiful fins to help them swim. As they cannot take off from land they must run on top of the water before flying. A wounded Coot is reputed to be able to dive to the bottom and hold onto weed until the danger has passed. Young Coots often take shelter under their mother's wings, sometimes with just a small foot sticking out to betray their presence. The generic *fulica* comes from the Latin *fuligo* meaning 'soot' while the specific *atra* is from the Latin *ater* meaning 'black'. The Irish *cearc cheannann* means 'bald hen'. In America, certain species of scoter duck are also called 'coot'.

While serene to look at, male Moorhen can be very aggressive and will defend their territories with great violence sometimes leading to death. While they might seem equally common on our local lakes and ponds, there are many times more Moorhen in Ireland than Coots. In Antrim Irish, the call of the Moorhen has a specific word: *sciúgán*.[26] The Irish *Cearc uisce* means 'water hen'. The generic *gallinula* is from Latin meaning 'little hen'. The specific *chloropus* is from Greek meaning 'green-footed'.

Proverbs & Similes:

As queer as a coot.
As bald as a coot.

CULINARY

Coot were eaten and seemingly were rather an acquired taste, the flesh being coarse[27] and tasting strongly of the marsh.[28] Payne-Gallwey highly regarded them.[29] Moorhen were also eaten in times of need.

NAMES

COOT

English: Bald Coot (Uls.), Baldcoot (Mayo), Baldpate (Uls.), Baldy (Uls.), Black Diver, Drink-a-penny,[30] Mudhen, Swamphen, White-faced Diver

Irish: Coileach ceannann (bald cock, male)

MOORHEN

English: Common Gallinule, (Common) Water Hen

Irish: Cearc fhraoigh[31] (heather hen), Coileach fraoich (heather cock, Mun.), Truisc

Uls. Scots: Watter Hen

Scientific: Fulica chloropus

FACTS & FIGURES

COOT

Resident omnivores. Widespread in all counties but locally scarce. Up to 10,000 pairs (88–91) with numbers inflated in winter. Live max twenty years. Collective name: a cover of coots, a raft of coots. Amber list.

MOORHEN

Resident omnivores. Widespread in all counties. Up to 100,000 pairs (88–91) with numbers inflated in winter. Live max eighteen years.

About 130 species in the *Rallidae* family, including eleven species of *Fulica* and ten species of *Gallinula* worldwide. Order: *Gruiformes*; Family: *Rallidae*.

3.5.8 The Skuas

Meirligh

The Great Skua	Meirleach mór	*Stercorarius skua skua*
The Arctic Skua[32]	Meirleach Artach	*Stercorarius parasiticus*
The Pomarine Skua	Meirleach pomairíneach	*Stercorarius pomarinus*
The Long-tailed Skua[33]	Meirleach earrfhada	*Stercorarius longicaudus*

Skuas are dark-coloured relatives of gulls known in North America as jaegers. Almost entirely seaborne, they are rarely encountered by most of us. Of the four species of skua to be seen in Irish waters, none is common. Great Skuas or Bonxies are perhaps the commonest and largest and Longtailed Skuas the least common and smallest. All are broadly dark brown with some white on the wings. Both the Arctic and Pomarine have dark and pale morphs (varieties), the pale having white on the underside and distinct yellow on the face. Long-tailed Skuas are elegant birds with long tails, white undersides and characteristic yellow faces. All arrive to visit in spring/autumn. Skuas are scavengers, known to harass and steal food from other birds. Great Skuas are formidable birds, about the size of Herring Gulls. They will attack and eat birds almost up to their own size (including petrels, gulls and waders). They will also eat fish offal or carrion. From this we get the apt Irish name *Meirleach* (*mara*) meaning '(sea) thief' or '(sea) villain'.

Skuas will sometimes force birds to disgorge swallowed food in mid-air, which led to the belief that they ate the excrement of other birds. From this, we get the delightful Ulster Scots name 'gabshite' and the Irish *Faoileán an chaca* 'shite gull'. On land, skuas are just as aggressive in defending their nests and will feign injury, like some waders, to distract attention (see Lapwing, Section 3.8.3 and Red Grouse, Section 3.7.1). They are also very aggressive to birds of prey and were once employed, in island communities in the north of Scotland, to protect lambs. They were also killed for their feathers, which were favoured over goose feathers.

The name 'skua' probably comes from *skuvar* from the Faeroe Islands and/or the Icelandic *skumar*. The alternative name 'Bonxie' may also come from the Faeroes and Shetlands possibly meaning 'fat woman'. The generic *Stercorarius* literally means 'from dung' so it is easy to see the reputation these birds had.

Weather: The presence of skuas close inshore indicated that a storm was on the way.

Great Skua

NAMES

ALL

English: Shitehawk (Uls.)

Irish: Faoileán an chaca (shite gull), Meirleach mara (sea thief), Seabhac cac faoileann (gull-shite hawk, Gal., May.), Seabhac mara (sea hawk, Uls.), Tomáisín chac na bhfaoileán (little Tommy gull-shite, Kry.)

GREAT

English: Black Gull (Tra., Kry.), Bonxie, Common Skua, Brown Gull, Dirt-bird, Jaeger (US, from the German jäger meaning 'hunter')

Irish: Caobach, Faoileán an chaca (shite gull), Meirleach (m) ([sea] thief), Tuilleóg

Uls. Scots: Gabshite

Scientific: Cataractes vulgaris, Catharacta skua, Larus cataractes, Lestris cataractes, Stercorarius catarrhactes

ARCTIC

English: Black Gull (Uls.), Black-toed Gull (Uls.), Dirt Bird, Parasitic Jaeger (stan.), Richardson's Skua

Irish: Meirleach na mara (sea thief)

Scientific: Cataractes parasiticus, Larus crepidatus, Larus parasiticus, Lestris crepidatus, Lestris parasiticus, Lestris richardsoni/richardsonii, Stercorarius cepphus, Stercorarius crepidatus

POMARINE

Scientific: Cataractes pomarinus, Lestris pomarinus, Lestris striatus

LONG-TAILED

English: Long-tailed Jaeger (stan.)

FACTS & FIGURES

GREAT

Spring and autumn coastal visitors. A couple of pairs now breeding (00–01). Weigh up to 1.5 kg. Live max thirty-two years.

ARCTIC

Spring and autumn coastal visitors. None breeding. Live max thirty-one years.

POMARINE

Spring and autumn coastal visitors

LONG-TAILED

Rare spring and autumn coastal visitors.

About seven species of *Stercorarius* worldwide. Order: *Charadriiformes*; Family: *Stercorariidae*.

3.6 BIRDS OF PREY – ÉIN CHREICHE

'Bird of prey' is a general term, which includes, in Ireland, hawks, falcons, kites, harriers, buzzards and eagles. Nocturnal owls are usually placed in a group of their own but are generally regarded as raptors. That said, there are over four hundred species of bird of prey worldwide. Birds of prey are carnivorous hunters usually equipped with sharp bills and talons. Vultures are birds of prey but do not appear in Ireland. Compared to Britain and continental Europe, Ireland has both fewer species of raptor and fewer numbers. This is probably a legacy of the last Ice Age, where fewer species have made it out to re-colonise our island. Raptors have also been persecuted greatly because of their perceived threat to farm animals.

Man got much of his early knowledge of raptors through the practice of falconry. Falconry developed in Asia in at least 1000 BC and was brought to Europe by Germanic tribes who in turn handed it on to the Romans. Wild falcons, hawks and other raptors were caught and others were bred specifically. Such birds were and still are used to hunt natural prey species. Traditionally favoured prey species were as diverse as Blackbirds, Skylarks, Grey Herons and Cranes. Falconry has its own language from which we get 'tiercel', the male Peregrine and 'musket', the male Sparrowhawk. Many of these archaic terms date to the Norman invasion of England and subsequently Ireland in the eleventh century.

Hawks were held sacred by the Egyptians, as a hawk was the form assumed by Ra or Horus. In Ireland, hawks were connected with the willow. They were regarded as messengers between this world and the 'Otherworld'. They symbolised clear sightedness and deep memory. Of the seventy or so species of hawk worldwide, only one, the Sparrowhawks are common in Ireland. Goshawks are rare visitors. Hawks get their generic name *accipiter* from the Latin *accipere* meaning 'to seize'.

Falcons were symbols of majesty, power and eagerness. Of the fifty or so species of falcon worldwide, three are reasonably common in Ireland: Kestrels, Peregrines and Merlins. In addition, Hobbies (*Falco subbuteo*) are sometimes seen along the south coast in summer and the huge Gyrfalcons make rare appearances. Falcons get their name from the Latin *falx* meaning 'sickle', after their talons!

Red Kites, unmistakeable with their forked tails were very common in Ireland in the Middle Ages. Having become extinct here, they were reintroduced to Wicklow in 2007. There are more than twenty other species of kite worldwide including Black Kites which vary rarely stray into Irish skies.

Hen Harriers are the only representative of the harrier family which are in any way common in Ireland. Of the nearly twenty other species of harrier worldwide, only two, the Marsh Harrier and Montagu's Harrier can be seen, albeit rarely, in Ireland.

Once effectively extinct in Ireland, buzzards have been making a comeback, re-colonising the country southwards from the north. Common Buzzards are the only representatives of the thirty or so species of buzzard worldwide.

Odd birds, in a family of their own, Ospreys may also be starting to re-colonise Ireland, albeit in much smaller numbers than buzzards.

Perhaps our most impressive raptors are the eagles. Eagles were symbols of nobility, ingenuity, speed of learning, judiciousness, magnanimity, power, sovereignty, courage, freedom and immortality. Two species of eagle, the Golden Eagles and the White-tailed Eagles, were once common in Ireland. The last ones were shot around the beginning of the twentieth century. Like the Red Kites, they are now making a comeback through re-introduction programmes: Golden Eagles in Donegal and White-tailed Eagles in Kerry.

3.6.1 The Hen Harrier[1]

Cromán na gcearc | *Circus cyaneus cyaneus*

NAMES

English: Blue Hawk (Wic.), Kite (Uls., Wat.), Marsh Hawk[6] (US), Northern Harrier (stan.), Ringtail (fem.), Seagull Hawk (Conm.), White Hawk/Kite (Don.)

Irish: Clamhán na gcearc (hen Buzzard), Préachán na gcearc (hen crow)

Scientific: Circus pygargus, Circus strigiceps, Falco cyaneus, Strigiceps pygargus

FACTS & FIGURES

Resident carnivores. Very scarce. Around 130 breeding pairs (98–00) and declining with perhaps 70 per cent of those in the Republic. Live max seventeen years. Red list. About fourteen species of *Circus* worldwide. Order: *Falconiformes*; Family: *Accipitridae*.

Conspicuously coloured raptors, Hen Harriers are now very rare in Ireland. Males are generally blue-grey with black wing tips. Females (called 'ringtails') are brown with bars on the tail. Both sexes have a distinct long tail. A Hen Harrier's face feathers are shaped into a disc that funnels sound waves to the ear openings like a parabolic microphone.[2] Like other harriers and owls, they are often seen 'quartering' over reed beds and marshes. They favour upland areas but have been hugely persecuted.

The specific *cyaneus* refers to the blue colour of the male. The Irish *Cromán na gcearc* means 'Hen Harrier'. Many European languages refer to the bird as the 'blue hawk'. Harriers tend to fly in circles whilst targeting their victims. From this, they probably get their generic name *Circus* but this may be a reference to their round faces.

The closely related Montagu's Harriers[3] (*Circus pygargus, Cromán liath*) are rare visitors to Ireland, probably even rarer than the Marsh Harriers (see Section 5.1.4 below). A pair bred in Wicklow from 1959 to 1961 and also in Kerry in 1971.[4]

Beliefs & Traditions: In the nineteenth century in Ireland, it was believed that if a Hen Harrier went missing from its usual hunting territory then some evil spirit had moved into the locality.[5]

3.6.2 The (Common) Buzzard

Clamhán | *Buteo buteo buteo*

'If I were reincarnated, I'd want to come back a Buzzard. Nothing hates him or envies him or wants him or needs him. He is never bothered or in danger, and he can eat anything.'[7]

Buzzards are large dull-coloured birds with mostly dark brown upperparts and mottled brown and white underparts and narrow bars on the tail. Once common in Ireland, they became extinct here in 1891. Numbers began returning from about 1933[8] and recently they have been continually expanding their range here. Buzzards are now locally common in Ulster, with strongholds in Antrim and Donegal and can be encountered all the way down the east coast as far as Wexford. Buzzards will eat almost any small animal, bird or carrion, and are often poisoned by tainted meat. A Buzzard's call, referred to as 'mewing', is very distinctive and sounds like a laboured two-syllable whistle. The UK population suffered greatly from myxomatosis in rabbits in the 1950s and 1960s. The Irish *clamhán* means 'mangy' or 'shabby-looking'. *Buteo* is Latin for hawk.

The closely related Rough-legged Buzzards[9] (*Buteo lagopus lagopus, Clamhán lópach*) are very rare visitors to Ireland.

NAMES

English: Goshawk, Kite

Irish: Clamhán goblach ('beaked' Buzzard, Conn.), Cromán (harrier), Gilm, Préachán geárr (bird-crow)

Scientific: Buteo vulgaris, Falco buteo

FACTS & FIGURES

Resident carnivores. Up to 200 breeding pairs and increasing (88–91) of which 50 to 60 per cent are in Northern Ireland. Live max twenty-eight years in the wild, thirty in captivity. Weigh up to 1.5 kg. Collective name: A wake of buzzards. Nearly thirty species of *Buteo* worldwide. Order: *Falconiformes*; Family: *Accipitridae*.

3.6.3 The (Eurasian) Sparrowhawk

Spióróg | *Accipiter nisus nisus*

Sparrowhawks are striking raptors common throughout Ireland. Males are mostly blue-grey on top with orange bars across the underparts. Females, twice the size of the males, have grey-brown upperparts with brown bars across the underparts.

Sparrowhawks hunt small to medium birds and large insects but will also take small mammals and carrion. They are clever hunters often catching birds by deception, either by hiding in ambush or typically flying along one side of a hedgerow only to swoop suddenly to the other, catching anything there unawares.

They are known to imitate a pigeon's flight to allow them to get closer to their prey. They have been seen to drown small birds in shallow water. In falconry, the male birds are known as 'muskets' from which the musket gun was named. We know that Sparrowhawks were present in Ireland as far back as the twelfth century, as Gerald of Wales mentions them in his travels here.[10] In the seventeenth century, the nobility used Sparrowhawks to hunt Blackbirds and there are documented reports of this taking place in Dublin's Phoenix Park.

In the 1950s and 1960s, the population was dramatically reduced through the use of DDT,[11] which, when brought into the diet of a bird, caused their eggs to be thin-shelled and not viable. Thankfully, numbers have recovered somewhat since.

The generic *accipiter* is from the Latin meaning 'hawk'. The specific *nisus* may be from the Latin meaning 'soaring'. The word 'hawk' is from the Anglo Saxon *hafoc* meaning 'seize'.

Beliefs & Traditions: Hawks were believed to have the best eyesight of all the birds. Gerald of Wales, on his travels in Ireland in the twelfth century, tells us that when winter frost gets severe, a Sparrowhawk is likely to seize a bat in the evening to which it clings through the night for the sake of warmth, only to release it in the morning.[12]

The Colloquy between Fintan and the Hawk of Achill, an Irish play copied in the fourteenth century but much older, and perhaps the oldest in existence, features 'The Hawk of Achill', said to be a wise creature, a messenger from the Otherworld and, the oldest of all the animals.

Proverbs & Similes:

Chomh meabhrach breabhsach le seabhac aille.
(As intelligent and sprightly as a sparrowhawk)

The eye of a hawk on a mountain top. (sharp-eyed)

PLACE NAMES

Carrickatuke, Co. Armagh (Carraig an tSeabhaic, hawk rock)
Craignashoke, Co. Derry, Co. Antrim (Creag na Seabhac, also hawks' rock)
Craigatuke, Co. Tyrone (Creag an tSeabhaic, crag of the hawk)
Hawk's Nest, Glenarm, Co. Antrim
Knockatouk, Co. Waterford (Cnoc an tSeabhaic, hawk's hill)
Monatouk, Co. Waterford (Muine an tSeabhaic, hawk's thicket)

NAMES

English: Blue Hawk (Uls.), Spar Hawk, Sprawk (sl.)

Irish: Gabhlán,[13] Naile, Ruán aille (cliff Sparrowhawk), Ruabhan alla, Ruadhán alla/aille (cliff red-bird, Aran.), Seabhac aille (cliff hawk), Seabhóg, Spioróg, Seabhac ruadh (red hawk), Séagh, Spéaróg, Spéir-chearc (hen-hawk), Spéire (Kry.), Spéireog (Ant.), Spéirge, Speirsheabhac, Spiorsóg, Spirreog

Uls. Scots: Kack, Sparrahakk

Scientific: Astur nisus, Falco nisus, Nisus communis, Nisus linnei, Nisus nisus

FACTS & FIGURES

Resident carnivores. Widespread in all counties. Up to 10,000 breeding pairs (88–91). Live max eleven years. Collective name: a cast of hawks, a kettle of hawks. About fifty species of *Accipiter* (Goshawks and Sparrowhawks) worldwide. Order: *Falconiformes*; Family: *Accipitridae*.

3.6.4 The (Common) Kestrel

Pocaire gaoithe | *Falco tinnunculus tinnunculus*

'. . . *dapple-dawn-drawn Falcon* . . .'[14]

The Windhover, the subject of Gerard Manley Hopkins' famous poem, is the old name for Ireland's most widely known falcon, the Kestrel. Present throughout Ireland, Kestrels are most often seen from the window of a moving car, hovering into the wind. They are among the few birds that have benefited directly from man's expansion. The development of large junctions and roundabouts has had the effect of leaving small areas of wild vegetation, which are seldom if ever disturbed by man. With little fear of moving traffic, Kestrels have made the most of these new oases. In the past, Kestrels were often kept near dovecotes because they frightened away Sparrowhawks and would not bother the doves themselves. It was even said that pigeons would seek out a Kestrel for protection if a Sparrowhawk were about.

The Irish name *Pocaire gaoithe*, translating as something like 'wind frolicker', is a good description. 'Kestrel' itself probably comes from the Middle English *kastil*, 'to rattle'. The specific name *tinnunculus* comes from the Latin *tinnio*, 'to ring'.

Poetry: from '*The Windhover*': To Christ our Lord

> *I caught this morning morning's minion,*
> *kingdom of daylight's dauphin,*
> *dapple-dawn-drawn falcon, in his riding*
> *Of the rolling level underneath him steady air,*
> *and striding*

Gerard Manley Hopkins (c. 1877)

NAMES

English: Sparrow Hawk (Uls.), Windhover

Irish: Bod/Bodaire gaoithe (wind tramp, Din.), Púicín gaoithe (little wind pooka), Seabhac buidhe/buí (yellow hawk, Din), Seabhac gaoithe (wind hawk), Seabhac(h) Géill (Ant.)

Scientific: Cerchneis tinnunculus, Tinnunculus alaudarius, Tinnunculus linnei, Tinnunculus tinnunculus

FACTS & FIGURES

Resident carnivores. Widespread in all counties. Up to 10,000 breeding pairs but declining (88–91). Live max sixteen years. The national bird of Belgium. Nearly forty species of *Falco* worldwide of which about thirteen are called Kestrel. Order: *Falconiformes*; Family: *Falconidae*.

3.6.5 The Merlin

Meirliún | *Falco columbarius aesalon,*
Falco columbarius subaesalon

Smaller than Jackdaws, Merlins are Ireland's smallest falcons. With little more than a hundred pairs in the country, you will not see Merlins every day. The males are slaty-blue on top and streaked below. Females and young are dark brown, looking something like small Kestrels. Strictly speaking, 'merlins' are female and 'jacks' are males. While Merlins do catch birds, they are small enough to live on a diet of insects, which they eagerly snatch on the wing. Merlins were used in falconry, mostly by ladies. Mary Queen of Scots herself owned one.[15] Medieval nuns also kept Merlins and were criticised for bringing them into church.[16]

The name 'Merlin' comes from the same root as *merle*, the Blackbird, and it is possible that they were used to hunt Blackbirds. They were certainly used, as ladys' falcons, to hunt Skylarks. The scientific name *Falco columbarius* translates as 'dove-falcon' and they are sometimes called 'pigeon hawks' in North America. Jeff Greenhalgh[17] reports a historic bird, in a record of 1616, referred to in falconry as an 'Irish Merlin', with green legs. As no Irish raptor with green legs fits the bill, the identity of this bird remains a mystery.

Poetry: from: *A Queer Book*

> *And the Merlin hang in the middle air,*
> *With his little wings outspread,*
> *As if let down from the heavens there,*
> *By a viewless silken thread.*

James Hogg (The Ettrick Shepherd, 1832)

NAMES

English: (Common) Pigeon Hawk, North European Merlin, Sparrow-hawk

Irish: Meirliun

Scientific: Aesalon lithofalco, Falco aesalon, Falco colombarius aesalon, Falco emerillon, Falco lithofalco, Falco merillus, Falco regulus

FACTS & FIGURES

Scarce resident carnivores. Migrate from lowland to upland in summer. Up to 130 breeding pairs (88–91) with some extra arrivals in winter. Live max twelve years. Amber list. Nearly forty species of *Falco* worldwide. Order: *Falconiformes;* Family: *Falconidae.*

3.6.6 The Peregrine (Falcon)

Fabhcún gorm | *Falco peregrinus peregrinus*

One of nature's greatest achievements, the Peregrine Falcon, can be found on all continents except Antarctica. Stocky birds, notably larger than Sparrowhawks, the females are larger birds, with similar colouring to the males. Both adults show blue-grey upperparts with heavily streaked white underparts and the appearance of a large down-curling moustache. Males are 'tiercels',[18] females are falcons and they pair for life. A pair's territory may cover up to 200 square kilometres.

Peregrines are supreme hunters, taking birds on the wing up to the size of pigeons. Regarded as the fastest birds on the wing, they have been measured at speeds of at least 160 km/h in a dive known as a stoop.

As the raptors of choice for kings and nobles, Peregrines were protected since at least the time of the Normans but the birds became victims of their own success and when the tide turned towards shooting rather than hawking game in the seventeenth century, the killing of Peregrines to protect game commenced. In Ireland, the number of Peregrines had dropped to only twenty-five to thirty breeding pairs by 1970 due to increased use of pesticides. With farmers introducing new pest control measures, their numbers are now on the increase again.

The name 'falcon' is from the Latin *falx*, meaning 'sickle', after the birds' talons. They were favoured falconry birds. The name 'Peregrine' is from Latin meaning 'wanderer'. The Irish *Fabhcún gorm* means 'blue falcon'.

NAMES

English: Blue Hawk, Cliff Hawk, European Peregrine, Game Hawk (Uls.), Goose Hawk (Uls.), Goshawk, Rock Hawk

Irish: Seabhac gorm (blue hawk, Din.), Seabhac reilige (graveyard hawk), Seabhac seilge (game hawk)

Scientific: Falco communis

FACTS & FIGURES

Resident carnivores. Migrate internally. Up to 350 breeding pairs and increasing (02) of which nearly 75 per cent are in the Republic. Winter numbers are inflated with overseas visitors. Up to half a metre in length. One metre wingspan. Weigh about 1 kg. Live max seventeen years. Amber list. Nearly forty species of *Falco* worldwide. Order: *Falconiformes*; Family: *Falconidae*.

3.7 OTHER LARGE LAND BIRDS

3.7.1 The Red Grouse[1]

Cearc fhraoigh | *Lagopus lagopus hibernicus* (Irish Red Grouse)

Our one species of grouse in Ireland, the Red Grouse is unlucky enough to be classified as a game bird. As a result, many are killed in the shooting season every year. Game birds, including Red Grouse, are so used to being hunted for hundreds if not thousands of years that they have evolved avoidance habits. Red Grouse spend a lot their time walking in heather or other thick cover. They will only fly as a last resort, then only to hug the ground as much as possible. The birds are very much dependent on heather for their diet and indeed the Irish name *Cearc fhraoigh* means 'heather hen'. They are plump, somewhat chicken-like birds. Males are a rusty red-brown, with white furry legs and a bright red wattle above the eye. Females are similar but smaller with subdued colours, sometimes almost yellow-marmalade in the breeding season. The birds are darker in winter. The male is the gorcock and the female the gorhen or moorhen. Nests are on the ground and chicks hatch well developed and able to fend for themselves. When threatened with danger, a hen grouse will feign injury, usually dragging a wing, to direct attention away from her chicks.

We have our own subspecies of Red Grouse in Ireland, the *hibernicus* race, though one would need to have a keen eye to note the differences from the British race *scoticus*. All Red Grouse have an intriguing breeding call sounding very much like 'go back go back go back go back', an entreaty perhaps to their would-be hunters. McGillivray speculated that the Celts, speaking Gaelic [sic], would have heard the grouse call '*co, co, co, co, mo chlaidh, mo chlaidh*' (who, who, who, who goes there? my sword, my sword).[2] The Red Grouse is the same species as the Willow Grouse or Willow Ptarmigan. Numbers are declining due to loss of habitat.

The scientific name *lagopus* comes from the Greek *lagos* meaning 'hare' and *pous* meaning 'foot' which obviously refers to the bird's furry legs.

Proverbs & Similes:

Sparáil na circe fraoigh ar an bhfraoch (the grouse sparing the heather, meaning 'unnecessary frugality').

CULINARY

Grouse have been hunted and eaten for hundreds if not thousands of years. They are usually roasted, as the flesh is too dry to broil. Bewick described them as 'delicate and wholesome'.

PLACE NAMES

Reanagullee, Co. Waterford (Réidh na gCoillighe, grouse plateau)

NAMES

English: Gorcock (male), Gorhen (fem.), Heath Cock/Hen, Heather Cock/Hen (Uls.), Moor Cock/Hen (Uls.), Moor-game, Moorfowl, Red Game, Willow Ptarmigan

Irish: Cearc fraoigh (heather hen), Coileach fraoigh/fraoich (heather cock)

Uls. Scots: Heath Powt

Scientific: Lagopus albus, Lagopus scoticus, Lagopus subalpina, Tetrao lagopus, Tetrao scoticus

FACTS & FIGURES

Resident omnivores. Widespread but locally scarce. Found on upland bogs and moors. Up to 2,500 breeding pairs and declining (88–91). Live max eight years. Collective name: a brace of grouse, a covey of grouse, a crumming of grouse, a pack of grouse. Red list. About three species of *Lagopus* worldwide. Order: *Galliformes*; Family: *Phasianidae/Tetraonidae*.

3.7.2 The (Grey) Partridge

Patraisc | *Perdix perdix*

Grey Partridges may be Ireland's rarest native breeding birds. Partridges look somewhat like small footballs on legs. They are largely mottled brown with grey underparts and breast and rusty face and a distinctive dark horseshoe mark on the lower breast. Gerald of Wales says partridges were absent here in the twelfth century[3] but we know they were introduced to the Phoenix Park, Dublin in the 1660s and were being taken by 'kites'. Around 1600, Fynes Moryson said that 'partridges are somewhat scarce'.[4] Unfortunately, the birds are still considered 'game' birds though there are precious few left, in pear trees or elsewhere. The birds may soon be extinct here. The constant decline in population over the last 200 years may be due to pesticides and fertilisers and harsh weather conditions. A pair of partridges is known as a brace, which comes from the Latin *bracchia* for arms (and embrace). The generic name *perdix* is Latin for partridge, used by the Romans. Partridges were symbols of cunning and guile.

Grey Partridges have cousins, the Red-legged Partridges (*Alectoris rufa, Patraisc chosdearg*) which are native to south-western Europe but are sometimes encountered as escapees.

Proverbs & Similes:
Chomh ramhar le patraisc (as fat as a partridge).

CULINARY

Considered game birds, Grey Partridges were widely hunted and eaten.

NAMES

Irish: Cearc coille (wood hen), Cearc ghearr (short hen, Kry.), Paitrisc (Kry.), Patraisce, Piotraisc

Uls. Scots: Paitridge (Ant.), Pitredge, Shear Leeks

Scientific: Perdix cinerea, Starna cinerea, Starna perdix, Tetrao perdix

FACTS & FIGURES

Live max five years. Perhaps fewer than twenty breeding pairs left, and declining (88–91). Collective name: a bevy of partridges, a covey of partridges. Red list. Three species of *Perdix* worldwide. Order: *Galliformes*; Family: *Phasianidae*.

3.7.3 The (Common) Pheasant

Piasún | *Phasianus colchicus colchicus*
(no ring) (Colchis Pheasant, Old English Pheasant)

Phasianus colchicus torquatus
(ring-necked) (Chinese Ring-necked Pheasant)

Among Ireland's most spectacularly coloured birds, Pheasants are an exotic species imported from Asia and were favoured game birds of the Romans. The males are the commonly known, brightly coloured birds, the females being a drab light brown. Some males of the *torquatus* race have a white ring around the neck. This race was mostly introduced by gun clubs. White and partial white birds are quite common.

CULINARY

Pheasants have always been highly prized for the table. Henry VIII introduced the practice of raising Pheasants for hunting. Older birds are considered tougher. Pheasant meat is all white and similar to chicken. Pheasant eggs were regarded as superior to hens' eggs.

Pheasants rarely fly. When they do, the flight is usually a short hop to clear a hedge or road. This is most likely an evolutionary trait, developing through hundreds of years of intensive hunting. Like most game birds, male Pheasants will attack each other on sight in the breeding season. Pheasants are often heard before they are seen, giving a very distinctive call reminiscent of a chicken.

Most likely, the birds were named after the River Phasis, in Colchis near the Black Sea,[5] from which we also get the generic name 'Colchis'.

History: Some reports suggest that the Normans introduced Pheasants to Ireland in the twelfth century but Gerald of Wales says there was none here at that time. Others suggest they did not arrive until the sixteenth century. We do know that King Henry III of England had some for his Christmas dinner in 1251. Fynes Moryson, in Ireland between 1599 and 1603 says there are 'such plenty of Pheasants, as I have known sixty served up at one feast'.[6] Today they are widespread throughout the country and are hunted in large numbers.

While Pheasant hunting was the preserve of the rich, that did not stop the common Irish people from hunting them and they were taken at night by dazzling with a lantern and then knocking to the ground with sticks in the same way as thrushes and Blackbirds.[7]

PLACE NAMES

Coolnabeasoon, Co. Waterford (Cúil na bPiasún, Pheasant's nook) Pheasant Glen, Glenarm, Co. Antrim

NAMES

English: Ring-necked Pheasant

Irish: Cearc coille (hen of the wood), Cearc fheá (hen of the wood), Coileach coille (cock of the wood), Coileach cruaigh, Coileach feá[8]/feadh (cock of the wood), Feasán

Uls. Scots: Fesan, Feysan, Phaisan (Ant.)

FACTS & FIGURES

Introduced resident omnivores, widespread in all but the extreme west and northwest. Up to 100,000 'wild' pairs (88–91) but perhaps over 1,000,000 Pheasants including gun-club releases. Gun clubs shoot about 200,000 Pheasants each year in Ireland. Weigh about 1 kg. Live max seventeen years. Collective name: a bouquet of Pheasants (when flushed) or a nide or nye of Pheasants (on the ground). Two species of *Phasianus* worldwide. Order: *Galliformes*; Family: *Phasianidae*.

3.7.4 The (Common) Quail

Gearg | *Coturnix coturnix coturnix*

Quail are exquisite birds no bigger than wagtails and resembling balls of fluff with stubby tails. The birds show an overall streaked light brown colour, darker above than below and thinly streaked white above. The head is a broadly light grey colour with multiple black stripes. Females are similar but lack the black head stripes and show a spotted breast. Unlike our other 'game' birds, Quail are summer visitors, coming to Ireland to breed. Like Corncrakes, they are becoming very uncommon and are close to extinction here. Huge numbers are shot in continental Europe every year. In some 'quail years' there are still small 'irruptions' of summer visitors. The most recent was 1989. Like Corncrakes, they call both day and night, are more often heard than seen and are very difficult to locate. Their infamous skulking nature is responsible for the verb 'to quail', i.e. to skulk and hide. When disturbed, like most 'game' birds they prefer to run rather than fly and will often freeze on the spot, blending into the background. The three-note-call has earned them numerous local names in Britain and the name 'Wet-My-Feet' here. The generic name *Coturnix* is Latin for quail. The Irish *gearg* is probably derived from *gearr* for 'short', meaning 'short bird'.

History: Gerald of Wales mentions that Quail were common in Ireland in the twelfth century.[9] In the nineteenth century, Watters tells us that Quail were the most common game birds in Ireland: 'In summer it is so abundant in the fields, that, in the suburban streets of the city, we may constantly hear their pleasing call-notes.'

Beliefs & Traditions: Quail were symbols of courage and victory in battle for the Romans.

CULINARY

As a favoured game bird, Quail were always eaten whenever they could be found. In Victorian times, Quail and their eggs were considered delicacies. Autumn birds were preferred to those arriving in the spring. The meat is white and tender. They were also caged for their pleasant call. Today their eggs are often served with sushi. Quail encountered in restaurants are likely to be of the domesticated Japanese species. Mrs Beeton referred to Quail as 'feathered game which have from time immemorial given gratification to the palate of man'. The Romans were wary of eating the birds as they were believed to eat poisonous plants.

NAMES

English: (Eurasian) Migratory Quail, Pharaoh Quail,

Irish: Gairg, Gearg coirt (Conn.), Geárr/Gearr (Guirt)[10] (small (field) bird), Gearr goirt, Gearr naosc (Kry.), Gearra (Ghoirt) (Kry.), Muirial

Uls. Scots: Weet-my-feet, Wet-my-fut

Scientific: Coturnix communis, Coturnix daclytisonans, Coturnix vulgaris, Ortygion coturnix, Perdix coturnix, Tetrao coturnix

FACTS & FIGURES

Summer visitors. Omnivorous. Up to twenty breeding pairs in (88–91). Live max eight years. Red list. Collective name: a bevy of quail. About 130 species of bird called Quail, including about eight species of *Coturnix* worldwide. Order: *Galliformes*; Family: *Phasianidae*.

3.7.5 The (Common) Cuckoo

Cuach | *Cuculus canorus canorus*

'Fáilte don éan is binne ar chraoibh.'[11]

The cuckoo family has well over one hundred species worldwide, including the infamous North American Roadrunner (*Geococcyx californianus*). Only about a third to a half of these are brood parasites (they lay their eggs in other birds' nests). Only one species, the Common or European Cuckoo, visits Ireland. Known as 'gowks' in Ulster Scots, Cuckoos arrive in Ireland, from southern Africa, in mid- to late April and depart in August.

CULINARY

Cuckoos are not eaten now and the Christian bible forbade it (Leviticus 11). Yet Pliny considered 'For sweetness of flesh, there is not a bird to be compared with the cuckoo'.[30]

PLACE NAMES

Ballycooge, Co. Wicklow (Baile Chuag, Cuckoo town) Derrycoogh, Co. Tipperary (Doire Cuach, Cuckoo's oakwood) Drumawhy, Co. Down. (Droim an Chuaigh, Cuckoo ridge) Gowks Hill, Co. Down (from Uls. Scots gowk, meaning 'Cuckoo') Gowkstown, Co. Antrim Knocknagoogh, Co. Tipperary (Cnoc na gCuach, Cuckoo hill)) paircín na cuaiche (numerous) (the little field of the Cuckoo) Tullycoe/Tullyco, Co. Cavan (Cuckoo hill)

NAMES

English: Cuccu, Cuckow

Uls. Scots: Gowk

Scientific: Cuculus hepaticus

FACTS & FIGURES

Summer visitors. Carnivorous. Present in all counties. Up to 10,000 breeding pairs and declining rapidly (88–91). Live max twelve years. Amber list. Almost 150 species in the *Cuculidae* family including over ten species of *Cuculus* worldwide. Order: *Cuculiformes*; Family: *Cuculidae*.

Cuckoos are just as well known for their unique 'cuck-oo' call as they are for their tendency to lay eggs in other birds' nests though it is the males who do the cuck-ooing and the females who lay the eggs.

Males 'cuck-oo' at the beginning of the season to attract a mate, their whole bodies expanding and contracting with the effort. Once this has been achieved, they become much quieter for the rest of the season. Females are reported to make a low bubbling sound but alas this author has yet to hear it.

A hen Cuckoo may lay several eggs in several nests. She may even eat or discard an existing egg to make room so it is no wonder she is not liked by other birds. If the nest is situated so that she cannot position herself to lay directly in it, she will lay the egg nearby on the ground, and carry it to the nest in her bill. A young hatched Cuckoo systematically removes any remaining eggs from the nest to gain the undivided attention of its surrogate parents, making use of the hollow of its back. For this reason and perhaps as they look a little like hawks to the human eye, and perhaps to the avian eye too, they are frequently mobbed and harassed by smaller birds.

Cuckoos lay in several birds' nests including Dunnocks, Meadow Pipits, Reed Warblers, Robins, Pied Wagtails and Blackcaps. This has led to a number of alternative Irish and English names for some of these birds:

* **Meadow Pipit:**
  * Cuckoo's Follower
  * Cuckoo's Maid
  * *Banaltra na Cuaiche*   (Cuckoo's nurse)
  * *Coimhdire na Cuaiche* (Cuckoo's chaperone)
  * *Éinín na Cuaiche*   (Cuckoo's little bird)
  * *Giolla na Cuaiche*   (Cuckoo's servant)
  * *Gobadán na Cuaiche*   (Cuckoo's bird)

* **Dunnock:**
  * *Caochán or Gealbhan caoch* (blind creature or blind sparrow . . . the Dunnock does not notice the Cuckoo's egg)

* **Yellowhammer:**
  * *Cuach bhuidhe*   (yellow Cuckoo)

In England, Wrynecks[12] (*Jynx torquilla*) were sometimes called 'Cuckoo's Mates' or 'Cuckoo's Maids' as they always arrived a few days before the Cuckoo.

Each Cuckoo may lay up to twenty-five eggs per season, one per nest[13] and each individual female Cuckoo only lays eggs in the nest of one species, probably the one with which she herself was raised. It is said that the egg colour of these specialised

The (Common) Cuckoo continued

female Cuckoos matches the colour of the foster-species eggs but it is not clear how this can be possible. Some Blackcaps and flycatchers have learned to abandon their nests and try breeding afresh if they find a Cuckoo's egg within. It is a huge effort for two small birds to rear a relatively huge Cuckoo. Physically, it is sometimes necessary for the parent birds to feed the young Cuckoo from atop the youngster's back. The enormous effort often means that the parents do not survive the following winter.

It is part of the Cuckoo mystery that young Cuckoos migrate alone and know where to go without tuition and can also recognise their own species to mate, despite never having seen another Cuckoo.

The word 'Cuckoo' comes from the Old French *cucu*. The scientific name *Cuculus canorus* broadly translates from the Latin as 'singing Cuckoo'. From old English we also have the word 'cuckold', meaning the husband of an unfaithful wife, after the behaviour of the female Cuckoo. Oddly, there seems to be only one word in Irish for Cuckoo: *Cuach*.

Beliefs & Traditions: There are a number of beliefs regarding the Cuckoo's call, varying to such an extent around the country as to be sometimes contradictory. It was believed that if you heard the Cuckoo's first call in spring then you could learn to whom you would be married. After hearing the Cuckoo, you must look under your right foot where you will see a white hair. Take the hair, keep it with you and the first name you hear thereafter will be that of your future spouse.[14] Variations suggest the colour of the hair will be that of your spouse.[15] However, if you heard the Cuckoo with your right ear you would have luck all summer long[16] but if you heard it with your left ear, the summer would not be fun for you.[17] Nonetheless, in whatever direction you were looking when you heard the first Cuckoo of the season, you would be travelling in that direction before the year was out.[18] If you heard a Cuckoo before your breakfast, you would be hungry for the year.[19] But that's not all, if you happened to be stooping when the Cuckoo made his first call, there would be a death in the family; similarly if you heard the Cuckoo in a graveyard.[20] In addition, the place where you heard the Cuckoo for the first time would be the place where you would spend the rest of your life.[21] It was also lucky to hear the Cuckoo on the morning of your wedding. If you heard it from inside a building it was contrastingly bad luck.[22]

It was thought very bad luck to kill a Cuckoo or destroy its eggs.[23] On Tory Island it was good luck to have a Cuckoo's nest on your land.

It was believed that Cuckoos were really hawks that lived in Ireland year round but went through a certain metamorphosis in springtime to change into Cuckoos. This is similar to the belief that Corncrakes changed into Moorhen or Water Rails in winter. It was also believed that, when Cuckoos disappeared in autumn, they were hibernating in hollow trees. Some believed the Cuckoos devoured their own parents before disappearing.[24] Later, it was believed that when the Cuckoo was flying to Ireland, it flew with a stick in its mouth so that, when it got tired, it could rest on the stick while still flying.

Cuckoo oats were oats that could not be sewn, on account of bad weather, until around the time the first Cuckoo was heard, about April.

It was believed in Ireland that the pipit was forever trying to get into the mouth of the Cuckoo and if and when this should happen, the world would end.[25] '*Titfidh an spear nuair a rachaidh an gobadán i mbéal na cuaiche*' (the sky will fall when the pipit goes into the mouth of the Cuckoo).

'Cuckoo Spit' is a secretion from a number of insects, which manifests itself as a frothy extrusion found on the stems and leaves of several plants. It tends to appear at about the same time that the first Cuckoo is heard and so was believed to be the 'spit' of the Cuckoo. It is caused by, among others, *Philaenus spumarius* (the aphid-like Froghoppers). The arrival of the first Cuckoo also corresponded with the appearance of *Arum maculatum* ('Lords and Ladies' or 'Cuckoo-Pint'[26]) and *Cardamine pratensis* ('Lady's Smock' or 'Cuckoo Flower').

Weather: In some parts of the country, early bad weather in May is referred to as *gairbhín na gcuach*,[27] the little rough patch that comes with the Cuckoo. In other parts, Cuckoos were believed to bring fine weather.[28]

Proverbs & Similes:

A common proverb advises the sale of cattle and the purchase of corn on the first call of the Cuckoo. This has some slight variations around the country:

Nuair a chanann an chuach ar chrann gan duilliúr, díol do bhó is ceannaigh arbhar. (When the cuckoo sings on a leafless tree, sell your cow and buy corn.)

Má labhríonn an chuach ar chrann gan duilliúr, díol do bhó agus ceannaigh arbhar. (If the cuckoo calls on a leafless tree, sell your cow and buy corn.)

An tráth a ghaireann an chuach ar an sceach lom, díol do bhó agus ceannaigh arbhar. (When the cuckoo cries on the bare thorn bush, sell your cow and buy corn.)

Is garbh mí na gcuach. (The month of the cuckoo is severe.)

Chomh ríméadach leis na cuacha. (As jubilant/proud as the cuckoo.)

The (Common) Cuckoo continued

Chomh leitheadach leis na cuacha. (As conceited as the cuckoo.)

Chomh sona le cuach i nead a comharsan.
(As happy as a cuckoo in it's neighbour's nest.)

Éan na cuaiche (cuckoo's chick – an only child)

Uls. Scots: 'cuckoo's lachter' – a one-child family ('pigeon's lachter' – a two-child family), 'gowk's ern' (a fool's errand), 'gowk storm' (spring storm, Antrim)[29]

Readers with their heads in 'cloud-cuckoo-land' may like to know that the phrase originated in the Athenian Aristophanes' comedy drama *The Birds* in the fifth century BC, meaning a perfect city between the clouds.

Curses:

Nár fheice tú an chuach ná an traonach arís.
(May you not live to see the cuckoo or corncrake again)

Nár airighir an chuach. (May you not hear the cuckoo)

Poetry:
from: '*Fáilte don Éan*'

> *Fáilte don éan is binne ar chraoibh,*
> *Labras ar chaoin na dtor le gréin;*
> *Domsa is fada tuirse an tsaoil,*
> *Nach bhfeiceann í le teacht an fhéir.*

> Welcome to the bird, the sweetest in the trees
> Who sings the beauty of the shrubs to the sun;
> For so long a time, I've been tired of life
> For I cannot see her when the grass is new.

Séamas Dall Mac Cuarta, (1650? –1732)

'*Repeat That, Repeat*'

> *Repeat that, repeat,*
> *Cuckoo, bird, and open ear wells, heart-springs, delightfully sweet,*
> *With a ballad, with a ballad, a rebound*
> *Off trundled timber and scoops of the hillside ground, hollow hollow hollow ground:*
> *The whole landscape flushes on a sudden at a sound.*

Gerard Manley Hopkins (c. 1879)

3.7.6 The (European) Nightjar

Tuirne lín | *Caprimulgus europaeus europaeus*

Perhaps Ireland's most remarkable birds, Nightjars are scarce and elusive breeding summer visitors. Nightjars are unusual in perching lengthwise along a branch where they sleep during the day, protected by their grey-brown military camouflage. Males and females are broadly similar, males having white patches on the wings and tail. They have a wide gape for catching insects on the wing, which completes their rather odd appearance. The birds make an extraordinary noise called a 'churr' and the delightful Irish name *Tuirne lín* (flax spinning wheel) derives from the sound. Churring can be heard up to a kilometre away on a still night. While formerly widespread and locally common in the summer, it is now a rare treat to hear or see one. Almost totally inactive during the day, Nightjars begin their nightly insect hunt at dusk. The flight profile is very much like that of a hawk and indeed their close relatives in North America are called nighthawks. However, the Nightjars are much closer to the owls. Another American relative, the Whip-Poor-Will is named after its distinctive whipping call. The scientific name *Caprimulgus europaeus* translates as 'European goat-milker'.

The (European) Nightjar continued

Beliefs & Traditions: Being very odd creatures, active at night, it is not surprising that Nightjars had a bad reputation in the countryside. They were often associated with death. The name 'goatsucker' derives from the erroneous belief that they would suck milk from goats at night and is reflected in the generic name *caprimulgus* from Greek. In Ireland, they have been associated with the Pooka (*Púca*) and in the UK with the corresponding mythical creature Puck. In Ireland, the *Púca* was regarded as a sometimes-evil, sometimes-mischievous and rarely helpful hobgoblin or spirit which could take the form of an animal, lurking around the farmyard or harassing travellers in the dead of night.

Poetry: '*Goatsucker*'

Old goatherds swear how all night long they hear
The warning whirr and burring of the bird
Who wakes with darkness and till dawn works hard
Vampiring dry of milk each great goat udder.
Moon full, moon dark, the chary dairy farmer
Dreams that his fattest cattle dwindle, fevered
By claw-cuts of the Goatsucker, alias Devil-bird,
Its eye, flashlit, a chip of ruby fire.

So fables say the Goatsucker moves, masked from men's sight
In an ebony air, on wings of witch cloth,
Well-named, ill-famed a knavish fly-by-night,
Yet it never milked any goat, nor dealt cow death
And shadows only—cave-mouth bristle beset—
Cockchafers and the wan, green luna moth.

Sylvia Plath (1959)

CULINARY

Nightjars were said to make good eating.[31]

NAMES

English: Churn Owl, Dor Hawk, Fern Owl, Goat-Sucker, Moth Hawk (Wat.), Night Hawk, Puck (Eng.), Reeler (Uls.), Spinner (Wex.)

Irish: Áinleog,[32] Cnagaire cnuic (hill knocker), Seabhac oidhche (night hawk), Túrna lín (Conn.)

Uls. Scots: Purrin Bird

Scientific: Caprimulgus punctatus, Nyctichelidon europoeus

FACTS & FIGURES

Scarce summer visitors. Now less than thirty breeding pairs and declining (88–91). Live max eleven years. Red list. Over ninety species in the *Caprimulgidae* family including about sixty species of *Caprimulgus* worldwide.
Order: *Caprimulgiformes*; Family: *Caprimulgidae*.

3.8 WADERS (SHORE BIRDS) – LAPAIRÍ

Waders[1] are, for the most part, birds of coastal mudflats, inlets and sandy beaches. Some frequent grassy meadows and remote uplands. Being an island, Ireland is visited by large numbers of waders, mostly in winter, with some in summer. To all but the experienced ornithologist, waders can be difficult to tell apart. Thousands of years of hunting have made them wary of man, so a close view is never easy. Many waders were taken for the pot in Ireland, especially in times of hardship. Of the two hundred or so species of wader worldwide, we can see over thirty in Ireland.

Waders give us the haunting 'legend of the seven whistlers'. Found in many parts of the world including Ireland, the legend tells of seven ghostly birds that are heard and sometimes seen flying overhead at night. Their haunting call is said to presage death or disaster. The legend has many variations. In one there are six birds forever searching for the seventh. When the seventh is found, the world will end. The birds are believed to be a mixed band of Curlews, Whimbrels and plovers (though sometimes geese or swans). Another variation has the birds carrying the grief-stricken souls of unbaptised babies, condemned to roam the skies forever. A third has the birds as the souls of drowned sailors come to warn their comrades at sea.

3.8.1 The (Eurasian) Oystercatcher

Roilleach | *Haematopus ostralegus ostralegus*

The (Eurasian) Oystercatcher continued

Some of our noisiest seashore birds, Oystercatchers are brightly coloured birds. With immaculate black plumage on top, white below and brilliant orange/red eye and bill and pink legs, Oystercatchers look like exotic tropical visitors. Curiously, although Oystercatchers are very partial to shellfish, including cockles and limpets, they rarely eat oysters. Worms are also a favourite. The bill is skilfully used either to prise or hammer open shellfish. Common all year round on all but the south coast, the birds are easily found on mudflats or nearby fields.

Beliefs & Traditions: Oystercatchers are marked with a faint cross on the breast, which was believed to be the symbol of Christ.[2] This is explained by an Ulster folktale that when Christ was hiding by the Sea of Galilee, an Oystercatcher covered him with seaweed so that he could not be found and was rewarded with the cross on his breast.[3] An alternative legend has it that St Bride was fleeing from her persecutors and collapsed at the seashore. Seeing her distress, Oystercatchers covered her with seaweed and hid her. In thanks, she blessed the birds and gave them the sign of the cross. From this, the birds are also known as St Bride's or St Brigid's birds. St Bride is usually described holding an Oystercatcher in each hand.

An old Irish folk tale tells of an Oystercatcher that foolishly lent its webbed feet to a seagull. The seagull never returned the feet and since that time the Oystercatcher's call is a forlorn screech. This tale lends us the proverb '*Iasacht an roilligh don fhaoileann iasacht na fillfidh go deo*' (the loan of the Oystercatcher to the seagull, loan never returned).

In Scots Gaelic an Oystercatcher was said to call *bí glic, bí glic* (be shrewd, be shrewd) when its nest was threatened.[4]

CULINARY

Oystercatcher eggs were eaten on Great Blasket Island.

NAMES

English: Bride's Bird, Fish Rook (Uls.), Limpet Picker (Uls.), Mussel Pecker/Picker (Uls.), Oysterpicker (Uls.), Oyster Plover, Rock Ouzel (Uls.), Sea Mag, Sea Magpie, Sea-pie (Uls.), Sea Pyot (Uls.), Wilkpicker (Uls.), St Brigid's Bird

Irish: Giolla Brighde/Bhríde (Brigid's Servant, Ach., Conn., Kry.), Gobadán, Riabhán (striped bird, Conn., Kry.), Roilleog (Din.), Scaladóir[5]

Uls. Scots: Breedyeen, Garrabrack (Don.)

Scientific: Ostralegus haematopus

FACTS & FIGURES

Resident carnivores. Up to 10,000 breeding pairs (88–91) with over 40,000 birds in winter (94–00). Live max forty-three years. The national bird of the Faeroe Islands. About eleven species of *Haematopus* worldwide. Order: *Charadriiformes*; Family: *Haematopodidae*.

3.8.2 The (Common) Ringed Plover

Feadóg chladaigh | *Charadrius hiaticula hiaticula*

Ringed Plovers are unmistakable small birds of the sandy shore. Despite the distinctive black banding on the head and breast, the birds can be very hard to spot on a sandy beach. Once spotted, the only confusion can be with their close cousins, the Little Ringed Plovers (*Charadrius dubius*), which are rare visitors from Europe.

A Ringed Plover's slow fluttering display flight is known as the 'butterfly flight'.

The generic name *charadrius* comes from Greek meaning 'a plover'. The specific *hiaticula* is from Latin, perhaps meaning 'dweller in a cleft'. The name plover itself comes from the Latin *pluvia*, meaning 'rain'. The Irish *Feadóg chladaigh* means 'shore whistler').

Beliefs & Traditions: Plovers were greatly respected and it was said that they were brought to Ireland by Brian Ború[6] because of their ability to warn of an impending attack but we do not know to which plover species this refers.

PLACE NAMES

See Golden Plover, Section 3.8.5.

NAMES

English: Bull's Eye, Jack Whaup (Uls.), Knot (Bel.), Mary-of-the-trousers,[7] Ring/Ringed Dotterel, Ring Plover, Sand Lark (Wat.), Sand Plover (Uls.), Sand Tripper (Dow., Kry.), Sea Lark, Stone Plover

Irish: Feadóg an fháinne (ringed whistler), Ladhrán trá (beach 'claw-bird', Aran.), Pilibín míogach[8] (little piping Philip), Tormachán na dtonn ('ptarmigan of the waves', Ant.)

Uls. Scots: Pliver (Ant.)

Scientific: Aegialitis hiaticula, Egialites hiaticula

FACTS & FIGURES

Resident carnivores. Present in coastal regions of every county. Move inland in local areas, in summer. Up to 2,500 breeding pairs (88–91) with up to 12,000 wintering birds (94–00). Live max twenty years. Nearly seventy species in the family *Charadriidae* (plovers, Dotterels & Lapwings) including over thirty species of *Charadrius* (plovers) worldwide. Order: *Charadriiformes*; Family: *Charadriidae*.

3.8.3 The (Northern) Lapwing

Pilibín | *Vanellus vanellus*

Lapwings are green plovers known for their acrobatic flying and 'peewit' calls for which they are also named. They are exotic birds with radiant green plumage above, snow-white below and a rampant crest. From the distance, they appear black and white. Adult Lapwings and other plovers protect their nests by running away and feigning a wing injury to draw would-be predators towards them and away from the nest. This is described in Irish as *cleas an Philibín* (the Lapwing's trick) and from it we get the Irish phrase '*is é seoladh (tionlacan) an Philibín óna nead aige é*' ('he has the Lapwing's guidance/escort from the nest', meaning he is evading the issue). During the breeding season, male Lapwings have a dramatic display flight. They will tumble down through the air in a series of lateral stalls, all the while calling loudly to the females.

The word Lapwing probably comes from the Anglo-Saxon *hleapewince* meaning one who turns about while running or in flight (for its twisting flight) or perhaps for the flapping sound of its wings. It was equally known around Ireland as the Peewit or Green Plover. The generic name *Vanellus* comes from the Latin meaning 'little fan' and refers to its slow, flapping flight. The Irish *Pilibín* may mean 'little Philip'.

Beliefs & Traditions: Plovers were greatly respected in Ireland, though Swainson says Lapwings were almost universally held in bad esteem.

CULINARY

Lapwings were eaten extensively in Ireland, usually roasted or in pies.[12] The flesh was highly regarded and they were often sold at city markets. Many more were exported to markets in England.[13] Their eggs were considered a delicacy (*uibheacha Pilibín*). In England, dogs were trained to find Lapwing eggs.

PLACE NAMES

Curraghphilipeen/ Curraghphillifreen, Co. Waterford (Currach Philibín, Lapwing's marsh)

NAMES

English: Bastard Plover, Black Plover, Green Plover (Uls.), Peevit, Peewit, Philip-a-week (Dub.), Phillapee, Phillipene (little Phillip), Pilibín Meek (Wat.)

Irish: Adhaircín (little horned bird), Adhaircleog, Adharcán, Adharclóg, Píbín, Pilibín glas (green plover), Pilibín míog[14] (cheeping plover, Din.), Sadharcóg (Don.), Saotharcán (busy bird), Saotharcóg (Don.)

Uls. Scots: Lappeen, Peesweep, Peeweep (Ant.), Peewheep, Pewiep, Pewit, Wallapy

Scientific: Tringa vanellus, Vanellus cristatus, Vanellus vulgaris

Weather: A Lapwing seen screaming, in wheeling flight in the evening was a sure sign of a dirty night[9] and the call of a Green Plover meant frost was coming.[10] Lapwings flying or coming down off the mountain were a sign of bad weather coming.[11]

Proverbs & Similes:

Is é seoladh (tionlacan) an philibín óna nead aige é. ('He has the lapwing's guidance/escort from the nest' – he is evading the issue)

FACTS & FIGURES

Omnivorous, resident in most counties. Some internal migration from summer to winter. Up to 10,000 breeding pairs and declining (88–91) with numbers inflated in winter. Live max twenty-three years. Collective name: a deceit of lapwings. Red list. Nearly seventy species in the family *Charadriidae* (plovers, Dotterels and Lapwings) including over twenty species of *Vanellus* (plovers) worldwide. Order: *Charadriiformes*; Family: *Charadriidae*.

3.8.4 The (Eurasian) Dotterel

Amadán móinteach | *Charadrius morinellus*

Of the plover family, Dotterels are rare autumn visitors to Ireland. They are included because of their unfortunate Irish name, *Amadán móinteach*. The 'bog idiots' are named as such as they are reputed to be easy birds to catch, putting up next to no resistance or flight at all. What they lack in intelligence, they make up for in colour. In summer/autumn, the birds look like exotic tropical vagrants. The blue breast is separated from the contrasting rusty underparts by a clear black and white line.

The (Eurasian) Dotterel continued

The throat and eye stripe are white while the top of the head is black. Wings are mottled brown. Like most brightly coloured birds, the brilliant hues fade to mottled buff-brown in winter but the birds can still be recognised by the cream bar above the eye. Dotterels prefer remote mountain regions but can be seen on coastal headlands on migration.

The word 'Dotterel' comes from the same root as 'dote' and perhaps gives us the word 'dotty'. The specific name *morinellus* means 'little fool'.

Beliefs & Traditions: Dotterels were said to imitate every motion of their attackers, as they approached, never running away.

CULINARY

Dotterels were eaten and considered a delicacy. Their unwillingness to flee has probably led to their rarity.

NAMES

Scientific: Eudromias morinella, Eudromias morinellus

FACTS & FIGURES

Rare autumn visitors. Insectivorous. Bred in Mayo in 1975. Collective name: a trip of dotterels. Live max eleven years. Nearly seventy species in the family *Charadriidae* (plovers, Dotterels and Lapwings) including over thirty species of *Charadrius* (plovers) worldwide. Order: *Charadriiformes*; Family: *Charadriidae*.

3.8.5 The (European) Golden Plover

Feadóg bhuí | *Pluvialis apricaria apricaria*

& the Grey Plover

Feadóg ghlas | *Pluvialis squatarola*

Golden Plovers inhabit upland blanket bogs in summer and wet coastal lowlands during the winter. The male's plaintive whistling in-flight call is distinctive and from it we get the Irish name *feadóg* meaning 'whistle' or 'whistler'. In summer, the birds are a fantastic golden colour as though wearing a golden cloak over black underwear. Females are slightly duller. Golden Plovers nest on the moors and mountains of Connacht and Ulster.

Grey Plovers might have been better named silver plovers as they look, for all intents and purposes, like silver versions of the Golden Plovers. They visit Ireland only in the winter, from Siberia, and stick to coastal areas. Winter colours are duller. The silver 'cloak' and black 'underwear' is replaced with pale grey and dark spotting.

Golden Plover

Grey Plover

The specific name *pluvialis* and indeed the English name 'plover' probably come from the Latin *pluvia* meaning 'rain'. The Irish *Feadóg bhuí* and *Feadóg ghlas* mean 'yellow whistler' and 'grey whistler' respectively. The specific *squatarola* may be from Italian meaning having a black belly or from Latin meaning 'spangled'.

Beliefs & Traditions: There are many regions where plovers were called the Wandering Jews, from an old legend that the birds were the transmuted souls of those Jews who assisted at the Crucifixion. This legend may be related to that of the Seven Whistlers (see Section 3.8). It was believed that the *feadóg* neither ate nor drank but fed upon the wind.

Proverbs & Similes:
It's a long way from home that the plover cries.

CULINARY

Golden Plover were eaten extensively in Ireland and were regarded for their delicate flavour. They were often sold in city markets. Payne-Gallwey regarded them as the best of the waders for eating and indeed better than the Grey Plover[15] which were also regarded highly. Watters also regarded the Grey as inferior to the Golden Plover.[16]

PLACE NAMES

Balfeddock, Co. Louth (Baile Feadóg, plover-town)
Barranafaddock, Co. Waterford (Barr na bFeadóg, hill top of the plover)
Glennavaddoge, Co. Galway (Gleann na bhFeadóg, plover valley)
Moanaviddoge, Co. Limerick (Móin na bhFeadóg, plover's bog/moor)
Reanavidoge, Co. Waterford (Réidh na bhFeadóg – plover's plateau)

NAMES

GOLDEN
English: Black-breasted Plover, Gray/Grey Plover (Uls.), Green Plover, Mountain Star (Uls.), Yellow Plover

Irish: Feadóg bhuidhe (yellow whistler), Feadóg rua (red whistler, Kry.), Feadóg sléibhe (mountain whistler, Ach., Din.)

Scientific: Charadrius apricaria, Charadrius apricarius, Charadrius pluvialis, Pluvialis apricarius, Squatarola pluvialis

GREY
English: Black-bellied Plover (NA.), Gray Plover, Mud Plover, Rock Plover (Wex.), Sand-cock, Sea-cock (Wat.), Sea Plover, Shore-cock, Stone Plover, Strand Plover (Crk.), Whistling Plover (Bel.)

Scientific: Charadrius helveticus, Charadrius squatarola, Squatarola cinerea, Squatarola helvetica, Squatarola squatarola, Tringa helvetica, Tringa squatarola

FACTS & FIGURES

GOLDEN: Resident on coasts and inland, but absent locally. Carnivorous. Breed in specific sites in the north and west. Up to 400 breeding pairs (88–91). Up to 120,000 wintering birds (94–00). Live max twelve years. Collective name: a congregation of plovers, a leash of plovers, a stand of plovers, a wing of plovers.

GREY: Carnivorous winter visitors to coasts. Up to 6,600 wintering birds (94–00). Live max twenty-three years. Amber list.

Nearly seventy species in the family *Charadriidae* (plovers, Dotterels and Lapwings) including about four species of *Pluvialis* worldwide. Order: *Charadriiformes*; Family: *Charadriidae*.

137

3.8.6 The Ruff

Rufachán | *Philomachus pugnax*

A truly spectacular species, the males are Ruffs, and the much smaller females are Reeves. Rather drab waders for most of the year, breeding male Ruffs grows spectacular head and neck plumes and wattles in variable resplendent colours looking something like African tribal chieftains. Ruffs breed in northern Europe and Russia. The flamboyant plumes are used in the Ruffs' exotic territorial dances. Their display areas are called 'leks'. In spring the males congregate day after day at the same spot. Here they engage in combat, not unlike fighting cocks, grabbing each other with their bills and striking with their wings, under the exacting eye of the females. The ruff of feathers around the neck is erected and is used as a sort of symbolic shield. Females may visit leks for up to a week.

The Irish name *Rufachán* translates as 'ruffed' or 'frilled bird'. The generic *philomachus* is from Greek translating broadly as 'battle-lover'. The specific Latin name *pugnax* comes from the bird's 'pugnacity' in defending its turf. Both refer to the birds' tendency towards combat.

CULINARY

In Britain, Ruffs and Reeves were regularly caught for the table where available.[17]

NAMES

Scientific: Machetes pugnax, Tringa pugnax

FACTS & FIGURES

Uncommon summer/autumn visitors. Omnivorous. Less than 100 wintering birds (94–00). Live max thirteen years. Over ninety species in the family *Scolopacidae* including one *Philomachus* worldwide. Order: *Charadriiformes*; Family: *Scolopacidae*.

3.8.7 The (Red) Knot

Cnota | *Calidris canutus islandica*

the Dunlin

Breacóg | *Calidris alpina schinzii, Calidris alpina arctica,
Calidris alpina alpina*

& the Sanderling

Luathrán | *Calidris alba*

These three waders are locally common on our shores in winter. Only Dunlin remain in the summer, mostly in the northwest. For the non-ornithologist, they are very difficult birds to tell apart, particularly in winter.

Knot and Dunlin are quite alike but there are about three times as many Dunlin here in winter. As they are winter visitors, we are usually deprived of the Knots' striking rusty-red summer colours. Knot in winter are largely streaked grey on top and white below with black bills and yellowish legs. They are noticeably larger than Dunlin. Knot form huge swirling flocks by the sea, flashing black to silver to white as they swing en masse as a single organism. They like to feed right at the water's edge, running back and forth with the crashing waves.

Among our commonest winter waders, Dunlin are small quaint birds, about the size of wagtails, which inhabit the shoreline in huge flocks. Most birds arrive in winter from Iceland and northern Europe. Some stay to breed in summer, mostly in the machair grass in the west and northwest. The birds are primarily light grey on top in winter with white underparts and jet-black bill and legs. In summer, adults take on a mottled rusty-chestnut colour on the upperparts and a distinctive jet-black patch on the belly.

The generic name *Calidris* means 'sandpiper' and was a bird originally referred to by Aristotle. The specific name *canutus* comes from the Knot's association with the eleventh century Danish king, Canute the Great, who unsuccessfully ordered the tide to retreat as a demonstration that he was not omnipotent. The name 'Knot' itself may be a reference to the birds' grunting call. The name 'Dunlin' means 'dun-coloured'. The specific *alpina* is from Latin meaning 'from the mountains' and the specific *alba* means 'white'. In Ulster Scots all small waders were referred to as 'Sanny Larks' (sand larks) or 'Cuttyweerys'.

The (Red) Knot, the Dunlin & the Sanderling continued

Sanderling

Dunlin

CULINARY

Knot were regarded as the best to eat of the small waders.[18]

NAMES

KNOT

English: Ash-coloured Sandpiper, Dun/Dunne (Bel.), Red Knot (NA.), Red Sandpiper, Sea Snipe (Cla., Dub.), Stone Row (Uls.)

Scientific: Erolia canutus, Tringa canutus, Tringa cinerea, Tringa islandica

DUNLIN

English: Mudlark (Uls.), Ox-bird, Purre,[19] Sandlark of the Shore, Sea-Snipe, Sea Lark (Uls.), Stint

Irish: Cearc ghainimh (sand hen), Circín trá/trágha (little beach hen, Din.)

Uls. Scots: Sanny Lark

Scientific: Erolia alpina, Pelidna alpina, Pelidna cinclus, Tringa alpina, Tringa variabilis

SANDERLING

English: Sand Lark, Sea Lark, Wave Chaser (Wat.)

Irish: Ladhrán/Laidhrín geal (bright 'claw-bird')

Scientific: Arenaria calidris, Calidris arenaria, Tringa arenaria

FACTS & FIGURES

KNOT: Winter visitors. Carnivorous. Up to 27,000 wintering birds (94–00). Live max twenty-five years. Amber list.

DUNLIN: Resident carnivores. Up to 250 breeding pairs (88–91) with up to 120,000 wintering birds (94–00). Live max twenty-eight years. Collective name: a fling of Dunlin. Amber list.

SANDERLING: Winter visitors. Carnivorous. Up to 6,100 wintering birds (94–00). Live max eighteen years.

Over ninety species in the family *Scolopacidae* including nearly twenty *Calidris* (typical waders) worldwide. Order: *Charadriiformes*; Family: *Scolopacidae*.

3.8.8 The Purple Sandpiper

Gobadán cosbhuí | *Calidris maritima*

Purple Sandpipers are beautiful little birds that visit Ireland in winter from Greenland, Iceland and northern Europe. The birds are generally a drab, dark bluish-grey with perhaps a hint of purple and generally streaked white below. A Purple Sandpiper's orange/red bill and legs may lead to confusion with a Redshank from the distance but the birds are noticeably smaller, darker and 'stubbier'. Highly entertaining and quite tolerant birds, Purple Sandpipers are usually seen in small flocks and consort with Turnstones on the shore's edge, chasing the rolling waves back and forth.

The Irish *Gobadán cosbhuí* translates as 'yellow-legged sandpiper'. The specific name *maritima* means 'of the sea'. The generic name *Calidris* means 'sandpiper' in Greek and was referred to by Aristotle. A *caladrius* was a medieval bird with the ability to draw sickness out of a human and into itself. It would then fly towards the sun to dispose of the sickness. If a *caladrius* looked at a sick person, that person would recover, but if it turned its back, the person would die.

NAMES

English: Rock Sandpiper

Scientific: Erolia maritima, Erolia striata, Tringa maritima, Tringa striata

FACTS & FIGURES

Winter visitors. Omnivorous. Sporadic around the coast. Up to 3,200 wintering birds (94–00). Live max nineteen years. Over ninety species in the family Scolopacidae including nearly twenty *Calidris* (typical waders) worldwide. Order: *Charadriiformes*; Family: *Scolopacidae*.

141

3.8.9 The (Ruddy) Turnstone

Piardálaí trá | *Arenaria interpres interpres*

NAMES

English: Sea Lark, Stone Raw (Arm.)
Scientific: Strepsilas interpres,
Tringa interpres

FACTS & FIGURES

Winter visitors. Carnivorous. Up
to 9,000 wintering birds (94–00).
Live max nineteen years. Over
ninety species in the family
Scolopacidae including two
Arenaria (typical waders)
worldwide. Order:*Charadriiformes*;
Family: *Scolopacidae*.

Delightful winter visitors, Turnstones are usually to be found on the rocky seashore busily turning over stones, as their name suggests, searching for small creatures to eat. In summer, Turnstones are a mottled rusty red-brown on top and white below, with a patchwork black and white head, neck, throat and breast. In Ireland, in winter, the colours are much duller. The Irish *Piardálaí trá* translates appropriately as 'beach ransacker'. The generic *arenaria* is from Latin meaning 'a sandy place'. The specific *interpres* is from Latin meaning 'messenger' and refers to the birds' shrill alarm call.

3.8.10 The (Eurasian) Curlew

Crotach | *Numenius arquata arquata*

& the Whimbrel

Crotach eanaigh | *Numenius phaeopus phaeopus*

Curlew

Whimbrel

Ireland's and indeed Europe's biggest waders, Curlews have huge down-curved bills from which they get their Irish name *Crotach*, meaning 'humped' or 'hump-backed', which could also refer to the birds themselves. The other name, *Guilbneach* means the 'beaked one' and is shared with the godwits. The male Curlew is called a 'rooster' and a group of Curlews is called a 'curfew'. They are well known for their haunting 'cooor-lee' call, which is often heard at night. Several Curlews calling at night or dusk was a sure sign of a coming storm.[20] Curlews have a very soft pliable bill with which they probe the mud for food. While underground, the very end of the bill can open to grasp the prey and is as nimble as an elephant's trunk. This ability, called *rhynchokinesis*, is shared with the Woodcock and some other waders. Curlews suffer greatly from the frost,[21] and are protected from hunting in Ireland. When flying in groups, Curlews often adopt a goose-like 'V' formation. In courtship, the males rise high in the air and sing a crescendo of notes as they glide back to earth on wavering wings.

The generic name *numenius* comes from the Greek 'neos mene' meaning 'new moon' and probably refers to the curved shape of the bill. The specific name *arquata* probably comes from the Latin, meaning an 'arc'.

Close relatives of the Curlews, Whimbrels are much rarer visitors to Ireland. Whimbrels are like smaller, more delicate versions of Curlews, with small down-turned bills and clearer striping on the head. They tend to use Ireland as a stopover on their migratory flights north and some stay for the summer on the south coast. They are famous for their 'seven whistlers' call (see Section 3.8).[22] They probably got their name from the 'whimpering' cry of repeated notes, usually heard on the birds' night migrations. *Crotach eanaigh* means 'swamp' or 'marsh Curlew'. The specific *phaeopus* is from Greek meaning 'grey feet'.

Beliefs & Traditions: Seeing a Curlew at sea was considered bad luck. It was believed that Curlews did

CULINARY

Curlews and Whimbrels were eaten in Ireland and both Payne-Gallwey and Swainson regarded them highly, especially young birds.

PLACE NAMES

Whappstown, Co. Antrim, (Curlew's Town)
Whaup Rock, Whaup Island, Co. Down
Curlew Mountains,[27] Curlew Pass (between Sligo and Roscommon). Actually has no connection with the birds but comes from the Irish corrsléibhte (rounded hills).

NAMES
CURLEW

English: Rainbird (Uls.)

Irish: Crotach mara (sea Curlew), Cuirliún (Din.), Goibíneach (beaked-bird, Kry.), Guilbneach (beaked-bird, Uls.), Pocaire (Omt.), Pucaire gaoithe (wind buffeter)[28] (Omt.), Rucaire gaoithe (Uls.),

Uls. Scots: Courliew, Whaap, Whap (Ant.), Whaup

Scientific: Scolopax arquata

WHIMBREL

English: Jack Curlew (Uls.), Little Curlew, Little Whaup, May Bird (Uls.), May Curlew (Uls.), May Fowl, Seven-Whistler (Uls.), Spool Whaup[29] (Uls.), Stone Curlew

Irish: Crotach samhraidh (summer Curlew), Cúirliún (samhraidh)

Uls. Scots: May Whaap, Jack Courliew

Scientific: Numenius pheopus, Numenius phoeopus, Scolopax phoeopus

143

The (Eurasian) Curlew & the Whimbrel continued

not build nests (because they could never be found). It was said that when St Patrick first visited the Isle of Man he heard the shrill call of a Curlew warning that a kid goat had fallen down the rocks. He blessed them both and from that day, no man was ever to find a Curlew's nest or to see a goat giving birth.[23] Today we know that Curlews make their nests on bogs and moorland. The nests are no more than a depression in the grass, which are easily overlooked.

See Section 3.8 for the legend of the Seven Whistlers.

The Ulster Scots word 'whaup', for Curlew, is also associated with the name of a long-beaked goblin that is said to move about in the roof space in the dead of night.[24]

Weather: When Curlews made a double whistle, it was a sign of coming rain.[25] Similarly, a Curlew seen inland was a sign of a storm on the way. A single long clear call from a Whimbrel (*Cúirliún*) meant fine weather was on the way while a quivery repeated call meant rain was on the way.[26]

Poetry: from: '*The Seven Whistlers*' (A Victorian Anthology)

> *Whistling strangely, whistling sadly, whistling sweet and clear,*
> *The Seven Whistlers have passed thy house,*
> *Pentruan of Porthmeor;*

Alice E. Gillington

'*He Reproves The Curlew*'

> *O curlew', cry no more in*
> *Or only to the water in the West;*
> *Because your crying brings to my mind*
> *Passion-dimmed eyes and long heavy hair*
> *That was shaken out over my breast:*
> *There is enough evil in the crying of wind.*

William Butler Yeats, 1899, from *The Collected Poems of W. B. Yeats* (Macmillan, 1993)

FACTS & FIGURES

CURLEW: Resident carnivores. In winter, some migrate, within Ireland, from farmlands to coastal mudflats. Numbers also increase in winter with migratory birds arriving from Britain and the Continent. Up to 10,000 breeding pairs and declining (88–91). Up to 50,000 wintering birds (94–00). Live max thirty-one years. Collective name: a herd or curfew of Curlew. Red list.

WHIMBREL: Common passage spring/summer/autumn visitors. Carnivorous. Exact numbers unknown. Live max sixteen years.

Over ninety species in the family *Scolopacidae* including about eight *Numenius* worldwide. Order: *Charadriiformes*; Family: *Scolopacidae*.

3.8.11 The Godwits

Guilbnigh

Black-tailed Godwit: Guilbneach earrdhubh   *Limosa limosa limosa/islandica*
Bar-tailed Godwit: Guilbneach stríocearrach   *Limosa lapponica lapponica*

Black-tailed Godwit

Bar-tailed Godwit

The Godwits continued

Godwits are large striking waders with very long bills. The two species seen in Ireland, the Bar-tailed and the Black-tailed look very similar to all but the well-trained eye. They are most easily distinguished in flight when the rump clearly shows as either full black or black bars. In Ireland, they can only be confused with Curlew or Whimbrel, both having noticeably down-turned bills. As these birds only visit in winter, we are generally deprived of their fantastic orange/red summer colours although this can be seen when they arrive in September and a few birds spend the summer here. Black-tails migrate from Iceland while the Bar-tails come from northern Europe.

In winter, Bar-tails have a much rougher/speckled appearance. In summer, Bar-tails show all red body and head while only the Black-tail's head turns red. The Bar-tail's bill is slightly upturned while the Black-tail's is straight.

Godwits, like Curlews, Woodcock and Snipe, have the ability to flex the very ends of their bills, allowing them to grasp prey underground. The Irish name *guilbneach* means 'sharp-beaked'. The name 'godwit' may be from Old English meaning 'good creature' or, perhaps imaginatively, may have derived from the simple 'good-to-eat'. *Limosa* is from the Latin meaning 'favouring mud', an apt name. The specific *lapponica* means 'from Lapland'.

CULINARY

Godwits were eaten and were highly regarded as a delicacy.

NAMES

BLACK-TAILED
English: Blackwit (sl.), Red Godwit, Whelp

Uls. Scots: Yarwhelp

Scientific: Limosa aegocephala, Limosa melanura, Scolopax melanura

BAR-TAILED
English: Barwit (sl.), Common Godwit, Godwin/Godwyn, Norwegian Whaup (Uls.), Red Godwit, Russian Curlew (Uls.), Spool Whaup[30] (Uls.)

Uls. Scots: Yarwhelp

Scientific: Limosa rufa, Scolopax lapponica

FACTS & FIGURES

BLACK-TAILED: Winter visitors. Carnivorous. Over 10,000 wintering birds (94–00) of which a handful breeds in summer (88–91). Live max twenty-three years. Amber list.

BAR-TAILED: Winter visitors. Carnivorous. Up to 18,000 wintering birds (94–00) of which a handful stay for summer. Live max thirty-one years. Amber list.

Over ninety species in the family *Scolopacidae* including about four *Limosa* worldwide. Order: *Charadriiformes*; Family: *Scolopacidae*.

3.8.12 The (Common) Redshank

Cosdeargán | *Tringa totanus totanus*

CULINARY

Redshank are edible but not good to eat.[32]

NAMES

English: Pool Snipe, Red-leg, Red-legged Snipe, Sandcock, Shake (Conm.), Shore Snipe

Irish: Cailleach/Coileach bhreac (spotted cock/witch, Mun.), Circín trá (little beach chicken),[33] Coisdeargán/Coisdheargán (red-leg, May.), Deargcosach, Faoilean cos dearg (red-legged gull), Gabhlán mara (sea-inlet,[34] Kry.), Glúineach dhearg (red knee bird), Laidhrín dearg[35] (little red-toe), Ladhrán trá/trágha (beach claw-bird, Aran.), Mónóg thrá (beach bog-bird, Ach.), Roilleach[36]

Uls. Scots: Kitteryweary, Ridshank (Ant.)

Scientific: Scolopax calidris, Scolopax totanus, Totanus calidris, Totanus totanus

Like the Blackbirds of the woodlands, Redshanks are the sentinels of the seashore. Like many waders, they show a dull grey/brown colour above and white below. The birds are distinct though, with their black-tipped red bills and red legs. Close cousins, the Spotted Redshanks (*Tringa erythropus, Cosdeargán breac*) are rare winter visitors to Ireland's south coast. *Cosdeargán* means 'red-footed bird'. The alternative *Laidhrín dearg* means 'red-toed/clawed bird'. The generic *Tringa* may be from the Greek *tryngas* meaning 'white-rumped wading bird'. The meaning of *totanus* is unclear but it may simply be a Latin word for Redshank.

Cures: Bright's disease was an old name for acute or chronic nephritis (inflammation of the kidneys). It could be cured by eating the joints of the Redshank.[31]

FACTS & FIGURES

Resident carnivores. Up to 1,000 breeding pairs and declining (88–91). Numbers greatly increased in winter. Migrate internally from summer to winter. Live max twenty-six years. Amber list.

Over ninety species in the family *Scolopacidae* including more than ten *Tringa* (Shanks & Tattlers) worldwide. Order: *Charadriiformes*; Family: *Scolopacidae*.

3.8.13 The (Common) Greenshank

Laidhrín glas | *Tringa nebularia*

Beautiful elegant waders with dull green/yellow legs, Greenshanks are winter visitors to Ireland from their breeding grounds in Scotland. Largely mottled grey and white, the birds have long slightly up-turned bills. A handful stays for the summer and they were recorded breeding in 1972 and 1974 in Mayo. The birds have a beautiful three-syllable whistle.

The Irish *Laidhrín glas* translates as 'little green-toe'. The specific *nebularia* is from Latin, meaning 'foggy or misty', referring to the birds' colouring or perhaps to their marshy habitat.

NAMES

English: Greenlegged Horseman, Sand Piper, Sand Tripper

Irish: Ladhrán glas (grey 'claw-bird')

Scientific: Glottis chloropus, Scolopax glottis, Scolopax nebularia, Totanus glottis, Totanus littoreus, Totanus nebularius

FACTS & FIGURES

Winter visitors. Carnivorous. About 1,000 birds wintering (94–00) with one pair recorded breeding (88–91). Live max twenty-four years. Over ninety species in the family *Scolopacidae* including more than ten *Tringa* (Shanks and Tattlers) worldwide. Order: *Charadriiformes*; Family: *Scolopacidae*.

The (Common) Sandpiper

3.8.14

Gobadán (coiteann) | *Actitis hypoleucos*

Common Sandpipers are tiny brown-grey and white birds of the seashore and lake's edge. They have a distinctive three-note call and a constantly bobbing 'teetering' tail. They visit Ireland only in summer. Green Sandpipers (*Gobadán glas, Tringa ochropus*) are less common summer visitors.

The Irish *Gobadán coiteann* means 'common beak-bird'. The generic *actitis* is from Greek meaning 'of the shore'. The specific *hypoleucos* is from Greek meaning 'white below'.

Proverbs & Similes:

Ní thagann an dá thrá leis an ngobadán.
(The sandpiper cannot be on two beaches at the one time.)

or

Ní féidir leis an ghobadán an dá thrá a fhreastal.
(The sandpiper cannot attend to two beaches.)

or

Ní thig leis an ngobadán an dá thrághadh do fhreastal. (The sandpiper cannot attend both ebb-tides [i.e. night & day].)

NAMES

English: Fresh-water Sandlark, Sand Lark (Kry.), Summer Snipe (Uls.)

Irish: Cuirceach, Curcach (Kry.), Curcag, Currachóg (Kry.), Éinín locha (little lake bird), Ladhrán locha (lake 'claw bird'), Muireatrach,[37] Saidhlín aeir (Gal.)

Scientific: Totanus hypoleucos, Tringa hypoleucos, Tringoides hypoleucos

FACTS & FIGURES

Locally common summer visitors. Mostly insectivorous. Up to 2,500 breeding pairs (88–91). A few birds spend the winter. Live max fourteen years. Collective name: a fling of sandpipers. Over ninety species in the family *Scolopacidae* including two *Actitis* worldwide. Order: *Charadriiformes*; Family: *Scolopacidae*.

3.8.15 The (Common) Snipe

Naoscach | *Gallinago gallinago gallinago,*
Gallinago gallinago faeroeensis

& the Jack Snipe

Naoscach bhídeach | *Lymnocryptes minimus*

Looking a little like the younger brethren of the Woodcock, Snipe are rarely seen, skulking birds. They remain frozen when approached and will not fly until the very last minute. The birds are masters of camouflage being a general brown colour with buff stripes. Sexes are alike. Regarded as game birds, large numbers are shot every year. It is from the shooting of the unfortunate Snipe that we get the word 'sniper'.

Snipe are active at dusk and at night. The males have a fantastic display flight known as 'drumming' or 'bleating'. During this flight, a male flies high (several hundred feet) and then dives, with its specially modified stiff outer tail feathers extended sideways and vibrating to produce an eerie wailing sound. Snipe also make a sort of 'scraping' call. Like Woodcock, Snipe have flexible tips to their bills for grasping prey underground.

In the nineteenth century, even larger relatives, the Great Snipe (*Gallinago media/major, Naoscán* (Ant.)) were reported in small numbers in Ireland[38] but are not seen today. A subspecies of the Common Snipe, Wilson's Snipe (*Gallinago gallinago delicata*) lives in North America and occasionally strays to Ireland.

The scientific name *gallinago* comes from the Latin *gallo* meaning 'hen'. The Irish *naoscach* may simply be an Irish name for the birds.

Jack Snipes, the smallest of the family and winter visitors from Scandinavia, are found on very wet land and make a sound like a goat, hence the Irish name *Gabharán Reo* meaning 'little goat of the frost'. Jack Snipe are called *Mini-Gabhair* (mini-goats) in County Clare. They are particularly associated with weather forecasting though beliefs were somewhat contradictory. In most areas, to hear the *Mini-gabhair* was a great sign of good weather and if you heard one before 20 March (or within ten days of St Patrick's Day [17 March]), you would be guaranteed a good summer. Kevin Danaher[39] reports that the call was a sign of frost to come. Both Snipe and Jack Snipe have a sewing-machine-like motion when probing for food in the mud, Jack Snipe having a characteristic almost hypnotic bobbing motion while scavenging. The Irish *bídeach* means 'tiny'.

The (Common) Snipe

The Jack Snipe

The (Common) Snipe & the Jack Snipe continued

Beliefs & Traditions: In Ireland, Jack Snipe and Common Snipe were often regarded as being of the same species, the 'Jack' being the male and the common or 'Jill Snipe' being the female.

Weather: The drumming of a snipe indicated a storm was on the way.

Proverbs & Similes:
An fhaid a bheidh naosc ar mhóin is gob uirthi.
(While there is a snipe in the bog – for ever and ever . . . literally, 'as long as there will be a snipe on the bog and a beak on her)
    or
An fad bhíos naosca ar móin nó gob uirthe.
(While there's a snipe on the bog or a bill on the snipe (e.g. forever).)

Poetry: '*Gabhairin Reo*'

> *Gabhairin Reo old Irish name for male snipe*
> *A songless bird one of the silent type*
> *A long billed bird that dwell in places poor*
> *Rushy wet meadow and the marshy moor.*
>
> *But Gabhairin reo make strange sound with his wings*
> *Above the marshy moorland in the spring*
> *When darkness fall above the moor he fly*
> *And with his wings he makes a goat like cry.*
>
> *From an Irish-English dictionary I quote*
> *The Irish word 'An Gabhar' means a goat*
> *The old Irish named him Gabhairin from the sound*
> *That he makes with flapping wings o'er marshy ground.*
>
> *And I have heard a nature lover say*
> *That this is gabhairin reo's courtship display*
> *That he fly across the sky when darkness fall*
> *And with his wings make goat like courtship call.*
>
> *Next time you walk down bog road on spring night*
> *And goat like bleats disturb the peace and quiet*
> *T'is not a goat you hear though it sound so*
> *But male snipe known to some as gabhairin reo.*

Francis Duggan

from '*Donal Óg*'

It is late last night the dog was speaking of you;
the snipe was speaking of you in her deep marsh.
It is you are the lonely bird through the woods;
and that you may be without a mate until you find me.

Anon (eighth century)

NAMES

COMMON SNIPE

English: Bog Bleater, English Snipe, Evening Goat (Uls.), Full Snipe, God's Goat (Uls.), Guttersnipe (Uls.), Heather-bleater, Jill Snipe, Mire Snipe (Uls.), Snib (Uls.), Weather-bleat/blade (Uls.).

Irish: Bod suic (frost bum, Ant.), Bonnán léana[40] (Bittern of the water meadow, Gal.), Gabhairín bainne (milk goat, Cla.), Gabhairín oíche (night goat, Kry.), Gabhairín reo (male, little frost-goat-bird, Din.), Gabhar deorach (male, little wandering goat), Gabhar reo (male), Mionnán aerach /Meannán aeir (little goat of the air), Mionntán,[41] Naoisc, Naosc (Uls.), Naosca, Naoscán (beaked bird, Don.), Naoscarnach, Naoscrán (Don.)

Uls. Scots: Blooterwheep, Heather Bleat/Bleet, Heatherbleat (Ant.)

Scientific: Capella gallinago, Gallinago coelestis, Gallinago gallinaria, Gallinago media, Gallinago scolopacina, Gallinago scolopacinus, Scolopax gallinago, Telmatias gallinago

JACK SNIPE

English: Half Snipe, Little Snipe (Wat.), Mini-Gabhair (mini-goat), Single Snipe (Uls.)

Irish: Cuachán (Cuckoo-bird, Crk.), Gabhairín bainne beirbhthe (boiled milk goat-bird), Gabhairín reo, Gabharán rua (red goat-bird), Meigilín an aeir (the little air bleater), Minaun aerach, Mionnán-aerach, Seáinín dírúach (little straight Seán)

Scientific: Gallinago gallinula, Limnocryptes gallinula, Scolopax gallinula, Telmatias gallinula

CULINARY

Both birds were highly prized for the table with a taste similar to Woodcock. As well as the meat, most of the innards, except the gizzard, were considered delicacies. Snipe bills were also eaten roasted.

PLACE NAMES

Móin na Mionnán, Co. Waterford (bog of the Jack Snipes)

FACTS & FIGURES

COMMON SNIPE: Resident omnivores. Up to 10,000 breeding pairs and declining (88–91). Live max sixteen years. Collective name: a walk of snipe, a wisp of snipe. Amber list.

JACK SNIPE: Winter visitors. Mostly carnivorous. Perhaps over 20,000 wintering birds. Live max twelve years. Amber list.

Over ninety species in the family Scolopacidae including about seventeen species of *Gallinago* and one *Lymnocryptes* worldwide. Order: *Charadriiformes*; Family: *Scolopacidae*.

3.8.16 The (Eurasian) Woodcock

Creabhar | *Scolopax rusticola*

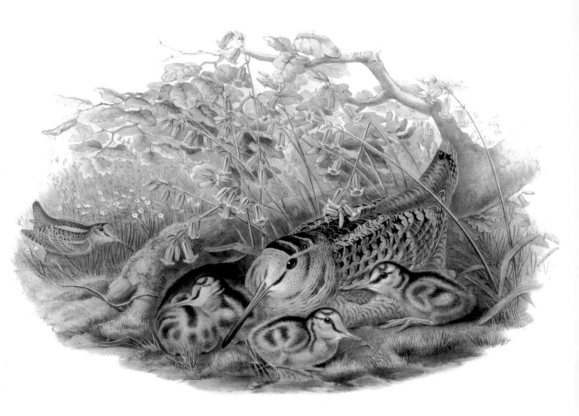

Woodcock are large brown birds seemingly in military camouflage. Very secretive woodland birds, they are unfortunately regarded as 'game'. Huge numbers are shot every year. While classed as waders, Woodcock are birds of quiet woodland, usually lying up during the day in deep cover and flying at dusk or dawn. A Woodcock's eyes are so placed on the side of its head that it has almost 360-degree vision in all planes. The males' display flights, known as 'roding' are very special. In spring, males display this zigzagging roding flight at dusk, low over the treetops while uttering squeaky, croaking whistles. They are reported to be the world's slowest-flying birds (5 mph). They are also very resistant to cold weather and, as very powerful flyers, are not easily discouraged by stormy weather. Like Snipe, they do not like snow.[42] Woodcock only began to populate Britain and Ireland in the early nineteenth century.

Woodcock have the extraordinary ability, called *rhynchokinesis*, to open the very end of their bills while probing in the mud for worms, avoiding the need to open the whole bill. The bill also has sensitive nerves at the tip and acts in some sense like an elephant's trunk. This ability is shared with the Curlew, godwits and Snipe and perhaps some other waders.

One of the Woodcock's most amiable attributes is its reputed ability to airlift its young with its feet while flying. It is by no means clear if the Woodcock really can do this. The author is willing to keep an open mind for the sake of a good story. It may also be the case that Woodcock feign carrying their chicks to mislead predators.

The tiny feathers located at the tip of the Woodcock's wings are referred to as 'pin feathers' and are much sought after by artists for fine painting work. They are also sought by game shooters, who place them in their hats to show that they have shot Woodcock. It is thought that the phrase 'a feather in his cap' is derived from this practice.

The Irish name *creabhar* is also the word for horsefly or tick, and a small haycock. The specific name *rusticola* means 'rustic' or 'from the country'. The generic *scolopax* comes from the Greek *scolopos* meaning 'pointed like a thorn' and 'Woodcock'.

History: A Woodcock appeared on the old Irish farthing coin (1928–1969) and later on the fifty-pence piece (1970–2000).

Beliefs & Traditions: Woodcock have an uncanny ability to 'predict' the weather and their migratory cycles are always in tune with the moon. Non-resident Woodcock tend to arrive in Ireland on the first full moon in November. As a result, it was believed that Woodcock spent their summers on the moon (See Section 2.5.3 for more on migration to the moon).

CULINARY

Regarded unofficially as 'game' birds, Woodcock have always been sought for the pot and are still served in top restaurants. As well as the meat, most of the innards and brain are considered delicacies. Best served 'pink', the meat is rich and dark, almost like venison.

PLACE NAMES

Gleann na gCreabhar, Co. Limerick (Anglesborough, Woodcock glen)
Gortnagrour, Co. Limerick (Gort na gCreabhar, Woodcock field)
Knocknagillagh, Co. Cavan (Woodcock hill)
Lackanagrour, Co. Limerick (Leaca na gCreabhar, Woodcock's slope)
Lugnaquilla, Co. Wicklow (Lug na gCoilleach) hollow of the cocks or Woodcocks or grouse).

NAMES

Irish: Coileach coille (literally wood-cock, Sco. and possibly parts of Uls.), Coileach feá/feadha (cock of the woods, Din.), Creabhar caoch (blind Woodcock), Fiodh-chearc (wood-hen, Ant.), Treabhar (Conn.)

FACTS & FIGURES

Resident omnivores. Widespread in all counties but absent in some areas in summer. Migrate internally from summer to winter. Up to 10,000 breeding pairs (88–91) with numbers greatly inflated in winter. Live max fifteen years. Collective name: a fall of woodcock. There are about eight species of woodcock worldwide. Over ninety species in the family *Scolopacidae* including about eight species of *Scolopax* worldwide. Order: *Charadriiformes*; Family: *Scolopacidae*.

3.8.17 The Phalaropes

Falaróip
Red:[43]   Falaróp gobmhór   *Phalaropus fulicarius*
Red-necked: Falaróp gobchaol   *Phalaropus lobatus*

Phalaropes are attractive, elegant waders. While none of the three species that can be seen in Ireland is by any means common, they are best seen in summer. The most likely birds to be seen are the Red Phalaropes, which can be seen, in passage, in late summer and autumn on all but the east coast. Red-necked Phalaropes, breeding birds we could be proud of into the 1990s, are now rare visitors. A third species, Wilson's Phalaropes (*Phalaropus tricolor, Falaróp Wilson*), are even rarer visitors from North America, seen only in autumn on the south coast. Like most waders, the Phalaropes are generally dull in winter but show beautiful rust red in summer. The Red-necked, as their name would suggest are bright red around the neck, extending up to the eyes. 'Reds' are primarily red on the neck, breast and underparts.

Red-necked Phalaropes are very unusual in the bird world as the females are the brightly coloured gender. The males are generally duller and rear the young. Red Phalarope sexes are alike. The phalaropes are also unusual among waders in spending a lot of their time swimming. They have downy breast feathers, which aid their buoyancy, and semi-webbed feet. While swimming, they often spin in tight circles, stirring up the mud in the hope of disturbing larvae. In the past, Red-necked Phalaropes have been reported to be seen picking food off the backs of whales at sea. Such reports could have given rise to legends of birds seen on floating islands.

The generic *Phalaropus* comes from the Greek *phalaris* meaning 'coot' and *pous* meaning 'foot', referring to the partially webbed coot-like feet. The specific *lobatus*, from Latin, also refers to the 'lobed' feet. The specific *fulicularius* is from the same Latin root as 'coot' (*fulica*) meaning 'sooty black', the females looking somewhat sooty black from the distance in winter. The Irish *gobmhór* means 'big-billed' while *gobchaol* means 'slender-billed'.

CULINARY

Watters[44] (1853) tells us that the flesh of a phalarope is excellent.

NAMES

English: Grey Phalarope (Red)

Irish: Faragán (Red-necked)

Scientific: Lobipes hyperboreus (Red-necked), Phalaropus fulicarius (Red), Phalaropus hyperboreus (Red-necked), Phalaropus lobatus (Red), Tringa lobata (Red)

FACTS & FIGURES

RED: Rare migrant visitors in autumn. Carnivorous.

RED-NECKED: A handful was breeding in Mayo in the 1990s but probably none now. Live max nine years. Red list.

Over ninety species in the family *Scolopacidae* including three species of *Phalaropus* worldwide. Order: *Charadriiformes*; Family: *Scolopacidae*.

3.9 GULLS & TERNS – FAOILEÁIN 'S GEABHRÓGA

There are about fifty species of gull in the world today. About twelve of these can be encountered in Irish waters. Of these, the Herring Gulls most aptly fit the bill of 'seagulls'. Male gulls are generally called 'cocks', females 'hens' and young, 'chicks'. Most live in colonies and are highly intelligent birds. Common Gulls are not so common and were known widely as mew gulls. The word 'mew' is Anglo-Saxon in origin and was a general word for gull, after their mewing call, up until about the fifteenth century.

Terns are the slimmer, more elegant cousins of gulls. There are over forty species worldwide. About seven of these can be encountered in Irish waters. They look a little like small gulls with berets. Arctic Terns make the longest migrations of any bird, flying 30,000 km every year from the Arctic to the Antarctic. Arctic and Common Terns in particular and indeed all terns in general were referred to as 'sea swallows'. European Little Terns (*Sternula albifrons*) were referred to as 'fairy birds'.

Some terns have a unique behaviour known as the 'dread'. Terns generally form large chattering breeding colonies. Periodically, these birds will simultaneously take to the air. They will circle the area for a number of minutes in complete silence before alighting once more and resuming their chattering concerto. The motive for this behaviour is unknown but it may be a response to predators, occasionally perhaps being triggered incorrectly. This behaviour is known in both Arctic and Roseate Terns. Terns are also energetic defenders of their nests, dive-bombing errant humans or other animals, sometimes striking the head with their bills with enough force to draw blood.

The word 'gull' is most likely Celtic in origin, probably from the Welsh *gwylan* (from the Celtic *wylo* meaning 'wail') or Cornish *gullan*, meaning 'gull'. It might also be from the Latin *gula* meaning 'throat'. From gull we get the words gulp, gullet and gullible. A gullible person is someone who will swallow anything, like a gull. Gull replaced the Old English *mæw* (mew). The generic name *Larus* probably comes from the Greek *laros*, a seabird. Tern is from the Norse *taerne* and the Old Norse *perna*.

Beliefs & Traditions: As with many other seabirds, Irish fishermen believed that gulls were the repositories of the souls of dead seamen and therefore should not be harmed in any way.

Three seagulls flying together, directly overhead, are a warning of death soon to come.

Weather: The presence of gulls inland was a sign that a storm was on the way.

Proverbs & Similes:
Chomh bán le faoileog. (As white as a seagull.)

Collective name: A colony of gulls, a screech of gulls, a squabble of seagulls.

PLACE NAMES

Gull Island, Co. Donegal
Oileán na bhFaoileán
(gull island), Co. Kerry
Roonivoolin (Rubha na bhFaolán,
seagull's point), Co. Antrim

GULL NAMES

Irish:

Éan faoilinne	(yng., Din.)
Faoile	(Don.)
Faoileadán	(Omt.)
Faoileagán	(Don.)
Faoileán	(Conn.)
Faoileann	(Mun.)
Faoileannán	(Omt., Mona.)
Faoileog	(Uls., Antrim)
Faológ	(north Conn.)
Grogaire	(young seagull, Din.)
Gulaí	(young seagull, Din.)
Scológ[1]	(young, Ant.)

TERN NAMES

English:

Sea Swallow	
Fish Swallow	(Uls.)
Purre[2]	(Uls.)
Skir/Skur	
Spurr(e)	
Sea Murre	

Irish:

Goireog	(caller, Kry.)
Giúróg	
Greabhróg	
Scréachóg thrá	(beach screecher)
Stearnálach	(Ant.)

Uls. Scots:
Jenny Dabber
Pirrie

FACTS & FIGURES

There are nearly fifty species of *Larus* and thirty species of *Sterna* worldwide.

3.9.1 The Great Black-backed Gull

Droimneach mór | *Larus marinus*

& the Lesser Black-backed Gull

Droimneach beag | *Larus fuscus graellsii*

Great Black-backed Gull

Huge menacing seabirds, Great Black-backs steal food from other gulls and even eat small birds and eggs. Lesser Black-backs are smaller and lighter in colour with numbers greatly diminishing. Both birds were often persecuted because of their predation and this had a very detrimental effect on numbers in the nineteenth century. Numbers have recovered since.

The scientific *Larus marinus* translates as 'gull of the sea' while *Larus fuscus* translates as 'dark gull'. The Irish *droimneach* obviously comes from the root *droim* meaning back, with *mór* and *beag* meaning 'large' and 'small' respectively.

Beliefs & Traditions: Hearing a Black-backed Gull at night was taken as a good sign as it meant that there were fish to be had.[3]

NAMES

GREAT BLACK-BACK

English: Carrion Gull, Cobb (Gal.), Goose Gull, Gray Gull, Greater Saddleback, King Gull (Uls.),(Great) Parson Gull (Gal.), Royal Gull (Kry.)

Irish: Caobhach (Iout, Din.), Cóbach (Din.), Cráinseach (fem., hag, Ach.), Droimneach mór, Druimneach mhór (Gal.), Éan óg breac (young spotted bird), Faoile mhór (big gull), Faoileán droma duibhe (Black-backed Gull, Din.), Faoileán druimneach (Black-backed Gull, Gal.), Faoileann dhromadhuí (Kry.), Prunntach

Scientific: Larus naevius, Larus niger, Larus noevius

LESSER BLACK-BACK

English: Gray Gull, Horse Gull (Uls.), Yellow-legged Gull

Irish: Caobach (Iout), Droimneach beag (little black-back), Faoile mhór (big gull), Faoileán droma duibhe (Black-backed Gull, Din.)

FACTS & FIGURES

GREAT BLACK-BACK

Resident omnivores. Weigh up to 2 kg. 2,200 breeding pairs and decreasing (99–02). Live max twenty-seven years.

LESSER BLACK-BACK

Resident omnivores. Nearly 3,000 breeding pairs and increasing (99–02). Live max thirty-four years.

Order: *Charadriiformes*; Family: *Laridae*.

3.9.2 The (European) Herring Gull

Faoileán scadán | *Larus argentatus argentatus,*
Larus argentatus argenteus

Herring Gulls are the true 'seagulls'. Large sea birds, they are happy to travel inland and have adapted well to human expansion. Herring Gulls do eat herring but also anything else remotely edible. They thrive on man's waste and are seen in large numbers at public dumps. They have learned to drop shellfish from a height to break them open.

Large gulls like Herring Gulls and the Black-backed Gulls are opportunistic predators. They are the raptors of the gull world, often intimidating and eating the young of other species and adult smaller species such as Puffins and Little Auks. While still a widespread species, numbers of Herring Gulls in Ireland have been in serious decline in recent years.

Recently there has been much debate on the subspecies of Herring Gull and indeed there seems to be several 'intergrades' between Herring Gulls and Lesser Black-backed Gulls. Several subspecies have been identified including Yellow-legged Gulls (*Larus a. michahellis, Larus a. cachinnans*), and American Herring Gulls (*Larus a. smithsonianus*)

The word 'gull' probably comes from the Welsh *gwylan* meaning 'to wail'. The specific *argentatus* means 'silver' while *larus* means 'gull' so the bird is the 'silver gull' and this is how it is known in most languages. The Irish *Faoileán scadán* translates directly as 'herring gull'.

Beliefs & Traditions: Three seagulls flying together, directly overhead, are a warning of death soon to come.[4]

Weather: It is said that seeing large numbers of Herring Gulls heading inland is a sign of bad weather on the way: 'Seagull, seagull, sit on the strand. There's an end to fair weather when you come to land'.[5]

NAMES

English: Laughing Gull (Bel.), Mew Gull (Wat.), Seagull, Silver Back, Silvery Gull

Irish: See Section 3.9.

Scientific: Larus argentatus argenteus, Larus argentatus michaellis (Larus cachinnans, Yellow-legged Gull), Larus argentatus smithsonianus (American Herring Gull)

FACTS & FIGURES

Resident omnivores. Often seen inland in winter. 5,500 breeding pairs and decreasing (99–02) with numbers inflated in winter. Weigh up to 1.5 kg. Live max thirty-four years. Order: *Charadriiformes*; Family: *Laridae*.

3.9.3 The Common Gull

Faoileán bán | *Larus canus canus*

Despite the name, Common Gulls are not so common in Ireland but visiting birds in winter increase numbers by a factor of ten. Beautiful, delicate, clean-looking gulls, they look somewhat like Kittiwakes, with all-white body, grey wings with black and white tips, black eye, bright yellow bill and greenish-yellow legs. Kittiwakes however have black legs.

In winter, Common Gulls can be found in all counties but they favour coastal regions. They breed in Ireland in summer but are confined to the west and north and the far tips of the Kerry fingers.

The Irish *Faoileán bán* translates directly as 'white gull'. The specific *canus* is from Latin meaning 'white/grey' (the word for greying hair). The English 'common gull' is a book term, the birds traditionally being referred to as 'mew gulls' after their call.

PLACE NAMES

Mew Island, Copeland Islands[6] (Oileáin Chóplainn), Co. Down

NAMES

English: Mew Gull, Sea Mew

FACTS & FIGURES

Resident carnivores. Migrate internally from summer to winter. Over 1,000 breeding pairs and declining (99–02) with numbers inflated in winter. Live max thirty-three years. Amber list. Order: *Charadriiformes*; Family: *Laridae*.

3.9.4 The (Common) Black-headed Gull

Sléibhín | *Larus ridibundus*

CULINARY

A hundred years ago, Black-headed Gull eggs were collected in large numbers for food, which lead to a great drop in numbers.[7] In the mid-nineteenth century, the eggs were sold in Dublin markets and were nearly as highly regarded as those of the Lapwing. They were also shot for sport and eaten. Watters, in the nineteenth century, reported the flesh as 'not disagreeable'.[8]

NAMES

English: Cob Pine, Crocker, Pine, Pine Maw (Ant.), Red-legged Gull, Redshank Gull

Irish: Faoileán an chaipín (gull of the cap), Faoileán beag na Tiarachta (small gull of An Tiaracht,[9] Din.), Faoileán ceanndhubh (black-headed gull)

Uls. Scots: Garrog

Scientific: Chroicocephalus ridibundus, Larus cinerarius, Larus erythopus/erythropus, Larus procellosus, Larus slesvicensis, Sterna obscura, Xema atricilla, Xema ridibundum/ridibundus

FACTS & FIGURES

Resident omnivores widespread in all counties but migrate within the country. About 4,000 breeding pairs and decreasing (99–02) with numbers increased in winter. Live max thirty years. Amber list. Order: *Charadriiformes*; Family: *Laridae*.

Black-headed Gulls are amongst the most common to be seen in Ireland. Smaller than Herring Gulls, they are often seen inland, but never far from water. The name is something of a misnomer as, for a large portion of their lives, the birds have mostly white heads. Like most gulls, they show light grey on top with white underparts and black wing tips. Only adult birds in summer plumage show a fully dark-brown to black head. They are well-adapted birds that will find food anywhere and will steal from their own and other species.

Some Black-headed Gulls are reported, from time to time, to have a pink hue particularly in the throat area. This occurs when the birds eat a lot of shrimp or krill and gain the beta-carotene colour in the same way that a wild salmon does. This is also reported in Common Gulls and other species of gull and tern and of course, flamingos.

The Irish *sléibhín* is an odd name, suggesting 'little mountain bird'. While the birds can be found almost anywhere, mountains are not a typical habitat for them. The specific *ridibundus* means 'laughing', referring to the birds' calls.

3.9.5 The (Black-legged) Kittiwake

Saidhbhéar | *Rissa tridactyla tridactyla*

Kittiwakes are small gulls characterised by their distinctive 'kitti-waaaaak' call. Looking like small Herring Gulls from the distance, Kittiwakes have much cleaner lines, bright yellow bills and black legs and wing tips. They are most similar to Common Gulls, which have distinctive yellow legs. Kittiwakes have black legs. They can be found around most Irish coastlines but rarely venture inland. Unlike most gulls, Kittiwakes dive into the water, somewhat Gannet-like to catch fish. They build their nests on narrow precipitous cliff ledges. The basic nest is usually constructed from mud. The chicks are silvery white.

The Scientific name *tridactyla* literally means 'three-toed'. *Rissa* is probably an Icelandic name. The meaning of the Irish *saidhbhéar* is unknown.

CULINARY

Young Kittiwakes were eaten in Scotland.[10] Kittiwake eggs were eaten in Ireland.[11]

NAMES

English: Tarrock[12] (yng.)

Irish: Éan geal fairrge (bright sea bird), Faireog (Kry.), Saidhbhséar (Conn.)

Uls. Scots: Chitty Wink

Scientific: Larus rissa, Larus tridactylus, Rissa tridactylus

FACTS & FIGURES

Resident carnivores. 33,000 breeding pairs (99–02). Live max twenty-eight years. Two species of *Rissa* worldwide. Order: *Charadriiformes*; Family: *Laridae*.

3.9.6 The Common Tern
Geabhróg | *Sterna hirundo hirundo*

& the Arctic Tern
Geabhróg Artach | *Sterna paradisaea*

Common Tern

Arctic Tern

The Common Tern & Arctic Tern continued

From a distance, Arctic and Common Terns are so alike that ornithologists sometimes refer to them as 'commic' terns. Like most terns, they look somewhat like small elegant gulls. Common Terns show largely grey on top, white below, a black cap and black-tipped red bill and red legs. Arctic Terns are similar, with smaller red bills. From their long tail-streamers, Arctic and Common Terns were often called Sea Swallows. Arctic Terns are renowned for vigorously defending their nests by dive-bombing human intruders, sometimes drawing blood. They can be seen hovering over water before plunging in to catch fish. Of all birds, they take the world's longest migratory flights, travelling about 30,000 km every year from the Arctic to the Antarctic. Apart from man and some marine creatures, they are the only animals that do this. Arctic Terns have a behaviour known as the 'dread' (See Section 3.9).

The generic *sterna* is originally from an old Norse word meaning 'tern'. The specific *hirundo* is from Latin meaning 'swallow' and refers to the birds' forked tails. The Irish *geabhróg* probably means 'chatterer' from the same origin perhaps that we get the word 'gabbing' in English.

Beliefs & Traditions: In Ireland, the appearance of a Common Tern was regarded as a sign of a good fishing season to come.[13]

CULINARY

Arctic Terns were eaten and enjoyed by royalty. Watters, in the nineteenth century, considered the flesh 'delicate'.[14] Common Tern eggs were eaten in Ireland, especially in time of famine.

NAMES
COMMON
English: Comic/Commic Tern (sl.), Fish Swallow (Uls.), Jourong (Gal.), Kingfisher (LN.), Pirre (Uls.), Sea Swallow (Uls.), Skirr (LI.), Spurre (Uls.), Swallow Sea-Gull

Irish: Giúróg, Scréachóg (thrá) ([beach] screecher, Din.)

Scientific: Hirundo marina, Sterna major

ARCTIC
English: Jourong (Gal.), Sea Swallow, Skirr

Scientific: Sterna arctica, Sterna macrura

FACTS & FIGURES

COMMON: Summer visitors. Fish eaters. 2,500 breeding pairs (99–02). Live max thirty-three years.

ARCTIC: Summer visitors (spend winter in the Antarctic). Fish eaters. 2,700 breeding pairs (99–02). Live max thirty years. Amber list.

Order: *Charadriiformes*; Family: *Laridae*.

3.9.7 The (Atlantic) Roseate Tern

Geabhróg rósach | *Sterna dougallii dougallii*

Perhaps the most beautiful of the Irish terns, Roseate Terns are birds of which Ireland can be truly proud. Rockabill Island off the coast of Dublin is the largest and most successful breeding colony in Europe and there is yet another at Lady's Island in County Wexford. Looking very similar to a 'commic' tern's (see Section 3.9.6) the birds are very white in colour with mostly black bills with red at the base. Elegant, graceful birds, they are masters of flight and a joy to watch. In summer, adult Roseate Terns have a pinkish hue on there undersides, from which they get their name. They can also be identified by their long streaming tail feathers. The birds are exquisite. Audubon wrote[15] '*beautiful indeed are terns of every kind, but the Roseate excels the rest, if not in form yet in the lovely hue of its breast. I had never (until April 1832) seen a bird of this species before, and, as the unscathed hundreds arose and danced as it were in the air, I thought them the humming-birds of the sea, so light and graceful were their movements*'.

The Irish *rósach* means 'rosy'. The specific name *dougallii* refers to Dr MacDougall from Glasgow who first 'discovered' this species in 1812. Man has been unkind to these birds and their numbers have suffered terribly over the years. Now they are conserved, at least in Western Europe, with Ireland at the forefront. They are still exploited at their West African breeding grounds.

NAMES

English: Purre Maw (Cck.), Skirr

FACTS & FIGURES

Summer visitors. Fish eaters. Over 700 breeding pairs and increasing (99–02). Live max twenty-one years. Red list. Order: *Charadriiformes*; Family: *Laridae*.

167

3.9.8 The Little Tern

Geabhróg bheag | *Sternula albifrons albifrons*

NAMES

English: Fairy Bird (Gal.), Jourongs (Gal.), Lesser Tern, Skirr

Scientific: Sterna metopoleucos, Sterna minor, Sterna minuta,

FACTS & FIGURES

Summer visitors. Locally common. Fish eaters. Over 200 breeding pairs and decreasing (99–02). Live max twenty-three years. Over thirty species of Sterna worldwide. Order: *Charadriiformes*; Family: *Laridae*.

Little Terns are easily identified by their small size and yellow bills. They nest on shingle beaches and are extremely noisy in the breeding season. Their eggs are very well camouflaged and ironically, this can lead them to being unwittingly trampled by people. They spend their winters in Africa. The Irish *Geabhróg bheag* means 'little tern'. The specific *albifrons* means 'white-browed'.

3.9.9 The Sandwich Tern

Geabhróg scothdhubh | *Sterna sandvicensis sandvicensis*

In contrast to Little Terns, Sandwich Terns are identified by their large size and black bills. Like Little Terns however, they too nest in noisy colonies on shingle beaches. Unlike Little Terns, they will nest inland. Numbers have been steadily increasing but of late the birds may be suffering persecution in the wintering grounds in Africa.

The name 'sandwich', reflected in the specific *sandvicensis*, comes from Sandwich in Kent, England the home of John Latham, the English naturalist, who named the bird in 1787. The Irish *scothdhubh* means 'black-tufted'.

CULINARY:

Sandwich Tern eggs were eaten.

NAMES

English: Big Skirr (Dub.)

Irish: Geabhróg dhuscothach

Scientific: Sterna boysii, Sterna cantiaca, Thalasseus cantiacus, Thalasseus sandvicensis

FACTS & FIGURES

Summer visitors. Fish eaters. Locally common on the southeast, west and north coasts. 1,800 breeding pairs (99–02). Live max thirty years. Amber list. Over thirty species of *Sterna* worldwide. Order: *Charadriiformes*; Family: *Laridae*.

3.10 AUKS – FALCÓGA

Though well capable of flight, auks are the penguins of the northern oceans. Of the twenty-three or so species of auk worldwide, five are likely to be seen in Irish waters: Razorbills, Guillemots, Black Guillemots, Puffins and Little Auks. There are over 200,000 breeding pairs in and around Ireland. Generally black and white, they have evolved to live in harmony together as they eat different sizes and types of fish. The sexes are generally alike. All auks are marvellous underwater swimmers and spend a great deal of time at sea. They suffer greatly from oil pollution and over-fishing.

Great Auks (or Garefowl, Gairfowl), *Falcóg mhór*, became extinct worldwide in 1844. The last Irish sighting of a Great Auk was off Waterford in 1834.[1] Huge flightless birds, they were exterminated by man for food and oil.

Auk is from the Scandinavian *alca* or *alka* meaning 'auk'. In North America, they are called 'murres'. The Irish *Éan dubh* (black bird) refers to any bird of the auk family. A breeding colony of Guillemots or other auks is called a 'loomery'. A group of them bobbing on the sea is called a 'raft'.

There are over twenty species in the family *Alcidae* (auks) worldwide.

3.10.1 The (Common) Guillemot[2]
Foracha | *Uria aalge albionis* (south), *Uria aalge aalge* (north)

& the Black Guillemot
Foracha dhubh | *Cepphus grylle grylle* (from Baltic)
Cepphus grylle arcticus (from Atlantic)

Guillemots and their cousins, Black Guillemots, spend much of their time at sea, coming to land only to nest. They lay their eggs on tiny windswept cliff ledges. There are scattered colonies along the east coast of Ireland and numbers are increasing. In the past, the birds have suffered from 'sport shooting' and egg collecting, from oil pollution and from being caught in fishing nets. Guillemots are dark chocolate-brown on top with white underparts. In winter, they turn black and white, with a white face.

Common Guillemot

Black Guillemot

The (Common) Guillemot & the Black Guillemot continued

Some Common Guillemots have a white ring around the eye with a white stripe behind. These Bridled Guillemots were once considered a separate species (*Uria lachrymans*).

Guillemot comes from the French *Guillaume* meaning 'little William'. The other common name for the guillemot, 'Murre' is derived from the dull murmuring background noise from a colony. The generic *uria* is from Greek meaning a 'water bird'. The specific *aalge* is a Scandinavian word, meaning 'guillemot'.

Black Guillemots are beautiful black birds with contrasting white wing patches and red feet. In winter, they are largely mottled white. Black Guillemots breed in small groups on our coasts and islands, in any nook or cranny they can find.

The generic *cepphus* is from Greek meaning a 'sea bird'. The specific *grylle* is derived from Latin and means 'cricket'. The old name 'Tystie' probably comes from the Old Norse/Icelandic *teista* meaning 'black guillemot'.

NAMES

GUILLEMOT

English: Foolish guillemot, Frybird (Uls.), Muir-eun (HH., Don.), (Sea) Murre (Crk., NA.), Murse (Crk.), Puffin (Uls.), Sea Hen

Irish: Cuilín (Kry.), Éan aille (cliff bird), Falc (Kry.), Forachan, Forathar, Forcha, Muiréan (sea bird)

Scientific: Colymbus troille, Uria lachrymans (Bridled Guillemot), Uria lomvia, Uria minor, Uria ringvia, Uria troille

BLACK GUILLEMOT

English: Black Puffin (Uls.), Dovekie, Greenland Dove, Parrot (Gal.), Rock Dove (Dub.), Sea Pigeon (Lar., Ll.), Tarrock,[4] Tystie

Irish: Bairéadach (from bairéad, a bonnet), Caltóg/Calltóg (Kry.), Casgán na long (ship's coffin, Kry.), Colúr tinne/toinne (pigeon of the waves, Din.), Colúirín tuinne (little sea-pigeon), Cubhar tuinne (carnivore of the waves), Éan dubh na scadán[5] (black herring-bird, Kry.)

Scientific: Alca grylle, Uria grylle, Uria minor

CULINARY

Both guillemots and their eggs were eaten in Ireland. Their eggs were also used in the manufacture of patent leather. While difficult to reach on cliff ledges, once approached, guillemots put up no defence, gaining them the reputation for being dim-witted birds and the name 'Foolish guillemot' (see Dotterel). Watters tells us, in the nineteenth century, of men lowered on ropes on Lambay Island, County Dublin, to collect guillemot eggs which were sold in the Dublin markets.[3]

FACTS & FIGURES

GUILLEMOT: Resident fish eaters. Migrate internally. 88,000 breeding pairs and increasing (99–02). Live max thirty-eight years. Collective Name: a bazaar of guillemots. Amber list.

BLACK GUILLEMOT: Resident fish eaters. Migrate internally. 3,400 breeding pairs (99–02) with populations expanding greatly in winter. Live max twenty-five years. Amber list.

Two species of *Uria* and three *Cepphus* worldwide. Order: *Charadriiformes*; Family: *Alcidae*.

3.10.2 The Razorbill

Crosán | *Alca torda islandica* (island Razorbill)
Alca torda torda (continental Razorbill)

Razorbills are sleek, graceful auks with immaculate black and white summer plumage. The birds are named after their razor-sharp bills, which they use to hold fish, and for defence. Fish are carried crossways in the bill, puffin-style, and several fish can be held at once. The bills have distinctive white banding marks looking something like war paint and a serious warning to 'keep-away' as they really are razor-sharp.

Razorbills nest on perilous ledges on the side of cliffs. When a young Razorbill reaches just two weeks old, it launches itself into the sea. They sometimes fall directly onto the rocks below, but are well protected by a layer of fat. Their eggs are notoriously pear-shaped, so that they will spin rather that fall off the narrow cliff edges. Their eggs are not so perilously placed as their cousins the guillemots with which they often associate. Sometimes the parents will place small stones or other material around the egg like 'chocks' on an aircraft wheel to help the egg stay put. The eggs are highly nutritious and are well favoured by foxes and avian predators. While numbers are strong in Ireland, many are killed off by illegal salmon drift nets and they always suffer badly from oil spills.

The generic *alca* is Scandinavian meaning 'auk'. *Torda* is probably a corruption of *tarda* meaning 'slow' or it may be from a Scandinavian word meaning 'droppings'.

Proverbs & Similes:

Blas an seachtú crosáin. (The taste of the seventh Razorbill – the feeling of having eaten to excess.)

CULINARY

Razorbills and their eggs were rarely used for food though they were certainly taken on Great Blasket Island.

NAMES

English: Auk, Falk, Frybird (Uls.), Marrot, Murre, Murren (Uls.), Puffin (Ant.), Scoot (Uls.), Razor-billed Auk, Scout, Sea-Pigeon

Irish: Creasán, Crosachán (Kry.), Duibhéan trágha (beach black bird, Don.), Éan dubh na scadán[6] (black herring-bird, Kry.)

Uls. Scots: Bridle-neb

Scientific: Alca pica, Utamania torda

FACTS & FIGURES

Resident fish eaters. Seen on every coast. Migrate internally. 17,400 breeding pairs (99–02). Weigh up to three-quarters of a kilo. Live max thirty years. Amber list. One species of *Alca* worldwide. Order: *Charadriiformes*; Family: *Alcidae*.

3.10.3 The (Atlantic) Puffin

Puifín | *Fratercula arctica grabae*

W. v. Wright del. & lit.

Once known as Sea Parrots or Lundys, Puffins are small seabirds of the auk family. They are unmistakable, showing black on top, white below and with enormous brightly coloured bills. Very amiable birds, they are unknown to most as they nest on remote cliffs and islands in huge colonies and spend most of the year at sea. Puffins are very affectionate birds, often rattling their bills together as if kissing. The huge bills become brightly coloured in the breeding season. They use them to store fish temporarily as they hunt under water. They are particularly fond of sand eels and collect several before eating or returning to the nest. One Puffin was recorded with over sixty sand eels in its bill. Puffins generally mate for life but go their separate ways at the end of the breeding season and reunite again the following year to use the same nesting burrows. Both adult and young Puffins are prey for many species of large gull and other seabirds. The young are sometimes called 'pufflings'. They are particularly vulnerable when they leave the nesting burrow. While at the nest, parents will defend their chick with their lives and can inflict a severe bite with their powerful bills. Burrows tend to be on the tops or sides of cliffs and the young flightless birds hurl themselves off the top and bounce down into the sea. As with most seabirds, human overfishing and oil and chemical pollution are seriously reducing their numbers.

There are thousands of them on Skellig Michael, and many more on other islands around the coast of Ireland including Cape Clear Island, the Cliffs of Moher, the Saltee Islands, and Rathlin Island.

The generic *fratercula* means 'little brother' and shows the affection with which the birds were held. The name 'puffin' itself comes from old English meaning 'puffed-out' or 'fat' and was originally applied to the shearwaters.[7] The Irish *Puifín* is probably borrowed directly from the English. The alternative *Albanach*, a Scotsman or Protestant reflects the birds' solemn expression and black colouring.

CULINARY

Puffins and their eggs were eaten in Ireland, particularly in soup and were reckoned by some to be a great delicacy. Younger birds were favoured. They were also barbecued on a tongs with a piece of burning turf or cinder, which would absorb some of the high fat content. In the seventeenth century, James Chaloner found fresh birds on the Isle of Man very distasteful because of their fishy taste and recommended pickling or salting them whereby they reminded him of anchovies and caviar. Actually catching a Puffin was a perilous endeavour, as they often make their burrows on inaccessible cliff ledges. The eating of 'alternative' animals such as Puffins may have become common again at the time of the famine. Roast Puffin is still eaten in the Faeroe Islands.

PLACE NAMES

Leac na gCánóg, Co. Waterford (puffins' flat rock)
Oileán na gCánóg (Puffin Island) and Puffin Sound, Co. Kerry (near Valentia)

NAMES

English: Ailsa Cock/Ailsa Parrot (Ant.), Bill (Gal.), Clown Pope (Kry.), Coliaheen/Collahene (Gal.), Lundy (Uls.), Puffing (old), Puffling (yng.), Red-neb (Uls.), (Sea) Parrot (Uls., Wat.), Welsh Parrot (Uls.)

Irish: Albanach (Scotsman or Presbyterian), Cadhnóg (old), Caifneog, Canán dearg, Cánóg[8] (puffin), Crosán,[9] Cuiltreachán, Éan dearg (red bird, Din.), Éan giúrainn/giughrainn[10] (barnacle bird, Ach.), Fuipín (yng., Din.), Foipín, Gobachán[11] (Din.), Poipín (poppy)

Uls. Scots: Bridle-neb,[12] Dooker, Fooran, Tommy Norrie

Scientific: Alca arctica, Mormon arcticus, Mormon fratercula

FACTS & FIGURES

Resident pelagic migrants. Fish eaters. 20,000 breeding pairs (99–02). Live max thirty-three years. Weigh under half a kilo. The national bird of the state of Newfoundland, Canada. Amber list. Three species of *Fratercula* worldwide. Order: *Charadriiformes*; Family: *Alcidae*.

3.10.4 The Little Auk

Falcóg bheag | *Alle alle alle*

Little Auks are the most abundant sea birds in the north Atlantic yet probably Ireland's least popularly known auks. Looking a little like flying penguins and being about the size of Starlings, Little Auks are our most diminutive auks. Quite a drab black and white in winter, the head becomes brilliant black in summer, a time unfortunately when Little Auks are absent from Irish shores. Spending most of their winter far out to sea, they are usually only seen in Ireland when they are blown in to the coast, or indeed far inland, in severe weather where they are often found to be very tame. Such events are called 'wrecks'. They can sometimes be found dead on the coast in winter. About the size of Starlings, they are (coincidentally) sometimes found following Starling flocks inland where they are hopelessly ill-adapted to flying amongst trees. Like other auks, they dive underwater for long periods. Being so small they are prey to other larger sea birds such as Glaucous Gulls, which can take a Little Auk on the wing and devour them whole.

The birds were more often referred to as 'Dovekie' or 'Rotch' in the past. The scientific *alle* may be a Scandinavian word meaning 'avenue' as the birds make huge long lines in the sea.

Beliefs & Traditions: 'Wrecks' of Little Auks in bad weather can lead to them being found dead on beaches in large numbers. This has led to a belief, similar to that about Barnacle Geese, (see Section 3.4.4) that Little Auks were more fish than fowl and grew on trees and dropped into the sea when 'ripe'.

CULINARY

There is no direct evidence of Little Auks being eaten in Ireland but the Inuit hunt them for food and use their skins for clothing.

NAMES

English: Common Sea Dove, Dovekie (little dove), Little Guillemot, Rotch, Rotche, Rotchie

Irish: Crosán[13]

Scientific: Alca alle, Mergulus alle, Mergulus melanoleucos, Plautus alle, Plotus alle, Uria alle, Uria minor

FACTS & FIGURES

Scarce winter visitors to Ireland's coasts. No breeding. Eat fish and plankton. One species of *Alle* worldwide. Order: *Charadriiformes*; Family: *Alcidae*.

3.11 PIGEONS & DOVES – COLÚIR 'S FEARÁIN

'The dove and very blessed spirit of peace.'[1]

Symbols of peace and wisdom, there are about three hundred species of pigeon and dove worldwide. Of the family *Columbidae*, broadly speaking, the larger birds are the pigeons, the smaller the doves. Sexes are generally alike. The flightless Dodos (Dódó, *Raphus cucullatus*) of Mauritius, were probably the most infamous members of the clan, rendered extinct by humans in the late seventeenth century, about a hundred years after their discovery in 1581. Passenger Pigeons (*Colm imirce,*[2] *Ectopistes migratorius*) of North America were among the most numerous birds of all time. Passenger Pigeons roamed America in flocks of millions of birds. Being regarded as a nuisance, they were systematically wiped out, the last one dying in 1914.

Pigeons and doves have a number of abilities unique in the avian world. They are the only birds that drink without tipping the head up. Pigeon's milk is a secretion from the crop, of members of the pigeon family, used for feeding the young. The proportion in the diet of the nestlings is reduced as they grow older. It is thought that pigeon's milk evolved to meet the needs of pigeons with their protein-free diet.

Pigeons have fantastic navigational abilities beyond that of many other birds including those that migrate. They seem to be able to pinpoint an exact location using several cues from the natural world, including the earth's magnetic field. This natural ability has been harnessed perhaps for thousands of years by domestic homing pigeons and their pigeon-fancying owners.

Several species can be seen in Ireland of which Woodpigeons are the most well known. Other native species include the Rock Doves (and feral pigeons) and Stock Doves. The only other common species, the

CULINARY

Pigeons and their eggs were eaten and kept in special, usually wooden, shelters called dovecotes. A dovecote provided protection from the cold in winter and a year-round food supply for the owner. A few of the stone-built ones can still be seen around Ireland. Pigeon guano was also used to fertilise gardens. Old pigeons are tough to eat while cooked young pigeons are called squabs.

PLACE NAMES

The Pigeons, Athlone, Co. Westmeath.

NAMES

Irish: Colbhar, Colm, Colm árais (tame), Colmán, (yng.), Colúirín, Colúr

COLLECTIVE NAMES

A cote of doves, a dule[5] or dole of doves, a flight of doves, a kit of pigeons, a loft of pigeons, a piteousness of doves, a pitying of doves, a prettying of doves.

FACTS & FIGURES

There are more than thirty species of *Columba* worldwide.

Pigeons & Doves – Colúir 's Fearáin continued

Collared Doves, arrived in Ireland as recently as the 1950s. While Turtle Doves used to be more common in Ireland, we now get only small numbers visiting from the UK.

In display, pigeons will often gently touch bills or caress each other. This is known as 'billing' or 'nebbing' from which we get the phrase 'billing and cooing'. The name 'pigeon' probably comes from the Latin *pipere* meaning 'to cheep'. The generic *columba* is Latin for pigeon/dove. The name 'dove' is from the Anglo-Saxon *dufan* meaning 'to dive' (from their flight).

Beliefs & Traditions: Tradition tells us that the dove is the only bird into which the devil cannot transform himself. It was believed that a sick person lying on a pillow of pigeon feathers could not die but instead would be terribly agonised and tormented. So it was often the practice to remove a pillow from under the head of the dying if it was felt they could not pass on. It was considered unlucky to have pigeons visit your haggard or farmyard, unless of course you kept pigeons yourself,[3] and it was very unlucky to see a pigeon entering a dwelling house.[4]

3.11.1 The Feral Pigeon/Rock Dove[6]

Colm aille | *Columba livia livia* (wild Rock Dove)
Columba livia domestica (domestic pigeon)

Some of our most familiar birds are feral pigeons; the 'flying rats' of the city. Common feral pigeons found in city parks and squares are descendents of domesticated Rock Dove escapees. Rock Doves have been domesticated for thousands of years and were often bred for their meat, eggs, manure and feathers in specially constructed dovecotes. The wide variety of trained homing, racing and messenger pigeons are also descended from Rock Doves. Pigeons were trained as message carriers by the early Persians and Greeks and later played an important role as message carriers in both world wars. Modern pigeon racing originated in Belgium in the early nineteenth century. 'Fancy' pigeons have exotic names like 'fan-tails', 'tumblers', 'rollers' and 'pouters'.

Feral pigeons are semi-wild, living in cities and towns mostly on the eastern side of the country and depending to a large extent, for their food, on man's garbage and handouts. Rock Doves on the other hand are truly wild birds and found

rurally, confined to remote coastal areas on all but the east coast. Feral pigeons come in an array of colours, from white to mottled, to their original wild colouring. The phrase 'stool pigeon' comes from the ugly practice of capturing pigeons by sewing the eyes of an already captured pigeon shut and then tying the flapping unfortunate to a stool, thereby attracting other pigeons. The slow increase in the population of Sparrowhawks and Peregrine Falcons may keep the expanding feral pigeon population in check.

The Irish *colm aille* translates as 'cliff pigeon'. The specific *livia* means 'blue-grey'. In Ireland they were widely called Rock or Sea Pigeons.

Proverbs & Similes: Chomh dúr doicheallach le colúr céileachais a mbeadh cochall air le ceann dá threibh. (As dour and churlish as a mating pigeon with the hackles up at one of his own.)

PLACE NAMES

Cuas na gColúr (pigeon's cave/cove, Co. Kerry)

NAMES

English: Blue Rock (Uls.), Carrier Pigeon, Common Pigeon, (Common) Rock Pigeon, Homing Pigeon, Sea Pigeon, Squab (yng.)

Irish: Colm aille (cliff dove), Colm fiatúil (wild pigeon), Colm frithinge (homing pigeon), Colm sráide (street pigeon), Colúr aille (cliff pigeon), Colúr gabhlach (fantail pigeon), Colúr gorm carraige (blue rock pigeon, Kry.), Fearán binne (melodious dove)

FACTS & FIGURES

Resident omnivores. Up to 2,500 wild breeding pairs (88–91) but perhaps up to 50,000 'feral' breeding pairs. Live max twenty years. Order: *Columbiformes*; Family: *Columbidae*.

3.11.2 The Stock Dove

Colm gorm | *Columba oenas oenas*

'Thou stock-dove, whose echo resounds thro' the glen.'[7]

Stock Doves are locally common doves, often overlooked or mistaken for Woodpigeons or Rock Doves. While a Stock Dove is about the same size as a Rock Dove, its colouring is much more that of a Woodpigeon, differing mostly in its smaller size and lack of white in its plumage. The birds often feed communally, sometimes in the company of Woodpigeons. Some think the call, sometimes described as 'roaring', sounds like 'ooh-look'. Stock Doves are considered less of an agricultural pest than Woodpigeons as they mainly feed on seeds of weed species.

The Irish *Colm gorm* means 'blue dove'. The specific *oenas* is from Greek meaning a 'wild pigeon'. The English name 'stock' refers to the birds making their nests in the stocks (trunks) of trees.

Poetry: from '*Afton Water*'[8]

> *Thou stock-dove, whose echo resounds thro' the glen,*
> *Ye wild whistling Blackbirds in yon thorny den,*
> *Thou green-crested Lapwing, thy screaming forbear,*
> *I charge you disturb not my slumbering fair.*

Robbie Burns, 1791

from '*O Nightingale! Thou Surely Art*'[9]

> *I heard a Stock-dove sing or say*
> *His homely tale, this very day;*
> *His voice was buried among trees,*
> *Yet to be come at by the breeze:*

William Wordsworth, 1807

NAMES

English: (Western) Stock Pigeon

Irish: Colmán gorm (blue dove)

Scientific: Columba aenas, Columba cavernalis

FACTS & FIGURES

Resident omnivores. Widespread but locally scarce. Up to 10,000 breeding pairs and declining (88–91). Live max twelve years. Amber list. Order: *Columbiformes*; Family: *Columbidae*.

3.11.3 The (Common) Woodpigeon

Colm coille | *Columba palumbus*

'Scarce with the cushat's homely song can vie.'[10]

Formerly known as Woodquests, Ring Doves or Cushats, Woodpigeons are renowned for their lazy bucolic cooing, often heard in the mornings and evenings. Largely grey, with a pinkish breast and white neck patch, the birds appear rotund and ungainly on the ground.

The species is doing so well it is periodically culled, though they do suffer greatly from frost. While the 'co-coo' call is widely recognised, the birds often make in-flight impressions of other birds.

Woodpigeons were once hunted in Ireland with sticks smeared with sticky 'birdlime'. Any alighting birds would become stuck to the branch and be caught. While this practice is now illegal, it is still carried out in some Mediterranean countries.

The generic *columba* is from Latin meaning 'dove' while the specific *palumbus* means 'wood pigeon'. The Irish *Colm coille*, meaning 'wood dove', may derive from the Irish St Colmcille (dove of the church), known as St Columba in Scotland. A very young dove or pigeon is a squab while an immature bird is a squeaker. The name 'Common Wood Pigeon' has recently been recommended by the International Ornithological Congress as the standard name for 'Woodpigeon'.

Beliefs & Traditions: It was considered very unlucky if a lone pigeon flew into your farmyard.[11]

Weather: A wild pigeon cooing in a tree was an indication of mild weather.[12]

CULINARY

Woodpigeons were widely eaten, typically roasted or in pies. The word 'squab' describes a young pigeon, and the dish derived from it.

PLACE NAMES

Craignagolman, Co. Antrim (Creag na gColmán, pigeon's crag)
Pollnagollum, Co. Fermanagh (Poll na gcolm, pigeon's hole)

NAMES

English: Cushat, Quest (Uls.), Ring Dove (Uls.), wild pigeon, Woodpigeon, Woodquest

Irish: Colmán (little dove), Colúr (coille) (Din., Mun.)

Uls. Scots: Croodlin Doo

Scientific: Columba palumba

FACTS & FIGURES

Resident omnivores. Widespread. Up to one million breeding pairs and increasing (88–91). Weigh 0.5 kg. Live max fifteen years. Order: *Columbiformes*; Family: *Columbidae*.

3.11.4 The (Eurasian) Collared Dove

Fearán baicdhubh | *Streptopelia decaocto*

& the (European) Turtle Dove

Fearán | *Streptopelia turtur*

'So shows a snowy dove trooping with crows, As yonder lady o'er her fellows shows.'[13]

Introduced to Ireland from Europe and first recorded as recently as 1959, Collared Doves are delicate, beautiful birds with a fantastic purring in-flight call. From a distance, a Collared Dove can sound like a Cuckoo and can cause confusion. Collared Doves, by nature of their recent arrival, do not have a folklore history in this country but such beautiful and widespread birds deserve an entry. A broadly fawn-pink colour with a black half-circle neck band, the birds have dark eyes and pinkish legs. They are easily distinguished from Ireland's other pigeons and doves. The only birds with which they could be confused are their cousins the Turtle Doves, rare summer visitors to the south and east coasts. Turtle Doves were visiting these shores long before the Collared Doves arrived. They have a distinctive purring call. Turtle Doves are slightly smaller than Collared Doves and have a scaly rust-black back and wings. They have a dramatic display flight where they slowly spiral downwards with wings spread and black and white tails fanned out. They spend their winters in western and southern Africa. As Turtle Doves are absent from Ireland in winter, your true love will probably not be sending you any for Christmas, in a pear tree or otherwise.

Doves of all kinds are emblems of peace and love and it was said that the Turtle Dove was the eternal partner, in love with the Phoenix.

NAMES

COLLARED DOVE

English: Collared Turtle Dove, Western Eurasian Collared-Dove

Scientific: Columba risoria decaocto

TURTLE DOVE

Irish: Colmán, Féarán, Féarán breac (mottled dove), Féarán eidhinn (ivy dove), Fearán fiaigh (game dove, Kry.)

Scientific: Columba risoria decaocto, Columba turtur, Turtur auritus

FACTS & FIGURES

COLLARED DOVE

Resident herbivores. Widespread but scarce in some counties. Up to 100,000 breeding pairs (88–91). Live max seventeen years.

TURTLE DOVE

Scarce summer visitors. Herbivores. A handful has stayed to breed. Live max thirteen years.

Sixteen species of *Streptopelia* worldwide. Order: *Columbiformes*; Family: *Columbidae*.

Turtle Dove

Fearán is the Irish for Turtle Dove. The Irish for Collared Dove, *Fearán baicdhubh* simply means 'black-naped turtledove'. The generic *streptopelia* comes from the Greek for 'collar' and 'dove'. The specific *decaocto* is from Greek meaning 'eighteen' and demands an explanation. Greek myth tells of a servant girl who was paid eighteen 'pieces' per year. On complaining to the gods, she was turned into a dove who would eternally call 'decaocto'. How this helped her is not clear. The specific *turtur* of the Turtle Dove is from Latin and describes the purring call.

History: Turtle Doves were mentioned in the Bible: 'Even the stork in the heavens knows its time; and the turtledove, swallow, and crane observe the time of their coming' (Jeremiah 8:7) and 'For now the winter is past, the rain is over and gone. The flowers appear on the earth; the time of singing has come, and the voice of the turtledove is heard in our land' (Song of Songs 2:11–12).

3.12 OWLS – ULCHABHÁIN

'Come doleful owl, the messenger of woe.'[1]

Owls were sacred to Athena, the Greek goddess of wisdom, and were regarded as symbols of vigilance, prudence, wit and wisdom. They also had a dark side, being associated with night and black magic. Today, there are about one hundred and seventy different species of owls. Three can be seen in Ireland. They and other nocturnal birds have specially adapted eyes, on the front of the head, giving binocular vision. The pupils are much larger than are those of a person and gather much more available light. Owls have many more rod cells (for gathering light) than cone cells (for gathering colour) and thus can see much better in the dark than a person, but only in black and white. Owls cannot move their eyes within their sockets as we can. In order to look around, they have to move their entire head, which has a range of movement of about 270°. Their fluffy feathers give them almost silent flight. Owls are at the top of the food web; they have no major predators save man and larger owls! Generally, owls hunt at dawn and dusk. Food is swallowed whole, head first, and the remains are ejected as characteristic pellets. The discovery of such pellets on the ground may indicate the presence of a roosting owl overhead.

Owls also have an acute sense of hearing. Their ears are not symmetrical. The ear on one side of the head is lower than on the other so that sound reaches one ear slightly before the other. This tiny difference permits the owl to know exactly whence a sound is coming. Because of this highly sensitive hearing, owls can find small animals when there is no light at all.

The Irish *ulchabhán* means 'bearded one'. A young owl is generally called an owlet (*gearrcach ulchabháin*) and a female is a jenny. The name 'owl' comes originally from the Latin *ulula*.

NAMES

Irish: Ulchabhán, Ubhlachán (Conn.), Ulcachán, Ulagán, Olchobhchán, Mulchán, Cailleach oíche (night witch), Cearc oidhche (night hen), Coileach oidhche (night cock), Scréachán reilige (graveyard screecher), Ceann cait (cat's head, Mun.)

3.12.1 The Barn Owl

Scréachóg reilige | *Tyto alba alba, Tyto alba guttata*

Barn Owls are ghostly birds of the night and the half-light. Largely fawn on top and white below, they were known as white or ghost owls and were very common in Ireland. Unfortunately, their numbers are declining today. Typically, they roost and nest in outhouses and barns or any undisturbed building and sleep during the day, only coming out at dusk to hunt for small rodents, flying silently. The very tips of the wings are extra fluffy to dampen sound. They are truly the vampires of the rodent world with the best hearing and night vision of any bird. They often hunt at dawn or dusk, flying low 'quartering' over fields. No rodent is safe.

When seen face-on, the head is distinctively heart-shaped and houses two huge night-vision eyes. Like most owls, the head can be rotated almost completely to look behind. The shape of the face channels incoming sound to the two ears, which are not of equal height. This allows the owls a certain 'depth-of-field' to the sound.

The Barn Owl continued

The generic name *Tyto* comes from the Latin, *tuto*, for owl while the specific alba means 'white'. The Irish *Scréachóg reilige* translates eerily as 'graveyard screecher'.

Beliefs & Traditions: Barn Owls may be responsible for at least some of the myths of the banshee (*Bean Sí*, fairy woman). Called ghost or white owls, they are active at night and undoubtedly can appear ghostly. They are not uncommon in graveyards, often nesting in old towers and church buildings where they are undisturbed and have excellent access to scurrying food. Many an Irishman on his way home in the dead of night has seen a ghostly white form making its way up the church path towards the graveyard. Though usually quiet at night, Barn Owls can produce a spine-tingling screech giving rise to the name Screech Owl and the Irish *Scréachóg reilige* (the graveyard screecher), adding to their mystique. There are also reports (not proven) that Barn Owls can show luminescence or bioluminescence,[2] positively radiating white light as they fly at night.

Poetry: from '*A Midsummer Night's Dream*'

The screech-owl screeching loud,
Puts the wretch that lies in woe
In remembrance of a shroud.

William Shakespeare

CULINARY

Though there may be no evidence of them begin eaten in Ireland, they were eaten in Norway and considered a delicacy.[3]

NAMES

English: Ghost Owl (Uls.), Screech Owl, Skrike Owl (Don., Uls.), White Owl

Irish: Corr scréacha (screech bird), Corr scréachóg, Corr screadóige, Mulcha, Mulchán, Scréachán reilige, Ulagadán (bearded one), Ulchabhán sciobóil (Barn Owl)

Uls. Scots: White Ool

Scientific: Stryx flammea

FACTS & FIGURES

Resident carnivores. Found in almost every county in Ireland. Up to 1,000 breeding pairs and declining (88–91) with more birds arriving in winter. Live max seventeen years. Collective name: a parliament of owls, a stare of owls. Red list. About sixteen species in the family *Tytonidae* (Barn Owls), including fourteen species of *Tyto* worldwide. Order: *Strigiformes*; Family: *Tytonidae*.

3.12.2 The Long-eared Owl

Ceann cait | *Asio otus otus*

& Short-eared Owl

Ulchabhán réisc | *Asio flammeus flammeus*

Short-eared Owl

The Irish name for a Long-eared Owl, *an Ceann cait*, means 'the cat's head', perhaps for obvious reasons. They are resident in most counties in Ireland but are rarely seen. During the day, the owls roost in dense tree cover, preferring conifers. At night, they hunt. The birds show largely a mottled grey-brown camouflage colour with a dull-amber face. They can be told from their cousins, the Short-eared Owls, by the two earlike feather tufts on the head but these are not always visible. While generally solitary, in cold weather many Long-eared Owls may roost together for warmth in a wren-like fashion. They fly completely silently so you will only see one if it happens to cross your path on a moonlit night. Long-eared Owls can sometimes be seen roosting in daylight hours.

Long-eared Owl

Unlike Long-eared Owls that like dense woodland, Short-eared Owls can be found in open marshes and moors. Their ear-like tufts are much smaller than are those of Long-eared Owls. While they show camouflage patterns largely similar to those of the Long-eared Owls, overall they are a much lighter mottled-fawn colour. As our least nocturnal owls, they are more often encountered hunting during the day even though they only visit Ireland in the winter. They will take any small mammal and some birds on the wing. They are also known to steal prey from other raptors like Kestrels. They are completely absent from most of the country and this may be down to the scarcity of their favourite food here, voles. They are most likely seen near the east and south coasts, in winter.

The generic *asio* is Latin for 'horned owl'. The specific *otus* comes from Latin meaning 'eared owl'. The specific *flammeus* refers to the birds' bright yellow eyes which are said to glow like fire in flight. The Irish *Ulchabhán réisc* translates as the 'marsh' or 'moor bearded-one'.

Beliefs & Traditions: Hearing the hoot of an owl was associated with bad luck. It was also bad luck to see an owl in the sunlight and an owl flying across your path was definitely a bad omen. To counter evil owls, people put irons in their fires or

The Long-eared Owl & Short-eared Owl continued

threw salt, hot peppers or vinegar into the fire. In doing so, the owl would get a sore tongue, hoot no more, and no one close would be in trouble. If that did not work, drastic measures could be taken. One solution suggests that if you heard an owl, you should take off your clothes, turn them inside out and put them back on to mitigate the bad luck. Luckily owls mostly appear at night! If the owl was not deterred and entered your house it was necessary to kill it at once, as if it flew out it would take the luck of the house with it.

In England, it was believed that if you walked around a roosting owl, in a full circle, the owl's head would follow you until it wrung its own neck.[4]

Another belief, which perhaps might be better not being brought to light, suggests that any man who eats owl served by his wife will be an obedient slave to her for life.[5]

Cures: In England, alcoholism was treated with owl eggs and owl eggs burnt to ashes were said to improve eyesight. Owl soup was a cure for whooping cough and salted owl was a cure for gout.

Proverbs & Similes:
As wise as an owl.

Poetry:

Come doleful owl, the messenger of woe,
Melancholy's bird, companion of Despair,
Sorrow's best friend and Mirth's professed foe
The chief discourser that delights sad Care.
O come, poor owl, and tell thy woes to me.
Which having heard, I'll do the like for thee.

Anon c. 1607

NAMES
GENERAL
Irish: Cailleach oíche (night witch, Uls.), Mulchán, Ollchaochán (Kry.), Scréachán reilige (graveyard screecher, Omt.), Ulagán, Ulcachán, Ulchabhchán

Scientific: Strix otus

LONG-EARED OWL
English: Cat's Head (Wat.), Fern Owl, Horned Owl,

Irish: Coileach oidhche (night cock)

Uls. Scots: Ool

Scientific: Otus albicollis, Otus vulgaris, Strix otus, Stryx otus

SHORT-EARED OWL
English: Fern Owl, Marsh Owl, Woodcock Owl

Uls. Scots: Ool

Scientific: Asio accipitrinus, Asio brachyotus, Brachyotus gmelini, Brachyotus major, Brachyotus palustris, Otus brachyotus, Strix accipitrinus, Stryx brachyotos, Strix flammea

FACTS & FIGURES
LONG-EARED OWL: Resident in most counties. Carnivores. Up to 2,500 breeding pairs (88–91). Live max seventeen years.

SHORT-EARED OWL: Scarce winter visitors to Ireland. Carnivores. A handful stay to breed in summer. Live max twenty years. Amber list.

Six species of *Asio* worldwide. Order: *Strigiformes*; Family: *Strigidae*.

3.13 SWALLOWS, MARTINS & SWIFTS – FÁINLEOGA 'S GABHLÁIN

Swallows, martins and Swifts are among the most adept flyers. In Ireland, we have four species: the Barn Swallows, House Martins, Sand Martins and Swifts. All are summer visitors that breed here and spend their winters in Africa. Although Swifts look somewhat like Swallows and martins, the birds have evolved independently and are placed in different bird orders. Together they form an example of convergent evolution. Of the four, the Swifts are the most at home in the air. With long pointed wings and almost no legs (just feet), they spend their lives in the air, only coming to settle on a rafter or beam to lay their eggs. Swifts, appearing black, were associated with the devil and bad luck. A mythical legless bird, the martlet (*mairléad*) appears like a cross between a Swallow and Swift and is used on many coats of arms worldwide, including those of the town council of Bray, County Wicklow. There are over eighty species of Swallow and martins worldwide and a similar number of Swifts.

Swallows and martins are associated with good luck while Swifts are associated with bad luck. It was especially lucky if a Swallow or Martin built its nest in your house and even more so if the bird returned the following year. Consequently, it was considered very unlucky to kill a Swallow or disturb its nest in any way. It is thought that this tradition goes right back to the Romans who regarded Swallows as sacred and especially loved by the Goddess Venus and other gods.

There are almost ninety species of the family *Hirundinidae* (swallows and martins) worldwide and about a hundred species of the family *Apodidae* (swifts) worldwide.

3.13.1 The (Barn) Swallow

Fáinleog | *Hirundo rustica rustica*

Delicate birds of summer, Swallows are largely blue on top, white below, with distinctive red throats and forked tails. Characterised by their chattering insect-catching flights on lazy summer evenings, Swallows arrive in March or April from Africa and return in October. Large chattering flocks gather on wires prior to departure. They often return to the same nest sites year after year.

The generic *hirundo* is Latin for Swallow. The specific *rustica* means 'rustic', i.e. of the countryside. The word Swallow probably comes from the Old Norse *svala* meaning 'a cleft stick', which refers to the tail. The Irish *fáinleog* may come from *fán* meaning 'wandering' or 'migrating'.

Beliefs & Traditions: Swallows were generally believed to bring good luck but people were still wary of them as it was thought that every Swallow had three drops of the devil's blood in it. However, like the Robin, the Swallow was believed to have its red throat from bringing fire to earth from the heavens.

It was generally regarded as being a very bad idea to disturb a Swallow or its nest. If you did so, being wise birds, they would watch and mark your conduct for punishment or favour. Disturbing a Swallow would also result in your cows' milk turning to blood.

If you had your hair cut, it was risky to leave the cuttings around. If a Swallow lined its nest with them, you would have headaches all summer long.[1] Another tradition tells us that there is a particular hair on our heads, which, if picked off by a Swallow, will lead to eternal perdition for the unfortunate individual.[2]

Notwithstanding this bad press, it was a very good omen for a Swallow to fly into your home. If a Swallow nested in your barn, it would not be hit by lightning as long as the nest was there. Seeing a Swallow at sea was considered good luck.

Before migration was understood, it was believed that Swallows hibernated through the winter on the bottom of ponds. There are even written reports of fisherman bringing up such hibernating Swallows in their nets:[3] '*In the beginning of Autumn they assemble themselves together among the reeds of ponds, where, allowing themselves to sink into the water, they join bill to bill, wing to wing, and foot to foot*'[4] (see also Barnacle Goose, Section 3.4.4).

Cures: In Roman times, it was believed that Swallows could cure all problems of the eyes. To quote Marcellus of Bordeaux: '*When you hear or see the first Swallow, go, without speaking, to the first well or fountain and there wash your eyes and pray God that that year they may not be dimmed, and so the Swallows will carry away all trouble from them.*'

Marcellus also tells us that Swallows could also cure toothache; when you see a Swallow, hold your tongue and go to 'pure shining water' and dip your middle finger of the right hand in and say:

'I say to thee, O swallow,
As this will never be in thy beak,
So may my teeth pain me no more for a year.'

A recipe from 1692, promising a cure for epilepsy (falling sickness) and 'sudden fits', calls for fifty Swallows to be ground up with mortar and pestle and added to an ounce of caster sugar and white wine vinegar.[5]

Every Swallow was believed to have a special stone in its stomach. If this stone was taken at the August full moon, it would cure epilepsy, blindness and stammering.[6] It was believed that Swallows sought out this stone on the shore when their young were sick, usually blind.[7]

Weather: Swallows flying low are said to be the sign of rain,[8] whereas Swallows flying high indicate sunshine to come.

Proverbs & Similes:

'One swallow does not a summer make,'

Aristotle, *Nicomachean Ethic*

'When the swallows fly high, the weather will be dry.'

Poetry: from '*Coole Park 1929*',

'They came like swallows and like swallows went . . .'

William Butler Yeats, 1993, from *The Collected Poems of W. B. Yeats* (Macmillan, 1993)

'The first spring swallow I have seen,
A lucky thing it was, I ween.
I ran to where the fountain flies,
And in its water washed my eyes,
Which were so long my pain and grief,
Yet no physician brought relief;
Yet the first swallow which I see
Has caused a happy cure to me.
Blest may the swallows ever be!'

Anon (Italian)

PLACE NAMES

Aghnavalloge, Co. Down (Achadh na bhFáinleog, Swallows' field)

NAMES

English: Chimney Swallow, Devil's Bird,[9] Eurasian Swallow

Irish: Ailleog/Áilleog (Uls., Omt.), Áinle (Kry.), Ainleag (Uls.), Áinleog, Fáinle, Faoinleog (Aran.), Sciathán leathair ('leather wing', a 'bat', Din.)

Scientific: Chelidon rustica, Hirundo domestica

FACTS & FIGURES

Summer visitors to all counties. Up to 250,000 breeding pairs (88–91). Live max eleven years. The national bird of Austria and Estonia. Collective name: a flight of swallows. Amber list. Fifteen species of *Hirundo* worldwide. Order: *Passeriformes*; Family: *Hirundinidae*.

3.13.2 The (Common) House Martin

Gabhlán binne | *Delichon urbica urbica*

House Martins are swallow-like birds that visit Ireland in summer. Often overlooked, they sometimes form joint insect-chasing flocks, with Swallows. They are blue/black on top with white under-parts and forked tails. They often make their mud nests in the eaves of houses. Like Swallows, House Martins spend their winters in Africa.

The Irish *Gabhlán binne* translates as 'sweet martin', probably referring to the birds' song. *Gabhlán* is an Irish word meaning something forked such as a tree branch or the gap between toes and refers here to the forked tail. The generic *delichon* is an anagram of the Greek word *chelidon* meaning 'swallow'. The specific *urbica* means 'urban'. The bird is named after St Martin, the fourth century bishop of Tours[10] or perhaps the god of war Mars, as some arrive in this part of the world in March.

Beliefs & Traditions: As with Swallows, disturbing a martin's nest led to bad luck. In County Wexford, it was believed that if a Martin's nest were destroyed, the cows' milk would be tainted with blood.[11] Interestingly, it was also considered 'bad manners' to destroy a martin's nest while it was migrating abroad.[12] In any case, it was said that martins would never build their nests on a house wherein there was strife.[13]

NAMES

English: Martlet, Northern House Martin, Window Martin, Window Swallow

Irish: Fáinle, Gabhlán duine (Conn.), Gobhlán gaoithe[14]

Scientific: Chelidon urbica, Chelidonoria urbica, Delichon urbicum, Hirundo urbica

FACTS & FIGURES

Summer visitors. Up to 100,000 breeding pairs and declining (88–91). Live max fourteen years. Three species of *Delichon* worldwide. Order: *Passeriformes*; Family: *Hirundinidae*.

3.13.3 The Sand Martin

Gabhlán gainimh | *Riparia riparia riparia*

Like their cousins the House Martins, Sand Martins are summer visitors to Ireland usually arriving in early March. They are generally a dull brown colour with white underparts and a brown band across the breast. They live up to their name and are often found, in this country, in nesting colonies, digging long tunnels in sandbanks for their nest, not unlike Kingfishers. They tend to favour riverbanks, sandpits, gravel pits and steep cliffs. Severe drought in the African wintering grounds in the 1990s has led to a big drop in the numbers visiting here.

The scientific name *riparia* comes from the Latin *ripa* meaning 'river-bank' and from which we get the word 'riparian' meaning 'of the river'. The name 'martin' comes from Mars, the Roman god of war or perhaps St Martin. The Irish *Gabhlán gainimh* translates directly as 'sand martin', *gabhlán* meaning something forked and referring to the birds' tails.

CULINARY

Sand Martins were eaten in Anglo-Saxon England.[15]

NAMES

English: Bank Swallow (NA.), Sand Swallow (Uls.), Shore Bird

Irish: Bruachalán (bank bird, Gal.), Fáinle, Gabhlán gainmhe (sand martin), Gabhlán puill (hole martin, Ant.)

Scientific: Cliviola riparia, Cotile riparia, Cotyle riparia, Hirundo riparia

FACTS & FIGURES

Summer visitors to Ireland. Up to 250,000 breeding pairs and increasing (88–91). Live max ten years. Amber list. Five species of *Riparia* worldwide. Order: *Passeriformes*; Family: *Hirundinidae*.

3.13.4 The (Common) Swift

Gabhlán gaoithe | *Apus apus apus*

While superficially similar to Swallows and martins, Swifts evolved independently. They can be distinguished from their hirundine cousins by their longer, sharper wings, looking almost like flying boomerangs. Generally jet-black, they have a pale patch on the throat. Sexes are alike. Like Swallows, Swifts are summer visitors and are even more at home in the air. They tend to be the last of the migrants to arrive, usually not turning up here until late April. They are truly a sign of the arrival of summer, appearing high over our towns and cities almost magically in screeching flocks.

Swifts have a simple undercarriage of tiny feet and almost no legs, from which they get their scientific name *apus*, from the Greek meaning 'no feet'. They do not perch on wires like Swallows because they are unable. They play, feed, mate, and even drink and sleep on the wing. The only thing they have not mastered is laying eggs and rearing young on the wing. For this, they must come to earth. They lay their eggs on old bare rafters and ledges. The only nesting material used is anything they find on the wing. They will roost in old buildings, where they cling to the walls with their tiny feet. Swifts usually return to the same breeding site every year and at the same time (about 1 May). When the young emerge, they immediately take to the air and are expert fliers. As it can take a young Swift three years to reach breeding age, those three years are spent entirely on the wing. Swifts leave on their return trip to Africa at the beginning of August.

As tiny birds, Swifts need to accumulate as much food as possible while consuming as little energy as possible, before their enormous migration flights. To this end, they will hunt insects incessantly in good weather. In bad weather they roost, going into a sort of mini-hibernation (a coma-like condition in which their metabolism slows to almost nothing), conserving as much energy as possible until good weather and insect-fuel returns. Even with this sort of commitment, it is believed that many are lost at sea because of insufficient 'fuel' on board.

Swifts have a habit known as 'banging'. A Swift will approach its nest and touch it with its wings without landing. Such a Swift is known as a 'banger' but the significance of the action is not known. Once thought to be related to Swallows, the birds may have been called 'Swift Swallows', later shortened to 'Swifts' The Irish *Gabhlán*[16] *gaoithe* translates as 'wind martin'.

Beliefs & Traditions: While Swallows and martins are well loved, black Swifts are generally regarded as birds of the devil.

NAMES

English: Black Martin (Uls.), Black Swallow (Wat.), Devil's Bird

Irish: Áinle[17]

Scientific: Cypselus apus, Cypelus murarius, Hirundo apus, Micropus apus, Micropus murarius

FACTS & FIGURES

Summer visitors. Insectivores. Live max twenty-one years. Up to 20,000 breeding pairs and decreasing (88–91). Seventeen species of *Apus* worldwide. Order: *Apodiformes*; Family: *Apodidae*.

3.14 PIPITS – RIABHÓGA

Pipits are small, drab, brown-streaked birds of remote mountains, meadows and shores. Though related to wagtails, they look somewhat like larks. They tend to eat insects and nest on the ground and are never far from water. Across the world, there are about forty species of which two, the Meadow Pipits and the Rock Pipits are common in Ireland.

The generic *Anthus* is Greek. In Greek mythology, Anthus was killed and eaten by his father's horses through sheer hunger. The gods Zeus and Apollo took pity on his family and transformed them into birds. The birds' song was said to mimic that of a horse and they were said to always fly away on sight of a horse. The pipits were named after them. Of course, the name also reflects the birds' 'peeping' call.

There are nearly seventy species of the family *Motacillidae* (wagtails and pipits) including about forty-five species of *Anthus* worldwide.

NAMES

Irish: Gobachán (Din.), Riabhóg (little speckled bird)

PLACE NAMES

Culrevog, Co. Tyrone (Cúil Riabhóg, pipit's nook)

3.14.1 The Meadow Pipit

Riabhóg mhóna | *Anthus pratensis whistleri* (Celtic Meadow Pipit)

Meadow Pipits are small brown-streaked songbirds with reddish legs, looking somewhat like Skylarks. The male's display song is also similar to the Skylark's but perhaps not as impressive. They are usually the commonest songbirds in upland areas. They are also known for their dramatic 'parachute' display flights. Meadows Pipits always land away from their nests and then walk the rest of the way, to avoid drawing attention. Cuckoos however have become masters (or more correctly mistresses) of discovering Meadow Pipits' nests.

The Irish *Riabhóg mhóna* means 'little streaky bog-bird'. The specific *pratensis* means 'of the meadow'. In Waterford they are called by the wonderful name 'Tittery Hay Birds'.

Beliefs & Traditions: Meadow Pipits' nests are among those favoured by Cuckoos in which to lay their eggs. As a result, it was said that the Meadow Pipit and the Cuckoo were constant companions. Meadow Pipits and other small birds often chase Cuckoos as they would hawks. It was believed in Ireland that the pipit was forever trying to get into the mouth of the Cuckoo and when this should happen, the world would end;[1] '*Titfidh an spéir nuair a rachaidh an gobadán i mbéal na cuaiche*' (the sky will fall when the pipit goes into the mouth of the Cuckoo).

NAMES

English: Bog-lark (Tyr., Kry.), Cuckoo's Follower, Cuckoo's Maid (Uls.), Heather Grey[2] (Uls.), Meadow Lark, Mippit (sl., UK)., Tattle (Uls.), Titlark/Tit Lark, Titling, Tittery Hay Bird (Wat.), Wekeen (Kry.)

Irish: Adharclóg (bog-lark, Mea.), Aoi áirleagach (bog lark, Farney, Mona.), Banaltra na cuaiche (Cuckoo's nurse, May.), Caológ riabhach (Aran.), Ciológ riabhach, Coimhdre/ Coimhdire/Coimhthíre na cuaiche (Cuckoo's escort, Der., Tyr.), Éan riabhach (brindled bird), Éinín na cuaiche (Cuckoo's little bird, Gal.), Fuiseog mhóna (bog lark), Fuiseoigín ruadh na móna (little red bog bird), Giolla (na) cuaiche (Cuckoo's servant), Gobadán na cuaiche (Kry.), Liabhóg (bog-lark, tit-lark, Tyr.), Réabhóg, Riabhachóg, Riabhóg bheag (little pipit), Riafóg, Seánín na lathaí (Johnny of the mud, Kry.)

Uls. Scots: Mosscheeper, Moss Cheepuck, Tittle (Ant.)

Scientific: Alauda pratensis, Alauda trivialis, Alauda campestris

FACTS & FIGURES

Resident omnivores. Widespread in all counties. Up to one million breeding pairs (88–91) with numbers increased in winter. Live max seven years. Sexes alike. Order: *Passeriformes*; Family: *Motacillidae*.

3.14.2 The (Eurasian) Rock Pipit

Riabhóg chladaigh | *Anthus petrosus petrosus*

Rock Pipits are unspectacular brown birds that can easily go unnoticed. Largely mottled brown-grey with spotted underparts, they can be told from their cousins the Meadow Pipits by their generally darker colours and blackish legs. Much less common than Meadow Pipits, Rock Pipits are most often encountered on quiet rocky shorelines going about their business with typical anonymity.

The Irish *Riabhóg chladaigh* means 'little speckled shore bird'. The generic *petrosus* is from Latin meaning 'of the rocks'.

NAMES

English: Dusky Lark, Field-Lark, Rock Lark (Uls.), Sea Lark (Kry.), Shore Pipit

Irish: Beagéan carraige (little rock bird, Kry.), Circín trágha[3] (beach chicken, Conn.)

Scientific: Alauda obscura, Alauda petrosa, Alauda pratensis, Anthus aquaticus, Anthus campestris, Anthus obscurus, Anthus rupestris, Anthus spinoletta

FACTS & FIGURES:

Resident omnivores. Up to 20,000 breeding pairs (88–91). Live max ten years. Order: *Passeriformes*; Family: *Motacillidae*.

3.15 WAGTAILS – GLASÓGA

There are nearly seventy species of the family *Motacillidae* (wagtails and pipits) including about twelve species of *Motacilla* worldwide. Of these, three can be seen in Ireland. The most common are Pied Wagtails. Next are the Grey Wagtails, which are predominantly yellow. Finally, Yellow Wagtails are rare all-yellow visitors. A subspecies of Pied Wagtails, the White Wagtails, are rare visitors.

3.15.1 The Pied Wagtail[1]
Glasóg shráide | *Motacilla alba yarrelli*

& the White Wagtail
Glasóg bhán | *Motacilla alba alba*

Known proverbially as 'Willie wagtails', Pied Wagtails are amiable birds often seen on the street or pavement chasing food. Wagtails are so named for the constant bobbing of their tails. A striking black and white, wagtails are relatively tolerant of people and can be approached quite closely. They have a distinctive undulating flight.

PLACE NAMES
Terryglassog, Co. Tyrone (Tír na nGlasóg, wagtails' territory)

NAMES
PIED, English: Common Wagtail, Cowbird (Uls.), Devil/Devil's Bird, Devilin/Deviling (Uls.), Gypsy Bird, Pied Dishwasher, Water Wagtail, (Wee) Willie/Willy Wagtail

Irish: An t-Éan beannuighthe (the blessed bird), Glaiseog gabhail (forked (tail) wagtail, Ant.), Glasán sailighe[5] (willow finch), Glasóg bhuaile (cow-yard wagtail), Siobhán ghlas an charn aoiligh (grey Joan of the dung-hill, Kry.), Suibháinín an bhóthair (little Joan of the street)

Scientific: Motacilla lotor, Motacilla yarrellii

WHITE, Scientific: Motacilla alba, Motacilla brissoni

FACTS & FIGURES
PIED: Resident omnivores. Widespread in all counties. Up to 250,000 breeding pairs (88–91). Live max eleven years.

WHITE: Uncommon visitors. Omnivores. Live max twelve years. The White Wagtail is the national bird of Latvia.

Order: *Passeriformes*; Family: *Motacillidae*.

The Pied Wagtail & the White Wagtail continued

While normally encountered as solitary birds, in winter they can form large communal roosts, one of which, in the middle of O'Connell Street, Dublin, is now well known.

Pied Wagtails have very close but very rare cousins, the White Wagtails (*Motacilla alba alba, Glasóg bhán*), which arrive in very small numbers in winter. From the distance, they are identical to the 'Pieds' but much of the Pieds' black is replaced with grey and they have clear white bellies.

The Irish, *Glasóg shráide* translates roughly as 'grey bird of the street' while *Glasóg bhán* translates directly as 'white grey-bird'. The generic name *motacilla* means 'little mover' while the specific name *alba* is Latin for white. The sub-species name *yarrelli* of the Pied comes from its discoverer, English ornithologist William Yarrell (1784–1856) who wrote a *History of British Birds* in 1837.

Beliefs & Traditions: A wagtail's grey-white and brown mottled eggs were never touched. The constant bobbing and upright nature of the bird's tail was regarded as unnatural and gained it the reputation of being the devil's minion and the name 'Devil's Bird'.[2] It was believed the bird had three drops of the devil's blood on its tail which meant it could not stop bobbing.[3] It was also thought that the only way to catch a wagtail was to sprinkle salt on its tail. Lady Wilde tells us 'a water wagtail near the house betokens bad news on its way to you'.[4]

Proverbs & Similes:

Chomh breabhsánta le glasóg. (As spruce/sprightly as a wagtail.)

'Oke Romano chiriklo dikasa e Kalen'
('Behold a wagtail and you shall see the gypsies', (Romani))

Poetry:

Wee Mister Wagtail, hopping on a rock,
Daddy says your pretty tail is like a Goblin's clock.
Wee Willie Wagtail, how I love to see,
Wee Willie Wagtail, wag his tail at me.
Wee Mister Wagtail, running by a pond,
Daddy says your pretty tail is like a Goblin's wand.

Old Irish Rhyme

3.15.2 The Grey Wagtail

Glasóg liath | *Motacilla cinerea cinerea*

Grey Wagtails are cousins of the much commoner Pied Wagtails (see Section 3.15.1). Wagtails are named in a very confusing way. While Pied Wagtails are black and white, the most striking feature of Grey Wagtails is their bright yellow colouring. However, Grey Wagtails must not be confused with the very rare summer visitors, the Yellow Wagtails (*Motacilla flava, Glasóg bhuí*) that are almost entirely yellow. To add to the confusion, Grey Wagtails were often called Yellow Wagtails in Ireland.

While Pied Wagtails are common on our roads and streets, Grey Wagtails prefer the peace and tranquillity of quiet waterways. Like Dippers, they nest by swift running water. They are severely affected by cold winters.

The Irish name *Glasóg liath* translates as 'grey grey-bird'. The specific name *cinerea* means 'ash-coloured', referring to the grey upperparts.

NAMES

English: Barley Bird, Western Gray Wagtail, Yellow Wagtail (Uls.)

Irish: Glasóg bhuidhe (yellow wagtail), Glasóg cheannliath (grey-headed wagtail), Glasóg shailighe (willow wagtail)

Scientific: Motacilla boarula, Motacilla melanopa, Motacilla sulphurea

FACTS & FIGURES

Resident carnivores. Present in all counties. Up to 20,000 breeding pairs (88–91). Live max eight years. Order: *Passeriformes*; Family: *Motacillidae*.

201

3.16 THRUSHES – SMÓLAIGH

There are about 300 species in the thrush family worldwide of which about 70 species are of the *Turdus* genus. Six of these can be seen in Ireland while only two are known by name: the Song Thrushes and the Mistle Thrushes. Some of our better-known garden birds, the Blackbirds, are also thrushes. Blackbirds have some very rare cousins, the Ring Ouzels, which live in the mountains and visit this country in small numbers in summer. The remaining two, the Fieldfares and Redwings are winter visitors. American Robins (*Turdus migratorius*) are members of the thrush family whilst our European Robins are only distant cousins.

Thrushes were symbols of solitude, poetry and concord. All are excellent singers and were often caged for their trouble. It was common to hunt and kill thrushes and Blackbirds throughout Ireland and they were roasted and eaten. This was particularly prevalent in times of need. In other times young boys carried on the tradition. It was the practice to go out at night with a bright light to dazzle the birds whereupon they were knocked to the ground with sticks.[1]

The generic *turdus* is Latin for thrush.

Proverbs & Similes:

The three most wholesome foods for the driver were the back of a herring, the belly of a salmon and the head of a thrush . . .[2]

'A blackbird or thrush which sings before Candlemas[3] will be sure to mourn many days afterwards' (Pomeroy, Tyr.).[4]

Similes: Chomh tirim le nead smólaighe. (As dry as a thrush's nest.)

NAMES

Smaol, Smaolach, Smeorach, Smíol, Smíolach, Smól, Smólán, Smórlach

COLLECTIVE NAME

A listening of thrushes, a mutation of thrushes.

Order: *Passeriformes*;
Family: *Turdidae*.

The (Common) Blackbird

3.16.1

Lon dubh/Céirseach | *Turdus merula merula*

'Stop, stop and listen for the bough-top is whistling . . .'[5]

The song of a Blackbird is amongst the most exquisite you will hear in the Irish countryside. This ethereal warble has moved many a bard to verse. Formerly known as Ouzels, male Blackbirds are stunning jet-black birds with orange bills and eye rings. Females (*Céirseach*) are brown. All-white and partial-white albino Blackbirds are not uncommon. Blackbirds are the sentinels of the forest. Disturbed unexpectedly, they emit a loud chirping crescendo, warning all species of an intruder. In Antrim this call was referred to as a 'yirp'.[6] The Irish *lon* means 'Blackbird' so, strictly speaking, *Lon dubh* means 'black Blackbird'. The specific *merula* is Latin for Blackbird.

History: As Blackbirds are fond of berries they and other thrushes were often hunted and killed. The Earl of Stafford (Lord Lieutenant of Ireland 1640–1641) commented that he 'flew hawks after Blackbirds' in the Phoenix Park which attracted as many as 200 mounted spectators. They were not liked by the common people from their habit of ripping thatch off the roof, in search of insects, or perhaps nesting material.[7]

In seventeenth- and eighteenth-century Ireland, a Jacobite was referred to as *londubh*. *Londubh* also referred to Ireland as a whole.

Beliefs & Traditions:

Blackbirds were said to impart mystical messages and it was believed that they could freely pass into the 'Otherworld'. They are associated with the druids and the Welsh goddess Rhiannon. The birds could put a person into a trance through singing. They could give a person access to the 'Otherworld' and were associated with witches.

Gerald of Wales relates a story about St Kevin of Glendalough and Blackbirds in the seventh century. Once, while St Kevin was alone on retreat in a cabin in the woods,[8] he put his hand out the window whilst praying to God. As he remained long in that position, in praise of God, a Blackbird came and landed on his hand, built a nest and laid eggs there. In pity for the bird, St Kevin remained in that position, enduring pain, until the chicks were hatched and departed.[9]

In Ireland in the nineteenth century, Blackbirds were supposed to hold the souls of those in purgatory until judgement day. It was said that whenever the birds' voices were particularly shrill, it was those souls, parched and burning, calling for rain. The rain always followed.[10]

If a Blackbird built its nest on or near your house, it was a good omen.

203

The (Common) Blackbird continued

CULINARY

Every member of the thrush family in Ireland has been eaten, especially when other foods were in short supply. This practice was also widespread on the Continent, especially in France. Both peasants and royalty ate Blackbirds and they were also kept by the well-to-do as pets. Mrs Beeton, in 1861, recommended 'one Blackbird to every two persons'. The Blackbirds referred to in the old nursery song 'Sing a Song of Sixpence' (p. 205) may have been Rooks but we do know that in the time of Henry II (1133–1189) live birds were sometimes enclosed in pies and brought to the table where they were released and hunted by falcons, to the dubious enjoyment of all.

Weather: The whistle of the blackbird at dawn warned of rain and mist for the coming day.[11]

Proverbs & Similes:

'When the blackbird sings before Christmas, she will cry before Candlemas' (Mea.).[12]

Chomh héadrom le lon ar sceach. (As light as a blackbird on a bramble.)

There'll be white blackbirds before an unwilling woman ties the knot.[13]

Poems & Quotations:

'Int én bec ro léic feit do rind guip glan buidi; fo-ċeird faíd os Loċ Laíg lon do ċraíb ċarn buidi.'

'A little bird has whistled from the tip of his bright yellow bill. A blackbird from the yellowed branch sends its call over Loch Loigh.'

Anon (Irish eighth/ninth century)

'*Ah blackbird, it is well for you where your nest is in the bushes; a hermit that rings no bell, your call is sweet, soft, and peaceful.*'

Anon (Irish eleventh/twelfth century)

from: '*The Blackbird of Derrycairn*'

He loved the breeze that warns the black grouse,
The shouts of gillies in the morning
When packs are counted and the swans cloud
Loch Erne, but more than all those voices
My throat rejoicing from the hawthorn.

Austin Clarke

from: *The Spectator* (6 September 1712)

'*I value my garden more for being full of blackbirds than cherries, and very frankly give them fruit for their songs.*'

Joseph Addison (1672–1719)
Writer & Chief Secretary for Ireland in *The Spectator*, c. 1712

'*Sing a Song of Sixpence*'

Sing a song of sixpence,
A pocketful of rye;
Four and twenty blackbirds,
Baked in a pie.
When the pie was opened,
The birds began to sing;
Wasn't that a dainty dish,
To put before the king?
The king was in the counting house,
Counting out his money;
The queen was in the parlour,
Eating bread and honey.
The maid was in the garden,
Hanging out the clothes;
When down came a blackbird,
And bit her on the nose.

Anon

PLACE NAMES

Bunalunn/Bunalun, Co. Cork (song of the Blackbirds or low place of the Blackbirds) Kilnalun, Co. Cavan, Co. Wicklow, Co. Tyrone, Co. Donegal. (Coill na Lon, Blackbird's wood)

NAMES

English: Merle (Uls.), Ousel/Ouzel (Cock) (AS. 'osle')

Irish: Cearc loin/luin (hen), Céirseach (hen), Ciairseach[14] (hen, Din.), Éan dubh (black bird), Gobadán buidhe (yellow-billed bird, Cla.), Londubh, Méire (prob. from merle, Uls.)

Uls. Scots: Blakburd

Scientific: Merula vulgaris

FACTS & FIGURES

Resident omnivores, present in all counties. Up to 2.5 million breeding pairs (88–91). Live max twenty-one years. The national bird of Sweden. Order: *Passeriformes*; Family: *Turdidae*.

3.16.2 The Ring Ouzel

Lon creige | *Turdus torquatus torquatus*

Looking very much like their common cousins the Blackbirds, Ring Ouzels are scarce summer visitors to mountain areas. The birds are distinguished by a broad swathe of white across the upper breast. Though common here a hundred years ago, the birds are now exotics, to be cherished if seen. There are about ten thousand times more Blackbirds breeding here than there are Ring Ouzels. To see one will take some effort as they visit us only in summer and favour remote mountain areas. Like many uncommon

birds, Ring Ouzels are becoming an enigma in Ireland, a holy grail of the bird world that may only be glimpsed on a carefully planned 'ouzel' quest. Even then, many will go disappointed. The Irish *Lon creige* means 'crag Blackbird'. The specific *torquatus* is from Latin meaning 'collared'.

Beliefs & Traditions: In Wicklow in the nineteenth century, it was believed that if a Mountain Star (Ring Ouzel) finished its song with a pause and then followed with a loud, prolonged, shrill note, it was a call to the fairy folk. The little people would congregate by moonlight in the Wicklow mountain hollows and dance until dawn. As a result, anyone who heard the Ring Ouzel would bar themselves behind closed doors for the night.[15]

NAMES

English: Cowboy (Tipp., Wic.), Mountain Blackbird, Mountain Ouzel, Mountain Star/Stare (Wic.), Ring Blackbird, Ring Rush (Uls.), Ring Thrush, Rock Blackbird, Rock Starling, Round-berry Bird (Conm.), Whistler (Wic.)

Irish: Fraochán[16] (heather bird, Don.), Lon abha (Din.), Lon abhann, Lon uisce

Scientific: Merula torquata

FACTS & FIGURES

Omnivorous summer visitors. Scarce. Up to 250 breeding pairs and declining (01–03). Live max nine years. Red list. Order: *Passeriformes*; Family: *Turdidae*.

3.16.3 The Song Thrush

Smólach (ceoil) | *Turdus philomelos clarkei* (British Song Thrush)

The top singers in the Irish countryside, Song Thrushes are the smaller, sweeter-singing brothers of the Mistle Thrushes. The birds are largely brown on top and heavily spotted-white below. The spots are elongated, almost like arrowheads. Song Thrushes are typically to be found hopping around the garden looking for worms, which they find by cocking the head to listen and pulling violently from the earth. They are rather unassuming birds and seem to go about their business almost apologetically. They also feed on snails, which they crack open by smashing on a stone. In some areas, favoured rocks, known as anvil-stones, are littered with the shelled remains of many a snail. The birds are perhaps our true native thrushes, as the Mistle Thrushes did not arrive here until the end of the eighteenth century.

The specific name *philomelos*, the Greek word used for 'nightingale'[17] is a reference to the bird's singing skills. The Irish *smólach* perhaps means 'ash-coloured' and *ceoil* means 'of music'.

Beliefs & Traditions: It was a common belief that thrushes acquired new legs and cast off the old ones when about ten years old.[18]

The Song Thrush continued

In Ireland in the nineteenth century, it was believed that the fairies insured that a Mavis (Song Thrush) built its nest low near the fairies' homes in the grass so that they could enjoy the bird's song. Consequently, if a Song Thrush built its nest high in a thorn-bush it was a sure sign that the fairies were unhappy and some calamity would soon befall the neighbourhood.[19]

Cures: Pliny believed that both Song Thrushes and Blackbirds, roasted with myrtleberries, were a cure for dysentery.[20]

Proverbs & Similes:

Chomh binn le smóilín. (As sweet as a little thrush.)

Chomh tirim le nead smólaighe.
(As dry as a thrush's nest.)

Poetry: from '*The Darkling Thrush*'[21]

At once a voice arose among
The bleak twigs overhead
In a full-throated evensong
Of joy illimited;
An aged thrush, frail, gaunt, and small,
In blast-beruffled plume,
Had chosen thus to fling his soul
Upon the growing gloom.

Thomas Hardy (c. 1900)

from '*The Throstle*'[22]

'Summer is coming, summer is coming,
I know it, I know it, I know it.
Light again, leaf again, life again, love again!'
Yes, my wild little Poet.

Alfred, Lord Tennyson (1889)

from '*The Thrush's Song*'[23] (from Gaelic)

Qui, qui, queen, quip;
Tiurru, tiurru, chipiwi,
Too-tee, too-tee, chin-choo,
Chirri, chirri, chooee
Quin, qui, qui!

William MacGillivray (1796–1852)

CULINARY

Every member of the thrush family in Ireland has been eaten, especially when other foods were in short supply. This practice was also widespread on the Continent, especially in France. In some areas, boys would go on periodic thrush hunts for the family pot.

PLACE NAMES

Glenasmole, Co. Dublin (Gleann na Smól, Song Thrush valley)
Glensmoil, Co. Donegal (Gleann na Smóil, Song Thrush valley)

NAMES

English: Common Thrush, Grey Bird, Mavis, Sit-ye-down, Throstle, Thrushling

Irish: Céirseach/Ciairseach[24] (poe.), Smaol (Dry.), Smaolach (Lou., Mona.), Smól, Smólach ceoil (music thrush), Smólach cnoic (hill thrush, Kry.), Smórlach (Din.)

Uls. Scots: Mavis (Ant.), Thrustle

Scientific: Turdus ericetorum, Turdus musicus, Turdus philomelogus, Turdus philomelus, Turdus viscivorus minor

FACTS & FIGURES

Resident omnivores. Widespread in all counties. Up to half a million breeding pairs (88–91) with winter population inflated. Live max seventeen years. Collective name: a listening or mutation of thrushes. Order: *Passeriformes*; Family: *Turdidae*.

3.16.4 The Mistle Thrush

Liatráisc | *Turdus viscivorus viscivorus*

Our largest thrushes, Mistle Thrushes are like the older brethren of the Song Thrushes. They are not regular visitors to the garden. They can be distinguished from Song Thrushes by their greater size, and coarser spotting on the chest. They stand upright on the grass in a 'haughty' posture and have an unforgettable rasping call. Like a Nightjar's, a Mistle Thrush's trill call is known as 'churring'.

Although badly affected by cold winters, Mistle Thrushes were called Storm Cocks from their habit of singing through a storm.[25]

Mistle Thrushes are relatively new to Ireland. They began to arrive in numbers at the beginning of the nineteenth century.[26] Thompson says the first one was shot here in the year 1800. By the end of the nineteenth century, they had totally colonised the island from east to west.

The 'mistle' in Mistle Thrush is indeed short for mistletoe. They are infamous for spreading the seeds of the parasitic Mistletoe[27] plant (*Viscus album*) whence they get their name. The specific name *viscivorus* is from the Latin meaning 'sticky' from the sticky mistletoe berries. The Irish *liatráisc* means 'grey thrush'. They were sometimes confused with Fieldfares with which they share the northern name 'Big Felt'.

Beliefs & Traditions: In Ireland in the nineteenth century, a large number of Mistle Thrushes feeding on hawthorn berries was a sign of a very cold winter.[28]

NAMES

English: Butcher Bird (Don.), (Holm) Screech, Holm Thrush,[29] Jay (Ant.), 'Master of the Coppice' (Wal.), Missel Bird/Thrush, Screech Thrush (Ant.), Squirley Thrush (Uls.), Storm Cock, White Thrush (Wat.), Wood-Thrush

Irish: Liath-thruisc[30] (grey thrush), Smólach m(h)ór (big thrush)

Uls. Scots: Big Felt (Uls.), Cornageerie, Corney Keevor (Ant.), Grey Felt (Ant.)

Scientific: Turdus viscivorus major

FACTS & FIGURES

Resident omnivores. Widespread in all counties. Up to 100,000 breeding pairs and declining (88–91). Live max twenty-one years. Order: *Passeriformes*; Family: *Turdidae*.

3.16.5 The Fieldfare

Sacán | *Turdus pilaris*

& the (Eurasian) Redwing

Deargán sneachta | *Turdus iliacus iliacus, Turdus iliacus coburni*

Fieldfares and Redwings visit Ireland in large numbers in winter, from Scandinavia. They are often seen, in mixed scavenging flocks, in open fields. A Fieldfare is a large, striking bird with grey head, chestnut-brown back and wings and brown chevron-spotted buff breast, grey rump and jet-black tail. From a distance, they can be confused with Mistle Thrushes. Redwings are the smallest members of the thrush family to be seen in Ireland. The birds are generally brown with spotted breast and underparts, white eye-line and distinctive characteristic rusty-red flash on the flanks, which is best seen in flight. Redwings and Fieldfares are true winter birds. The birds breed in northern Europe and Asia. In particularly bad winters, they will visit gardens in large numbers but will only take fruit. Both birds are highly nomadic and may winter in different countries every year.

The Irish *sacán* and *siocán* are probably from *sioc* meaning 'frost' (frost bird) as the birds come here in winter. *Deargán sneachta* translates roughly as 'red snow bird'. The specific *pilaris* is from Greek meaning 'hair'. The reason is unclear. The specific *iliacus* is originally from Greek meaning 'thrush'.

NAMES

FIELDFARE

English: Blue Pigeon, Feldefare, Frost Bird (Uls.)

Irish: Glaisneach (grey-bird, Conn.), Liathtráisc, Siocán sneachta (snow frost-bird), Socadán ruadh (red frost-bird), Socán

Uls. Scots: Big Felt, Blue Felt (Ant.), Felt, Feltyfare, Pigeon Felt, Scrachen Felt, Snabird, Snaeburd (Ant.), Snowburd[31]

REDWING

English: 'Swedish Nightingale' (Scan.), Swinepipe, Wind Thrush

Irish: Siocán (frost-bird, Kry.), Socán

Uls. Scots: (Small) Felt

Scientific: Turdus musicus

FACTS & FIGURES

FIELDFARE: Winter visitors. Omnivorous. Numbers vary greatly from year to year. About 750,000 visit Britain and Ireland on average. Live max eighteen years.

REDWING: Winter visitors. Omnivorous. Numbers unknown but vary greatly from year to year. Live max seventeen years. The national bird of the Republic of Turkey.

Order: *Passeriformes*; Family: *Turdidae*.

3.17 WARBLERS – CEOLAIRÍ

Warblers are small songbirds that visit this country mostly in summertime. There are more species of warbler than any other group of small birds. Named for their singing ability, they tend to be generally dull in colour and hard to tell apart. Ornithologists identify them primarily by song.

Warblers are split into two large groups: Old World warblers (Europe, Africa, Asia, and Oceania) and New World warblers (North America). The Old World warblers, of which several species visit Ireland, are further split into more groups. Primary amongst these groups are the *Phylloscopus* (leaf-warblers, c. 60 species, two common in Ireland), *Acrocephalus* (marsh and tree warblers, c. 40 species, two common in Ireland), *Locustella* (c. 10 species, one common in Ireland), *Sylvia* (true warblers, c. 20 species, two common in Ireland) and *Hippolais* (c. 8 species, none common in Ireland).

Sylvia comes from the Latin *sylva* meaning 'wood', *phylloscopus* from the Greek *phullus* meaning 'leaf' and *skopus* meaning 'watchman'. *Acrocephalus* means 'sharp-headed'. *Locustella* means 'little grasshopper'.

As warblers tend to be shy and secretive, and tend to look very similar, there is scant folklore about them.

NAMES
Irish: *Éan ceoil* (music bird),
Ceolaire (music bird).

3.17.1 The Goldcrest

Cíorbhuí | *Regulus regulus regulus*

Goldcrests are our smallest European birds. They belong to a six-species family of birds, known as kinglets in North America and are as *Roitelets* (little kings) in French. A Goldcrest is largely olive-green in colour with a distinct black-lined orange-yellow stripe running the length of the top of its head and distinct white wing-bars. The underparts are a dull white-green colour and the beady black eye is prominent. Females have a pure yellow head stripe. The wheezy song of a Goldcrest has been described as like a tiny bicycle pump.

In summer, most of them live among pine trees and other conifers where their tiny needle bills can pull seeds from cones. They are very sensitive to cold weather, with a bad winter sometimes killing 80 per cent of the population.[1]

Goldcrests have much rarer cousins, the Firecrests (*Lasairchíor, Regulus ignicapillus*) which live in the UK and continental Europe in winter and rarely visit the south coast of Ireland in summer. Looking almost identical from the distance, Firecrests have a less timid appearance, with dark eyebrow stripes and 'spectacle' marks.

The scientific name *regulus* means 'royal' or 'king/prince'. The Irish name *Cíorbhuí* means 'yellow crest'. Goldcrests were historically called Gold-crested Wrens, which may account for their alternative names, Kinglet or *Roitelet* as the Wren was regarded as the king of the birds. In England, Goldcrests were also called 'Woodcock Pilots' because when they arrived, Woodcock were sure to follow within a few days.[2]

NAMES

English: Bishop Wren (Wat.), Gold-crested Regulus, Gold-crested Wren, Golden-crested Wren, Half-moon (Uls.), Kinglet (US, UK), Marigold Bird, Nettle-Creeper,[3] Pope's Eye (Uls.)

Irish: Caipín dhearg (red cap), Diairmín ('little Dermot', Din.), Diarmín riabhach[4] (little streaked/striped Dermot), Dreoilín ceannbhuí (yellow headed wren), Dreoilín easbuig (Conn.), Dreoilín easpaig/easpoig (bishop wren), Éan a cinn bhuí (yellow-headed bird, Kry)

Scientific: Motacilla regulus, Regulus cristatus, Regulus flavicapillus, Regulus linnei, Sylvia regulus

FACTS & FIGURES

Resident insectivores. Widespread in all counties. Up to 250,000 pairs (88–91). Live max five years. Weigh 6 g. The national bird of Luxembourg. There are six species of *Regulus* worldwide, making up the entire family of *Regulidae*. Order: *Passeriformes*; Family: *Regulidae*.

3.17.2 The Willow Warbler

Ceolaire sailí | *Phylloscopus trochilus trochilus*

& the (Common) Chiffchaff

Tiuf-teaf | *Phylloscopus collybita collybita*

Left: Willow Warbler

Right: Chiffchaff

'Why does a silly bird go on saying "chiff-chaff" all day long? Is it happiness or hiccups?'[5]

Willow Warblers and Chiffchaffs are very similar summer visitors to Ireland. Willow Warblers are very small yellow/olive-coloured birds with pale legs and a very different song from the Chiffchaff. Chiffchaffs are slightly smaller and duller with darker legs. These birds are so alike that ornithologists will sometimes use the word 'willowchiff' to hedge their bets, when they are uncertain which of the two has been seen. Chiffchaffs are named after their distinctive 'chiff-chaffa' song. Both birds weigh in the order of just 9 g. Willow Warblers are very common in summer. Males are often polygynous (they have more than one mate at a time). They winter in West Africa, south of the Sahara. Chiffchaffs have shorter wings and do not migrate so far. Chiffchaffs spend their winters in the Mediterranean and south of the Sahara in Africa. A few Chiffchaffs spend the winter in Ireland.

The specific *collybita* means 'money changer' as the song sounds like rattling coins, while the specific *trochilus* is from the Latin meaning 'wren' or 'small bird'.

NAMES

WILLOW WARBLER

English: Gold-crested Wren, Golden Wren, Hay Bird, Lady Bird (s.), Sallypecker, Sally Picker, Sally Wren, Willow Wren (Uls.), Willochiff (sl.), Yellow Wren

Irish: Éinin sailighe (little willow bird, Gal.), Glasán sailighe (willow finch)

Uls. Scots: Sally-Wran

Scientific: Motacilla trochilus, Phyllopneuste trochilus, Phyllopseustes trochilus, Sylvia trochilus

CHIFFCHAFF

English: Green Two-note (Wat.), Least Willow Wren, Lesser Pettychaps,[8] Sallypecker, Sally Picker, Willochiff (sl.)

Scientific: Ficedula abientina, Motacilla rufa, Phyllopneuste rufa, Phyllopseustes collybita, Phylloscopus rufus, Sylvia abientina, Sylvia collybita, Sylvia hippolais, Sylvia rufa

213

The Willow Warbler & the (Common) Chiffchaff continued

The Irish *Ceolaire sailí* translates as 'willow singer'. The alternative 'sally wren' refers again to the willow tree. The reference to 'willow' in both the Irish and English languages might suggest the birds are particularly partial to willow trees in some way. Although this is not particularly evident, some observers do suggest that the birds are found often in areas with high concentrations of Goat Willows (*Salix caprea*).[6] The alternative name, used in Ireland, Sally Picker, may refer to the birds' use of fluffy willow seed heads in their nests.[7]

FACTS & FIGURES

Willow Warbler: Summer visitors. Omnivorous. Widespread in all counties. Up to one million breeding pairs (88–91). Live max eleven years. Weigh 9 g.

Chiffchaff: Summer visitors. Carnivorous. Widespread in all counties. Up to 100,000 breeding pairs and declining (88–91). A few stay for winter. Live max seven years. Weigh 8 g.

About sixty species of Phylloscopus (leaf warblers) worldwide. Order: *Passeriformes*; Family: *Sylviidae* (established)/ *Phylloscopidae* (new).

3.17.3 The (Eurasian) Reed Warbler

Ceolaire giolcaí | *Acrocephalus scirpaceus*

Reed Warblers are small, elusive summer visitors to our reed beds. Broadly brown above and white below, males and females are alike. Flanks are a warm tan colour. Their numbers have been on the increase in Ireland, probably due to our warming climate. A pair first bred in Ireland in 1953 (County Down). The birds are usually heard before they are seen, a repetitive chattering coming from deep within the reeds. Nests are cup-shaped, tied between the reeds. They winter in Africa.

The Irish *giolcaí* means 'of the reeds'. The generic *acrocephalus* is from Greek meaning 'sharp-headed' while the specific *scirpaceus* means 'pertaining to reeds'.[9]

NAMES

English: Night Warbler, Reed Wren

Irish: Ceolaire giolcaighe (reed singer, Conn.)

Scientific: Acrocephalus streperus, Calamoherpe arundinacea, Salicaria arundinacea, Sylvia arundinacea

FACTS & FIGURES

Uncommon summer breeding visitors. Omnivorous. Live max twelve years. Up to 100 breeding pairs with numbers rising every year (95–96). Amber list. About forty species of *Acrocephalus* worldwide. Order: *Passeriformes*; Family: *Sylviidae* (established)/ *Acrocephalidae* (new).

3.17.4 The (Common) Grasshopper Warbler

Ceolaire casarnaí | *Locustella naevia naevia*

When you hear a Grasshopper Warbler, you never forget. Uttering a continuous high-speed clicking, day or night, they sound not unlike the reel of a fishing rod. While spectacular of song, the birds are a rather dull streaked brown on top with dirty white below and on the throat. Sexes are alike. With a tapering tail, they are not unlike oversized wrens in their skulking habits. They are more often heard than seen, as they like to hide in dense bushes. Pinpointing them is very difficult as the sound seems to travel.

The Irish *Ceolaire casarnaí* translates roughly as 'scrub warbler'. The generic *locustella* means 'little grasshopper' while the specific *naevia* means 'spotted'.

NAMES

English: Brakehopper, Cricket Bird, Grasshopper Lark, Gropper (sl.), Torie Bird (Uls.)

Scientific: Locustella avicula, Locustella ravi, Salicaria locustella, Sylvia locustella, Threnetria naevia

FACTS & FIGURES

Summer visitors to all counties. Insectivorous. Up to 10,000 breeding pairs and declining (88–91). Amber list. About nine species of *Locustella* (grass warblers) worldwide. Order: *Passeriformes*; Family: *Sylviidae* (established)/*Megaluridae* (new).

3.17.5 The Sedge Warbler

Ceolaire cíbe | *Acrocephalus schoenobaenus*

Sedge Warblers are known as Irish Nightingales because of their melodious night-time singing. Their emulations of other birds' calls are well known. They can sing continuously for over a minute, the song consisting of a long rambling series of chattering and musical notes.

Warblers can be hard to tell apart at the best of times but Sedge Warblers are relatively straightforward. The birds are generally light brown with a distinctive black-bordered white line above the black eyes. Underparts are dirty white. Sexes are alike.

The male's courtship display consists of singing whilst flying directly upwards and then descending with wings and tail fanned out. The birds winter in southern Europe and Africa south of the Sahara.

The Irish name *Ceolaire cíbe* translates as 'sedge singer'. The specific *schoenobaenus* is Greco-Latin meaning 'rush-dwelling'.

Beliefs & Traditions: When Sedge Warblers sing at night, and particularly at midnight, their voices are believed to be those of dead babies who choose to return temporarily from the 'other side' to sing, to soothe the hearts and minds of their poor keening mothers.[10]

Poetry: from: '*Serenades*' (Wintering Out)

> *The Irish nightingale*
> *Is a sedge-warbler,*
> *A little bird with a big voice*
> *Kicking up a racket all night.*

Seamus Heaney (1972)

NAMES

English: Hedge Warbler, Hedgewarbler, Irish Nightingale, Night Singer, Noisy Wren (Wat.), Sally Pecker[11]/Picker, Sedge Bird, Sedge Wren

Irish: Seascán[12]

Uls. Scots: Wee Nightingale

Scientific: Acrocephalus phragmitis, Calamodus phragmitis, Calamodus schaenobaenus, Calamodyta phragmitis, Calamoherpe schaenobaenus, Motacilla salicaria, Motacilla schaenobaenus, Salicaria phragmitis, Sylvia salicaria

FACTS & FIGURES

Summer breeding visitors to all counties. Omnivorous. Up to 100,000 breeding pairs (88–91). Live max ten years. About forty species of *Acrocephalus* worldwide. Order: *Passeriformes*; Family: *Sylviidae* (established)/ *Acrocephalidae* (new).

3.17.6 The (Eurasian) Blackcap

Caipín dubh | *Sylvia atricapilla atricapilla*

Blackcaps are perhaps amongst our most distinctive warblers. Both males and females are generally dark grey. A male's black cap identifies it immediately while females have a chestnut cap. Together they have the air of a distinguished well-dressed couple.

Blackcaps are regarded by many as the sweetest-singing birds in Ireland. They share the name Irish Nightingale with Sedge Warblers. As the true Nightingales, famous for their melodious midnight song, are not Irish birds, the title has fallen to the Blackcaps and Sedge Warblers, accomplished singers in their own right.[13]

Like most warblers, Blackcaps are mostly summer visitors to Ireland but more are staying for the winter, perhaps due to our warming climate.

The Irish name *caipín dubh* translates directly as 'little black cap' while the alternatives, *Donnchadh an chaipín* (Denis of the cap) and *Máirín an triúis* (Maureen of the trousers) are more attractive. The generic *sylvia* comes from Latin, meaning 'wood' or forest. The specific *atricapilla* comes from the Latin *ater* meaning 'black' and *capillus* meaning 'hair'.

Beliefs & Traditions: In Cyprus, it was believed that migrating storks carried Blackcaps on their backs as two voices can be heard when the storks are flying overhead.

CULINARY

Unfortunately for Blackcaps, they have long been considered a culinary delicacy and many of them are still killed for food in the Mediterranean area during migration. They are caught with illegal mist nets or 'lime sticks' which are twigs covered with glue placed in bushes or on poles. Having alighted on these sticks, the birds are not strong enough to pull away (see also Woodpigeon). These practices, now illegal in Ireland, were once widespread.

NAMES

English: Irish Nightingale, Western Blackcap

Irish: Bod na dtor (bush vagrant), Donncha/Donnchadh an chaipín[14] (Denis with the cap), Máirín an triubhais/truis (Maureen with the trousers), Seán an chaipín (John of the cap)

Uls. Scots: Blakkep (Ant.)

Scientific: Corruca/Curruca atricapilla, Motacilla atricapilla

FACTS & FIGURES

Resident omnivores. Widespread in summer and locally common in the east in winter. Up to 20,000 breeding pairs and increasing (88–91). Live max eleven years. Over twenty species of *Sylvia* (typical warblers) worldwide. Order: *Passeriformes*; Family: *Sylviidae*.

3.17.7 The (Common) Whitethroat

Gilphíb | *Sylvia communis communis*

Whitethroats are distinctive warblers, the males having grey heads, white throats and a pink tinge to the breast. Summer visitors to Ireland, Whitethroat numbers are increasing here, probably due to our warming climate and despite a big drop in numbers in the 1960s. Previously they may have been much more common. They have a distinctive display flight and a 'scratchy' song. Males tend to arrive a week earlier than females, which gives them time to set up territories. They spend their winters south of the Sahara and across northern tropical Africa.

The specific *communis* is from Latin meaning simply 'common'. The English name Whitethroat is self-descriptive. The Irish *gilphíb* is from *geal-píb* and means the same thing, 'white throat'. Other names such as Nettlerunner and Nettle-creeper from Ulster, refer to the habit of frequenting thick foliage, as does the delightful 'Hedge Chicken' which was sometimes shared with the Dunnock.

NAMES

English: Hammerhead (Uls.), Haychat, Hedge Chicken (UK), Nettle-creeper, Nettle-grey (Uls.), Nettlerunner (Uls.), Peggy Chaw, Polly Whitethroat

Irish: Gilphiob (Conn.), Gilphíob

Scientific: Curruca cinerea, Motacilla rufa, Motacilla sylvia, Sylvia cinerea, Sylvia rufa, Sylvia sylvia

FACTS & FIGURES

Summer visitors. Omnivorous. Widespread in most counties. Live max six years. Up to 100,000 breeding pairs (88–91). Over twenty species of *Sylvia* (typical warblers) worldwide. Order: *Passeriformes*; Family: *Sylviidae*.

3.17.8 The Flycatchers

Cuilirí

Spotted Flycatcher	Cuilire liath	*Muscicapa striata striata*
(European) Pied Flycatcher	Cuilire alabhreac	*Ficedula hypoleuca*
Red-breasted Flycatcher	Cuilire broinnrua	*Ficedula parva*

Pied Flycatcher

Spotted Flycatcher

Flycatchers are small summer visitors. Of the three species that can be seen in Ireland, none is common. The commonest, the Spotted Flycatchers, can be seen in all counties in summer, in parks and gardens, but are easily overlooked. Both the Pied and Red-breasted Flycatchers are very scarce, only seen along the south coast in summer. There are about twenty-five species of *Muscicapa* flycatchers and thirty species of *Ficedula* flycatchers worldwide from a total of about 300 species of flycatcher-like birds.

Red-breasted Flycatcher

The Flycatchers continued

Spotted Flycatchers are speckled brown birds that visit Ireland in summer, usually arriving in mid-April. More often recognised by their feeding habits, they tend to favour prominent perches where they assess passing insects and fly out to catch the unlucky, only to return to the same perch. They are usually found in woodlands, parks and gardens. They spend their winters in Africa, south of the Sahara, sometimes travelling as far as South Africa.

The Irish *Cuilire liath* means 'grey flycatcher'. The generic *muscicapa* is Latin meaning 'flycatcher' while *striata* means 'striped'.

Though rare, Pied Flycatcher numbers are increasing in Ireland. They are most often seen on the south coast in summer. The males are primarily black on top with white below hence the 'pied' name. The females are grey-brown where the males are black.

Looking superficially like Robins but no bigger than Blue Tits, Red-breasted Flycatchers are much rarer autumn visitors to Ireland usually seen along the south coast. They are greyer than the mostly brown Robins with the upperpart of the tail black with white flashes. Robins' tails are brown.

The Irish *alabhreac* means 'pied' while *broinnrua* means 'red-breasted'. The generic *ficedula* is Latin meaning 'small garden bird' while the specific *hypoleuca* is Greek meaning 'white below'. *Parva* is from Latin meaning 'little'.

Beliefs & Traditions: In Somerset, it was said: 'If you scare the flycatcher away, no good luck will with you stay'.[15]

NAMES

SPOTTED FLYCATCHER

Irish: Breacán glas (grey speckled bird, Kry.), Breacán scióbóil (speckled bird of the barn, Kry.) Cuilsealgaire liath (grey fly-hunter),

Scientific: Butalis grisola, Motacilla ficedula, Motacilla striata, Muscicapa ficedula, Muscicapa grisola

PIED FLYCATCHER

Irish: Cuilsealgaire alabhreac, Cuilsealgaire breac

Scientific: Ficedula atricapilla, Muscicapa atricapilla, Muscicapa luctuosa

RED-BREASTED FLYCATCHER

Irish: Cuilsealgaire broinnrua

Scientific: Erythrosterna parva, Muscicapa parva, Siphia parva

FACTS & FIGURES

SPOTTED: Uncommon insectivorous summer visitors to most counties. Live max eleven years. Up to 100,000 breeding pairs and declining (88–91). Amber list.

PIED: Rare insectivorous summer visitors. Live max ten years. Up to ten breeding pairs (88–91). Amber list.

RED-BREASTED: Rare insectivorous summer visitors. Probably none breeding here.

About twenty-four species of *Muscicapa* and over thirty species of *Ficedula* worldwide. Order: *Passeriformes*; Family: *Muscicapidae*.

3.18 TITS – MEANTÁIN

Known as chickadees or titmice in the US, there are three separate families of tit worldwide, the 'long-tailed tits and bushtits', the 'penduline tits' and the 'true tits'. Of these, four species can be seen in Ireland: Great Tits, Blue Tits, Coal Tits and Long-tailed Tits. Rarely, the reed-loving Bearded Tits make an appearance but these birds are misnamed and are really of the 'babbler' family. There are about fifty-five species in the family *Paridae* (tits and chickadees) worldwide.

Several species of tit will often feed together, roaming from tree to tree in large marauding multispecies flocks, chirping incessantly and dropping pieces of seed from the high branches. Beautifully coloured birds, all four common Irish species are regular visitors to our gardens in search of nuts and seeds. Blue Tits have become infamous for opening our milk bottles in the early morning. Despite their ubiquity in Ireland, they have generated very little lore. This suggests a more forest-bound past away from human interaction.

The word 'tit' may come from the Old Icelandic *titr* meaning 'small' or from the Greek *titis* meaning 'a small chirping bird'. The generic *Parus* is Latin for tit.

Collective name: a titillation of tits.

NAMES

Irish: Caochán, Cíochán (Mun.), Finnín feoir (Finín of the river edge), Mionntán

3.18.1 The Coal Tit

Meantán dubh | *Periparus ater hibernicus* (Irish Coal Tit)

Periparus ater britannicus (British Coal Tit)

Coal Tits look somewhat like Blue Tits in 'black-and-white'. They are common garden birds in Ireland, but not as common as the Blue. In Ireland, we have our own race of Coal Tit, *Periparus ater hibernicus*. Irish Coal Tits have subtle sulphur-yellow tones on the face, breast and underparts and have a somewhat pale rump. The British race is also quite common here. Coal Tits will live anywhere in gardens and woodland but are particularly at home in conifers and have benefited greatly from coniferous tree planting throughout Ireland.

The specific name *ater* is from Latin meaning 'black'. The Irish name *Meantán dubh* means simply 'black tit'. The taxonomy of the *Paridae* family has changed, the Coal Tits being moved from *Parus* to the new genus *Periparus*. While *Parus* is Latin for 'tit' *peri* here has the meaning 'at the boundary of' or 'near'.

NAMES

English: Blackcap, Cole Tit, Colemouse, Tomtit

Irish: Mionntán dubh (black tit)

Scientific: Parus ater

FACTS & FIGURES

Resident omnivores. Widespread in all counties except the extreme northwest. Up to 250,000 breeding pairs and increasing (88–91). Weigh max 10 g. Live max nine years. Six species of *Periparus* worldwide. Order: *Passeriformes*; Family: *Paridae*.

3.18.2 The (European) Blue Tit

Meantán gorm | *Cyanistes caeruleus obscurus* (British Blue Tit)

'Where is he that giddy Sprite, Blue-cap, with his colours bright.'[1]

Brilliantly coloured, Blue Tits are very common Irish garden birds. In the era of the delivered milk bottle, they became renowned as early morning milk-thieves, piercing the thin foil caps and sipping the cream. Green upperparts, yellow underparts, white faces and blue bonnets distinguish them. Sexes are alike. Birds of woodland, they will often form large flocks which sometimes merge with flocks of Great and Long-tailed Tits to form marauding superflocks. Such flocks can produce a din of overhead seed picking as they systematically pick trees free of their seeds. Being small, they are sensitive to harsh winters.

Both the Irish *Meantán gorm* and the scientific *Parus caeruleus* simply mean 'blue tit'. The species has recently been moved to the new genus, *Cyanistes*.

Weather: The call of a Blue Tit was said to warn of cold weather.[2]

Poetry: from '*The Kitten and Falling Leaves*'

> *Where is he that giddy Sprite,*
> *Blue-cap, with his colours bright,*
> *Who was blest as bird could be,*
> *Feeding in the apple-tree;*
> *Made such wanton spoil and rout,*
> *Turning blossoms inside out;*
> *Hung--head pointing towards the ground--*
> *Fluttered, perched, into a round*
> *Bound himself, and then unbound;*
> *Lithest, gaudiest Harlequin!*
> *Prettiest Tumbler ever seen!*
> *Light of heart and light of limb;*
> *What is now become of Him?*

William Wordsworth

NAMES

English: Billy-biter (Uls.), Blue Bonnet or Bluebonnet (Uls.), Bluecap, Nun, Stonechat, Tam Titty Mouse (Uls.), Tittymouse (Uls.), Tomtit

Irish: Cailleach chinn ghuirm (blue-headed hag or cock), Diarmaid beag (little Dermot), Diarmaid breac (speckled Dermot, Conn.), Mionntán gorm (blue tit)

Scientific: Parus caeruleus, Parus coeruleus

FACTS & FIGURES

Resident omnivores. Widespread in gardens and woods in all counties. Up to one million breeding pairs (88–91). Weigh max 11 g. Live max nine years. Two species of *Cyanistes* worldwide. Order: *Passeriformes*; Family: *Paridae*.

3.18.3 The Great Tit

Meantán mór | *Parus major major*

Parus major newtoni (British Great Tit)

The largest of our domestic tits, Great Tits are distinctive sturdy tits. The smaller Blue Tit's blue bonnet is replaced by the glossy black cap of the Great. The contrast between this and the broad white cheeks makes the entire head look like a large eye, leading to one of the bird's colloquial names, the Oxeye. Great Tits get their fabulous green/yellow colour from carotenoid[3] pigments which they get from ingesting green herbivorous larvae (e.g. caterpillars), in the same way that wild salmon get their pink colour from the carotenoid pigments in shrimp. Nonetheless, females are somewhat duller than males.

Great Tits often join other species of tit in large foraging groups. The call varies enormously but the 'teacher teacher teacher' call is very distinctive. The call is often described as the sound of a saw being sharpened hence the other colloquial name, Sawsharper.

The Irish *Meantán mór* simply means 'big tit'. '*Mean*' may derive from *miontas* meaning 'mint'. The scientific *Parus major* simply means 'great tit'. Tit is short for 'titmouse', the mouse part coming from the old English *mase* meaning 'small thing'.

Weather: The call of a Great Tit was said to warn of rain.[4]

PLACE NAMES

Ballinaminton, Co. Offaly (Béal Átha na Meantán, the mouth of the ford of the tits.)

NAMES

English: Black Skull (Uls.), Blackcap, Great Titmouse, Oxeye, Sawsharper, Teacher (Wat.), Tomtit

Irish: Meanntán, Meantas, Mionntán (Conn.), Miontas (mint)

FACTS & FIGURES

Resident omnivores. Widespread in all counties. Up to half a million breeding pairs (88–91). Weigh max 22 g. Live max fifteen years. There are about twenty-four species of *Parus* worldwide and at least thirty races of Great Tit. Order: *Passeriformes*; Family: *Paridae*.

3.18.4 The Long-tailed Tit[5]

Meantán earrfhada | *Aegithalos caudatus rosaceus*

(British Long-tailed Tit)

Tiny bundles of delight, Long-tailed Tits are locally common birds, found in small foraging flocks, often with other tit species. Though easy to overlook, once spotted, the Poke Puddings or 'flying spoons', as they were once called, are easy to identify. The tail is as long as the rest of the body. The black and white striped head and white underparts fade into a delicate pink. The upperparts and wings are mottled black, white and pink. Like Wrens, Long-tailed Tits are known to clump together in large numbers but unlike Wrens, will do so even in good weather. Even captive pairs will squeeze together at night for warmth. They make a beautiful, enclosed, slightly elongated nest with a small entrance hole. Long-tailed Tits are not true tits. They belong to the bushtit family *Aegithalidae*.

The Irish *Meantán earrfhada* translates directly as 'long-tailed tit'. The generic *Aegithalos* is from Greek meaning 'titmouse' while the specific *caudatus* is from the Latin meaning 'tailed'.

NAMES

English: Bottle Tit, Flying Spoon (sl., Dub.), Long-tailed Bushtit, Long-tailed Titmouse, Poke Pudding, Ragamuffin

Irish: Cíochán, Meantán fada (long tit), Mionntán earbaill fhada (long-tailed tit, Conn.)

Scientific: Acredula caudata, Acredula rosea, Mecistura caudata, Orites caudatus, Parus caudatus

FACTS & FIGURES

Resident insectivores. Locally common in all counties. Up to 100,000 breeding pairs and increasing (88–91). Live max ten years. About eleven species in the *Aegithalidae* (bushtit) family including seven species of *Aegithalos* worldwide. Order: *Passeriformes*; Family: *Aegithalidae*.

3.19 CROWS – PRÉACHÁIN, CARÓGA

Crows are amongst the most intelligent of birds. They have been the subject of not a few scientific experiments and books on bird intelligence. Despite their size, crows are 'passerines', that is, perching song birds, and they are the largest of the group.

There are more than 120 species in the *Corvidae* family (Crows, Jays and Magpies) including over 40 species of *Corvus* worldwide. Of these, seven can be seen in Ireland. The birds that most of us know as crows are Rooks. Our other common crows are the Jackdaws, renowned for making nuisances of themselves in chimneys. Jackdaws are smaller than Rooks with a grey sheen to their heads, silver/white eyes and a self-confident swagger. Then there are the Hooded or Scald Crows, which, with their distinctive black and grey colouring, are easy to spot. Those are the common ones. Ravens live in Ireland too but are not so accessible. They are huge black birds that like to live where people do not. Choughs are very uncommon crows, but very easy to recognise. They live in remote areas around the north, west and south coasts and have bright red bills and legs. Lastly, our two most colourful crow species are the Magpies and the Jays. The brilliantly coloured Magpies are now omnipresent while Jays are much more secretive. Woodland birds, Jays show an elegant brown/pink colour with beautiful blue wing stripes displayed in flight.

In days past, knowing the exact species of a bird was not as important as it is today. A 'black bird' was a Hooded Crow, Rook, Raven or even a Blackbird. As a result, we cannot always be sure, when we read crow lore, which species is being referred to. Crows were associated with the gods Badhbh, Macha and the Morrigan. They were symbols of conflict, war, and death. Their skills were wisdom, combined with trickery. They were the protectors of the sacred records.

The generic *corvus* is Latin for crow. 'Crow' comes from the Anglo-Saxon *crawe*, an imitation of the crow's call.

The Old Crow Teaches the Young Crow

There was an old crow long ago, and he made a nest. After a time, only one of his brood remained with him. One day the old crow took the young one out into the field to teach him how to fly.

When the young crow had learned how to fly and was able to go to any part of Ireland, the old crow said, 'I think that you are able to fly anywhere now and make your living by yourself. Before you go, I want to give you a little advice that will protect you from danger, as it has protected myself.'

'Tell it to me,' said the young crow. 'If you are ever in a potato field or cornfield and see a man coming toward you with something under his arm or in his hand, fly off immediately, fearing he may have a gun and may shoot you.' 'I understand,' said the young crow. 'Another bit of advice to you,' said the old crow. 'If you see a man bending down as he comes toward you in the field or on the road, fly off as fast as you can, for he will be picking up a stone to throw at you. If he has nothing under his arm and if he doesn't bend down, you're safe.' 'That's all very well,' said the young crow, 'but what if he has a stone in his pocket?' 'Off you go,' said the old crow. 'You know more than myself!'[1]

Collective Noun: A congress of crows, a hover of crows, a murder of crows, a storytelling of crows.

3.19.1 The Rook

Rúcach | *Corvus frugilegus frugilegus*

The Rook continued

Rooks are amongst Ireland's best-known birds. When we talk about crows in Ireland, we are generally talking about Rooks. Highly intelligent birds, they live in communities called rookeries. They are entirely black with a dark blue metallic sheen. They have distinctively shaped heads with a greyish/white base to the silvery bills. Rooks can pair for life and often stay together all year round. Each year they repair last year's nest, often stealing from a neighbour. Young Rooks lack the whitish base to the bill and can be confused with British Carrion Crows (*Corvus corone corone, Caróg dhubh*) which are uncommon visitors here.

Rooks have a reputation for eating fruit and vegetables, hence the specific name *frugilegus*. Nonetheless, insects make up a large part of their diet. It has long been a practice in Ireland, for keeping Rooks away from crops, to hang or nail up a dead Rook in a prominent position, the sight of which will keep its brethren away.

Rooks get their name from the Old Norse *hrokr* describing the voice.

Beliefs & Traditions: A Rook was a symbol of long, settled life. Rooks feeding in a village or close to their nest in the morning meant bad weather was coming, whereas Rooks flying far from their nests meant good weather was on the way. A flight of Rooks over an army spelt imminent defeat and a flight of Rooks over a house or a group of people walking or driving meant a death was imminent.[2]

The building of a new rookery (*garrán préachán*) near a house was regarded as good fortune. Consequently, if a rookery near your home was abandoned, it was a bad omen known as the 'curse of the crows'.[3] By tradition, Rooks are supposed to start building their nests on 1 May but if this falls on a Sunday, they will wait until the next day.[4]

CULINARY

Rooks were eaten in Ireland but it was thought best to catch as young a bird as possible as the 'old crows' were very tough and needed much cooking. Watters[5] tells us (1853): In many parts of Ireland young rooks are shot after a certain day in June, and concocted into a dish dignified by the name of a 'crow pie', the merit of which is believed to be considerably enhanced if eaten in ignorance of the contents.

NAMES

English: (Praheen) Crow

Irish: Cnáimh-Fhiach (bone-Raven, Don.),[6] Drechan, Préachán dubh (black crow, Din., Uls.), Rúca, Rúfa

Uls. Scots: Corbie/Corby (also Hooded Crow), Cra (Ant.), Croupy, Crow (Ant.)

Scientific: Trypanocorax frugilegus

FACTS & FIGURES

Resident omnivores. Widespread in all counties. Up to half a million breeding pairs (88–91). Live max twenty years. Collective name: a building of Rooks, a clamour of Rooks, a parliament of Rooks. Order: *Passeriformes*; Family: *Corvidae*.

3.19.2 The Hooded Crow

Feannóg[7] | *Corvus cornix (Corvus corone cornix)*

'Hoodies' are large members of the crow family known for their scavenging and eating of carrion. Very distinct, Hooded Crows are largely grey with a black head, wings and tail. They are of the same species as the British Carrion Crow (*Corvus corone corone, Caróg dhubh*) and tend to occur where the Carrion Crow does not. Sexes are alike. You will see 'hoodies' in Ireland and Scotland but not throughout most of England. The two subspecies do inter-breed where their ranges overlap so inter-mediate colouring can be found. The birds will eat anything, including carrion, and behave somewhat like birds of prey.

Several alternative names have been used in Ireland, the most common being scald crow and grey crow. 'Corbie' was used in Ulster. One of the English names, Royston crow, also used in Ireland, comes from the English village of Royston in north Hertfordshire where the birds were once common. The Irish *Feannóg* means 'crow'. The specific *corone* is from Greek, meaning 'crow'.

Beliefs & Traditions: Morrigan or Badhbh was the Celtic goddess of war and death, who could take the shape of a Hooded Crow or Raven. The banshee was associated with the Morrigan and could appear as a variety of other animals associated in Ireland with witchcraft; a Hooded Crow, a stoat, a hare or a weasel.

Roystons (Hooded Crows) were generally considered unlucky in county Clare and they were believed to be incarnations of the war goddess, Badhbh. It was believed that the fairies often exercised their powers in the form of Roystons and as a result, the birds were always avoided whenever possible. If a Hooded Crow rested on a house, it meant death or great misfortune to a member of the house-hold. Similarly, a crow flying directly over a home was also an omen of death. Finding a dead crow on the road was good luck but crows in a churchyard were bad luck.

In Ireland in the nineteenth century, it was believed that when a Praheen cark[8] (hen crow) was found in solitude in a mountain glen, away from habitation, it contained the soul of a wandering sinner.[9]

The Hooded Crow continued

Proverbs & Similes:

A crow on the thatch, soon death lifts the latch.

As the crow flies (mar théid an t-éan).

Ravens' knowledge (seeing and knowing everything).

You'll follow the crows for it (you will miss it after it is gone).

Chomh dubh le préachán (As black as the crow).

D'inis fiach é agus shéan feannóg é (the raven said it and the hooded crow showed it).

Ná creid feannóg agus ná creid fiach (believe neither hooded crow nor raven – don't believe in omens).

Lá a mbeadh an fiach dubh ag cur amach a theanga (a day when a raven would put out its tongue – a very hot day).

Curses:

With all your money, airs and graces, may you be left where the crows don't shite.[10]

Mallacht na bpréachán ort (the curse of the crows [or Ravens] on you – may you stop before you enjoy the fruits of your labour).

PLACE NAMES

Altnavannog, Co. Tyrone (Alt na bhFeannóg, hill of the crows)
Ardnapreaghaun, Co. Limerick (Ard na bPréachán, the height of the crows)
Bawnnavinnoge (Bán na bhFeannóg, scald crow's field), Co. Waterford
Binnafreaghan, Co. Tyrone (Binn an Phréacháin, peak of the crows)
Corby Knowe, Co. Antrim
Cornafanog/Corrnafannoge, Co. Fermanagh (Corr na bhFeannóg, hill of the crows)
Druminnick, Co. Cavan (Droim Fhionnog, ridge of the scald crow)
Faill na bPréachán, Co. Waterford (The crows' cliff)
Garrán na Fionnóige/Feannóige (scald crow's rookery), Co. Waterford
Gleanntán na bhFionnóg, Co. Waterford (little glen of the Hooded Crows)
Knockaphreaghaun, Co. Clare, Co. Galway (Cnoc na Phréachán, hill of the crows)
Mulnavannoge, Co. Leitrim (hill of the scald crows)

NAMES

English: Black-neb (Uls.), Blue-backed Crow, Bunting Crow, Grey Backed Crow (Uls.), Grey Crow, Hen Crow, Hoody, Hoodie (sl.), Praheen Cark, Royston, Scal Crow, Scald-Crow

Irish: Badhbh, Feannóg dubh, Caróg dhubh (Black Crow), Caróg liath (grey crow, Din.), Córnach, Coróg/Corróg (Gal.), Créamaigheach (crow, Der.), Créamhaíoch (Der.), Cromán riabhach (grey crow), Feannóg chorrach, Feannóg liath, Fionnóg, Iascaire cóirneach[11] (tonsured fisherman), Préach, Préachán (crow), Préachán liath (grey crow, Kry.), Préachán na gcearc[12] (hen crow)

Uls. Scots: Corbie/Corby,[13] Cra (Ant.), Hoodie

Scientific: Corvus cornix

FACTS & FIGURES

Resident omnivores, Common in all counties. Up to 250,000 breeding pairs (88–91). Live max seventeen years. Order: *Passeriformes*; Family: *Corvidae*.

3.19.3 The (Northern) Raven

Fiach dubh | *Corvus corax corax*

'At the end of forty days Noah opened the window of the ark which he had made, and sent forth a Raven; and it went to and fro until the waters were dried up from the earth.' [14]

Ravens can live for sixty years. The largest of the crow family, they are intelligent and sociable birds and can learn to talk. Ostensibly like any other crow, Ravens are immediately identifiable by their large size. Glossy black, adults have prominent furry feathers under the chin and fly with a fanned-out tail, hawk-like.

Ravens are uncommon in Ireland and like to live away from human settlement. They prefer remote areas where they usually reveal their presence by their distinctive inflight 'caw'. Ravens will eat almost anything and are highly adaptable. They will attack small birds and animals and will readily eat carrion. They cache food under rocks and in crevices in anticipation of harder times. They have a distinctive courting dance. The male performs a series of hair-raising aerial acrobatics to impress the female. When she joins in, his acrobatics increase. He can fly upside down and offer her food while flying. They usually mate for life.

The specific *corax* is from the Greek *korax* meaning a 'croaker'. The name Raven itself probably comes from the Old Norse *hrafn* meaning 'to clear one's throat'.

History: Viking chiefs sometimes used Ravens as their representative symbols. They were believed to be Odin's (the Raven God) messengers and were depicted on banners, representing him. Such a banner may have been used at the Battle of Clontarf (AD 1014). A Raven also appears with a falcon on the coat of arms of the

The (Northern) Raven continued

Isle of Man as it does on the old coat of arms of County Dublin and the flag of Fingal county, recalling the Viking settlements there in the ninth and tenth centuries.

Beliefs & Traditions: Much Irish Raven lore is similar to that found in Scandinavia, indicating the influence of the Vikings in this regard.[15] Ravens were symbols of virility and wisdom and had huge importance in Irish historical myth. They were also symbols of death with a reputation for eating eyes. In early Celtic mythology, the birds were associated with the enemy, and were thought to be their message carriers. They were known as Bran or Dómhnall dubh (black Dónal). The god Lugh, father of Cúchulainn, was often linked with the Raven. The war goddess Badhbh Catha (Raven of Battle) or Morrigan, often appeared in the shape of a crow or Raven. In a famous battle, Cúchulainn tied himself to a stone as he was dying. It was only when a Raven alighted on his shoulder that his enemies and fellow fighters knew for sure he was dead, as no bird would do such a thing with a living person. Though we generally think of this bird as a Raven, it might have been any type of crow. In the story of Deirdre and Naoise, one morning Deirdre watched a calf being skinned on the fresh snow and a Raven coming to feast on the scraps. She decided that her ideal man would have 'hair as black as a Raven, cheeks as red as blood and a body as white as snow'.

The druids effectively worshipped Ravens and watched them carefully to learn the future. With the arrival of Christianity, the cult of the Raven was suppressed and it became Satan's own bird.[16] According to the Bible, the Raven was the first bird sent out from the ark by Noah.

In England, to kill a Raven was to harm the spirit of King Arthur who visited the world in the form of a Raven or a Chough. It was also said that England would never fall while there were Ravens in the Tower of London and presently, tame Ravens are kept there by the British government.

It was believed that Ravens, like Blackbirds could travel back and forth to the 'Otherworld'. The appearance of a Raven in or near a house meant a death was imminent.[17] In the nineteenth century, it was believed that if a Raven hovered near a herd of cattle or sheep, the animals would be found to be diseased.[18] It was also believed that a baby would die if a Raven's eggs were stolen. Lady Wilde gives us a means of becoming invisible: Get a Raven's heart. Split it open with a black-hafted knife. Make three cuts and place a black bean in each cut. Then plant it and when the beans sprout, put one in your mouth and say 'By virtue of Satan's heart, and by strength of my great art, I desire to be invisible'. And so it will be as long as the bean is kept in the mouth.[19]

Lady Wilde also tells us a way to win love: write the following love charm with a Raven's quill with blood from the ring finger on the left hand: '*By the power that Christ brought from heaven, mayest thou love me, Woman! As the sun follows its course, mayest thou follow me. As light to the eye as bread to the hungry as joy to the heart may thy presence be with me O woman that I love, till death comes to part us asunder*'.[20]

Gerald of Wales relates a story of St Kevin of Glendalough and Ravens. When St Kevin was a student, Ravens are alleged to have spilt his milk. St Kevin cursed them and from that day on, on his feast day, the Ravens of Glendalough are not able to land on the ground or to take any food.[21]

In Ireland in the seventeenth century, it was believed that a Raven with white on its wings and flying to the right hand side of a person, while croaking, was a certain sign of good luck for that person.[22]

Cures: It was thought that Ravens had healing powers. An alleged cure for baldness was to burn a Raven and boil its ashes with mutton fat. The resulting 'paste' should be rubbed on the head when cool.[23]

Poetry: from *'The Raven'*

> *Then this ebony bird beguiling my sad fancy into smiling,*
> *By the grave and stern decorum of the countenance it wore,*
> *'Though thy crest be shorn and shaven, thou,' I said, 'art sure no craven,*
> *Ghastly, grim and ancient raven wandering from the nightly shore—*
> *Tell me what the lordly name is on the Night's Plutonian shore!'*
> *Quoth the raven, 'Nevermore.'*

Edgar Allan Poe, 1845

Proverbs & Similes:

There is a saying '*He is in the book of the raven*' which means he is not to be trusted.

Chomh dubh leis an bhfiach (As black as the raven).

Chomh dubh le cleite an fhéich (As black as a raven's feather).

D'inis fiach é agus shéan feannóg é (The raven said it and the hooded crow showed it).

Is geal leis an bhfiach dubh a ghearrcach féin. (The raven thinks its own nestling fair).

233

The (Northern) Raven continued

PLACE NAMES

Aillenaveagh, Co. Galway (Aill na Bhfiach, Raven's cliff)

Altnaveagh/Altnaveigh, Co. Tyrone (Alt na bhFiach, Raven's hill)

Ardnaveagh, Co. Limerick (Raven's hill)

Bauraneag, Co. Limerick (Barr an Fhiaigh, high point of the Raven)

Carnanee, Co. Antrim (Carn an Fhiaigh, cairn of the Raven)

Carraig na bhFiach, Co. Kerry (Raven Rock)

Carrigeen, Co. Tipperary (Carraigín na bhFiach, little rock of the Ravens)

Cornaveagh, Co. Roscommon, Co. Cavan (Corr na bhFiach, the hill of the Ravens)

Drumfea, Co. Carlow (Droim Féich, Raven ridge)

Foynes, Co. Limerick (Faing, Raven)

Mullynaveagh, Co. Tyrone (Mullach na bhFiach, Raven's summit)

Neadnaveagh, Co. Roscommon, (Nead na bhFiach, Raven's nest)

Ravenhill, Co. Antrim[24] (Ballynafy, Baile na bhFiach, Raven town)

Shelburne, Co. Wexford (descendents of Bran)

NAMES

English: Bran, Brendan, Brion, Corbie, Corey, Fay

Irish: Bran, Bran-Éan, Bran-Fhiach, Branán, Cnáimh-Fhiach (bone-Raven),[25] Domhnall/Dónall/Dónal dubh (black Donald, Din.), Féich, Féichín (yng.), Fiach dubh (black Raven or perhaps black hunter), Fiach sléibhe (mountain Raven), Fiach tíre (country Raven), Préachán an teampaill (churchyard crow, Kry.), Préachán chnámhach (bony crow, Kry.), Préachán cnáimhightheach, Troghan[26]

FACTS & FIGURES

Resident omnivores. Locally scarce. Up to 10,000 breeding pairs (88–91). Live max twenty-one years. The national bird of Bhutan and the Yukon Territory, Canada. Collective name: a conspiracy of Ravens, a constable of Ravens, an unkindness of Ravens. More than ten species worldwide are called Raven. Order: *Passeriformes*; Family: *Corvidae*.

The (Western) Jackdaw

3.19.4

Cág | *Corvus monedula spermologus*

The smallest members of the crow family, Jackdaws are very intelligent birds. Like most crows, they are generally black in colour, but have a distinct grey 'scarf' around the throat and nape of the neck and have largely grey underparts. The head is capped black and the piercing silvery eye is distinctive. Sexes are alike. The rusty high-pitched 'caw' marks the Jackdaws out from other crows. They are social birds with a recognised leader and pecking order. In the Middle Ages, Jackdaws were 'daws' until the familiar name Jack was added. Their habit of nesting in chimneys and reputation for stealing money and other shiny objects has brought them into close proximity with humans and given them a somewhat unsavoury reputation. Still, they are generally regarded as likeable rogues.

The specific *monedula* is Latin for Jackdaw as is the Irish *Cág*. There is an alternative etymology: 'Jack' Daw, as in Jack Snipe, can mean 'small daw'.

NAMES

English: Chough (Uls.), Greyhead (Uls.), (Jack) Daw

Irish: Cabhag, Cabhóg[29] (Don.), Caog, Cathóg,[30] Coc-bhran, Éan murach

Uls. Scots: Jeckda (Ant.), Ka, Kay

Scientific: Coloeus monedula, Lycos monedula

FACTS & FIGURES

Resident omnivores, widespread in all counties. Up to 250,000 breeding pairs (88–91). Live max nineteen years. Two species worldwide are called Jackdaws. Order: *Passeriformes*; Family: *Corvidae*.

Beliefs & Traditions:

It was said that if Jackdaws did not frequent a ruined castle or tower, then it was surely haunted.[27]

The arrival of a solitary Jackdaw was taken as a portent of some approaching calamity.[28] More particularly, a Jackdaw falling down the chimney was a portent of bad luck.

3.19.5 The (Red-billed) Chough

Cág cosdearg | *Pyrrhocorax pyrrhocorax pyrrhocorax*

Previously known as sea crows, Choughs are perhaps the least known, most elusive and most enjoyable of our crows. They can only be found on remote coastal areas on cliffs or machair. Known as *Cág cosdearg* (the red-legged Jackdaw) in Irish, they are very distinctive black birds, with bright red legs and bill. Choughs seem to rejoice in flight and several are often seen flying together, riding the updrafts off cliffs.

Previously found in much greater numbers, Choughs are easily tamed and were often kept as pets in Ireland, along coasts where they were plentiful.[31]

The scientific *Pyrrhocorax* is from Greek meaning 'red crow'. The name 'chough' itself is derived probably from their cawing call. Pronunciation varies. Most say 'chuff', but 'chaff' is common in Ireland. In Cornwall, it can be pronounced 'koff' and has in the past been pronounced 'chaw' or 'chow'. Some of the alternative Irish names, *Préachán na drochaimsire* (bad-weather crow) and *Préachán róid* (storm crow) records the birds' apparent delight in 'surfing' heavy winds.

PLACE NAMES

Cuas na Cáige, Co. Kerry
(Chough's Cave/Cove)

NAMES

English: Cliff Daw (Kry.), Cornish Crow, Red-billed Jackdaw, Red-legged Crow/Jackdaw (Uls.), Sea Crow

Irish: Cabhóg[33] (Don.), Cág deargchosach (red-legged Jackdaw), Cathóg dheargchosach (red-legged Jackdaw, Aran.), Coróg[34] (Ach., Cl.), Cosdhearg (red-leg, Kry.), Éan na gcos dearg (red-legged bird), Préachán cosdearg (red-legged crow), Préachán na drochaimsire (bad-weather crow), Préachán róid (storm crow)

Scientific: Corvus graculus, Fregilus graculus, Pyrrhocorax graculus

FACTS & FIGURES

Resident omnivores. Found uncommonly in remote areas along the north, west and south coasts. Less than 900 breeding pairs (02–03). Two-thirds of the British and Irish population live in Ireland. Live max sixteen years. Collective name: a chattering or clattering of Choughs. Red list. Two species of *Pyrrhocorax* worldwide. Order: *Passeriformes*; Family: *Corvidae*.

Beliefs & Traditions:

Choughs are protected in Cornwall, because the soul of King Arthur was said to have migrated into a Chough.[32] Today the bird is the 'national' bird of Cornwall.

3.19.6 The (Eurasian) Magpie

Snag breac | *Pica pica pica*

Magpies are amongst the most resplendent birds to be seen in Ireland. They show a magnificent melange of white, black and shimmering blue-green. Though perhaps not obvious, Magpies are members of the crow family. Good vocal imitators, they are extremely adaptable birds and are now abundant in urban areas, their numbers increasing markedly in the last thirty years. The increase seems to be largely because of the decline in their previous persecution. Victims of their own success, their large numbers now pose a problem, as they will happily feed on the young of other birds, although the extent of the problem is debated.

It takes a pair of Magpies around forty days to build their large, domed nest. As part of the crow family, they are intelligent birds: Magpies will cache surplus food during times of plenty. They have a loud, sharp three-beat alarm call, usually encountered in urban areas when a cat appears. Their apparent communication is called chattering (or chittering in Northern Ireland). They are good mimics and can be taught to speak parrot-style, in captivity. Regarded at best as nuisances, Magpies are reputed to steal shiny objects such as rings with which to decorate their nests.

Originally the birds were called 'Pies' until the familiar name Mag (for Margaret) was added in the Middle Ages. It may also be that the birds were called Maggot Pies. It is not clear from where the 'pie' part came, but from it, we get the word 'pied' meaning 'jumbled' or 'mixed up' (black and white, piebald). Black and white wood-peckers can also be called 'pie' and there are also the black and white Pied Wagtails and Pied Flycatchers. The Latin *pica* translates directly as Magpie. The Irish name *Snag breac* translates roughly as 'pied Magpie'. The word *Snag* has roots meaning 'creeping/crawling' and 'hacking/coughing', perhaps referring to a Magpie's rasping call. *Snag* is also the name for woodpecker and Treecreeper in Irish. Magpies are also known as *Francach* (Frenchman or foreigner) in Irish, probably referring to their late arrival here in the seventeenth century. *Francach* was also a word used for rat.

History: Magpies are relative newcomers to Ireland though there is some bone evidence that they may have been here in prehistoric times. Gerald of Wales confirms there was none here in the twelfth century.[35] In 1617, Fynes Moryson noted that '*Ireland hath neither singing nightingall, nor chattering pye, nor undermining moule*'.[36] Charles Smith, in his *History of the City and County of Cork* c. 1750 notes that there were no Magpies there seventy years previously.[37] A number of them are said to have been blown across the Irish Sea by a strong east wind in 1676, to arrive in County Wexford. Yet Jonathan Swift, in his letter to Stella of 1711 says of Wexford, '*Magpies have been always there, and nowhere else in Ireland, till of late years*'. The birds were first noticed breeding in Dublin in 1852.

The (Eurasian) Magpie continued

According to George Griffith's *Chronicles of the County Wexford*, a Colonel in Cromwell's army, Solomon Richards while living in Wexford, commented in 1682: '*One remark more is that there came with a black easterly wind, a flight of Magpies, under a dozen, as I remember out of England or Wales, none having been seen in Ireland before. They lighted in the Barony of Forth where they have bred and are so increased that they are in every wood and village in the county. My own garden, though in the town of Wexford is constantly frequented by them and they are spread more thinly into other counties and parts of the kingdom. The natural Irish much detest them, saying they "shall never be rid of the English while these Magpies remain"*.'[38]

Beliefs & Traditions: Magpies were believed to be repositories of the souls of evil-minded or gossiping women.[39] They were also regarded as harbingers of death. A Magpie tapping at the window was a death warning.[40] The travelling people were particularly wary of Magpies. Hearing a Magpie on top of a wagon meant you would hear of a death within a week. If you heard Magpies having an argument then you would soon hear some bad news. If a lone Magpie crossed your path then it was necessary to turn back immediately to avoid bad luck.[41] So it is not surprising that the 'one for sorrow' rhyme came into being. It was widely considered an ill omen to meet a single Magpie on the road. This belief is still widespread in Ireland. While it was unlucky to see a single Magpie, the ill effects could be mitigated or altogether avoided by taking off your hat and bowing to the bird.[42] In Dublin, children were encouraged to say 'Hello Mr Magpie, how do you do? How is your wife and your children too?' to mitigate the bad luck.

Despite the bad reputation, it was considered unlucky to kill a Magpie.[43] Lady Wilde tells us that to see three Magpies on the left-hand side when on a journey is unlucky; but two on the right-hand side is a good omen.[44] In Mayo, against the trend, Magpies were regarded as heralds of good news usually connected with a future postal delivery.[45] If a Magpie appeared near the door, a letter bearing good tidings could be expected. Sending good news or money to someone was referred to as 'sending the Magpie'.

In Christian tradition, it was also said that the Magpie got its black and white colouring at the death of Christ when all the birds went into mourning and the Magpie did it only half-heartedly.[46]

Kevin Danaher tells the story of how a Magpie tried to teach the other birds how to make a good nest. Thinking the Magpie was teaching them what they already knew, all of the birds flew off in disgust except the Wren who waited until the end. Now it is said that only Magpies and Wrens know how to roof a nest.[47]

Curses: A Magpie on your wheat field gate.[48]

Poetry:

One for sorrow,
Two for joy,
Three for a girl,
Four for a boy,
Five for silver,
Six for gold,
Seven for a secret
Never to be told,
Eight for a wish
Nine for a kiss
Ten for a time of
joyous bliss.

My mother's version:

One for sorrow,
Two for joy,
Three for a girl,
Four for a boy,
Five for Ireland,
Six for France,
Seven for a fiddler
Eight for a dance.

A version from Ulster:

One for sorrow, two
for mirth,
Three for a wedding,
four for a birth.

FACTS & FIGURES

Resident omnivores. Present in all counties. Up to 100,000 breeding pairs (88–91). Live max twenty-one years. The national bird of South Korea. Collective name: a tiding of Magpies. There are several species of bird worldwide called Magpie but only about three species of *Pica*. Order: *Passeriformes*; Family: *Corvidae*.

NAMES

English: Black-billed Magpie (US), Pie, Pighead,[49] Pye

Irish: Bocaire na mbánta (beggar of the pastures), Breac na n-ál (Tyr.), Cabaire breac (pied babbler, Aran.), Colmán ard (high pigeon, Mun.), Diarmuid beag na dtruslóg (little Dermot of the hopping, Mun.), Domhnaillín breac (little pied Donald), Éan péan/peana (play name, Omt.), Francach (Frenchman, foreigner), Magaide, Meaig, Meigeadán breac (pied chatterer, Der.), Míogadán breac (pied chirper, Omt.), Pean (Der.), Pioghaid (old Irish), Pocaire na mbánta (frolicker of the pastures), Poitheunad (Der.), Préachán breac (pied crow, Uls.), Préachán lachán (Der.), Sceagaire breac (north Conn.), Smagaide, Snagaide

Scientific: Cleptes pica, Corvus pica, Pica caudata, Pica fennorum, Pica melanoleuca, Pica rustica

3.19.7 The (Eurasian) Jay

Scréachóg | *Garrulus glandarius hibernicus*   (Irish Jay)
Garrulus glandarius rufitergum   (British Jay)
Garrulus glandarius glandarius   (European Jay)

'What: is the Jay more precious than the lark because his feathers are more beautiful?'[50]

Jays are beautiful yet secretive birds of deciduous woodland. They show primarily an exquisite buff-pink colour contrasted with a brilliant blue wing flash, best seen in flight. In the breeding season Jays are truly secretive and completely silent, to avoid detection. At other times they make a very sharp crow-like screech from which they get the Irish name *Scréachóg* and the generic Latin name *garrulus*. *Scréachóg* is shared with the Barn Owl (*Scréachóg reilige*) which has an even more haunting screech. Jays are well capable of mimicking other birds. Along with Magpies, they are our most colourful members of the crow family. They share many of the habits of their crow brothers and will take nestlings of smaller species to feed their young. Jays have a penchant for acorns and will gather and hide them for the winter, each individual burying several thousand. With deforestation, Jays declined across Ireland. They were also pursued for their beautiful plumage for fly-tying and for the millinery trade.[51] Ireland has its own subspecies of Jay, *G. g. hibernicus*. Irish birds tend to be darker than British and continental races.

The generic *garrulus* mean noisy and the specific *glandarius* comes from the Latin *glans*, meaning 'acorn', so a *Garrulus glandarius* is a 'noisy acorn bird'.

NAMES

Irish: Cabhóg[52] (Don.), Scréachóg choille (wood screecher)

Scientific: Corvus glandarius, Pica glandaria

FACTS & FIGURES

Resident omnivores. Widespread but not present in all counties. Absent particularly in the north, west and southwest. Up to 10,000 breeding pairs (88–91). Live max sixteen years. Collective name: a band of Jays, a party of Jays. About three species of *Garrulus* worldwide. Order: *Passeriformes*; Family: *Corvidae*.

3.20 FINCHES – GLASÁIN

Of the twenty-five or so species of true finch worldwide, nine can be seen in Ireland: Chaffinches, Greenfinches, Goldfinches, Bullfinches, Linnets, Bramblings, Siskins, Redpolls and Twites, with occasional rare visits from Hawfinches and Scarlet Rosefinches. Of these, the most common garden birds are Chaffinches and Greenfinches, with Goldfinches and Bullfinches locally common. Siskins are becoming more common in gardens and Linnets and Redpolls are widespread and well known in rural areas. Bramblings only visit us in the winter and Twites, while with us all year round, are the rarest of the bunch, found mostly in remote areas of the far west and north.

The name 'finch' comes from the Anglo-Saxon *finc*. The Irish *Glasán* literally means 'grey-bird' or 'green-bird' and should not be confused with *Glasóg*, a wagtail. The Irish surname Gleeson means 'descendant of *Glasán*'. *Glasán* is also the Irish word for the Black Pollock or Coley fish (*Pollachius virens*) and the 'Sea Lettuce' algae (*Ulva lactuca*). St Glasán was an Irish saint with feast day on 1 October.

PLACE NAMES

Ardglassan, Co. Meath (the high place of the finches or perhaps Linnets).

COLLECTIVE NAMES:

A charm of finches, a trembling of finches, a trimming of finches.

NAMES

Irish: Glasán (grey/green bird), Diairmín (little Dermot, little creature)

3.20.1 The (Common) Chaffinch

Rí rua | *Fringilla coelebs gengleri*

& the Brambling

Breacán | *Fringilla montifringilla*

Chaffinch

Brambling

Perhaps the most numerous birds in Ireland, Chaffinches are much loved, often frequenting our gardens and favouring beech trees. Male Chaffinches have blue-grey heads, brownish backs and pinkish bellies and underparts. In winter, these colours are much duller. The birds have the characteristic forked tails of a finch. In the garden, Chaffinches are most easily identified by their metallic 'chink' call. Like many birds, Chaffinches mimic the songs and calls of other birds and have different dialects in different areas.

The males have been called 'bachelor finches' from the habit of the sexes splitting up for the summer and migrating in different directions. However, most breeding pairs return to the same nest site year after year. From this behaviour, we get the specific name *coelebs*, from Latin, meaning 'unmarried'. The generic *fringilla* is from Latin meaning a 'small bird'.

Close relatives of the Chaffinches, the Bramblings or 'Mountain Chaffinches' are scarce winter visitors to Ireland. Bramblings have the same general shape as Chaffinches but have ashy-black heads and backs and rusty orange breasts and underparts. In some winters, huge numbers of Bramblings arrive. The specific *montifringilla* is from Latin meaning 'little mountain bird'.

CULINARY

Bewick tells us that the flesh of a Brambling was good to eat, though bitter, and better than that of a Chaffinch.[1]

NAMES

CHAFFINCH

English: Beechfinch, Horsefinch, Pink, Red-breasted Finch (Wat.), Shilfa, Whitewing (Arm., Don.)

Irish: Bricín beatha (lively speckle-bird), Coinleog (stubble-bird, Kry.), Coinlín cáithe/cátha[2] (chaff stubble-bird), Gealbhan/Gealún cátha (chaff sparrow, Din.), Gealbhan gleoránach (noisy sparrow), Rí rua (red king), Spinncín

Uls. Scots: Caff

BRAMBLING

English: Lulean Finch, Mountain Finch

Irish: Gealbhan breac (speckled sparrow)

Uls. Scots: Brammle Finch (Ant.)

Scientific: Fringilla lulensis

FACTS & FIGURES

CHAFFINCH: Resident omnivores, widespread in every county. Population increased in winter by birds from overseas. Up to 2.5 million breeding pairs (88–91). Live max fourteen years.

BRAMBLING: Rare winter visitors, mostly absent from the west. Live max fourteen years.

Three species of *Fringilla* worldwide. Order: *Passeriformes*; Family: *Fringillidae*.

3.20.2 The (European) Goldfinch

Lasair choille | *Carduelis carduelis britannica* (British Goldfinch)

Goldfinches are spectacularly coloured birds often seen in gardens and on bird-tables. The birds show a base dull-brown colour set off by a brilliant red, white and black head and yellow wing flashes. Sexes are alike. Particularly fond of thistles, the scientific name *Carduelis* comes from the Latin *carduus* meaning 'thistle'. Apart from the birds' striking colours, they have a melodious twinkling call, which led to many being kept as cage birds. The Irish name *Lasair choille* is as enchanting as the bird itself, translating as 'flame of the woods'. Most of the alternative names refer to the gold on the wing or the love of thistles.

Beliefs & Traditions: The red patches on a Goldfinch's face were said to be the blood of Christ left when a Goldfinch tried to remove the crown of thorns.[3]

On St Valentine's Day, the first bird a girl would see would give a clue as to the man she would marry. If it was a woodpecker, she would not marry at all. If it was a Robin, he would be a sailor, if a Blackbird, a clergyman, if a sparrow, he would be poor man (though they would be happy) or a farmer, if a Crossbill, an argumentative man, if a dove, a good man, and if it was a Goldfinch, he would be a millionaire. This tradition and others like it probably arises from the belief that 14 February was the date on which the birds chose their mates. 'On St Valentine's Day, when every bird cometh to choose his mate.' (Geoffrey Chaucer).

Poetry: from: *'I Stood tip-toe upon a little hill'*[4]

Sometimes Goldfinches one by one will drop
From low hung branches; little space they stop;
But sip, and twitter, and their feathers sleek;
Then off at once, as in a wanton freak:
Or perhaps, to show their black, and golden wings,
Pausing upon their yellow flutterings.

John Keats (c. 1817)

NAMES

English: Draw-water, Goldspink (Uls.), Goldspring (Uls.), Pink (Uls.), Thistle Finch, Thistle Sparrow, Yellow Finch (Wat.)

Irish: Barra cinn óir (gold-bar-head, Don.), Buigheán óir[5] (gold yellow-bird, Fanad, Don.), Buíóg an chinn óir (gold-headed yellow-bird), Buíóg[6] an óir (gold yellow-bird, Kry.), Buíon óir (gold yellow-bird, Uls.), Cinnín óir (little gold head), Coinnleoir Muire[7] (Mary's candle bearer), Finseog (Kry., Conn.), Gealbhan feothadain (thistle sparrow), Gealbhan fothanáin (thistle sparrow), Gealbhan órdha (golden sparrow), Glasair coille

Uls. Scots: Corney of the Cap, Gooldie/Gouldie (Ant.),

Scientific: Acanthis carduelis, Carduelis elegans, Carduelis linnei, Fringilla carduelis

FACTS & FIGURES

Resident omnivores, widespread in all counties. Up to 100,000 breeding pairs and increasing (88–91). Live max eleven years. Collective name: a charm of Goldfinches, a drum of Goldfinches, a troubling of Goldfinches. Over thirty species of *Carduelis* worldwide. Order: *Passeriformes*; Family: *Fringillidae*.

3.20.3 The (European) Greenfinch

Glasán darach | *Carduelis chloris harrisoni*   (British Greenfinch)

Carduelis chloris chloris   (European Greenfinch)

Although uncommon a century ago, Greenfinches are now commonly seen at bird tables and feeders. They tend to be a very noisy bunch, twittering loudly and often squabbling together. Overall a light dull green in colour, they have a characteristic yellow bar on the wing and the forked tail of a finch. Males can have more than one female, which tend to be a little duller in colour. Both are duller in winter. Largely herbivorous, they are particularly fond of sunflower seeds. As well as feeding together, they nest closely together in small evergreen bush colonies.

The Irish name *Glasán darach* means 'oak finch' from *doire*, an oak wood. The generic *Carduelis* comes from the Latin for 'thistle' while the specific *chloris* refers to the green colour.

Poetry: from: '*The Green Linnet*'

> *Hail to Thee, far above the rest*
> *In joy of voice and pinion!*
> *Thou, Linnet! in thy green array,*
> *Presiding Spirit here to-day,*
> *Dost lead the revels of the May;*
> *And this is thy dominion.*

William Wordsworth (1803)

CULINARY

Greenfinches were eaten and regarded as a delicacy.

NAMES

English: Green Grosbeak, Green Linnet, Peasweep

Irish: Bricín beithe[8] (speckled birch-bird, north Conn.), Gealbhan glas (green sparrow), Gealbhan liath (grey finch, Ant.), Gealbhan linne/lín (flax sparrow), Glasán dorach, Glasúinin (little-green-one, Mun.)

Scientific: Chloris chloris, Chlorospiza chloris, Coccothraustes chloris, Fringilla chloris, Ligurinus chloris, Linaris chloris, Linota chloris, Loxia chloris

FACTS & FIGURES

Resident omnivores. Widespread in all counties. Up to 250,000 breeding pairs (88–91) with numbers inflated in winter. Live max thirteen years. Over thirty species of *Carduelis* worldwide. Order: *Passeriformes*; Family: *Fringillidae*.

The (Eurasian) Siskin

3.20.4

Siscín | *Carduelis spinus*

Siskins are small finches, often overlooked. Denizens of coniferous forests, they have been appearing more and more in our gardens. Males are generally a dull yellow colour with black on the head, chin and wings and olive-green cheek and back and the forked tail of a finch. Females are a dull olive grey with yellow-green highlights. They eat a wide variety of tree seed but are fond of mature pine cones, and alder and birch, hence one of their Irish names *Gealbhan fearnóige* (alder sparrow). It is likely that Siskins first arrived in Ireland in the 1850s when there was a large population irruption and have thrived since in the new conifer plantations. They are often seen mixing with Redpolls. For years, Siskins were favoured cage birds and many escapees have thrived in the wild.

The name Siskin comes from the Swedish *siska* meaning 'chirper'. The specific *spinus* is from Greek meaning 'small bird' or from Latin meaning 'thorn' or 'blackthorn'.

The name 'Aberdevine' was once common and was probably a bird fancier's name.[9] The origin is unclear but Swainson tells us it means 'alder-finch'.[10] The Irish *Siscín* is probably just borrowed from the English name.

Beliefs & Traditions: In parts of Germany and Switzerland, it was believed that Siskins used a special stone with which to make themselves invisible.[11]

NAMES:

Irish: Gealbhan fearnóige (alder sparrow), Píobaire (piper), Seascán[12] (Der.)

Uls. Scots: Aberdavine (Ant.)/ Aberdevine

Scientific: Acanthis spinus, Chrysomitris spinus, Fringilla spinus, Spinus spinus

FACTS & FIGURES

Resident herbivores. Widespread in all counties but locally uncommon. Migrate internally from summer to winter. Up to 100,000 breeding pairs (88–91) with numbers increasing in winter. Live max thirteen years. Over thirty species of *Carduelis* worldwide. Order: *Passeriformes*; Family: *Fringillidae*.

3.20.5 The (Common) Linnet

Gleoiseach | *Carduelis cannabina cannabina*

& the (Lesser) Redpoll

Deargéadan coiteann | *Carduelis cabaret*

Linnet   Redpoll

'*. . . and evening full of the Linnet's wings . . .*'[13]

Linnets are small sparrow-like finches that live throughout Ireland on rough ground. Males have a distinctive red mark on the forehead and breast in summer and can only be confused with the less common Redpolls. In winter, males lose the red patches and look similar to the females.

The word Linnet comes from the Latin *linum* (flax) because the birds feed on the seeds of flax and hemp (hence the specific *cannabina*).

Redpolls look somewhat like small Linnets. A small black mark on the chin distinguishes them. Both have the distinctive forked-tail of the finch. Redpolls have a penchant for birch catkins. Lesser Redpolls were once considered part of the species *Carduelis flammea* (Redpoll), then the subspecies *Carduelis flammea cabaret* and are now regarded by most authorities as a separate species, *Carduelis cabaret*. The Irish *Deargéadan coiteann* means 'common red-face'. The 'poll' in Redpoll means the top of the head between the ears.

Beliefs & Traditions: Linnets have a very mournful yet pleasing song. It was believed that their voices were those of unhappy souls trapped in the Otherworld.[14]

Poetry: A Linnet features prominently in one of W. B. Yeats' best known poems:

from '*The Lake Isle of Inisfree*'

*There midnight's all a glimmer and noon a purple glow
And evening full of the linnet's wings.*

William Butler Yeats, 1893, from *The Collected Poems of W. B. Yeats* **(Macmillan, 1993)**

CULINARY

Both birds are edible and were regarded as a delicacy.

FACTS & FIGURES

LINNET: Resident omnivores. Widespread in all counties. Up to 250,000 breeding pairs (88–91). Live max nine years. Collective name: a glow of Linnets.

REDPOLL: Resident. Widespread in all counties. Up to 100,000 breeding pairs and increasing (88–91). Live max ten years. Amber list.

Over thirty species of *Carduelis* worldwide. Order: *Passeriformes*; Family: *Fringillidae*.

NAMES

LINNET

English: Brown Linnet, Chaff Cock, Flax Sparrow, Gray/Grey (Uls.), Gray/Grey Linnet, Greater Redpole, Rosy Gray/Grey (Uls.), Rose Linnet, Thorn-grey, Whin-grey (Uls.)

Irish: Coilichín cátha (little chaff cock), Coinnleoir óir (golden candle bearer), Éinín bun na punainne (little bird of the sheaves, Kry.), Gealbhan croige (crag sparrow), Gealbhan liath (grey sparrow, Ant.), Gealbhan lín (flax sparrow, Din.), Gealbhan rois (flax sparrow), Glasán lín (flax finch), Glasán linne (flax finch)

Uls. Scots: Lilty, Lintie (Ant.), Whunny-Grey[15] (Ant.)

Scientific: Acanthis cannabina, Cannabina cannabina, Cannabina linnei, Cannabina linota, Fringilla cannabina, Fringilla linota, Linaria cannabina, Linota cannabina

REDPOLL

English: King Harry (Uls.), (Lesser) Redpole, Speedy Grey (Uls.), Thorn Gray

Irish: Gleoisín cúldearg (red-reared chatterer)

Uls. Scots: Nettley-Grey (Ant.)

Scientific: Acanthis flammea, Acanthis linaria, Carduelis flammea cabaret, Carduelis linaria, Fringilla brevirostris, Fringilla cabaret, Fringilla flammea, Fringilla linaria, Linaria alnorum, Linaria betularum, Linaria borealis, Linaria minor, Linota linaria, Linota rufescens

3.20.6 The Twite

Gleoiseach sléibhe | *Carduelis flavirostris pipilans*

Twites are dull-brown-streaked mountain birds with a beautiful pink flash (in summer) at the base of the finch-like tail and a dull-yellow bill (in winter). The birds are quite uncommon in Ireland and are becoming even more so. They occupy upland areas or lonely rocky shorelines where Linnets are not found, and are quite elusive. Twites are relatively tolerant of man and can be quite approachable. In winter, they can form large flocks roving on the ground. In summer, they build colonial nests together on coastal grassland and heath. There has been a 50 per cent reduction in the number of Twites in Ireland over the last eighty years. The name Twite is probably descriptive of the birds' call. The Irish name *Gleoiseach sléibhe* means 'mountain Linnet'. The specific *flavirostris* is from Latin meaning 'yellow-beaked'.

NAMES

English: Bog Linnet (Kry.), Heather-Grey[16] (Uls.), Heatherling (Uls.), Mossy Grey (Uls.), Mountain Linnet, Twitty (Wat.)

Irish: Gealbhan/Gealún sléibhe (mountain sparrow, Kry.)

Scientific: Acanthis flavirostris, Cannabina flavirostris, Fringilla flavirostris, Fringilla montium, Linaria flavirostris, Linaria montana, Linota flavirostris, Linota montium

FACTS & FIGURES

Resident omnivores. Found in coastal areas in the far west and northwest. Rarely on the east coast in winter. Up to 1,000 breeding pairs and declining (88–91) with numbers increased in winter. Live max six years. Red list. Over thirty species of *Carduelis* worldwide. Order: *Passeriformes*; Family: *Fringillidae*.

3.20.7 The (Eurasian) Bullfinch

Corcrán coille | *Pyrrhula pyrrhula pileata*

Bullfinches are beautiful chunky pink/red finches with striking black caps. Both males and females have the distinctive stocky neck, the head merging directly into the body. While the males are almost crimson in colour in summer, the females are a demure tan/pink. They are locally common in Ireland in all but the extreme northwest and west but often go unnoticed. In the nineteenth century, Bullfinches suffered greatly from their striking appearance and were greatly valued as cage birds. In captivity, they can learn and recite human music, adding to their 'value'. After making a comeback in the early part of the twentieth century, their numbers are now in decline again. They are nearly always seen in pairs and are very fond of fruit buds, bringing them into conflict with fruit farmers.

The name Bullfinch comes from the birds' thickset bull-like neck and head. The scientific name *Pyrrhula* comes from the Greek *purrhos* meaning 'flame-red-coloured'. The Irish *Corcrán coille* translates roughly as 'purple bird of the wood'.

NAMES

English: Alp, Budfinch (Uls.), Holly Sparrow, Nope, Pope, (Red) Hoop (male)

Irish: Corcán coille, Cothaoin, Cuithin, Gealbhan/Gealún cuilinn (holly sparrow)

Scientific: Loxia pyrrhula/pyrrhyla, Pyrrhula europaea, Pyrrhula linnei, Pyrrhula major, Pyrrhula rubicilla, Pyrrhula vulgaris.

FACTS & FIGURES

Resident omnivores. Up to 100,000 breeding pairs (88–91). Live max twelve years. Collective name: a bellowing of Bullfinches. Over thirty species of *Carduelis* worldwide. Order: *Passeriformes*; Family: *Fringillidae*.

3.21 BUNTINGS – GEALÓGA

Buntings are small birds now largely uncommon in Ireland. Of the forty-plus species worldwide, perhaps three are native to Ireland: Corn Buntings, Reed Buntings, and Yellowhammers. Alas, Corn Buntings, once common throughout the country, are now close to extinction here. A few rarer buntings show up from time to time, mostly along the south coast: Little Buntings, Rustic Buntings, Ortolans, Lapland Buntings and Snow Buntings, the latter two occasionally appearing in numbers in winter. Family: *Emberizidae*. See Section 5.1.13 for Corn Bunting.

3.21.1 The (Western) Yellowhammer

Buíóg | *Emberiza citrinella caliginosa*

Yellowhammers are some of our most brightly coloured birds. Members of the bunting family, male Yellowhammers, as can be guessed from their name, are primarily yellow in colour, looking somewhat like grubby canaries. Along with their colour, Yellowhammers are renowned for their singing. To some, the birds' call sounds something like '*a little bit of bread but no cheese*'. Like many of our smaller birds, their numbers have been decreasing in Ireland. They particularly suffer from removal of hedgerows.

The Irish name *Buíóg* means 'little yellow creature'. The English 'Yellowhammer' probably comes from the old English *yelambre* describing its colour, yellow-amber or may come from the German *ammer* meaning 'bunting'. There are a number of other names in English, the most unusual of which is the 'Writing Lark', which derives from the writing-like scribbles on the birds' eggs. The scientific name *Emberiza citrinella* means 'little yellow bunting'.

Beliefs & Traditions: In Irish religious myth, it was believed that if a Yellowhammer began to sing at three in the afternoon, it was a summons to prayer for souls in purgatory.[1] It was also said that a Yellowhammer fluttered around Christ on the cross and was stained with blood, which is still evident in the birds' dirty brown staining. The birds were sometimes called 'Devil's Birds' and in Scotland and Northern Ireland it was believed that they drank a drop of the devil's blood every day in May.[2] A variation says the birds have three drops of the devil's blood within them. A children's rhyme from south Down shows how the birds were regarded:

> *Yellow, yellow, yarling,*
> *You're the devil's darling.*[3]

Cures: It was believed that if a person with jaundice could fix his gaze on a Yellowhammer, the patient would be cured but the bird would die.[4]

CULINARY

Like many small birds, Yellowhammers were a food source in continental Europe and Britain. In Italy especially, they were highly regarded and were often fattened for the table.[5]

NAMES

English: Goldspink,[6] Writing Lark, Yellow Ammer, Yellow Bunting, Yellow Yoldring, Yellow Yellow Yorlin, Yolling (Uls.), Yowling

Irish: Baidheog (yellow bird), Buidéal buí (yellow bottle, Don.), Buidheán[7] (yellow bird), Buidheog (an chinn óir) (golden-headed/yellow bird, Omt.), Cuach bhuidhe (yellow Cuckoo, north Conn.), Diairmín riabhach[8] (little striped Dermot/Jerry), Gealán/Gealún/Gealbhan buidhe (yellow sparrow), Siobháinín bhuí (little yellow Joan, Din.)

Uls. Scots: Chitterareery, Gouldie (Dow.), Yedda Yeldern (Ant.), Yeldren, Yellayoit (Ant.), Yella-Yorlin, Yellayornin, Yellayowt, Yeltie

Scientific: Emberiza flava

FACTS & FIGURES

Resident omnivores. Up to 100,000 breeding pairs and declining (88–91). Live max thirteen years. More likely to be seen in the east. Red list. About forty species of *Emberiza* worldwide. Order: *Passeriformes*; Family: *Emberizidae*.

3.21.2 The Snow Bunting

Gealóg shneachta | *Plectrophenax nivalis*

Beautifully coloured brown and white birds, Snow Buntings visit Ireland in winter from the Arctic north, Iceland and Scotland. The birds are uncommon here, even in winter, but are a delight when found, usually in small flocks. They tend to be quite tolerant of people. As the birds only visit in winter, we are deprived of their beautiful black and white summer plumage. They have a distinctive whistling call. In Northern Ireland, they have the delightful name 'Snowflake'.

The Irish *Gealóg shneachta* means 'bright snow-bird'. The generic *Plectrophenax* is from Greek and refers to the long hind claw. The specific *nivalis* means 'of the snow'.

CULINARY

Snow Buntings were regarded as delicious to eat.

NAMES

English: Mountain Bunting (fem., yng.), Snowflake (Uls.), Tawny Bunting (fem., yng.)

Irish: Liath thruis (Uls.), Liath-thruisc[9]/thraisc/truisc (grey thrush, Ant.)

Scientific: Emberiza glacialis, Emberiza montana, Emberiza mustelina, Emberiza nivalis, Passerina nivalis, Plectrophanes nivalis

FACTS & FIGURES

Rare winter visitors. Omnivores. Live max nine years. Two species of *Plectrophenax* worldwide. Order: *Passeriformes*; Family: *Emberizidae*.

3.21.3 The (Common) Reed Bunting

Gealóg ghiolcaí | *Emberiza schoeniclus schoeniclus*

Small but distinctly coloured birds of reed beds and marshes, Reed Buntings are present in every county in Ireland. The males have unmistakeable black heads and throats, with white moustache-stripes leading down to what looks like a white fur collar. Females are generally dull brown with a distinctive pattern on the head. Males are most often seen sitting prominently on a reed or branch and singing their repetitive song. The birds move to lowlands in winter.

The Irish *giolcaí* means 'of the reeds'. The specific *schoeniclus* is from Greek meaning 'a bird of the reeds'. The birds were widely called Reed Sparrows up to the nineteenth century.

FACTS & FIGURES

Resident omnivores. Widespread. Up to 250,000 breeding pairs (88–91). Live max eleven years. About forty species of *Emberiza* worldwide. Order: *Passeriformes*; Family: *Emberizidae*.

Poetry: from: '*The Song of the Reed Sparrow*'

Mounted on a bended reed
Chanting as my fancies lead,
Tender tales I oft repeat,
Clear, harmonious, soft and sweet.

Anon (eighteenth century)

NAMES

English: Black-headed Bunting, Black-headed Sparrow (Wat.), Black Bonnet (Uls.), Blackcap (Uls.), Blackhead (Uls.), Chink (Uls.), Irish Nightingale,[10] Mary of the trousers[11] (Uls.), Reed Sparrow (Uls.), Ring Rasher (Uls.), Rush Sparrow (Uls.), Water Sparrow, White-winged Moss Cheeper (Uls.)

Irish: Brian na giolcaí/giolcaighe (Brian of the reeds, Gal.), Clochrán cinn duibh (black-headed stone-bird, Ant.), Gealbhan ghiolcaí (reed sparrow), Gealóg ceanndubh (black-headed bunting), Gealóg dhucheannac (black-headed bunting), Gealún giolcaighe (reed sparrow), Strapadóir giolcaighe (reed climber)

Uls. Scots: Corney of the Cravat[12]

Scientific: Cynchramus schoeniclus, Fringilla schoeniclus, Synchramus schoeniclus

3.22 OTHER SMALL LAND BIRDS – ÉANLAITH BEAGA EILE

3.22.1 The (Common) Kingfisher

Cruidín | *Alcedo atthis ispida*

'It was the Rainbow gave thee birth. And left thee all her lovely hues.'[1]

Perhaps Ireland's most brilliantly coloured birds, the elusive Kingfishers are a treasure to find. Favouring quiet streams and nesting in excavated tunnels in alluvial riverbanks, they are most often seen fishing from a favoured perch. The first view of a Kingfisher is usually of an azure streak in flight. About the size of a finch, at rest the magnificent azure-blue back is not so obvious. The wings have a turquoise hue and the lower parts are a rusty red-orange. A white flash on either side completes the colouring of the seemingly oversized head. The bill is dagger-sharp for fishing. Her red/orange lower bill distinguishes the female from the male, the male's being almost all black. The tail is small and stubby.

The nest is a burrow in a vertical sand bank by, or at least close to, a river. The entrance can sometimes be underwater but always leads upwards to a dry nest burrow. Females have been known to fight over males in the breeding season and may have several broods in a good season. They visit the sea only in times of frost and ice, being sensitive to cold weather and river pollution.

The birds have been victims of their own beauty and rarity, being hunted in the nineteenth century for their feathers and simply for their beauty. Many ended up in taxidermists' shops.

In Ireland, Kingfishers were first mentioned by Gerald of Wales in the twelfth century although he does seem to confuse the birds with Dippers.[2]

The specific, *atthis*, means 'Athenian'. *Alcedo* refers to the Greek goddess Alcyone (or Halcyon). The origin of the Irish *cruidín* is unknown. They are known as 'ice birds' in many European languages.

Beliefs & Traditions: Kingfishers were symbols of peace and prosperity. They were a promise of abundance, warmth, prosperity and love. When Noah freed the animals from the ark after the deluge, a Kingfisher was the first to fly away. He got the orange of the setting sun on his breast and the blue of the azure sky on his back.

In Greek myth, Halcyon or Alcyone was the daughter of Aeolus, the god of the wind, and the widow of Ceyx. When Ceyx was tragically drowned, Halcyon drowned herself in grief. The gods took pity on both of them and turned them

255

The (Common) Kingfisher continued

into Kingfishers. Zeus declared that for seven days before and after winter solstice, the winds should not blow. To this day, that two-week period is referred to as the Halcyon Days, now generally taken to mean a calm and happy period of youth. Kingfishers were also believed to have the power to calm the sea during the winter solstice.

> *Alcyone compress'd*
> *Seven days sits brooding on her watery nest,*
> *A wintry queen; her sire at length is kind,*
> *Calms every storm and hushes every wind.*

Ovid,[3] Metamorphoses XI (translated by Dryden)

from: '*The Indian Emperor*' (a play)

> *In this safe place let me secure your fear:*
> *No clashing swords, no noise can enter here.*
> *Amidst our arms as quiet you shall be*
> *As halcyons brooding on a winter sea.*

John Dryden (1665)

It was believed that a Kingfisher in full plumage is an antidote against certain diseases. In addition, when stuffed and suspended by a thread its bill points in the direction of the prevailing wind.[4] Variations suggested that the suspended bird's bill would point in one direction for good weather and another for bad weather.[5] Gerald of Wales believed that their dead bodies would not rot and recommended keeping them between clothes in order to keep moths away and give a pleasant perfume. He also believed that if they were hung by the bill (when dead), they would get a new set of feathers every year. Gerald also mentions 'martinets' which he described as frequenting rivers. He seems to confuse Kingfishers and Dippers, which he may have taken as male and female.[6]

PLACE NAMES

Bealach an Chruidín (Co. Cavan) (the Kingfisher's way).

NAMES

English: Halcyon

Irish: Biorra an uisce (water spear[7]), Cáirneach, Cruideán, Earrach[8] (tail), Gabha uisce[9] (water blacksmith), Iascadóir (fisher), Iascaire coirneach[10] (tonsured fisherman), Murlach (mara) (sea Kingfisher), Rí-iascaire (king-fisher, Conn.)

Scientific: Alcedo ispida, Gracula atthis

FACTS & FIGURES

Resident carnivores. Present in almost every county, except in the far west. Up to 2,500 breeding pairs (88–91). Live max twenty-one years. Common name: a concentration of Kingfishers. Amber list. About 100 species of *Alcedinidae* (Kingfishers) including about seventeen species of *Alcedo* worldwide. Order: *Coraciiformes*; Family: *Alcedinidae*.

3.22.2 The (Eurasian) Skylark

Fuiseog | *Alauda arvensis arvensis,*
Alauda arvensis scotica (Celtic Skylark)

Hail to thee, blithe Spirit![11]

What Skylarks lack in colour, they make up for in song. Of all birdsong, the Skylark's has perhaps inspired more poetry than has any other. There is hardly a greater expression of freedom and beauty than a Skylark singing high in the clear morning air.

Spotted brown birds about the size of wagtails, Skylarks have a crest that is not always visible. The unusually long rear claw is probably an adaptation for walking on grass. Sexes are alike and they are monogamous and lifelong mates. The birds are more often heard than seen. They sing high in the sky (up to sixty metres up) and are quite difficult to pick out, often seen as just a hovering speck. On completion of the trilling song, they descend vertically into vegetation, usually long grass. If the spot is noted, the Skylark can be approached and identified on the ground. Skylark numbers have suffered greatly in the past for their culinary value. When caught they were either eaten or exported, usually to France, for food. More recently, numbers have declined greatly since changes in farming methods have removed many of their favoured grass meadows.

The generic *Alauda* is from Latin, meaning 'lark' while the specific *arvensis* is from the Latin *arvus* meaning 'field', so, an *Alauda arvensis* is a 'field lark'. The etymology of the Irish *fuiseog* is unclear.

The (Eurasian) Skylark cont'd

Beliefs & Traditions: Skylarks were symbols of merriment, hope, happiness, good fortune and creativity and it was thought very unlucky to interfere with a lark's nest. Skylarks were purported to have three spots on their tongues. Each spot represented a curse and if you ate a Skylark, you would bring the three curses down upon you. Larks were supposed to be sacred to St Brigid as they woke her to her prayers each morning.[12] If a lark was heard on the morning of St Brigid's Day,[13] the day would be sunny and those who heard it would enjoy great fortune throughout the year.[14] Some thought that hearing a lark in the morning on any day would bring good weather.[15]

Proverbs & Similes:

As happy as a lark . . .

As melodious as a lark . . .

Every bird as it is reared and the lark for the bog . . . (The innate nature of things.)

There is an old saying, 'up with the lark', referring to those of us who rise early in the morning . . . it was one of the first birds to sing in the morning.

When the sky falls we will all catch larks. (Said to mock someone with high-flying plans.)

Chomh binn leis an fhuiseog . . . (As sweet as the skylark.)

Poetry: from '*To a Skylark*'[16]

Hail to thee, blithe Spirit!
Bird thou never wert,
That from Heaven, or near it,
Pourest thy full heart
In profuse strains of unpremeditated art.

Percy Bysshe Shelley (c. 1820)

CULINARY

Skylarks were widely eaten in Ireland and continental Europe. They were also kept as pets in Dublin and Belfast.

PLACE NAMES

Carnwhissock, Co. Antrim (Carn Fuiseog, lark's cairn)
Clogheenafishoge, Co. Waterford (Cloichín na Fuiseoige, little rock of the lark)
Cnocán Fuiseóige, Co. Waterford (the lark's hill)
Herbertstown, Co. Limerick (Cathair Fuiseog, lark city)
Kilnahushogue, Co. Tyrone (Coill na hUiseoige, lark wood)
Larkhill, Co. Dublin (Cnoc na Fuiseoige, lark hill[17])
Rathnafushogue, Co. Carlow (lark fort)

NAMES

English: Field Lark, Common Lark

Irish: Circín starraiceach/ struiceach (crested little hen, Din.), Fuise, Fuiseog stairiceach (crested lark), Riabh (streak), Riabhóg[18] (bheag) ([little] pipit, fem., Uls.), Uiseog (Omt., Uls.)

Uls. Scots: Laverock, Leverock (Ant.)

Scientific: Alauda vulgaris

FACTS & FIGURES

Resident omnivores. Widespread in all counties. Up to a half million breeding pairs (88–91) with wintering numbers increased by visiting birds. Live max nine years. Collective name: An exaltation of Skylarks. Amber list. About 100 species of *Alaudidae* (larks) including three species of *Alauda* worldwide. Order: *Passeriformes*; Family: *Alaudidae*.

3.22.3 The Dunnock

Donnóg | *Prunella modularis hebridium* (Celtic Dunnock)
Prunella modularis occidentalis (British Dunnock)

Dunnocks or Hedge Sparrows are very common Irish birds. They are the only Irish members of the group called Accentors that live largely in the mountains of Europe and Asia. Quite shy, they tend to scavenge on the ground beneath bird tables rather than visiting the tables themselves. They are a spotty brown on top with a gunmetal grey on the breast and face. Males and females are alike. The common Irish name *Donnóg* translates as 'brown bird' while the scientific *Prunella modularis* translates as 'little brown singer'. The Irish language also has the delightful names *Bráthair an dreoilín* (Wren's brother) and *Máthair chéile* (Mother-in-law).

Beliefs & Traditions: The Dunnock's blue-green eggs were regarded as charms against witches' spells when strung out along the hob. They were especially good for keeping witches and spirits from coming down the chimney.[19]

NAMES

English: Black Wren, Blue Wran (Uls.), Field Sparrow (Uls.), Grey Robin (Uls.), Hedge Accentor, Hedge Sparrow, Hedge Warbler, Hedgeling (Uls.), Reefouge (ríabhóg: a pipit), Shuffle Wing (Uls.), Whin Sparrow (Uls.), Winter Fauvette

Irish: Bod ar dris (bramble vagrant, s. Conn.), Bráthair an dreoilín (Wren's brother), Caológ riabhach (Aran.),[20] Ciológ, Dreoilín gorm (blue Wren, May.), Gealbhan bruaigh (bank sparrow), Gealbhan caoch (blind sparrow[21]), Gealbhan claí/claidhe/cloidhe (fence sparrow), Gealbhan coille (wood sparrow), Gealbhan garrdha (garden sparrow, Conn.), Gealbhan gleoidh (quarrelsome sparrow, Mun.), Gealbhán tor (bush sparrow, Kry.), Gob ramhar (fat beak, Kry.), Máthair chéile (mother-in-law, Conn.), Riabhóg (streaked-bird)[22]

Uls. Scots: Futtock

Scientific: Accentor modularis, Motacilla modularis, Tharraleus modularis.

FACTS & FIGURES

Resident omnivores. Widespread in all counties. Up to one million pairs and increasing (88–91). Live max eleven years. About thirteen species of *Prunella* (accentors) worldwide making up the entire family of *Prunellidae*. Order: *Passeriformes*; Family: *Prunellidae*.

3.22.4 The (European) Robin

Spideog | *Erithacus rubecula melophilus*

'A Robin Redbreast in a cage, puts all Heaven in a Rage.'[23]

Robins are among Ireland's most well-known and well-loved birds. Adult males and females are alike, being largely brown above, white below and with the conspicuous red breast and face, edged with grey. Being relatively comfortable in human company, they are apt to follow close behind in hope of a disturbed meal. This familiar behaviour is only seen in Britain and Ireland; elsewhere they are shy from years of hunting. Known alternatively as Christmas Birds or Robin Redbreasts, they are very territorial and fights between males are not uncommon, some resulting in death. They will chase other species, such as Dunnocks, out of their territories, as they compete for the same food. A Robin's song is probably one of the most beautiful to be heard in the Irish countryside and often, neighbouring birds can be heard answering. They are the only Irish birds that sing all year round, and outside the breeding season both males and females sing. In spring, males sing from prominent perches to attract females and declare the boundaries of their territories. When a prospective female approaches a singing male, she has to be quite careful as the highly aggressive male can mistake her for a rival and attack, both sexes seemingly looking alike even to a Robin. Once bonded, a pair can have more than one brood of chicks per year. In conveyer-belt-like procession, the male will feed chicks from the first brood while the female sits on the eggs of the next.

The generic *Erithacus* comes from the Greek *erithakos* meaning 'solitary' and the specific *rubecula* is from Latin meaning 'little red one'. The etymology of the Irish *spideog* is not clear but it may derive from *spid* meaning 'activity' or 'energy', or it may simply be an old name for the species.

Beliefs & Traditions: Robins were symbols of domestic peace and tranquillity and the mariner's symbol of hope and it was particularly bad luck to kill or even capture one. '*Whoever kills a Robin Redbreast will never have good luck were they to live a thousand years*'.[24] It was also said that the hand of he who killed a Robin would shake endlessly or that a large lump would appear on the right hand. If the Robin-killer owned cows, the milk would become blood-coloured. Even the breaking of a Robin's eggs would result in something belonging to the breaker being broken.

In counties Kerry, Limerick and Tipperary, if not elsewhere, it was the custom amongst boys never to kill a Robin caught in a trap. If one was found in a trap instead of a desired Blackbird or thrush, the Robin was brought home and a small piece of printed paper was placed in the Robin's bill. The Robin was addressed: '*Spideog, you must promise an oath on the book in your beak that you will send a blackbird or a thrush into my trap. If you do not, the next time I catch you, I'll kill you, and I now pull out your tail as a sign, that I'll know you from any other robin*'. The tail feather was then pulled out and the Robin released, usually up the chimney. The threat was an idle one, as no one would dare kill a Robin. If a Robin without a tail was found again, it was merely threatened a second time and released.[25]

People used to say that a cat would not chase a Robin. Others believed that if a cat killed a Robin, the cat would subsequently lose a limb.[26] This is not borne out in practice as young Robins are killed by cats in large numbers.

In Irish religious belief, a Robin is said to have helped Christ on the cross by trying to pick thorns from his head and staunch the flow of blood. As a result, blood splashed on the Robin, from which he got his red breast.[27] Other traditions say that Robins got their red breasts from taking water into Hell for sinners, whilst others say that a Robin helped the baby Jesus by keeping the fire alight in the stable with the flapping of his wings. A Robin was also said to have helped the Virgin Mary on her flight into Egypt. Mary was cut by brambles and dripped blood but the Robin followed behind and covered the blood trail with leaves.[28] A similar story has a bleeding Christ fleeing from pursuing soldiers when a Robin mops up each drop of blood with its breast and Christ escapes.[29]

There was an old tradition that the Robin and the Wren were husband and wife: '*The robin redbreast and the wren are God's almighty cock and hen*'.[30] As noted in the chapter on Wrens, in pre-Christian tradition in Britain and Ireland, the Robin Redbreast and Jenny Wren may have represented summer and winter and thus light and dark respectively. Wrens were hunted at the end of winter to usher

The (European) Robin continued

in the summer while Robins were hunted at the end of summer to usher in the winter. Robins were associated with the Celtic god of light, Bel[31] (or Bile or Belenos) while Wrens and Ravens were associated with Bran who was fond of battle and carnage. The tales of Robin Hood and his fight against the forces of darkness may further reflect this tradition. The hunting of the Robin is recorded in the children's rhyme 'Who Killed Cock Robin', below.

A Robin entering the house was a sign of a death in the family in most parts of Ireland but a sign of good luck in other parts. A wish made upon seeing the first Robin in spring will come true, but only if the wish is completed before the Robin flies away.

It was widely believed that if a Robin came across the body of a dead person, it would carefully cover it with leaves and other vegetation until it was completely hidden.[32]

Cures: Robins were believed to provide a cure for depression. The remedy suggests a Robin must be killed and its heart removed. The heart should then be stitched into a sachet and worn around the neck on a cord.[33]

Weather: In the southeast it was believed that if a Robin entered a house it was a sign of snow or frost.[34] A Robin singing likewise indicated a coming storm.

Proverbs & Similes:

Chomh haibí le spideog.
(As frisky as a robin, i.e. as fresh as a daisy.)

Poetry: from: '*Who killed Cock Robin?*'

'*I,*' said the Sparrow,
'*With my bow and arrow,*
I killed Cock Robin.'

Anonymous

PLACE NAMES

Graignaspidogue/
Graignaspideog/
Graigue-na-Spideog, Co. Carlow
(hamlet of the Robin)

NAMES

English: Christmas Bird, God's Bird (Uls.), Redbreast, Ruddock

Irish: Broinn-dearg (Ant., Insh.), Broinndearg (red breast, Insh., Ant.), Broinndeargán, (Spideog) Spideog mhuintir Uí Shúilleabháin (Robin of the O'Sullivan clan), Spideog Mhuire (the Virgin Mary's Robin, Kry.), Spiordóg (Din.)

Uls. Scots: Roabin (Ant.), Spiddiock

Scientific: Dandalus rubecula, Erythaca rubecula, Luscinia rubecula, Motacilla rubecula, Sylvia rubecula

FACTS & FIGURES

Resident omnivores. Up to 2.5 million breeding pairs (88–91). Live max seventeen years. The national bird of the United Kingdom. Three species of *Erithacus* worldwide. Order: *Passeriformes*; Family: *Muscicapidae*.

3.22.5 The (Common) Redstart

Earrdheargán | *Phoenicurus phoenicurus phoenicurus*

& the Black Redstart

Earrdheargán dubh | *Phoenicurus ochruros gibraltariensis*

Redstart

Black Redstart

Redstarts are rare yet consistent visitors to Ireland. Strikingly coloured, the name 'redstart' means 'red tail' and the birds are renowned for, and almost uniquely identified by, their bright rust-red tails. About the size of a House Sparrow, males have a distinctive black face and throat, rust-red underparts and delicate grey head and upperparts. Females are generally a dull brown but have the distinctive red tail. The Irish *earrdheargán* means 'red tail'. The scientific *phoenicurus* is from Greek also meaning 'red tail'.

Close cousins of the Common Redstarts, Black Redstarts are rare visitors to Ireland in winter. Unlike Common Redstarts, Black Redstarts tend to favour industrial sites and old ruins. Both male and female Black Redstarts have the rust-red tail but the males are largely black, fading to charcoal and then grey on the lower parts with distinctive white barring on the wings. The females are like female Common Redstarts but generally darker in colour. In winter, when we are most likely to see the birds, their colours are dulled. The females of both species can only be confused with the slightly larger Nightingales, which also have rust-red tails, but are hardly ever found in Ireland. The Irish *Earrdheargán dubh* means 'black red-tail' and the specific *ochruros* means 'ochre-coloured'.

NAMES

REDSTART
English: (Fanny) Redtail, Firetail, Quickstart

Irish: Ceann dearg (red-head, Kry.), Ceanndeargán (red-head, Don.),

Scientific: Motacilla phoenicurus, Phoenicura ruticilla, Ruticilla phoenicurus, Sylvia phoenicurus

BLACK REDSTART
English: Tithys Redstart

Scientific: Motacilla phoenicurus, Motacilla tithys, Phoenicura tithys, Ruticilla tithys, Sylvia tithys

FACTS & FIGURES

REDSTART: Rare summer visitors. Omnivorous. No more than ten breeding pairs (88–91). Amber list. Live max ten years.

BLACK REDSTART: Rare winter visitors. Omnivorous. A handful visit. Live max ten years.

About ten species of *Phoenicurus* worldwide. Order: *Passeriformes*; Family: *Muscicapidae*.

263

3.22.6 The (European) Stonechat

Caislín cloch | *Saxicola rubicola*[35] *hibernans* (Western Stonechat)

& the Whinchat

Caislín aitinn | *Saxicola rubetra*

Stonechat   Whinchat

Of the fourteen species of chat or Stonechat worldwide, only two, the European Stonechats and Whinchats can be seen in Ireland. Very distinctive birds in terms of colour and voice, Stonechats are often seen and heard perched atop a bush. Male Stonechats have a black head, dark uppers and wings, a white collar and wing flashes, and a deep amber breast. Females appear like dulled pastel versions of the males. Both are duller in winter. The 'chat' call, sounding a little like two stones banging together, distinguishes the birds from all others except perhaps their close cousins the Whinchats. The Irish *Caislín cloch* translates roughly as 'stone chatterer'. The generic *saxicola* is from Latin meaning 'rock-dweller' and the specific *rubicola* probably means 'bramble dweller' from the Latin *rubus* meaning 'bramble'.

Whinchats arrive in Ireland only in summer. From a distance, they look somewhat like drab Stonechats though they are somewhat more slender. Males have a dark head with prominent white collar and eye stripe. The upperparts and wings are mottled brown with white flashes and the breast is dull amber. The underparts are a dirty white. Females look like highly faded males and can be confused with female

NAMES

STONECHAT

English: Blacky Cap, Blacky Top, Blackcap (Uls.), Chatter-Stone, Furzecap (Wat.), Stone Chatterer

Irish: Bod an dris[37] (bramble vagrant), Caipín aitinn (little-capped-furze-bird, Conn.), Caisdín cloiche (stone-bird), Caislín dearg (red chat [male], Don.), Caistín fá chloich[38] (stone-bird, Kry.), Claochrán (stone-bird, Farney, Mona.), Donncha an chaipín (male, Denis with the cap, Din.), Guistín cloiche (stone chat, Cla.),[39] Máirín an triúis (fem., little Mary with the trousers, Din.), Siobhán an chinn duibh (black-headed Joan)

Uls. Scots: Corney of the Cravat[40]

Scientific: Motacilla rubicola, Motacilla torquata, Pratincola rubicola, Saxicola torquata, Sylvia rubicolla

STONECHAT

English: Furzechatterer, Stonechat, Whinny Gray[41] (Uls.)

Irish: Gorán (Whinchat, Kry.)

Scientific: Motacilla rubetra, Pratincola rubetra, Sylvia rubetra

Stonechats from a distance. They are very sensitive to winter cold. The specific *rubetra* means 'of the brambles'. The Irish *Caislín aitinn* means roughly 'whin chatterer'.

Beliefs & Traditions: It was believed that each Stonechat contained a drop of the devil's blood and that it's young were hatched by a toad (see also the Wheatear).[36]

Poetry: from '*Addressed to a Young Lady*'
    Where scarce the foxglove peeps, or thistle's beard;
    And restless stone-chat, all day long, is heard.

William Wordsworth, 1787

FACTS & FIGURES

STONECHAT: Resident omnivores. Present in most counties. Up to 20,000 breeding pairs and increasing (88–91). Live max eight years. Amber list.

WHINECHAT: Scarce summer visitors. Omnivores. Present in the midlands and northwest. Up to 2,500 breeding pairs (88–91). Live max five years. Amber list.

About fourteen species of *Saxicola* worldwide. Order: *Passeriformes*; Family: *Muscicapidae*.

3.22.7 The (Northern) Wheatear

Clochrán | *Oenanthe oenanthe oenanthe* (Northern Wheatear)
              Oenanthe oenanthe leucorhoa (Greenland Wheatear)

Elusive summer visitors to Ireland, Wheatears are interesting for their name, if for nothing else, the current name being derived from the original 'white arse'. Male Wheatears are generally grey on top, orange-buff fading to white below with dark wings, a dark 'mask' and a characteristic white rump. As the summer goes on the grey slowly fades to brown-grey. They can be recognised from a distance by the upturned black 'T' pattern at the base of the tail. Females are less distinctive looking generally dull-brown above with faded amber face and breast but with the same white rump and inverted black 'T' on the tail. Wheatears are often the first migrants to arrive in early summer. Their call is something of a *check* sound, which probably gives rise to the northern name 'Stone Checker'. Wheatears spend winter in Africa, south of the Sahara.

The (Northern) Wheatear continued

The Irish *Clochrán* translates roughly as 'stone bird'. The scientific *oenanthe* is from Greek meaning 'grape flower' and may date back to the days when Wheatears migrated to Greece in spring in time for the grape vine blossoms.

Beliefs & Traditions: An unusual belief about Wheatears pertained also to Stonechats and Yellowhammers. These birds were persecuted in parts of the UK and perhaps Ireland because it was believed that toads sat on and hatched their eggs and toads were universally disliked. It has been suggested that this may be because toads would sometimes legitimately frequent the stones where these birds built their nests.[42]

Like many migratory birds that come to us in summer, Wheatears were believed to hibernate underground, in a torpid state, for the winter.

In Scotland, Wheatears were known (in Scots Gaelic) as *Fear na Feill Padruig*, the St Patrick's Day bird, because they were said to first appear on that day (17 March).[43]

Proverbs & Similes:

Ar dhath ubh an chlochráin
(the colour of the Wheatear's egg, e.g. blue-grey).

PLACE NAMES

Clochran (Clochrán), Co. Dublin, Carraig Na Clochrán (Wheatear rock), Bluestack Mountains, Co. Donegal

NAMES

English: Fallowchat, Stagger Stone (Uls.), Stone-Checker (Uls.), Stonechat, Stonehammer (Tipp.), White-Arse, Whitetail

Irish: Caislín cloch (Stonechat), Caislín tónbhán (white-rumped Stonechat) Din.), Caistín fá chloich,[44] Casúr-fá-chloch, Casúr cloch (stone hammer, Tipp.), Claochrán (Farney, Uls.), Claothrán, Cloibhrean cloich (north and west), Coistín faoi cloich[45] (Kry.), Guirtín cloiche (stone chatterer, Cla.)[46]

Uls. Scots: Stanechacker

Scientific: Motacilla oenanthe, Pratincola rubetra, Saxicola oenanthe, Sylvia oenanthe, Vitiflora aenanthe

FACTS & FIGURES

Summer visitors to coastal areas. Largely insectivorous. Up to 10,000 breeding pairs (88–91). Live max nine years. Over twenty species of *Oenanthe* worldwide. Order: *Passeriformes*; Family: *Muscicapidae*.

CULINARY

At one time Wheatears were much more common in Ireland and were readily eaten and considered a delicacy. Bewick reported that many were taken in England, with snares placed in square holes cut into the turf where they like to hunt for worms, and were sold for sixpence a dozen.

In Victorian times, in particular, they were taken in big numbers for the restaurant, particularly in autumn when they had fattened themselves for winter.

3.22.8 The (White-throated) Dipper

Gabha dubh | *Cinclus cinclus hibernicus* (Irish Dipper)

Cinlcus cinclus gularis (British Dipper)

Dippers look like oversized Wrens with white aprons and this may contribute to their Irish name *Gabha dubh* or blacksmith. They are generally brown all over with white throat and breast and narrow chestnut breast band. The British and continental races vary slightly. The Irish race, (*C. cinclus hibernicus*) has a narrower chestnut band than the British Dipper and the Continental Dipper has no chestnut band at all.

Though resident in most counties, they are rarely seen. Dippers live on fast-flowing rivers and usually build their nests as close to water as possible. Strong and sturdy, they can walk and swim through fast currents, hopping from rock to rock. They can be seen standing stoutly in the midst of a torrent, constantly 'dipping' in a curtsey-like fashion.

The word 'Dipper' itself refers to the bobbing motion while standing in water. The old name Water Ouzel means 'water-blackbird', which corresponds with the alternative Irish name *Lon abhann* (river blackbird). They were believed, incorrectly, to be of the thrush family, though they are distantly related. *Cinclus* is from Greek meaning 'tail-wagging bird'.

Beliefs & Traditions: In parts of England, Dippers were believed to be female Kingfishers.[47] Gerald of Wales describes 'martinets' in Ireland which he described as frequenting rivers. He seems to be confusing Kingfishers and Dippers, which he may have taken as male and female.[48] In Ireland in the nineteenth century, if a large number of Water Ouzels (Dippers) appeared at an unfrequented locality, it was not only a sign of abundant freshwater fish but also a warning of the approach of malignant disease.[49]

Cures: A Dipper-skin worn on the stomach was said to be an aid for indigestion.[50]

NAMES

English: Kingfisher, River Pie/Pye, Water Blackbird, Water Ouzel, Water Owl

Irish: Gabha/Gobha (dubh) uisce (water blacksmith), Lon abhann (river Blackbird/ouzel), Lon uisce (water Blackbird), Tomaire/ Tumaire (Dipper)

Uls. Scots: Bessy Dooker, Ducker

Scientific: Cinclus aquaticus, Cinclus europaeus, Cinclus melanogaster, Hydrobata cinclus, Sturnus cinclus

FACTS & FIGURES

Resident carnivores. Up to 10,000 breeding pairs (88–91). Live max ten years. The national bird of Norway. About five species of *Cinclus* worldwide making up the entire *Cinclidae* family. Order: *Passeriformes*; Family: *Cinclidae*.

3.22.9 The (Winter) Wren

Dreoilín | *Troglodytes troglodytes indigenus* (British Wren)
Troglodytes troglodytes troglodytes (European Wren)

'The wran, the wran, the king of the Birds, St Stephen's Day was caught in the furze.'

Today, the 'king of the birds' is common in Ireland. Known as *Dreoilín* in Irish, Wrens have a very distinctive call and are some of the loudest birds you will hear, despite their size. They are short, dumpy birds, with a stubby tail and showing an all-round mottled brown colour. Sexes are alike. Highly territorial, they have been known to fall off their perches with the exhaustion of singing. Although the official name is the 'Winter Wren', heavy winters take their toll on their tiny bodies. While normally quite solitary during daylight, they are known to huddle together in large Wren 'clumps' to shelter from the cold at night. They suffer greatly in cold winters. They are not the smallest birds in Ireland, or indeed Europe. That honour goes to the Goldcrests (*Cíorbhuí*), another locally common species. Male Wrens are cocks, females are jennys. Males will often build several nests as part of the courtship ritual. If successful, a female will select one and the others will be abandoned.

The name 'wren' probably comes from the old English *wrenne* meaning 'a short tail'. The scientific name *troglodytes* means 'hole-' or 'cave-dweller'. The Irish *Dreoilín* is an ancient name and may be a derivative of *drui-éan* meaning 'druid-bird' as the birds are believed to have had a long history of use in augury by the ancient druids and were referred to, in English, as 'druid's birds'.

Beliefs & Traditions: The antipathy of the church towards Wrens may reflect their historic association with the druids of Ireland who regarded Wrens as sacred and used their musical notes for divination. They were called *magus avium* (the magic or 'druid' bird) and auguries were taken from them. They were regarded as messengers of the gods, and the goddess Clíona was said to sometimes take the form of a Wren. The story of St Moling supports the Christian Church's antipathy. St Moling was said to keep three animals, a fox, a fly and a Wren. One day the Wren killed the fly. In anger and grief, the saint cursed the bird with the words 'let his dwelling be forever in empty houses, with a wet drip therein continually, and may children be destroying him'.[51]

In any case, in later years, Wrens were regarded as treacherous. According to legend, a Wren is reputed to have betrayed Irish warriors fighting the Vikings at Doolin, by beating its wings on their shields and pecking on a drum, giving them away.[52] Another tradition suggests that while Irish troops were preparing an attack on Cromwell, Wrens came and tapped on the Irish drums, rousing Cromwell's soldiers who proceeded to kill the Irish soldiers.[53] Yet another tells that a Wren saved the forces of King William from those of James II in the seventeenth century. In a different variation, a Wren is charged with betraying St Stephen, the first Christian martyr, to the Romans.[54] Finally, a chirping Wren is blamed for giving away Christ in the Garden of Gethsemane to the soldiers and the servants of the high priest.[55]

For one or more of these reasons, Wrens were hunted on St Stephen's Day and, perhaps originally, on days leading up to and including Christmas Day. They were hunted with two sticks; one to beat the bushes and one to throw at the bird.[56] Today, the 'Wran Boys' (*Lucht an Dreoilín*) or 'Mummers' enact the hunting of the Wren every 26 December (St Stephen's Day, *Lá an Dreoilín* – The Day of the Wren). Groups of locals dress up in a range of costumes, the most traditional being a three-piece straw suit (Jack Straw). Some men dress as women. Originally, the dead Wrens were tied to a pole or nailed to a holly or birch branch[57] and carried from house to house. Money was demanded. If none was given, the Wren was buried on the doorstep, which was a great insult to the family living therein.[58] Money gained in this way was often used to pay for a New Year's dance. Today, the Wren Boys take to the streets singing and dancing and sometimes still call to houses for money. Wrens are no longer caught. The actual hunting of the Wren probably died out in the nineteenth century, at least in some places. In 1845 the Mayor of Cork issued a proclamation with the intention to 'prevent cruelty to animals' in which the hunting and killing of the Wren on St Stephen's Day was forbidden.[59] The tradition is largely absent from most parts of Ulster.

The mummers' song follows:[60]

'The Mummer's Song'

> The wran, the wran, the king of the birds
> St Stephen's Day was caught in the furze
> Up with the kettle and down with the pan
> Give 's a penny to bury the wran.

And another variation:[61]

> The wren, the wren, the king of all birds,
> St Stephen's Day was caught in the furze;
> Although he is little, his family's great,
> I pray you, good landlady, give us a treat.
>
> My box, it would speak, if it had but a tongue,
> And two or three shillings would do it no wrong,
> Sing holly, sing ivy – sing ivy, sing holly,
> A drop just to drink, it would drown melancholy.

The (Winter) Wren continued

And if you draw it of the best
I hope your soul in heaven may rest;
But if you draw it of the small,
It won't agree with the wren-boys at all.

The following version is from the Waterford and Youghal areas. The last three verses are from Waterford:[62]

To Mr . . . we've brought the wran,
He is the best gentleman in the land:
Put in your hand, pull out your purse.
And give us something for the poor wran!!

The wran, the wran, the king of all birds,
St Stephen's Day was caught in the furze;
Although he's little, his family's great, –
I pray, young landlady you'll fill us a treat!

Chorus: *Sing overem, overem, droleen:*
Sing overem, overem, chitimicore, hebemegola, tambereen

If you fill it of the small
It won't agree with our boys at all:
But if you fill it of the best,
I hope your soul in Heaven may rest!

Chorus . . .

It is the wran, as you may see,
'Tis guarded in a holly tree;
A bunch of ribands by his side,
And the . . . boys to be his guide.

Chorus . . .

On Christmas Day I turned the spit,
I burned my fingers, I feel it yet:
Between my finger and my thumb
I eat the roast meat every crumb.

Chorus . . .

We were all day hunting the wren,
We were all day hunting the wren;
The wren so cute, and we so cunning,
He stayed in the bush while we were running.

Chorus . . .

When we went out to cut the holly
All our boys were brisk and jolly;
We cut it down all in a trice,
Which made our Wren boys to rejoice.

Chorus . . .

Similar traditions can still be seen in parts of Scotland, England and France. On the Isle of Man, a Wren caught during the St Stephen's Day hunt was kept for the rest of the year and was brought aboard a herring boat to keep bad spirits at bay. Sometimes only the feathers were brought aboard.[63]

It may be that the tradition of the hunting of the Wren is an echo of an older pre-Christian tradition across Britain and Ireland. The origin of this tradition is lost in time but it was believed the god Midir went Wren hunting. The Wren represented winter or indeed the gods of winter, while the Robin represented spring or summer. The hunting of the Wren was symbolic of the death of winter and the birth of spring/summer. Similarly, there may have been a now-lost tradition of hunting the Robin at the end of summer. This may be recorded in the children's rhyme 'Who killed Cock Robin' (see entry under Robin). Despite the antipathy towards it, it was considered very bad luck to kill a Wren or destroy its nest on any day other than St Stephen's Day. Such an act would result in a death in the family.

On a lighter note, most Irish schoolchildren know the 'king of the birds' fairytale. The birds held a parliament one day to decide who would be their king. Whoever could fly the highest would be sovereign. Ultimately, the eagle flew highest but the Wren had hitched a ride on his back and flew out to win the day. The origin of this fable is probably very old indeed as the Roman historian Pliny[64] referred to the *trochilus*[65] as the 'king of the birds' in AD 77 and the story is widespread across Europe. Swainson tells us that there is a sequel to this story common in Ireland and Norway. Having lost the competition, the eagle flew into a rage. He caught the Wren and flew up high in the sky and dropped him to the ground. As a result of the trauma the Wren lost half of his tail and has been without ever since.[66]

The (Winter) Wren continued

Proverbs & Similes:

'A wren in the hand is better than a crane to be caught.'

'Cé gur beag díol dreoilín caithfidh sé a sholáthar.'
(Little as a wren needs, it must gather it.)

Chomh beag le dreoilín.
(As small as a wren)

Chomh meidhreach le dreoilín teaspaigh.
(As gay as an exuberant wren.)

Is leor don dreoilín a nead.
(A wren only has need for its nest.)

Dealbh an dreoilín (Mona.),
'the size of the wren' meaning tiny or nothing.

The fox is the most cunning beast in the world, barring the wren.[67]

The robin and the wren are God's two holy men.

PLACE NAMES

Carndroleen, Co. Waterford
(Carn an Dreolín, Wren's cairn)
Drumdran, Co. Fermanagh/
Co. Tyrone (Droim Drean,
Wren ridge)
Loch na nDreolan (The Wren's
Hollow, Bluestack Mountains, Don.)

NAMES

English: Chitty Wren, Common Wren, Cutty (small) Wren, Devil's Bird, Druid's Bird, God's Hen (Uls.), Jenny Wren, Kitty Wren, Northern Wren, Sally,[68] Tit (Uls.), Titty Wren (Uls.), Wran

Irish: Deireoilín, Draoi éan (druid bird), Drean (Uls., from Scots Gaelic), Dreoileacán, Dreolán (Uls.), Dreolín

Uls. Scots: Chitty-Wran (Ant.), Jinny-Wran (Ant.), Wran

Scientific: Anorthura troglodytes, Motacilla troglodytes, Nannus troglodytes, Sylvia troglodytes, Troglodytes europaeus, Troglodytes parvulus

FACTS & FIGURES

Resident omnivores. Widespread in all counties. Up to 2.5 million breeding birds and increasing (88–91). Weigh 9 g. Was the sacred bird of the Isle of Man. Live max six years. About ten species of *Troglodytes* worldwide. Order: *Passeriformes*; Family: *Troglodytidae*.

3.22.10 The (Bohemian) Waxwing

Síodeiteach | *Bombycilla garrulus garrulus*

The (Bohemian) Waxwing continued

Waxwings are stunning, exotic birds, with outrageous colouring and prominent crests. Waxwings show a base pinky-brown colour, darker above than below, with black chin, face mask and wing markings. They show white flashes on the face and wings, yellow wing flashes and yellow and black tail ends. The picture is completed with bright waxy red wing flashes, and the prominent crest. Now very rare winter visitors, they are amongst a number of uncommon species that 'irrupt' in great numbers from time to time. Waxwings live in Arctic Scandinavia and Russia. After a year with an excessive berry crop their numbers grow enormously and they must travel overseas, to countries like Ireland and Britain, to find food. They are usually seen on trees with small berries or other fruit and can be quite approachable. The birds are very similar to their American cousins, the Cedar Waxwings (*Bombycilla cedrorum*).

Waxwings get their name from their protruding secondary feathers which look like red sealing wax, from which we get the Irish name *síodeiteach* meaning 'silk-wing'. The root word *síod* also refers to fairies and 'fairy-wing' is at least a plausible name in light of the relationship of the birds with banshees, for which see section on 'Beliefs'. The scientific name *Bombycilla garrulus* translates roughly as 'chattering silk-tail'.

Beliefs & Traditions: It was believed that banshees used Waxwings as torches to guide them through the night.[69] It was also said that no man has ever found a Waxwing's nest,[70] which is probably true in Ireland as they mostly nest in Scandinavia. Waxwings' nesting habits were unknown until some nests and eggs were found in Lapland in 1856 by a British ornithologist.

Weather: The appearance of Waxwings presaged a harsh winter.

NAMES

English: Bohemian Chatterer, Silk Tail, Waxen Chatterer

Irish: Sciathán céarach (wax wing)

Scientific: Ampelis garrulus, Bombycilla garrula, Bombyciphora garrulus, Lanius garrulus

FACTS & FIGURES

Winter visitors. Omnivores. Mostly absent. Normally only a handful in winter with large numbers along the east coast in irruption years. Live max six years. Eight species of *Bombycillidae* including three species of *Bombycilla* worldwide. Order: *Passeriformes*; Family: *Bombycillidae*.

The (Eurasian) Treecreeper

3.22.11

Snag | *Certhia familiaris britannica*

Treecreepers are beautiful but secretive brown birds of the forest and on occasion, the garden. They show a light mottled-brown on top, with dirty white under-parts, a white eye-stripe and a small curved bill. Sexes are alike. In Irish, they are named *Snag*, which they share with woodpeckers and Magpies (*Snag breac*). In fact, their habit of continually 'cleaning' trees of insects has gained them the alternative name woodpecker in Ireland although there are no true woodpeckers here. Treecreepers make a habit of clearing a tree trunk of insects from bottom to top whilst slowly spiralling up the trunk, looking a little like adventurous mice. They have specially adapted curved needle-bills for reaching those hard-to-get morsels. They fan out their specially adapted tails, which they use for leverage against the tree whilst probing for food. On finishing, they move on to the next tree, dutifully cleaning the forest of insects and fulfilling their need for nourishment. Although relatively common in Ireland, spotting a Treecreeper is always a thrill. Very small birds, many are lost in harsh winters, but in recent years, they have spread west in Ireland into Connemara.

The generic *certhia* is from Greek meaning 'Treecreeper'. The specific *familiaris* means 'familiar' or 'common'.

PLACE NAMES

Ennisnag, Co. Kilkenny (river-meadow of the Treecreeper (or woodpecker).

NAMES

English: Creeper, Tomtit, Woodpecker

Irish: Beangán, Beanglán (branch shoot, twig), Brionglán (a branch), Meanglán, Streapach

FACTS & FIGURES

Resident insectivores. Up to 100,000 pairs (88–91). Live max eight years. About nine species of *Certhia* worldwide. Order: *Passeriformes*; Family: *Certhiidae*.

3.22.12 The (Common) Starling

Druid | *Sturnus vulgaris vulgaris*

For entertainment value, Starlings cannot be beaten. The adult birds appear black but have a distinct purple and dark-green sheen and become distinctly spotted in winter. The bill is a dull yellow in summer and grey-brown in winter. Sexes are similar. Very sociable birds, they often gather in large noisy flocks on favoured wires or tree roosts. Such roosts can number thousands of birds.

Starlings are excellent mimics and will readily copy any sound they hear. They will repeat sounds as heard, and will often make the sound of a very distant bird. They have been caught and caged for their trouble. Pliny tells us that Starlings were trained to speak Latin and Greek words for the amusement of young Caesars.[71] Their song rambles along in a series of clicks, chuckles, tweets, twitters, wheezes, whistles and bomb-dropping sounds. Quite tolerant of people, Starlings will appear wherever food is available, as if they have some sort of food radar. They sometimes smoke-bathe, deliberately visiting a smoking chimney and basking in the smoke as a means of removing parasites.

Starling numbers have declined markedly in Ireland, probably because of increased use of pesticides, but the population has never been stable. We know them as very common birds but they were not always so. The birds were absent from the southeast up to forty years ago[72] and before the 1800s were only winter visitors to Ulster from which they were christened 'Snabirds' (snowbirds).

The word 'Starling' is the diminutive of 'stare', an old name for the birds in Ireland. This probably comes directly from its Anglo-Saxon name *staer*. In winter, Starlings are dotted white like stars in the night sky. This might suggest the origin of the name, or it may derive from 'sterling' silver coins minted by Edward the Confessor in the eleventh century, each marked with four Starlings.[73] However, the opposite may be the case – the coin was named after the bird. The generic *sturnus* is Latin for Starling while the specific *vulgaris* means 'common'. The Irish *druid* is an ancient name for the birds.

Beliefs & Traditions: It was said that if Starlings did not follow grazing cattle, then some witch's spell had been put upon them,[74]

Branwen was a Welsh princess, mistreated by her Irish husband. She trained a Starling to take a message to her brother Bran in Wales. What followed was a great war between Wales and Ireland in which Bran and all but seven of his men were killed.

Starlings are associated with warriors and war due to their aggressive manner with other birds and with members of their own kind. An Irish ballad records a tremendous battle between two groups of Starlings in Cork in 1621. 'The Battell of the Birds' (1621) from Samuel Pepys' collection of ballads[75] tells of two huge but opposing bands of Starlings which gathered on either side of the city of Cork. On the day of battle they made a huge din of unusual noise before rising simultaneously and entering into aerial battle, one group against the other, until huge numbers were left dead and dying around the streets of Cork.[76]

While such an avian battle might seem improbable, another is reported, as late as 1930 in Fermoy, County Cork. On this occasion, the warring groups were a flock of Starlings on one side and a flock of Rooks on the other. On the evening of 2 November 1930, the Starlings, estimated at over 10,000 individuals, circled the town of Fermoy. They fell on the heavily outnumbered Rooks, seemingly attempting to dislodge them from their roost. The battle lasted several hours and was continued every night for a week. By 9 November the physically larger Rooks had sought reinforcements and 2,000 or so rose against the Starlings. By 11 November, the Starlings were defeated and returned to their roost. The Rook reinforcements departed. This story was most recently told in the 'Holly Bough' section of the *Evening Echo* newspaper of Christmas 2007, but has been told before. The author has not tracked down the numerous witnesses reputed to have viewed the incident.

Such bird battles have been recorded in folklore in Ireland, Gaelic Scotland, and Eastern Europe and nowhere else.[77]

Weather: A congregation of Starlings was a sign of frost.[78]

Proverbs & Similes:

Chomh haerach le druid.
(As chirpy as a starling.)

Poetry: from '*The Stare's Nest by My Window*'

> The bees build in the crevices
> Of loosening masonry, and there
> The mother birds bring grubs and flies.
> My wall is loosening; honey-bees,
> Come build in the empty house of the stare.

**W. B. Yeats, 1928, from *The Collected Poems of W. B. Yeats*
(Macmillan, 1993)**

PLACE NAMES

Cois Druide, Co. Waterford (Starling's Foot)

NAMES

English: Blacstair/Blackstare (Wex.), Curlew (Uls.), Slater (Uls.), Stare (west)

Irish: Druide (Don.), Druideog (Ach. Don., Mona.), Truid (Don.), Truideog/Troideog (Ach., Don., Mona.)

Uls. Scots: Snaabird (snowbird[79]), Snabird, Snaeburd (Ant.), Snowburd,[80] Star (Ant.), Stucky

FACTS & FIGURES

Resident omnivores. Widespread in all counties. Up to a half million breeding pairs (88–91) with numbers inflated in winter. Live max twenty-two years. Collective name: a murmuration of Starlings. About 120 species of *Sturnidae* including about fifteen species of *Sturnus* worldwide. Order: *Passeriformes*; Family: *Sturnidae*.

3.22.13 The (Red) Crossbill

Crosghob | *Loxia curvirostra curvirostra*

Crossbills are uncommon yet remarkable birds living in our coniferous forests. There are only a thousand pairs in the country so you will not see them every day. Males are brick-red and females faded green, looking not unlike Greenfinches and with the same forked tails. However, Crossbills are unmistakeable. Their crossed bills are exclusive to the five species of crossbill worldwide. The bill is a special adaptation for prizing conifer seeds from cones, so remote coniferous forests are where they are most likely to be seen. As they are so dependent on coniferous trees, their numbers fluctuate in direct correlation to the success of the conifers from year to year. Crossbills have a number of cousins that appear in Ireland rarely: Scottish Crossbills (*Loxia scotica*), the Two-barred Crossbills (*Crosghob báneiteach, Loxia leucoptera*) and the Parrot Crossbills (*Loxia pytyopsittacus*).

The Irish *Crosghob* means 'crossbill'. The generic *loxia* is from Greek meaning 'crosswise'. The specific *curvirostra* is from Latin meaning 'curved beak'.

Beliefs & Traditions: It was believed that a Crossbill tried to pull the thorns from the head of Christ on the cross and was given the crossed bill as a reward.[81] A variation suggests a Crossbill was trying to pull the nails from Christ's limbs and twisted its bill in the process. The males' red colour was also attributed to the blood of Christ.

On St Valentine's Day, the first bird a girl would see would give a clue as to the man she would marry. If it were a woodpecker, she would not marry at all. If it was a Robin, he would be a sailor, if a Blackbird, a clergyman, if a sparrow, he would be poor man (though they would be happy) or a farmer, if a Crossbill, an argumentative man, if a dove, a good man, and if it was a Goldfinch, he would be a millionaire.

Poetry: '*The Legend of the Crossbill*'

On the cross the dying Saviour
Heavenward lifts his eyelids calm,
Feels, but scarcely feels, a trembling
In his pierced and bleeding palm.

And by all the world forsaken,
Sees he how with zealous care
At the ruthless nail of iron
A little bird is striving there.

Stained with blood and never tiring,
With its beak it doth not cease,
From the cross 't would free the Saviour,
Its Creator's Son release.

And the Saviour speaks in mildness:
'Blest be thou of all the good!
Bear, as token of this moment,
Marks of blood and holy rood!'

And that bird is called the crossbill;
Covered all with blood so clear,
In the groves of pine it singeth
Songs, like legends, strange to hear.

Julius Mosen (1803–1867)
German poet and author (translated by Henry Wadsworth Longfellow)

NAMES

English: 'The Parrott of the Northern Woods' (UK)

Irish: Camghob (twisted bill), Cathóg[82]

FACTS & FIGURES

Resident omnivores. Locally common. Up 2,500 breeding pairs (88–91). Live max six years. About five species of *Loxia* worldwide. Order: *Passeriformes*; Family: *Fringillidae*.

279

3.22.14 The House Sparrow

Gealbhan binne | *Passer domesticus domesticus*

& the (Eurasian) Tree Sparrow

Gealbhan crainn | *Passer montanus montanus*

House Sparrow

Tree Sparrow

'I watch and am like a sparrow alone on the house top.'[83]

House Sparrows are some of Ireland's commonest and best-loved birds. They are perhaps our closest friends in the bird world, eating from our bird tables and nut dispensers, chattering noisily in our trees and dust bathing in our gardens to remove parasites. Males are small handsome birds with streaked-brown uppers, a light underside, grey cap and black bib. Females show an overall dull streaked-brown. While still common, House Sparrows have suffered a serious decline in numbers here in recent years. Yet they remain, almost certainly, the most widespread birds in the world.

Close relatives of the House Sparrows, Tree Sparrows are much scarcer birds. Though resembling House Sparrows at first glance, Tree Sparrows have magnificent chestnut crowns. A sure-fire way of identifying a Tree Sparrow flock is by recognising that all the birds are the same. Male and female Tree Sparrows are alike. Nonetheless, if you see a sparrow in Ireland, it is most likely a House Sparrow.

Passer is the Latin word for sparrow, from which ornithologists get the word 'passerine' meaning 'a small bird'. The specific *domesticus* means common or 'domestic'. The specific *montanus* means 'of the mountains' which is something of a misnomer as Tree Sparrows can be found in several habitats. The Irish *Gealbhan binne* means 'melodious sparrow'[84] while *Gealbhan crainn* means 'tree sparrow'.

Beliefs & Traditions: Sparrows carry the souls of the dead and as such, it is unlucky to kill them.[85] They were also believed to have prophetic powers.[86]

Weather: Sparrows hopping on the road were an indication of bad weather.[87]

Proverbs & Similes:

Cuireadh an ghealbhan chun arbhair na gcomharsain. (The sparrow's invitation to its neighbour's corn – somebody generous with something that does not belong to them)

Éirí le giolcadh an ghealbhain. (To rise with the dawn, to rise with the sparrows' chirping.)

Chomh héadrom le gealbhan, chomh héasca le gealbhan. (As light as a sparrow.)

PLACE NAMES

Altnagelvin, Co. Derry (Alt na nGealbhan, sparrow's hill)
Lisnagelvin, Co. Derry (Lios na nGealbhan, sparrow's fort[88])

CULINARY

House Sparrows are edible and were regarded as a delicacy.

NAMES

HOUSE SPARROW

English: Galvin, Grey Spadger (Ant.), Spug (Uls.), Squidger (Dub. Sl.)

Irish: Gealbhán (Uls.), Gealbhan sciobóil (barn sparrow), Gealbhan tí/tighe (House Sparrow), Gealún (sparrow), Seán an chaipín (Mun.)

Uls. Scots: Sparra

Scientific: Fringilla domestica, Passer domestica, Pyrgita domestica

TREE SPARROW

English: Mountain Sparrow

Scientific: Fringilla montana, Loxia hamburgia, Passer arboreus, Passer montana, Pyrgita montana

FACTS & FIGURES

HOUSE SPARROW: Resident omnivores. Up to one million breeding pairs in Ireland (88–91). Live max nineteen years. Collective name: a host of sparrows, a quarrel of sparrows, a ubiquity of sparrows.

TREE SPARROW: Uncommon residents. Locally common on coasts. Up to 2,500 breeding pairs (88–91). Live max thirteen years.

About forty-five species of *Passeridae* including about twenty-three species of *Passer* worldwide. Order: *Passeriformes*; Family: *Passeridae*.

4. Poultry & Domestic Birds – Éanlaith Chlóis, Éin Tí

4.1 POULTRY & DOMESTIC BIRDS – ÉANLAITH CHLÓIS, ÉAN TÍ

Birds have probably been domesticated since human beings first began to make permanent settlements. They have been bred for their meat, eggs and feathers, and for their aesthetics and companionship. As with most domesticated animals, man has bred birds to his own needs, selecting for taste and muscle size. As a result, many of our domestic birds are white, their camouflage colours no longer an important trait. The word 'fowl' was originally used for large birds, with 'bird' confined to only the small ones. With the wider adoption of 'bird' to describe all birds, 'fowl' is used selectively to describe water fowl, wild fowl and our subject of interest here, domesticated fowl.

Probably the most common domesticated birds worldwide are chickens. The first chickens may have been domesticated around 6000 BC.[1] These birds are domesticated forms of Asian Red Junglefowl (*Gallus gallus*) and probably came to Ireland through trade with the Romans. The Vikings and Normans increased their numbers here. Domestic geese probably followed the same path, the first being domesticated around 1500 BC. Some came to Ireland from trade with the Romans and more came later with the Normans. Most farm geese in Ireland are descendents of wild Greylag Geese (*Anser anser*). Domesticated ducks probably arrived with the Normans too. They were first domesticated between 2000 and 1000 BC. Worldwide, Mallards, along with Muscovy ducks (*Cairina moschata, Lacha Lochlannach*[2]) are the ancestors of almost all domesticated ducks. In Ireland, they are almost entirely descended from wild Mallard ducks. Turkeys only came to Ireland in the late sixteenth or early seventeenth century and over the next few hundred years replaced geese as the main feast birds. They were probably first domesticated in Mexico around 500 BC. Other 'game' birds such as quail and partridge have, at times, been domesticated in small numbers. Pheasants were introduced for hunting and ultimately for the pot and are regarded as semi-domesticated. Rock Doves and other pigeons were also domesticated and kept for their meat and eggs. The first pigeons were probably domesticated around 3000 BC. In modern Ireland some new species (to Ireland) such as guineafowl and Ostrich are now being raised for their meat. Peafowl have been widely if uncommonly domesticated in Ireland but although they can be eaten they are mostly kept for aesthetic reasons. They were first domesticated for this reason in India around 500 BC. Mute Swans were semi-domesticated in the Middle Ages but are now a protected species and have returned to the wild.

In the Irish farmyard, each animal had its own call to feed: geese were summoned with 'biddy, biddy, biddy', ducks with 'fian fian fian' and hens with 'tuc, tuc, tuc' or 'chuck chuck chuck' or 'pee pee pee' (pigs were called with 'wat wat wat' or '*staití, staití*'). Turkeys in Antrim were called with 'pee pee'.[3]

Domestication generally refers to a whole species of animal whereas a tame animal can be a member of any wild or domesticated species. Some birds have been tamed as pets (*éin gualainne*) and, like any other developed country, Ireland is full of budgerigars, canaries, parrots and many other caged birds. These birds were domesticated relatively recently (canaries around AD 1600, budgerigars around the 1850s, finches around the 1900s) and have not developed much in the line of folklore and as such have not been included in this work.

Roughly speaking, there are 30 million poultry birds on the island of Ireland at any time, including chickens, ducks, turkeys and others.[4]

The Mallard

Mallard | *Anas platyrhynchos platyrhynchos* (wild)

& the Domestic Duck

Lacha tí | *Anas platyrhynchos domesticus* (domesticated)

Mallards are Ireland's commonest wild ducks. Strictly speaking, the word 'mallard' only refers to males of the species, while females are the 'ducks'. Mallards are also the ducks from which domestic farm ducks are descended, being domesticated in China some 4,000 years ago. In Ireland, domestic ducks probably first arrived with the Normans. Wild Mallards are very adaptable and are found throughout Ireland, in town and countryside. They are among those birds that, at least to some extent, have benefited from man's expansion. Though common, drake Mallards are resplendent with a shimmering metallic-green head, white neck ring, brown breast and yellow bill. They show a general grey-brown above and grey below. They have characteristic curled feathers above the tail, which incidentally, were sported

285

The Mallard & the Domestic Duck continued

by Donald Duck, so perhaps Donald was a Mallard. Females show an overall mottled brown. Both sexes have a characteristic blue wing flash trimmed with white. The birds vary widely in size and colouring. A Mallard's *uropygial* or preen gland, found at the base of the tail, provides an oil with which the duck water-proofs its feathers and gives them more strength and flexibility. The edges of a Mallard's bill are specially adapted to sieve plants, seeds, and small animals from mud and water. Female Mallards are the source of the typical duck 'quack'. Mallards are particularly fast flyers, topping 100 km/h (60 mph).

Males mate with single females in succession. Males in large groups are also known to force themselves on single females and are one of the few animals known to do this. The males leave all child-rearing to the females. A female Mallard leading her fluffy chicks to water is a touching sight and we humans have gone out of our way to facilitate such mothers, in some cases building special bridges or tunnels to cross roads. Unfortunately many chicks are lost early, often to scavenging pike or indeed herons, Magpies, mink and otters.

In Ireland, the resident population is annually increased by the arrival of migrant visitors. These visitors tend to be smaller and do not associate with the locals. Resident Irish Mallard were known as 'heavy duck' and fetched a higher price than their foreign relatives.[5]

Through domestication and the natural occurrence of many varieties, quite a number of Mallard varieties and genetic anomalies can be encountered. Farm ducks are pure white. Rouen ducks are large goose-like Mallard bred through several generations in northern France. 'Top-knots' are Mallards with characteristic feather-crests on their heads appearing to have something like a Japanese chonmage haircut. Other well-known Mallard varieties include the Pekin and Aylesbury ducks. Another form of domestic duck is the Barbary Duck, which is a cross between the Mallard and the domesticated Muscovy duck (*Cairina moschata, Lacha Lochlannach*).

The word 'mall' of 'Mallard' may come from the Latin *masculus* meaning 'male'. The 'ard' ending indicates something done to excess, relating to the males' constant sex drive. The specific *platyrhynchos* means 'broad-billed'.

Cures: Pliny believed that Mallard blood was good for a number of ailments, and was kept in solid form until needed.[6]

Belief: Mallards were used in divining the future. The wishbone of a duck or goose was carefully observed. A dark wishbone indicated a bitter winter to come. Today, we make a wish over the pulling of a wishbone; a remnant of the ancient custom.

Proverbs & Similes:

It's as hard to see a woman crying as it is to see a barefooted duck.

Time enough lost the ducks. (Procrastination . . . the ducks should have been secured immediately from the fox.)

CULINARY

Whether wild or domesticated, Mallards are widely regarded as amongst the tastiest of ducks and are the most likely species to be found in restaurants or supermarkets. Payne-Gallwey regarded them as fourth in line for taste after Pintails, Shoveler and Teal.[7] He regarded the ducks (females) as tastier than the Mallard (males).

PLACE NAMES

Ardnasodan, Co. Galway (high place of wild ducks)
Duckspool, Co. Limerick (Clais na Lachan, ducks' gully)

NAMES

English: Coarse Duck, Flapper (yng.), Gross Duck, Harvest Duck, Heavy Duck, Mountain Duck, Wild Duck

Irish: Bardal/Bárdal, (male), Cráin lachan (breeding fem.), Crann-lacha (tree duck, fem.), Éan lachan (duckling, Din.), Fiadh-lacha (wild duck), Gaill-chearc (foreign duck), Lach (Ant., Don.), Lacha bhreac (Kry.), Lacha fhiáin/fhiadhain (wild duck), Lacha riabhach (streaked/striped duck, Kry.), Lachaidhe (male), Mallárd (Mea.), Tonnóg (yng., Ant.)

Uls. Scots: Dyuck (Ant.)

Scientific: Anas boscas/boschas, Anas platyrhyncha, Anas platyrhynchus.

FACTS & FIGURES

Resident omnivores. Widespread in all counties. Up to 20,000 breeding pairs of wild Mallard (88–91) with numbers inflated in winter. Live max twenty-three years in the wild. Weigh over 1 kg. Collective name: a flush of Mallard, a paddling of ducks, a sord of Mallard. About fifty species of *Anas* ducks worldwide. Order: *Anseriformes*; Family: *Anatidae*.

4.1.2 The Greylag Goose

Gé ghlas | *Anser anser anser* (wild)

& the Domestic Goose

Gé | *Anser anser domesticus* (farm)

Like domestic chickens, domestic geese were probably introduced to Ireland in the first few centuries AD having first been domesticated in Egypt 3,000 to 4,000 years ago. Domestic geese are direct descendents of wild Greylag Goose (*Anser anser*). Geese were kept for their meat, eggs, feathers and oil and are sometimes used in place of guard dogs. Like domestic turkeys, domestic geese are now all white, having had the natural grey colour bred out. Wild Greylag are generally grey all over with a hint of brown, from which we get the Irish *Gé ghlas* (grey goose). They have bright orange bills, orange/pink legs and are clearly streaked both above and below. From the distance, they are easy to confuse with other 'grey-geese' species, the White-fronted Geese, Pink-footed Geese and Bean Geese. Greylag visit us in winter, from breeding grounds in Iceland.

The 'lag' in Greylag is often thought to refer to 'lateness' as it lagged behind other geese in migrating. However, the true explanation is much simpler. 'Lag' is an old word for goose. The scientific *anser* is the Latin word for goose.

Beliefs & Traditions: Greylag Geese were symbols of resourcefulness. They were once considered sacred by the Romans. When the Gauls were attacking Rome in 390 BC they tried to climb in over the walls, but the Greylag Geese (presumably domesticated) warned the Romans with their honking calls. Following this, geese were celebrated and revered in Rome every year on the anniversary of the attack.

In some tales, Áine of Munster, Tuatha Dé Danann goddess of love and fertility, is 'married by force' by Gearóid Iarla. In revenge, she changes him into a goose, eventually killing him. In a related story, a variation of the swan-maiden tale, she marries Gerald, the Earl of Desmond when he finds her bathing in Lough Gur, County Limerick. He picks up her cloak and refuses to give it back until she marries him. After she does, a son, Gearóid Iarla is born. She tells her husband that he must never show surprise if his son does something unusual. One day, his son Gearóid jumps in and out of a bottle and his father instantly exclaims in shock. The son immediately turns into a goose and flies away. Áine turns into a swan and flies after him. Now if a lone swan and goose are seen swimming together on Lough Gur, it is said to be Áine and Gearóid swimming together.

Cures: Ailments of the mouth could be cured by bringing a live goose (sometimes a fasting gander) and placing its bill in the patient's mouth for five minutes for nine successive mornings.[8]

Not only the goose, but the goose's droppings were very versatile in treating illness. Jaundice could be cured by boiling goose droppings in milk and drinking while still hot![9] Fresh goose droppings mixed with camomile petals and newly churned, unsalted butter was a cure for burns, and goose droppings massaged into the area would cure sore throat![10]

An ointment made from goose grease and crushed tansy[11] (*Tanacetum vulgare*) was a cure for sores.[12]

Curses:
May you ride Rogan's gander to the dickens.[13]
The curse of the goose that lost the quill that wrote the Ten Commandments.

Weather: The appearance of wild geese forewarned a severe winter[14] and the appearance of a goose's breastbone could foretell the severity of the winter: if it was dark, the weather would be harsh; if it was light, the weather would be milder.

Poetry:

> *Goosey, goosey, gander,*
> *Where shall I wander?*
> *Upstairs, and downstairs,*
> *And in my lady's chamber.*
> *There I met an old man*
> *Who wouldn't say his prayers!*
> *I took him by the left leg*
> *And threw him down the stairs.*

Anonymous

Proverbs & Similes:

Chomh h-anásta le gé a bheadh ag siúl ar rópa. (As clumsy as a goose walking on a rope.)

Chomh lag le héan gé. (As weak as a gosling.)

Chomh lom le gé bhearrtha. (As naked as a plucked goose.)

Chuir na cránta chuige ina mhála i bhfochair na ngandal. (He bagged the geese as well as the ganders.)

PLACE NAMES

Gay Island, Co. Fermanagh (Inis na nGédh, goose island)
Monagay, Co. Limerick (goose bog)

NAMES

English: Grey Goose, Grey Lag Goose, Stubble Goose, Swan Goose, Wild Goose

Irish: Cráin ghé (fem. breeding goose), Cráinseach lachan (fem.), Crann-ghé (tree goose), Éan gé/géidh (gosling, Din.), Gé fiadhain (wild goose), Gé mhór fhionn (big white goose), Géidh, Geodh, Ghé dhubh (black goose, a Trent goose), Patall/Putall an ghé (gosling), Patallóg (gosling), Patlachán (Don.)
Plural: Géabhaí (May.), Géacha (Don.), Géadhna, Géana, Géidhe (west Cla.)

Uls. Scots: Giss (Ant.)

Scientific: Anas anser, Anser cinereus, Anser ferus

The Greylag Goose & the Domestic Goose continued

Ní faide gob na gé ná gob an ghandail.
(The goose's beak is no longer than the gander's.)

. . . If you eat goose on Michaelmas Day, you will not

be in want for the rest of the year . . .

Everything about a goose is used except the honk.

May you never be sent to the gander paddock.
(May you never be in your wife's bad graces.[15])

What's sauce for the goose is sauce for the gander.

'Ye sit yer time like many a good goose.'
(Uls. Scots, said to a person who overstays
their welcome.)

FACTS & FIGURES

WILD GREYLAG: Mostly herbivorous. Locally common at certain favoured locations but absent from most parts of Ireland. Some escapees from private collections. Up to 1,000 wild breeding pairs (88–91) with numbers inflated in winter by migrating birds. Live max twenty-three years in the wild. Weigh up to 4 kg. Collective name: a gaggle of geese (on the ground), a nide of geese, a skein of geese (in the air), a wedge of geese. Amber list. About eight species of *Anser* geese worldwide. Order: *Anseriformes*; Family: *Anatidae*.

CULINARY

The Celts were the first to begin trapping and domesticating migrating geese, initially at least, for religious and ceremonial purposes. There is still a tradition in some parts of Ireland where eating goose is taboo. In other parts of Ireland, there is a tradition of eating geese at or around the summer solstice. This apparent regional contradiction is unexplained. Traditionally, there have been two types of bred domestic goose: the small and the large, the small being regarded as tastier. It is a tradition across Europe to feed the larger, sometimes to extreme proportions. In France, *pâté de fois gras* (fat liver pate) is now a mass-produced delicacy. Notwithstanding the taste, over-feeding of the geese produces such liver and the *pâté* derived from it. The geese are plucked for their feathers for quills and pillows and live geese would be plucked only as far as it would not kill them and they could recover. In Ireland, when it snowed, children were told that geese were being plucked 'up above'.[16]

In Ireland, young or 'green' geese were particularly favoured while the older or 'stubble' geese were tougher in taste and texture. While a domestic goose could be served whole, this was not advised for any sort of wild goose, as it was widely said that 'Pat Hegarty's leather breeches' would make a better dish.[17] Green geese were often corralled two weeks before slaughter and fed a mixture of milk and potatoes to make the meat pale and tender.

'Aitin the Gander'[18] was a wedding tradition in parts of Ireland where the bridegroom was invited to the bride's family home before the wedding and a goose was cooked in his honour. This is perhaps where we get the adage 'his goose is cooked'!

A myth from the 'historical cycle' tells of the Banquet of Dún na nGedh[19] and the Battle of Magh Rath[20] which date from the seventh century. The High King of Ireland, Domnall mac Áedo, needed some goose eggs to serve at a feast, for some guests from Ulster, in his new fort on the banks of the River Boyne. Goose eggs were held in high regard and were hard to come by. He sent servants out to collect goose eggs across Ireland. The servants came across a hermit bishop Earc who lived exclusively on goose eggs and watercress. Ignoring the pious man's need for his daily meal and the dire warning of his servant, Domhnall's servants stole the eggs on which Earc subsequently put a curse. When Domhnall heard of the curse, he decided to serve some of his guests chicken eggs on wooden plates. This so insulted some of the Ulster guests, including his foster son Congal that the feast led to a fierce battle, the Battle of Magh Rath that Domhnall ultimately won.[21]

4.1.3 The (Domestic) Chicken

Cearc clóis | *Gallus gallus domesticus*

While the cock with lively din[22]
Scatters the rear of darkness thin,
And to the stack, or the barn door,
Stoutly struts his dames before.

Domestic chickens, common to every farm in the land, are direct descendents of wild Red Junglefowl (*Gallus gallus*) and Grey Junglefowl (*Gallus sonneratii*) from southern Asia. After thousands of years of domestication, domestic roosters are less brilliantly coloured than their wild cousins. These domesticated birds have spread to every corner of the planet. There are now hundreds of varieties worldwide ranging from black to white and every colour in between. In general, cocks are larger than hens, have more pronounced colouring, tail and head feathers and more prominent bare-skin wattles on the head. They can live for up to ten years. They have a very strict pecking order, or rather two pecking orders, one for the hens and one for the cocks. The dominant cock rules the roost. When he dies, the next rooster in line takes over. Females are hens or biddys or partlets and males are cocks, roosters, or stags. Wild hens lay from eight to ten eggs in a symbolic nest of a few old leaves and grass in a secluded spot. It is said that domesticated hens will breed stronger chicks if allowed to pick their own natural nesting spots.

The scientific *gallus* is the Latin for cock and poultry. The Irish *Cearc clóis* means 'yard-hen'.

History: A hen and chicks appeared on the old Irish penny coin (1928–1969).

Chickens were probably introduced to Ireland by trade with the Romans in the first few centuries AD but were not common here until the fourteenth century. In Ireland, chickens were generally allowed to roam where they wanted during the day. Although this often led to conflict with neighbours, the chickens knew their home and never strayed far. At night, chickens were brought into the house, usually to the warm kitchen and this was especially important in winter. A hen's main contribution was her eggs, which were available all year round. The chickens themselves were rarely eaten. If a chicken was to be eaten, it was usually the fattened cock. When they were killed, it was for a great and well-planned occasion. The feathers were used for pillows and mattresses. Because of the cocks' intolerance of other cocks, they were often used for cock fighting but this practice is now illegal.

The (Domestic) Chicken continued

Beliefs & Traditions: Symbols of St Peter, roosters were considered watchful protectors of humankind. Their crowing was believed to keep pookas and fairies away at night. Hens, on the other hand, were not so brave. The mere sight of a pooka[23] was enough to prevent hens from laying. A 'March cock' (*Coileach Márta*) was a cock that hatched in March from a cock and hen also hatched in March. It had certain powers and was particularly good at keeping the fairies at bay. Any cock crowing at midnight presaged the death of someone close. The travelling people believed that if a bantam cock crowed after midnight then something would go wrong.[24] A cock crowing through a door or window gave a similar warning of a death in the family.[25] A rooster crowing near the threshold or entering the house was an omen that visitors would arrive.[26] If you were setting out on a journey and a crowing cock blocked your door, it was best to cancel the trip immediately.[27] The fairy people went about their business at night and it was not safe to venture out until the cock crew in the early morning and sent the little people running.[28] The old Irish saying '*God between us and all harm*' was always said on hearing the crow of a rooster and particularly at night.[29] In England, it was a death omen if a cock crowed three times between sunset and midnight. Crowing at other times was often a warning against misfortune too. If a cock crowed while perched on a gate, or at nightfall, the next day would be rainy. Gerald of Wales in the twelfth century tells us that cocks in Ireland crow differently from cocks in other countries.[30]

The cock's 'cock-a-doodle-doo' was described as 'cock-a-leerie-crow' in Antrim.[31] There are a number of Irish phrases for 'cock-a-doodle-doo': '*mac-na-hÓighe-slán*' ('the son of the Virgin is well') may derive from the story that two people were discussing the resurrection of Christ while awaiting a cock in a pot to boil. One said 'tis more likely that that cock will rise out of the pot than a dead man could rise from the dead'. With that, the cock jumped up out of the pot with the words '*mac na hÓighe slán*'.

There was a custom to respect the last sheaf of wheat harvested. The custom varied greatly across the country. In County Laois, the grain from the last sheaf was fed to the chickens. The first rooster to get to it (*Coileach Mártan*) was marked for the table for St Martin's Eve (10 November). There was a widely held belief across Ireland as well as most of Europe that St Martin had been betrayed by either a flock of geese or a black cock. In revenge, the blood of the goose, black cock or white hen killed on St Martin's Eve was sprinkled across the floor, threshold and in some cases, the four corners of every room in the house. Sometimes the blood was sprinkled on all members of the household. Sometimes a cloth was soaked in the cock's blood and kept in the rafters. This cloth had the power to stop bleeding.[32]

White roosters were considered very lucky, and were not to be killed, as they protected the farm on which they lived; black cocks, however, were more ill-omened, being often associated with sacrifice.[33] A black hen was said to be smarter than a white hen as the black hen could lay a white egg but the white hen could not lay a black egg.[34] This tradition was particularly strong on the islands off the west coast.

An old Irish tale tells how to have money forever: 'kill a black cock, and go to the meeting of three roads where a murderer is buried! Throw the dead bird over your left shoulder, after nightfall, in the name of the devil, and holding a piece of money in your hand all the while. Ever after, no matter what you spend, you will always find the same piece of money undiminished in your pocket.'[35]

Hens that roosted in the morning were said to be foretelling a death, usually that of the farmer or someone in his household. A crowing hen, a whistling girl, and a black cat were considered very unlucky, particularly so in a house.[36] On the rare occasion that a hen would crow (*cábún*) it was considered that she was bewitched with fairies and the bird was sold or killed as soon as possible.[37] It was very lucky for a hen and her chickens to stray into your house.[38]

For religious reasons, the consumption of meat was prohibited throughout the period of Lent.[39] This helped to develop the tradition of using up all the excess eggs in advance, which in turn led to the tradition of Shrove Tuesday[40] when pancakes were eaten. Eggs were preserved for long periods by rolling them in butter immediately after laying, the butter being absorbed into the egg and forming a watertight seal. Eggs laid on Good Friday[41] were considered blessed and these, marked with crosses, were cooked for breakfast on Easter Sunday.[42] Egg shells were regarded as being the dwelling places of witches and fairies so they were always crushed when the egg was eaten.[43] In some parts of Ireland, a hole poked in both ends of the used shell did the same trick.[44] In Limerick in the sixteenth century, people would hang eggshells in the roofs of their houses to prevent kites from stealing their chickens.[45] It was also believed that if a horse should eat eggs, care should be taken that it eat an even number lest it become ill. Jockeys were not allowed to eat eggs.[46] It was widely believed that fishermen would get protection by eating the first egg laid by a hen.

There was a common custom in Ireland, still carried through to this day, where the seller in a business transaction would return some 'luck money' to the buyer. This was common too when selling hens' eggs. When eggs were sold, a luck penny was returned to the buyer to prevent the buyer from having bad luck with the eggs.[47]

It was believed (correctly) that chickens were not native Irish creatures and that the Vikings brought them to Ireland (though it is likely that they first arrived in Roman times). In any case, it was believed that when hens scratched the ground, they were trying to either burn the house down or dig their way back to Scandinavia!

The (Domestic) Chicken continued

On Valentia Island, County Kerry, in the late nineteenth century it was believed that the first egg laid by a little black hen, eaten the very first thing in the morning, would keep you from fever for the year.[48]

Similes:

There are nearly as many similes for cocks and hens as there are days in the year:

As mad as a wet hen . . .

As bold as a cock on his own dunghill.

Chomh caoch le cearc. (As blind as a hen.)

Chomh corrthónach le cearc ar ghreideall. (As restless as a hen on a griddle.)

Chomh dall le cearc san oíche. (As blind as a hen at night, i.e. when you suddenly find yourself in the dark).)

Chomh glórach le cearc ghoir. (As vocal as a broody hen.)

Chomh lag le cearc. (As weak as a hen.)

Chomh salach le teach na gcearc. (As dirty as the hen house.)

Chomh te teolaí le hubh i dtóin circe. (As cosy as an egg in a hen's rear end.)

Proverbs

A whistling woman and a crowing hen will bring no luck to the house they are in . . .

or 'A whistling girl and a crowing hen make the devil dance in his den.'

As rare as hen's teeth . . .

As the old cock crows, the young cock learns.

Curses, like chickens, come home to roost. Curses fall on the head of the curser, as chickens, which stray during the day, return to their roost at night . . .

Eating and complaining like the greedy hen . . .

An chearc a dhíol lá na báistí.
(To sell the hen on a rainy day, i.e. to pick the worst time to do something.)

Chuirfeadh sé cosa faoi chearca duit. (He would build a nest in your ear.)

Tá coiscéim coiligh ar an lá.
(There's a cock's footstep on the day – the day is getting longer.)

Is olc an chearc ná scríobfaidh di féin.
(It's a poor hen which will not provide [scrape] for herself.)

Is maith an cearc ná beireann amuigh. (The good hen does not lay outside.)

Is minic ubh mhór ag cearc bheag. (A small hen often has a large egg.)

Is trom cearc i bhfad. (A hen is heavy when carried far . . .)

Mar a bheadh cearc ghoir ann. (Like a brooding hen, i.e. overly fussy.)

Ná comhair do chuid sicíní nó go dtaga siad amach.
(Do not count your chickens before they are hatched.)

Oany cock can crow in its ain midden.
(Anyone can be aggressive from the safety of their own home)[49] (Uls. Scots).

Whun the owl cock crows the young yin knows.
(We learn from our parents' example) (Uls. Scots).

Curses:

May your hens take the disorder, your cows the crippen [phosphorosis] and your calves the white scour! May yourself go stone-blind so that you will not know your wife from a haystack.

Six eggs to you and half of them rotten.

The fate of Ned's cock to you!

PLACE NAMES

Cark, Co. Donegal (hen)
Carrickahilla, Co. Waterford.
(Carraig an Choiligh, The Cock's Rock[50])
Keeraunnagark, Co. Galway (Caorán na gCearc, hen moor)
Monakirka, Co Waterford (Móin na Circe, the hen's bog)
Quillia, Co. Limerick (Coilleach, cock)

NAMES

English: capon (castrated rooster), chick, chicken, cock (male), cockerel (young cock), fowl, hen, partlet, pullet (yng. hen), rooster (male)

Irish: cábún (capon), cearc (hen), cearc na n-éan (hatching hen), ceircín/circín (small, pullet or bantam), circeoil (culinary chicken meat), coileach (cock), éan circe (chicken), eireog (pullet), éirín (pullet) gaill coiligh (large cock), gall, sicín (chicken)

Uls. Scots: chookie (hen, Ant.), clocker (broody hen, Ant., Cav.), errak (young laying hen) (Ant.)

Scientific: Phasianus gallus, Gallus domesticus (domestic), Gallus ferrugineus, Gallus bankiva

FACTS & FIGURES

Present in Ireland only in the domesticated form. Can live for ten years. Collective name: a brood of hens, a clutch of chicks, a peep of chickens, a run of poultry. The cockerel is a national symbol of France. About four species of *Gallus* worldwide. Order: *Galliformes*; Family: *Phasianidae*.

4.1.4 The (Domestic) Turkey

Turcaí

Wild Turkey   *Meleagris gallopavo*
Ocellated[51] Turkey   *Meleagris ocellata*

'God has never told us what a turkey means. And if you go and stare at a live turkey for an hour or two, you will find by the end of it that the enigma has rather increased than diminished.'[52]

Domestic turkeys are direct descendents of both the Wild Turkeys of North America (*Meleagris gallopavo*) or the Mexican Ocellated Turkeys (*Meleagris ocellata*). They are regarded as game birds and are related to Pheasants.

Wild turkeys are large birds. The males show an overall mottled metallic blue-green colour, looking black from a distance. The breast-tuft, bare-skinned head and red wattle complete the unique appearance. The tail can be fanned. Females are smaller and duller. Domestic all-white turkeys tend to be twice the size of their wild counterparts. Wild turkeys can fly and, like Pheasants, spend the night in low tree branches. Male are known as stags or gobblers, females are hens, and chicks are known as poults. Males gobble and females cluck. In Antrim, males bubble or 'glunther'.[53] Turkey hens can sometimes produce young from unfertilised eggs. This process is called parthenogenesis, the young being genetically identical to the parent.

The generic *meleagris* is from the Greek meaning 'speckled' and 'guineafowl'. The name 'turkey' comes from the mistaken belief that the birds came from Turkey. At the time turkeys were arriving in Europe, other exotic birds such as guineafowl (*Numida meleagris*, aka turkey-cocks) were also arriving from Asia. Anything exotic was thought to come from Turkey or India. The French word for turkey, *dinde*, comes from *coq d'Inde* (cock from India).

History: It is generally believed that the first turkeys were brought to Europe by the Spanish conquistador Hernándo Cortés on his return from the Americas in the sixteenth century though they were known in England in 1524.[54] Soon after, turkeys became the most popular 'feast' birds in Europe. They probably arrived in Ireland in the seventeenth century.

Beliefs & Traditions: Turkeys displaced geese as the traditional birds eaten at Christmas. Henry VIII[55] is reputed to have been the first king to enjoy turkey. It was later popularised by Charles Dickens' *A Christmas Carol* (1843) and later

Edward VII[56] helped make eating turkey at Christmas fashionable. Nonetheless, turkeys were still uncommon at Christmas up to the 1950s and 1960s when refrigerators began to become more common.

The wings of turkeys and geese were often used as dusters.

Proverbs & Similes:

Chomh leochaileach leis an éan turcaí.
(As tender as a young turkey.)

A turkey never voted for an early Christmas.

'If I have another drink I'll be driving turkeys on the way home.'
(Staggering from too much alcohol.)[57]

CULINARY

Turkeys are traditionally baked or roasted in Ireland and eaten in huge numbers at Christmas. Domestic turkeys taste very different from their wild-caught cousins. Almost all wild-turkey meat is dark, with a more intense gamey flavour.

PLACE NAMES

Páirc na dTurcach, Co. Waterford (turkeys' field [perhaps])

NAMES

English: Gobbler (male)

Irish: Gaill-éan, Cearc Fhrancach (French or foreign hen), Coileach Francach/Franncach (French cock)

Uls. Scots: Glunthercock, Gobbler (male, Ant.)

Scientific: Agriocharis ocellata (Ocellated Turkey)

FACTS & FIGURES

Present in Ireland only in the domesticated form. Omnivorous. Turkeys weigh up to 11 kg. Collective name: a muster of turkeys, a raffle of turkeys, a rafter of turkeys. Two species of *Meleagris* worldwide. Order: *Galliformes*; Family: *Meleagrididae*.

4.1.5 Other Irish Domestic Birds – Peafowl & Guineafowl

A number of other non-native birds have been introduced to Ireland for ornamental and commercial reasons. These include peafowl, guineafowl and Ostrich.

Peafowl Péacóg | *Pavo cristatus* (Indian Peafowl) *and Pavo muticus* (Green Peafowl)[58]

Described as having the plumage of an angel, the voice of the devil and the guts of a thief, peacocks are, strictly speaking, the males of the peafowl species, the unfortunate females or peahens usually being forgotten. The Blue Peacocks are by far the commonest seen in captivity, known for their startling eyed tails or trains, which

Other Irish Domestic Birds –
Peafowl & Guineafowl continued

they display during courtship. Males show a dark blue-green head, neck and breast with striking crest feathers, a mottled dark green body and bronze, black and mottled-grey wings. Albino varieties are relatively common. Male peafowl are often seen in large parks and country houses, kept for their stunning display feathers. Originally from Asia, the two species *Pavo cristatus* (blue) and *Pavo muticus* (green) have been domesticated since at least 2000 BC. They are a hardy species and have easily adapted to the Irish climate.

The generic *Pavo* is Latin for peafowl but may have come originally from the Sanskrit *pavana* meaning 'purity'. The phrase 'stuck-up', meaning having superior airs, may derive from the habit of the peacock 'sticking up' its huge tail feathers, and portraying his superiority over others.

History: It is likely that the Phoenicians first brought peafowl to Europe via Egypt. They were certainly in the parklands of the nobility, across Europe, by the fourteenth century. We also know that King Henry III had some for dinner in 1251. Gerald of Wales noted in 1185 that wild peacock abounded in the woods here. As peafowl are not native, it may be Capercaillie to which he was referring. Birds, which some have identified as peacocks, appear in the Book of Kells. Peafowl are not farmed commercially for food in Ireland. In Greek mythology, Hera, the wife of Zeus, had the hundred eyes of her servant, the giant Argus Panoptes, preserved in a peacock's tail forever. Peacocks pulled her wagon and were sacred to her.

CULINARY

Peacocks have long been a delicacy for kings and nobles, and birds were usually fattened up long in advance of major feasts. The Greeks and Romans were particularly fond of them. As with many birds, the younger are favoured over the elder.

NAMES

English: Blue Peafowl, Common Peafowl (*cristatus*)

Irish: Cearc phéacóige (pea hen), Coileach péacóg/péacóige (Peacock north Conn.), Péacóg choiteann (common peafowl)

FACTS & FIGURES

Present in Ireland only in the domestic form. Live max fifty years. The national bird of India and Sri Lanka. Collective name: a muster of peacocks, an ostentation of peacocks. Two species of *Pavo* worldwide. Order *Galliformes*, Family *Phasianidae*.

Beliefs & Traditions: It was thought bad luck in parts of Ireland to have any representation of a peacock inside the house as the 'eyes' on the display feathers were thought to bring bad luck. A peacock's harsh call signalled the approach of rain.

Peacocks represented the incorruptibility of Christ, reflecting the ancient belief that a peacock's flesh was incorruptible. In Ireland, it was thought that they never died but flew away to heaven.

Similes: As proud as a peacock.

The (Helmeted) Guineafowl

Cearc Ghuine | *Numida meleagris*

Guineafowl are large turkey-like birds from Africa. They have recently made their way onto the plates of Irish restaurants. A few are kept with farm poultry around Ireland. While there are several species of guineafowl, the most common to be seen in domestication is the Helmeted Guineafowl (*Numida meleagris*), looking somewhat like camouflaged military helmets on legs. They have spotted dark-grey plumage with blue-white featherless heads sporting a red wattle. Guineafowl can mate with domestic chickens but the offspring are sterile. Young are known as 'keets'. The generic *numida* means coming from Numidia, the ancient name for part of northwest Africa. The specific *meleagris* is Greek for 'guineafowl'.

CULINARY

Guineafowl are bred for meat and are said to taste like Pheasant.

NAMES

English: Guinea Fowl, Guineahen, Helmeted Guineafowl, Pintada/Pintado, Poorman's Pheasant

Irish: Giní, Coileach Guine

Scientific: Phasianus meleagris

FACTS & FIGURES

Present in Ireland only in the domestic form. Omnivorous. Weigh over 1 kg. About six species of the Numididae family including one *Numida* worldwide. Order: *Galliformes*; Family: *Numididae*.

5. Birds from our Past

5.1 BIRDS FROM OUR PAST

'Ní bheidh ár leithéid arís ann.'[1]

A number of birds have become extinct in Ireland over the years. Some are making a comeback; some are perhaps gone forever. Those listed here include, Bitterns, Cranes, Bean Geese, the Golden and White-tailed Eagles, the Red and Black Kites, the Ospreys, Great Auks, Marsh Harriers, Goshawks, Gyrfalcons, Corn Buntings and Capercaillies.

Over the years though there may have been many more. There are many British species that are absent from Ireland (e.g. the woodpeckers and Nuthatches) that may once have lived here. Other exotic species, which may have lived here include Dalmatian Pelicans, Great Bustards and Eagle Owls. There are historical references to a 'Great Irish Owl'. Birds, such as Barnacle Geese, which still visit, may once have bred here.

Yet other breeding birds are close to extinction here. Corncrakes are seriously endangered. Corn Buntings are almost certainly gone, as are Quail. Grey Partridges and Red Grouse are endangered. Birds like Ring Ouzels, Nightjars and Cuckoos are becoming increasingly uncommon. Even common garden birds like Song Thrushes and House Sparrows have suffered serious declines in numbers. Red and amber list birds can be found listed in Section 6.

There are a large number of factors causing these extinctions and reductions and indeed some species' populations wax and wane in cyclic fashion over long periods. Nevertheless, new large-scale building projects, changed farming methods and use of pollutant chemicals have led to habitat destruction and loss of traditional food sources. Potential global warming is also bringing change. Not only birds, but the rest of our fauna and flora are also suffering.

While we have lost many birds, we have also gained some. Most recently, warmth-loving Little Egrets have been populating our southern shores and are now being followed by Cattle Egrets. In the twentieth century, we gained Collared Doves. Fulmars, Mistle Thrushes, Siskins and Stock Doves arrived a century earlier. Our ubiquitous Magpies arrived here only in the seventeenth century. Nonetheless, the trend seems to be a downward one and large-scale survey work and action are needed if we are not to lose more of our native species.

While these birds are no longer with us, they have left their mark in our lore. The birds are laid out in this section in standard taxonomic order.

5.1.1 The (Eurasian) Bittern

Bonnán (buí) | *Botaurus stellaris stellaris*

Bitterns are large water birds, slightly smaller than herons. The birds show an overall streaked light-brown camouflage colour, with a long black 'moustache' and cap and a white throat. The stout yellow bill is long and pointed. The sexes are alike. They are birds of quiet reed beds, far from the madding crowd.

Bitterns have an extraordinary plan of defence. When approached, a Bittern will point its bill straight up towards the sky and stretch out as far as it can, as if in imitation of the reeds around it. They have even been reported to sway gently with the reeds. While this behaviour may sound somewhat like that of an Ostrich burying its head in the sand, a Bittern's sensational military-style camouflage blends it into the background almost perfectly. If not successful in hiding, Bitterns will defend themselves vigorously against all attackers, including man. The bill is reputed to have inflicted grievous wounds on many a poacher and they allegedly target the eyes of their assailants.[2] A Bittern's eyes look downwards when the bill is horizontal and look straight forwards when the bill is pointing up.

Bitterns are perhaps best known for the 'booming' call of the males. The sound is somewhat similar to that produced when one blows across the open top of a bottle. To hear a Bittern in the reeds in the small hours of a sunny morning is one of life's 'must-dos'. The sound is an otherworldly expulsion of air. Oliver Goldsmith described it as 'dismally hollow' and seeming to come from 'some formidable being that resided at the bottom of the waters'.[3] You will be very privileged indeed to hear a Bittern in Ireland but they can still be seen and heard at a few locations in Britain.

The generic *botaurus* comes from the Latin *boatum tauri* meaning 'bull's bellow' relating to the booming call. The specific *stellaris* refers to the star-like spotty camouflage. The Irish, *Bonnán buí* translates roughly and perhaps poetically as 'yellow siren'. They were known, quite delightfully, as 'butter-bums' in parts of Britain.

History: Bitterns were once relatively common breeding birds in Ireland. Their numerous names in the Irish language, multiple literary references and occurrence in many place names attest to their being here in big numbers in antiquity. In fact, they have been here right up to the middle of the nineteenth century. Nesting ceased here around 1840.[4] Since then although being regarded as 'absent' from Ireland, increasingly more visitors are seen. This, in part, may be due to more birds arriving from Britain where they are uncommon. It may also be the case that the highly secretive Bitterns have always been visiting, albeit in small numbers, unbeknownst to the human world. A greater general knowledge of ornithology today means that more rare birds are seen and recorded on a regular basis. As the birds are sensitive to cold winters the increase in numbers is slow. Many of our larger mires and bogs were drained in the nineteenth century. Now we may no longer have any reeded wetlands big enough to sustain an indigenous pollution.

Beliefs & Traditions: The boom of a Bittern was regarded as a warning from the spirit world and this may be one possible origin for the wailing of the banshee.[5] Like many birds, it was believed that a Bittern's boom was the cry of a departed soul from purgatory. Goldsmith, who grew up in Ireland in the eighteenth century, tells us that in his childhood he remembers the locals were terrified by the birds' call. They believed it presaged some sad event. If someone subsequently died, the Bittern, which they called the 'night raven' was blamed.[6]

Some people thought that Bitterns made their airy call by blowing through a hollow reed or by ducking their heads under water and blowing hard!

Poetry: from '*An Bonnán Buí*'

> *A bhonnán bhuí, is é mo léan do luí,*
> *Is do chnámha sínte tar éis do ghrinn,*
> *Is chan easba bidh ach díobháil dí*
> *a d'fhág i do luí thú ar chúl do chinn.*
> *Is measa liom féin ná scrios na Traoi*
> *Tú bheith i do luí ar leaca lom',*
> *Is nach ndearna tú díth ná dolaidh sa tír,*
> *Is nárbh fhearra leat fíon ná uisce poll.*

Cathal Buí Mac Giolla Gunna (1680–1756)

from '*The Yellow Bittern*'

> *Yellow Bittern I'm sad it's all over.*
> > *Your bones are frozen and all caved in.*
> *It wasn't hunger but thirst and craving*
> > *That left you foundering on the shore.*
> *What odds is it now about Troy's destruction*
> > *With you on the flagstones upside down,*
> *Who never injured or hurt a creature*
> > *And preferred bog-water to any wine?*

Translated by Seamus Heaney (from 'An Bonnán Buí', Cathal Buí Mac Giolla Gunna)

The (Eurasian) Bittern continued

CULINARY

In Ireland, as in Britain, Bitterns were highly regarded for the table, by nobility and royalty. They were also believed to be a cure for many an ill. They were sold at food markets in Ennis, Co. Clare and in Dublin.[7] Their culinary and medicinal popularity may have contributed to their extinction here.

PLACE NAMES

Viewers of RTÉ's *Killinaskully* will be aware that Jacksie Walsh's pub is called 'An Bonnán Buí'.
Curraghbonaun, Co. Sligo (Bittern-bog)
Feabunaun, Co. Cork (Bittern of the rushes)
Inishbobunnan, Clew Bay, Co. Mayo (Inis-Bó Bunnán, cow island of the Bitterns)
Tievebunnan, Co. Fermanagh (Taobh an Bhonnáin, Bittern's side [of a river, possibly])

NAMES

English: Bitter Bum, Bog Drum, Bog Drummer, Bog Trotter, Brown Crane, Great Bittern, Mire Drum (Uls.), Night Raven

Irish: Béicire (yeller, Kry.), Bonnán léana (the water-meadow siren), Bunán, Bonnán/Bunnán buidhe/buí (yellow Bittern), Bunnán léana, Corr, Stearnal,[8] Tarbh curraig (bog bull), Troghan[9]

Uls. Scots: Bog Bluiter

Scientific: Ardea stellaris

FACTS & FIGURES

Now only very rare visitors to Ireland. Carnivorous. Live max eleven years. Collective name: a sedge of Bitterns, a siege of Bitterns. About four species of *Botaurus* and thirteen species of Bittern in total worldwide. Order: *Ciconiiformes*; Family: *Ardeidae*.

5.1.2 The (Common) Crane

Grús | *Grus grus grus*

Cranes were once common in Ireland but probably became extinct here in the fourteenth century. Huge yet elegant birds, in recent times they have been returning to Ireland, albeit in very small numbers. Males are largely grey, with black and white heads, red cap, and rump feathers not unlike those of an Ostrich. Sexes are alike. They are considerably taller than herons, coming up to the shoulder of a human being. European birds winter in southern Europe and Africa with huge migrating flocks flying in typical 'V' formation. Spain still hosts about 80,000 birds in winter (99–00).

The English name 'crane' and the general Irish name for a crane, *corr*, probably come from the Indo-European root 'gar' or 'kar' meaning to cry out. Though now officially called *Grús* in Irish, they were traditionally referred to as *Corr mhóna*. They have loud far-reaching calls generated in their metre-long curled tracheae.[10] Cranes are symbols of long life, fidelity, grace, prosperity and peace.

History: Gerald of Wales mentions the presence of Cranes in Ireland in the twelfth century[11] but we cannot be sure that this is not a reference to herons. He says that Cranes were so numerous that you could see a hundred or more in one flock alone. We know they were here earlier as their bones turn up in midden sites. They may have been gone by the fourteenth century and certainly by the seventeenth. Long absent, a few still stray to Ireland on migration. They are beginning to recolonise the Norfolk Broads in Britain and as they establish themselves more there, we may see more birds in Ireland again.

The word 'pedigree' comes from the French *pied de grue* (Crane's foot) which in turn comes from a Crane's common stance with one foot raised, which was later used in heraldry; a crane depicted with a stone held in one claw symbolising vigilance. It was believed that Cranes stood thus so that if the bird nodded off, the stone would drop and the bird would wake.[12] In fact, it is likely that the Crane stands like this to keep one foot warm.

Beliefs & Traditions: Cranes were associated with both the Cailleach witch and the sea god Manannán Mac Lir who possessed a bag of magical treasures made from crane skin. They were birds of the moon, magic, shamanic travel, secrets, and deep mysteries. Cranes also represented the logical mind, as well as patience while healing occurs.

It was said that the body of a Crane should be buried for a month in a keg or other suitable container in a manure heap. At the end of the month, greasy oil will have collected at the bottom of the container and this oil is an excellent treatment for burns.[13] (It is possible this refers to a heron.)

It was believed that migrating Cranes swallowed a stone before they departed. The stone acted as ballast, keeping the Cranes on course even in heavy winds.

The (Common) Crane continued

The regurgitated stone was thought to be a touchstone (tester) for gold. Gerald of Wales believed a Crane's liver was so powerful it could digest iron.[14]

It was believed that one of the wonders of Ireland was a Crane that was to be found on the island of Inis Kea, in County Mayo, where it had lived since the beginning of the world.

Legend tells us that the Tuatha Dé Danann god King Midir owned three magical Cranes, which stood outside his castle as sentries.[15]

In the mountains of Ulster, St Beanus[16] was said to give sanctuary from the locals to Cranes and grouse (possibly herons and Cranes).[17]

Proverbs & Similes:

A wren in the hand is better than a crane to be caught.

CULINARY

The nobility ate Cranes in Ireland and their popularity may have contributed to their extinction here. They were favoured above birds of the heron family because of the high percentage of vegetation in their diets; the herons ate only fish. The Normans hunted Crane in large numbers, with hawks and arrows, and we know that King Henry II ate some in Dublin in the twelfth century.[18] The invention of guns may have hastened their decline. There is evidence of a taboo against eating Crane flesh among the ordinary Irish people and they may have had druidic significance.[19] There is evidence that they were kept as pets, in the Middle Ages and perhaps before, in a similar way to peacocks.[20] St Colmcille may have kept one.

PLACE NAMES

Inishnagor, Co. Donegal, Co. Sligo (Inis na gCorr, Crane or heron island) Monagor, Co. Monaghan (crane or heron-bog) Many islands on lakes in counties Cavan and Monaghan are called Crane Island. As is always the case with these birds, it is unknown if these names stretch far enough back in time to refer to real Cranes or were used later to refer to herons, when the Cranes were gone.

NAMES

English: Craneling (yng.)

Irish: Bunnán léana (Bittern of the water-meadow),[21] Corr ghlas (grey crane), Corr mhóna/mónadh (bog crane), (and any heron name)

Scientific: Ardea grus, Grus cinerea, Grus communis

FACTS & FIGURES

Extinct in Ireland. A handful now visit every year. Omnivores. Live max seventeen years. Collective name: a sedge of cranes. About fifteen species in the *Gruidae* family including eleven species of *Grus* worldwide. Order: *Gruiformes*; Family: *Gruidae*.

5.1.3 The (Taiga) Bean Goose

Síolghé | *Anser fabalis fabalis*

Bean Geese are now rare winter visitors to Ireland but it is likely that they were much more common in the past. A Bean Goose looks very much like a typical large 'grey goose', superficially similar to a Greylag or White-fronted Goose and particularly so to a Pink-footed Goose (*Anser brachyrhynchus, Gé ghobghearr*). Indeed Bean Geese were not distinguished from Pink-footed Geese until 1833. The birds show an all-over brown-grey with distinct white edges to the feathers. Rear underparts are white. The bill is bright orange and black and the feet are bright orange.

The birds were called 'bog geese' in Ireland, a name shared with the White-fronted geese. The English name 'bean' comes from the birds' habit of grazing in bean-field stubble.[22] This is reflected in the specific *fabalis*, coming from the Latin *faba* meaning 'bean'. The Irish *síolghé* means 'seed-goose'.

NAMES

English: Bog Goose,[23] Great Harrow Goose (possibly White-fronted Goose), Wild Goose

Scientific: Anas fabalis, Anas segetum/segtum, Anser arvensis

FACTS & FIGURES

Very rare winter/spring visitors to Ireland from continent. Herbivores. Live max twenty-five years. About eight species of *Anser* worldwide. Order: *Anseriformes*; Family: *Anatidae*.

307

5.1.4 The (Western) Marsh Harrier

Cromán móna | *Circus aeruginosus aeruginosus*

Stunning birds, the largest of the harriers, Marsh Harriers can be told from other harriers by their large size and lack of white on the rump. Males are largely brown with slate-blue-grey wing markings and fawn-coloured heads. Females are larger and dark chocolate-brown with very distinct fawn-gold heads. The birds live up to the name 'harriers', harrying and harassing water birds, mammals and reptiles. Like other harriers, they are often seen 'quartering' over reed beds and marshes. Oddly enough, this hunting flight, with eyes constantly looking down, can lead to accidents when they collide with other objects. They are also known for their courtship aerobatics. In 1853, Watters tells us that Marsh Harriers were the 'most abundant of our larger birds of prey' and 'widely distributed'.[24] They were extinct in Ireland by 1917 probably as a result of shooting, egg collection and wetland drainage. By the turn of the millennium, however, they were back making regular summer visits. The Irish *Cromán móna* means 'bog harrier'. The specific *aeruginosus* is Latin for 'rusty coloured'.

PLACE NAMES

Curraghatouk, Co. Kerry (Corrach an tSeabhaic, bog/marsh of the hawk)

NAMES

English: Brown Hawk, Duck Hawk, Kite (Uls.), Moor Buzzard, Moor Harrier, Snipe Hawk, Western Harrier

Irish: Clamhán móna (bog Buzzard), Préachán na gcearc (hen crow)[25]

Scientific: Falco aeruginosus

FACTS & FIGURES

Extinct as a breeding species here. Now rare summer visitors to the southeast. Carnivorous. Live max twenty years. About fourteen species of *Circus* worldwide. Order: *Falconiformes*; Family: *Accipitridae*.

5.1.5 The Golden Eagle

Iolar fíréan | *Aquila chrysaetos chrysaetos*

'*He clasps the crag with crooked hands.*'[26]

Ireland was once home to large numbers of magnificent wild eagles. What's more, we had two species, the Golden Eagles and the White-tailed or Fishing Eagles.

The Golden Eagle continued

Golden Eagles are huge birds and cannot be confused with any other in this country at close range. The adults are generally a brown colour with a light-brown/gold head but in certain light, an all-over golden sheen can be seen. The feet are bright yellow. Sexes are alike with females larger. Young birds show white panels on the wings. They mate for life and build their eyries on perilously high, inaccessible cliffs. Golden Eagles will hunt a variety of birds and animals. They are big enough to take animals up to the size of a small lamb but such attacks are rare. There are anecdotal tales of eagles taking small babies but these remain unproven.

The generic *Aquila* means 'eagle' whilst the specific *chrysaetos* means 'Golden Eagle'. The Irish *Iolar firéan* means 'true eagle'.

History: Eagles suffered unmercifully at the hands of farmers, gamekeepers, egg collectors and trophy hunters. They were killed off in the nineteenth century by shooting, poisoning and trapping, finally dying out altogether early in the early twentieth century. Breeding may have stopped in Ireland by 1912.[27] Since then they have been reported in the far north of the country, probably as visitors from Scotland. They were obviously present in Connacht, appearing on that province's flag. Now there is a major effort to re-establish birds in Glenveagh National Park in Donegal with birds from Scotland, by the Golden Eagle Trust Ltd. (GET[28]). A chick hatched there in early 2007, the first in almost a century.

Gerald of Wales mentions eagles in his travels in Ireland in the twelfth century.[29] He says you will see as many eagles in Ireland as you will kites elsewhere. Given that we know how numerous the Red Kites were in urban Europe, there must have been very many eagles in Ireland indeed. Gerald also believed that eagles were a golden-brown colour from being scorched from flying to close to the sun.[30]

The birds appear on the coats of arms of many countries, provinces and cities right across the world. They often appear in churches as golden lectern supports, dedicated to the apostle St John. St John is also represented in the Book of Kells as an eagle.

Beliefs & Traditions: Eagles were symbols of wisdom and long life. They represented keen sight, knowledge of magic, and swiftness and were believed to be the most long-lived birds.[31] Euripides tells us that 'birds in general are messengers of the gods, but the eagle is king, and interpreter of the great deity Jupiter'.

There are stories in Ireland of eagles taking human children. Payne-Gallwey[32] tells such a story from the island of Achill (the island of the eagle): A woman with a young infant was trying to defend her chickens from a fox. She laid her infant down to chase after the fox but when she returned she discovered a large eagle making off with her child. The eagle soon became just a speck in the distance, heading towards Clare Island, five miles off shore. Soon she had the local men in boats heading out to the island. There they discovered the eagle's nest on a ledge of rock and men were soon lowered on ropes. To everyone's amazement, the young eaglets were busy eating their way through a fresh lamb carcass and ignoring the child who was sleeping nearby, totally unharmed, still wrapped in the thick red flannel in which Achill women wrapped their babies. Soon mother and child were reunited.

It is a traditional belief that Adam and Eve exist as eagles on the island of Inisbofin off County Galway.[33]

In Waterford and Wexford, the Pooka appears as an eagle with a massive wingspan.

Poetry: from: '*The Eagle*'

He clasps the crag with crooked hands;
Close to the sun in lonely lands,
Ring'd with the azure world, he stands.
The wrinkled sea beneath him crawls;
He watches from his mountain walls,
And like a thunderbolt he falls.

Alfred, Lord Tennyson (1842)

Proverbs & Similes:

Chomh hard leis an iolar. (As high as an eagle.)

Chomh liath leis an iolar. (As grey as an eagle.)

'You cannot fly like an eagle with the wings of a wren.' – William Henry Hudson

PLACE NAMES

Bunanilra, Co. Mayo (eagle's holm)
Carraig an Iolair, Co. Donegal (eagle's Rock, Bluestack Mountains)
Coumaniller, Co. Tipperary (eagle's hollow/valley)
Craiganuller, Co. Tyrone / Derry (eagle's rock)
Drumillard, Co. Monaghan (eagle's ridge)
Drumiller/Drummillar, Co. Down, Co Cavan (Droim Iolair, eagle ridge)
Eagle Craig, Glencloy, Co. Antrim
Eagle's Hill, Co. Kilkenny, Co. Waterford
Eagle's Rock, Co. Leitrim
Gleneagles, Co. Kerry (Gleann Iolair)
Knockinelder, Co. Down (Cnoc an Iolair, eagle hill)
Knockiniller, Co. Tyrone (Cnoc an Iolair, eagle hill)
Meenanillar, Co. Donegal (Mín an iolair, smooth place of the eagle)
Mounteagle, Co. Limerick (Cnoc an Iolair, eagle's hill)
Mount Eagle, Dunquin, Co. Kerry[34] (Sliabh an Iolair, eagle mountain)
Nadanullar, Co. Cork (Nead an iolair, eagle's nest)
Nead na nFolr, Co. Donegal (Eagles' nest, Bluestack Mountains)
Slieveanilra, Co. Clare (eagle mountain)

NAMES

English: Black Eagle, Ring-tailed Eagle

Irish: Fiolar (Din.), Fiolar buí (yellow eagle, Kry.), Ilear, Ilrín (eaglet), Iolar buí/buidhe (yellow eagle, Kry.), Iolarán (eaglet, Kry.), Iolra (Conn.), Iolrach (north Conn.), Rí na n-éan (king of the birds)

Scientific: Aquila fulva, Falco chrysaetos

FACTS & FIGURES

Rare visitors, formerly extinct, now being reintroduced in Donegal. Carnivorous. Weigh 3–6 kg. Two-metre (6-foot) wingspan. Live about fifteen years in the wild (thirty-two max). Collective name: a convocation of eagles. About twelve species of *Aquila* worldwide. Order: *Falconiformes*; Family: *Accipitridae*.

5.1.6 The White-tailed Eagle

Iolar mara | *Haliaeetus albicilla*

NAMES

English: Erne, Sea Eagle, White-tailed Fish-Eagle

Irish: Éan fionn (fair bird),[37] Fiolar mara (sea eagle, Kry.), Iolar earrach (tailed eagle), Iolar ingneach[38] (eagle with talons, Kry.)

Scientific: Aquila albicilla, Falco albicilla

FACTS & FIGURES

Extinct in Ireland. Carnivorous. Some birds reintroduced to Kerry and some may visit from Scotland. Almost one metre in length and weigh 5 kg. Live max twenty-eight years. The national bird of Poland. About eight species of *Haliaeetus* (sea eagle) worldwide. Order: *Falconiformes*; Family: *Accipitridae*.

'When thou seest an eagle, thou seest a portion of genius; lift up thy head!'[35]

Now rare vagrants from Britain and Europe, White-tailed Eagles or Ernes were once at least as common in Ireland as Golden Eagles. They were Ireland's largest birds of prey. Larger even than Golden Eagles and more vulture-like, the 'White-tails' are largely dark brown with a pale brown head and a distinctive white tail. The large bills and feet are bright yellow. Sexes are alike. The larger females can have wingspans of up to 2.5 metres. Particularly fond of fish, they will also take birds, small animals and carrion. They are much more gregarious than the Golden Eagles and in countries where they are common, they can be seen in large groups. From their fondness for fishing we get the Irish name *Iolar mara* meaning 'sea eagle'.

The generic *Haliaeetus* comes from the Greek *halos* meaning sea and *aetos* meaning eagle/hawk. The specific *albicilla* is a contrived word meaning 'white-tailed'. The bird is closely related to the American Bald Eagle (*Haliaeetus leucocephalus, Iolar maol*), the national bird of the United States. The old Irish name 'Erne' probably comes from the Old Norse/Icelandic *örn*, meaning eagle.

History: Many commentators attest to the ubiquity of 'White-tails' in Ireland right up to the nineteenth century. As with Golden Eagles, the increased importance of gamekeeping in Victorian Ireland led to more and more birds being killed. With the arrival of better guns and poisons such as strychnine, they were wiped out in large numbers towards the end of the nineteenth century. Egg collecting also took its toll and, as was the case with many species, as the birds became rarer they became the targets of trophy collectors who would often work to order. They were extinct here by 1910.

Like the Golden Eagles in Donegal, an attempt is now being made to reintroduce the White-tails to Killarney National Park, County Kerry, by the Golden Eagle Trust Ltd. (GET).

Beliefs & Traditions: The Anglo-Saxons believed that the bones of sea eagles possessed curative properties and the body fat was used in a complex ointment.[36]

5.1.7 The Osprey

Coirneach | *Pandion haliaetus haliaetus*

Ospreys are magnificent fishing raptors looking like undersized black and white eagles. They show largely a chocolate-brown colour on top with dirty white below. The head is mostly white with dark streaks, looking something like a cross between a tonsured monk and a masked bandit. The feet are a distinctive pale blue-grey. Sexes are similar. Many Ospreys winter in Africa.

Ospreys live on fish, which they catch by dipping into the water, on the wing, and pulling out with their considerable talons. The fish is always turned so it faces forwards and the Ospreys have special spiky pads on their feet to hold the wriggling fish.

The Irish word *coirneach* means 'tonsured'[39] as an adjective or 'tonsured monk' as a noun and obviously refers to the birds' monk-like bald patches. The original Irish name in full may have been *Iascaire coirneach* (tonsured fisherman). The name 'Osprey' comes from the Latin *ossifragus* meaning 'bone breaker'. The generic *pandion* was a legendary king of Attica (Greece) and the specific *haliaetus* means 'sea hawk'.

The Osprey continued

History: Formerly plentiful in Ireland, Ospreys were extinct here by the late eighteenth century. They are now making a slow recovery. More are seen in summer every year along the east and south coast. While reported as extinct here in 1779, Payne-Gallwey says they were commonly seen in Killarney in the nineteenth century.[40] They have a distinctive regal white crown and long legs in proportion to their bodies. They are sensitive to DDT and other chemicals and have suffered at the hands of farmers and other hunters in the past.

Beliefs & Traditions: Gerald of Wales mentions the presence of Ospreys in Ireland in the twelfth century.[41] He says they were numerous here and relates an erroneous belief that each of an Osprey's feet was uniquely distinct. It was believed that one of the Osprey's feet was equipped with talons to catch fish and that the other was more webbed and used for swimming. Today we know that both feet have talons. Molyneux in 1684 believed that Ospreys dropped fat out of their rear ends, which attracted and stunned fish!

It was also believed that Ospreys had the power to put fish under a spell and that they were covered in an oily substance that was irresistible to fish.[42]

In the nineteenth century in Ireland, it was believed that if an Osprey was shot along the coast, all the herring and mackerel would immediately disappear.[43]

PLACE NAMES

Knocknagornagh, Co. Limerick (Cnoc na gCoirneach, Osprey's (or monk's) hill)
Osprey Island, Osprey Rock, Lough Leane, Co. Kerry

NAMES

English: Fishing Eagle, Fish/Fishing Hawk, Sea Eagle, Sea Hawk

Irish: Cóirneach, Cóirnigh ghlasa, Éan fionn (fair bird),[44] Fáspróg, Fiolar mara (sea eagle, Kry.), (Iascaire) Cairneach/Coirneach, Iolar ingneach[45] (eagle with talons, Kry.), Iolar mara (sea eagle), Ospróg, Préachán ceannann (bald crow), Seabhac(h) cuain (harbour hawk) (Ant.)

Scientific: Falco haliaetus, Falco ossifragus

FACTS & FIGURES

Were extinct in Ireland. Now rare summer visitors along the east and south coast, becoming more common. May stay to breed. Fish eaters. Live max twenty-six years. Weigh up to 2 kg. State bird of Nova Scotia, Canada. One species of *Pandion* worldwide. Order: *Falconiformes*; Family: *Accipitridae*.

5.1.8 The Red Kite

Cúr rua | *Milvus milvus milvus*

& the Black Kite

Cúr dubh | *Milvus migrans migrans*

Red Kite

Black Kite

Common in Ireland in the Middle Ages, Red Kites are large rusty-brown raptors with light grey heads and distinctive light-brown forked tails. White underwing patches show up in flight. Sexes are alike. They can be seen in open country, hunting harrier-style, low over fields and marshes and will take small animal and carrion. The distinctive forked tail always identifies a kite.

Even rarer cousins, the Black Kites make the odd rare appearance here. They appear black from a distance. Up close, they show a general dark chocolate-brown colour with greyish head. Under parts are lighter. Yellow legs contrast the dark appearance. Like their red cousins, they will eat any small animal and carrion. They rarely stray far from water.

History: Kites had a reputation for taking poultry but there are reports that they themselves could be taken by larger raptors, presumably Peregrines, Gyrfalcons or eagles. They may also have been used as targets, in this way, in falconry.

Historically, Red and Black Kites were found in big numbers across Europe and still are in some Asian countries. Germany still hosts over 10,000 pairs of Red Kites

The Red Kite & the Black Kite continued

(95–99) and France well over 20,000 pairs of Black Kites (00–02). In some Asian countries, they can be found still in huge numbers in urban locations and are regarded as scavengers and thieves. British soldiers of the Raj in India referred to them as 'shite hawks' because of their indiscriminate defecation. In *A Winter's Tale*, Shakespeare noted 'when the kite builds, look to your lesser linen'. They may have once haunted Irish cities in a similar way.

Historically, Red Kites are hard to track in Ireland, as Buzzards, harriers and other raptors were sometimes referred to as kites. In the 1660s, Col. Edward Cooke, a park keeper in the Phoenix Park, Dublin, mentions that 'kites and poachers' were taking all the partridges. Thompson records a few in the 1830s.[46] They probably became extinct in Ireland in the early nineteenth century. Red Kites were reintroduced to County Wicklow in 2007 and to County Down in 2008.

Beliefs & Traditions: In some parts of Ireland, and particularly Limerick in the sixteenth century, to prevent kites from taking chickens, the shells in which they were hatched were hung up in the roof of the house.[47]

Poetry: from: '*An Evening Walk*'

> *While, near the midway cliff, the silvered kite*
> *In many a whistling circle wheels her flight;*

William Wordsworth (1787)

Similes:

Chomh fial leis an éan fionn.
(As generous as a kite, i.e. not generous!)

PLACE NAMES
Carrickacroman, Co. Cavan (kite rock (or harrier rock))

NAMES
RED KITE
English: Glead, Glede, Pricane-na-cark

Irish: Cromán (harrier), Cubhar (kite), Éan fionn (fair bird),[48] Garbh-sheabhac (rough-hawk), Préachán ceirteach (rag crow), Préachán geárr (bird crow), Préachán gobhlach (beaked crow), Préachán na gcearc (hen crow)

Scientific: Falco milvus, Milvus ictinus, Milvus regalis

BLACK KITE
Irish: Cnáimhfhiach (bone Raven)

Scientific: Falco migrans, Milvus ater, Milvus korschun, Milvus niger

FACTS & FIGURES
RED KITE: Extinct as a breeding bird in Ireland. Now rare visitors usually from Wales or Scotland and re-introduced in Wicklow. Carnivorous. Live max twenty-five years . Weigh up to 1.5 kg.

BLACK KITE: Extremely rare visitors from Europe. Carnivorous. Live max twenty-three years.

Three species of *Milvus* worldwide. Order: *Falconiformes*; Family: *Accipitridae*.

The (Northern) Goshawk

Spioróg mhór | *Accipiter gentilis gentilis*

Goshawks are spectacular large raptors looking like huge Sparrowhawks (hence the Irish name *Spioróg mhór*). As the females are substantially larger than males, it is possible to mistake a female Sparrowhawk for a male Goshawk. Sexes are broadly alike in terms of colouring. Males show an overall grey colour with distinct lateral grey-white barring on the breast, underparts and feathery legs. A broad white eyebrow and piercing yellow-orange eyes complete the distinguished look. Females show more of a brown sheen but this can vary with light, across different subspecies and, across different individuals. While the *gentilis* subspecies is the most likely to be seen in Ireland, other subspecies are possible but extremely rare. Young birds replace grey with mottled brown. In early spring, adult males give a spectacular roller-coaster display.

The larger size of a Goshawk allows it to take larger prey than a Sparrowhawk. Goshawks will take pigeons and corvids and larger rabbit-sized mammals.

The name Goshawk derives from an Anglicisation of the Anglo-Saxon for goose hawk. In the Middle Ages, only nobles were allowed to 'hawk' with Goshawks hence the Latin name *gentilis* meaning 'noble, and *accipiter* meaning 'hawk'.

History: Goshawks have been unmercifully persecuted across Europe. They are safe only in the huge, sparsely populated forests of northern Europe. The birds probably became extinct in Ireland in the early nineteenth century but they were in all probability more widespread here. Numerous literary references attest to their presence here in numbers. As with other raptors, the reasons for their demise are many. With the popularity of falconry, Goshawks may have been protected and managed since the coming of the Normans. Sometime around the beginning of the eighteenth century, the gentry turned their favours from falconry to game shooting. With the emphasis now on the protection of game birds such as grouse

The (Northern) Goshawk continued

and Pheasant, Goshawks and other raptors saw a rapid change in their status from heroes to villains and were systematically wiped out. While very rare now in Ireland, a few may be staying to breed.

NAMES

Irish: Meirliún (Merlin), Seabhac mór (big hawk)

Scientific: Astur gentilis, Astur palumbarius, Falco gentilis, Falco palumbarius

FACTS & FIGURES

Formerly extinct, a handful may now breed here. Carnivorous. Live max eighteen years.
Collective name: a flight of Goshawks. Amber list.
Fifty species of *Accipiter* (Goshawks and Sparrowhawks) worldwide. Order: *Falconiformes*; Family: *Accipitridae*.

5.1.10 The Gyrfalcon

Fabhcún mór | *Falco rusticolus*

The world's largest falcons, Gyrfalcons are huge birds from the Arctic, larger even than Peregrines. Gyrfalcons have white, grey and dark phases. The darkest phase looks like a huge menacing Peregrine. The all-white 'Greenland' falcon and the pale-grey 'Iceland' Falcon were previously considered separate species and then subspecies known as *Falco rusticolus candicans* and *Falco rusticolus islandus* respectively. Today, no subspecies are officially identified. They are simply regarded as different colour morphs.

The Irish *Fabhcún mór* simply means 'big falcon'. The specific *rusticolus* means 'of the country'. The English 'gyr' may derive from 'gyrate', referring to the birds circling in the air while hunting.

History: Though never common in Ireland, they may have been more numerous in the past. There are numerous reports of 'Greenland' and 'Iceland' falcons shot in Ireland in the nineteenth century and we now know these to be different colour phases of the Gyrfalcon. The birds turn up in very small numbers in Ireland and Britain now with several sightings in some years, for example in counties Clare and Antrim.

Along with Goshawks, Gyrfalcons were the preferred birds of kings, in falconry.

NAMES

English: Gerfalcon, Greenland Falcon, Iceland Falcon, Jer Falcon, Norwegian Falcon

Scientific: Falco candicans, Falco groenlandicus, Falco gyrfalco, Falco islandicus, Falco obsoletus, Falco swarthi, Hierofalco grebnitzkii, Hierofalco gyrfalco, Hierofalco islandus, Hierofalco rusticolus.

FACTS & FIGURES

Very rare vagrant winter visitors to Ireland. Weigh up to 2 kg. Live max twelve years. The national bird of Iceland and the state bird of the Canadian Northwest Territories. Nearly forty species of *Falco* worldwide. Order: *Falconiformes*; Family: *Falconidae*.

Gyrfalcon

5.1.11 The (Western) Capercaillie

Capall coille | *Tetrao urogallus*

These magnificent grouse, now confined to the highlands of Scotland[49] and the forests of Europe, may once have been common in Ireland. About the size of turkeys, the males are generally blue-black in colour with brown wings, white markings, a red wattle above the eye, a beard and huge fantail. Females are barred brown above and white below. During courtship, the males fan their tails and make an extraordinary 'clip-clop' sound rising to a crescendo and ending with a large distinct 'pop'. This may have given rise to the original Gaelic name *Capall coille*, 'the horse of the woods', or *Capall coilleach*, 'the horse-cock' from which we get the modern name Capercaillie. *Gabhar coille*, 'goat of the woods', is another possibility. The courtship is carried out on a special 'lek' display on the ground, which the birds defend against all comers. At this time, the birds can become aggressive towards humans and are of sufficient size that visitors should beware. They are close enough to Pheasant and Black Grouse to be able to hybridise occasionally.

One other species, the Black-billed Capercaillie (*Tetrao parvirostris*) breeds in eastern Russia and China.

The generic *Tetrao* is from Greek/Roman meaning 'black grouse' while the specific *urogallus* translates as 'tail-cock'. The Irish alternative *Coileach feá* translates as 'cock of the woods'. It was most likely referred to as 'Cock of the Wood' in English, in Ireland.

History: Although the historical presence of Capercaillies in Ireland is not proven, Gordon D'Arcy in *Ireland's Lost Birds* makes a good case for their being here.[50] Gerald of Wales noted the presence of what might have been Capercaillies in Ireland in large numbers in the twelfth century[51] which he called peacocks or pavones. They may have become extinct here in the late eighteenth century, probably as a result of habitat destruction. Capercaillie-like fossils have been found at a number of sites in Ireland but their identity is not confirmed beyond doubt. Two unsuccessful attempts to reintroduce them were made in the nineteenth century in Sligo and west Cork.[52] There are still about 1 million pairs across Europe and Russia with up to 300,000 pairs in Finland alone (98–02).

CULINARY

Fossil evidence shows they were eaten long ago. They were also hunted more recently before becoming extinct in the eighteenth century. Because of their favoured winter food, conifer needles, they are said to taste of turpentine. If Irish Capercaillies were perhaps accustomed to mixed woodland as they are in some parts of Europe then they may have tasted much better here. Various Irish literary references imply that the birds were highly esteemed for the table.

NAMES

English: Caper-cock (male), Capercailye, Capercailzie, Cock of the Wood(s), wild turkey, Wood Grouse

Irish: Coileach feá[53] (cock of the woods), Caileach coille (hag of the woods), Gabhar coille (goat of the woods)

Scientific: Tetrao major

FACTS & FIGURES

Omnivores, extinct in Ireland. Males weigh 4–6 kg. Live max nine years. Collective name: a tok of Capercaillies. Two species of *Tetrao* worldwide. Order: *Galliformes*; Family: *Tetraonidae*.

5.1.12 The Great Auk

Falcóg mhór | *Pinguinus impennis*

Probably only discovered in the sixteenth century, Great Auks have been extinct worldwide since the 1850s. Looking somewhat like a cross between a Razorbill and a penguin and standing about twice as tall as a Razorbill, they were flightless birds with small flipper-like wings. In summer plumage, the birds were largely black on top, white below, with a white face spot and huge bill. Winter birds showed paler colours with a mottled black and white head.

Great Auks lived on islands right across the north Atlantic and probably migrated south (by swimming) in winter. The original name 'penguin', may be from the Welsh *pen gwyn* (white head). Alternatively, it may derive from the generic Latin name *pinguinus* meaning 'pin-winged' (i.e. the bird cannot fly) or *pinguis* meaning the adjective 'fat' or the noun 'grease'. The alternative *alca* is from Latin meaning 'auk' but may originally have meant 'stupid bird'. The specific *impennis* means 'non-winged' or 'flightless'.

History: Great Auk bones have been discovered in Ireland in prehistoric 'middens' on the coasts of Antrim, Donegal, Clare and Waterford.[54] It is not known if the birds in Irish waters were residents or visiting migrants. Despite not being able to fly they were excellent swimmers and did migrate. There are reports in the eighteenth century, as late as 1802 of large penguin-like birds on the islands and waters around Ireland but these are not confirmed. Later in the nineteenth century, lists of Irish birds compiled by the leading naturalists of the time do not mention the Great Auks. According to Thompson, Ussher and Watters,[55] a live bird was caught off Brownstown Head, Waterford, in 1834 and was kept in captivity for four months before dying. This is likely to be the same bird that Payne-Gallwey refers to as being in the 'University Museum', Dublin, and which Dr Burkitt presented to the museum of Trinity College in 1844 (now in the National Museum). There is some evidence that Great Auks, like many other sea birds, were allowed to be eaten during Lent[56] as they was regarded as more fish than fowl.

Great Auks were exploited and eventually hunted to extinction by man for their eggs, meat, fat and down and because they were easy targets. They were constantly targeted by transatlantic sailors who raided their huge colonies to replenish their supplies, with no thought to conservation. It is thought that the last few colonies persisted in the waters around Iceland. The last few were probably dead by 1850.

A lovely story from Scotland tells of some locals who were on the island of Stac an Armin, in the St Kilda archipelago in 1840. They were looking for seabirds for food when they came across a Great Auk. They brought it home alive, as a curiosity. When the weather turned bad, the Great Auk was blamed. They took the bird for a witch, put it on trial, found it guilty and killed it! This was the last Great Auk seen in Britain.

CULINARY

The Great Auk's edibility, and that of its huge eggs, led to its extinction.

NAMES

English: Garefowl, Gair-Fowl, (Northern) Penguin

Scientific: Alca impennis

FACTS & FIGURES

Extinct worldwide. Carnivorous. Half to one metre long. Weighed about 5 kg.
Order: *Charadriiformes*;
Family: *Alcidae*.

5.1.13 The Corn Bunting

Gealóg bhuachair | *Emberiza calandra*[57] *clanceyi*

Once widespread across Irish farmland, Corn Buntings have been in decline since the early 1900s and are now probably extinct here.

They are drab brown-streaked birds, roughly the same colour and size as a Skylark. Underparts are dirty white. Birds in winter are duller and the sexes are alike, but males are larger. The song sounds like keys jangling and is delivered from a prominent position like a fence post. Each male is known to have a harem of several females. They are very dependent on arable farmland.

The Irish *Gealóg bhuachair* translates literally as 'bright cow-dung bird'! The generic *Emberiza* is from Latin, perhaps through German, meaning 'bunting'. The specific *calandra* is from Greek meaning 'lark'. The delightful name 'Corn Dumpling' appears in Ulster.

History: Ussher reports, in his *Birds of Ireland* c. 1900, that the birds were widespread on the mainland and islands of Ireland.[58] Throughout the twentieth century, the birds steadily declined. By the end of the millennium there were probably none breeding here. The few birds that are seen here now are probably passage migrants. Some breeding may still occur in the west and northwest. The birds still breed across Eurasia and northern Africa so it is not impossible that they will return some day. They have a mixed diet of insects and weed seeds. We should note the near extinction of such plants as the Corn Cockle (*Agrostemma githago*) in parallel with the disappearance of the Corn Bunting. The intensive removal of agricultural 'weeds' in Ireland and the global drop in insect numbers may be responsible for the bunting's extinction here. Twenty-two million pairs yet remain across Europe, Russia and Turkey.

CULINARY

The birds are edible and were regarded as a delicacy.

NAMES

English: Barley Bunting (Uls.), Briar Bunting (Uls.), Brown Bunting, Bush Lark, Common Bunting, Corn Bird (s.), Corn Dumpling (Uls.), 'the fat bird of the barley' (UK), Hornbill Bunting, Horse Lark (UK), Lark Bunting

Irish: Gealbhan coirce (oats sparrow), Gealbhan scióbóil/sgioboil (barn sparrow), Gealún guib reamhair (fat-billed sparrow), Geárr guirt[59] (small bird of the field)

Scientific: Crithophaga miliaria, Emberiza calandra, Emberiza miliaria, Miliaria calandra, Miliaria europaea

FACTS & FIGURES

Very rare resident omnivores. A handful perhaps yet breed in Ireland. Some winter visitors. Live max nine years. Red list. About forty species of *Emberiza* worldwide. Order: *Passeriformes*; Family: *Emberizidae*.

6. Bird Conservation in Ireland

6. BIRD CONSERVATION IN IRELAND

BirdWatch Ireland and the RSPB NI[1] work together to agree a list of bird species to be given priority treatment for conservation action. These species are called 'Birds of Conservation Concern in Ireland' (BoCCI). The species are classified into three separate lists, Red, Amber and Green, based on the conservation status of the species.

THE RED LIST of birds lists those with high conservation concern (i.e. those whose population or range has declined rapidly in recent years; and those that have declined historically and not shown a substantial recent recovery).

Red-listed species meet one or more of the following criteria:

- Their breeding population or range has declined by more than 50 per cent in the last twenty-five years.

- Their breeding population has undergone a significant decline since 1900.

- They are of global conservation concern.

THE AMBER LIST of birds is of those with medium conservation concern (i.e. those whose population or range has declined moderately in recent years; those whose population has declined historically but made a substantial recent recovery; rare breeders; and those with internationally important or localised populations).

Amber-listed species meet one or more of the following criteria:

- Their breeding population has declined by 25–50 per cent in the last twenty-five years.

- They are rare or sporadically breeding species.

- Their breeding or wintering population is internationally important and/or localised.

- They have an unfavourable conservation status in Europe.

The rest of the Irish birds make up the green list species. These are birds that are regularly occurring and have favourable conservation concern.

In addition, rare birds in the Republic of Ireland are assessed by the Irish Rare Birds Committee (IRBC) under the auspices of BirdWatch Ireland. Rare birds in Northern Ireland are assessed by the Northern Ireland Birdwatchers' Association (NIBA) Records Committee.

6.1 RED LIST

There are currently eighteen birds on the Red list (2007)

Barn Owl
Black-necked Grebe
Chough
Common Scoter
Corn Bunting
Corncrake
Curlew
Grey Partridge
Hen Harrier
Lapwing
Nightjar
Quail
Red Grouse
Red-necked Phalarope
Ring Ouzel
Roseate Tern
Twite
Yellowhammer

6.2 AMBER LIST

There are currently seventy-five birds on the Amber list.

Arctic Tern	Merlin
Bar-tailed Godwit	Peregrine
Bewick's Swan	Pied Flycatcher
Black Guillemot	Pintail
Black-headed Gull	Pochard
Black-tailed Godwit	Puffin
Black-throated Diver	Razorbill
Brent Goose	Red-breasted Merganser
Common Gull	Redpoll
Common Tern	Redshank
Coot	Redstart
Cormorant	Red-throated Diver
Cory's Shearwater	Reed Warbler
Cuckoo	Sand Martin
Dunlin	Sandwich Tern
Eider	Scaup
Gadwall	Shelduck
Gannet	Short-eared Owl
Garganey	Skylark
Golden Plover	Snipe
Goldeneye	Sooty Shearwater
Goosander	Spotted Crake
Goshawk	Spotted Flycatcher
Grasshopper Warbler	Stock Dove
Great Crested Grebe	Stonechat
Grey Plover	Storm Petrel
Greylag Goose	Swallow
Guillemot	Teal
Jack Snipe	Tufted Duck
Kingfisher	Water Rail
Knot	Whinchat
Leach's Petrel	White-fronted Goose
Lesser Whitethroat	Whooper Swan
Little Egret	Wigeon
Little Gull	Wood Warbler
Little Tern	Woodcock
Manx Shearwater	Yellow Wagtail
Mediterranean Gull	

GLOSSARY

anserine	Of the goose family.
aquiline	Of the eagle family.
arboreal	Living in trees.
Badhbh	An Irish war goddess who took the form of a Hooded Crow, Raven or wolf. Also known as a witch or banshee. A sister of Macha and Morrigan. (var: Badb, Badhb) (pronounced 'bov', 'bive').
banshee	An Irish female fairy spirit who appears in several forms, mostly associated with certain families and appearing at night wailing, to forewarn a death in the family. (var: bean-sidhe, bean sí).
bill	Ornithologists' name for a bird's beak.
billing/nebbing	Touching bills together, often by pigeons and doves.
bleating	The sound of air passing through the spread tail feathers of a Snipe (*Gallinago gallinago*) or similar bird as it dives during its display flight (also known as 'drumming').
booming	The far-carrying vocal sound produced by the male Bittern (*Botaurus stellaris*) and having the functions of a song. It is reminiscent of the noise produced by blowing sharply across the mouth of an empty bottle.
busking	The aggressive display of the male Mute Swan (*Cygnus olor*) in which he advances across the water towards an intruder with his neck drawn back and his wings arched, proceeding with a jerky movement and paddling with both feet in unison.
butterfly flight	A slow, fluttering and often erratic type of display flight found, for example, in the Ringed Plover (*Charadrius hiaticula*).
cailleach	In Irish mythology, a hag or witch with god-like powers, sometimes said to feast on the bodies of men.
chack	The short rasping call of a thrush or similar bird.
churring	Producing a continuous deep trill. The best example to be heard in Ireland is the song of the Nightjar (*Caprimulgus europaeus*), which can be sustained for up to five minutes without a break. Many other species have churring call notes, for example the Mistle Thrush (*Turdus viscivorus*).
clumping	Huddling together in a roost in order to conserve body heat. It is characteristic of very small species in winter or when young, examples being the Wren (*Troglodytes troglodytes*) and the Long-tailed Tit (*Aegithalos caudatus*). These tiny birds lose heat more quickly than larger ones.
cock's nest	A nest built by a male bird as part of the courtship ritual. Several such nests may be built by one male, one of which will be selected

	by the female. This behaviour is well seen in the Wren (*Troglodytes troglodytes*).
corvid	A member of the crow family.
croaking	The call of a Raven, and sometimes of a Woodcock.
dovecote	A man-made pigeon house.
drumming	(woodpecker) The sound made by a woodpecker while banging its bill against a tree or other object.
drumming	(snipe) The sound of air passing through the spread tail feathers of a Snipe or similar bird (*Gallinago gallinago*) as it dives during its display flight (also known as 'bleating').
dread	The behaviour of certain tern colonies where the whole colony will take to the air at once and circle a number of times in complete silence before re-alighting and resuming their business.
equinox	One of two times a year when the 'sun crosses the equator' and day and night are about the same length (vernal equinox [about 20 March] and autumnal equinox [about 23 September]). The equinoxes occur at the midpoint between the solstices and vice versa.
Fulmar oil	An evil-smelling oily substance ejected by the Fulmar (*Fulmarus glacialis*) as a defence against a predator. It originates in the stomach and may have food mixed with it.
grebe fur	The soft tippet feathers of the Great Crested Grebe (*Podiceps cristatus*), which were once in such great demand for the millinery trade that by the late nineteenth century the bird had become rare in Ireland and Britain.
grinding	A noise made by some warblers (e.g. Great Reed Warbler).
hirundine	Of the swallow family.
jingling	Description of a Corn Bunting's song.
jugging	The roosting of a covey of partridges (family *Phasianidae*), the group in the roost being called a 'jug'.
larid	A member of the gull family.
lek	An assembly of birds for the purposes of communal (or social) display, originally referring to those of the Black Grouse (*Tetrao tetrix*) and Capercaillie (*Tetrao urogallus*) but now also applied to the similar gatherings of the Ruff (*Philomachus pugnax*). On the display-ground ('arena' or, in the case of the Ruff, 'hill') the males defend small patches of ground called 'courts'.
Lear, Lir	In Irish mythology, god of the sea and father of Manannán Mac Lir.
loafing	Behaviour not connected with feeding or breeding. The term includes preening and resting and does not imply that time is being wasted. Some types of birds, such as wildfowl, have habitual 'loafing places'.
Lugh	In Irish mythology, a hero god and high king and father of Cúchulainn.

Macha	In Irish mythology, a battle goddess and third aspect of the Morrigan.
machair	A type of fertile raised beach or sand dune.
Manannán Mac Lir	In Irish mythology, the god of the sea, son of Lear, with strong ties to the Isle of Man.
martlet	A mythical legless hirundine bird often used in heraldry.
Midir	In Irish mythology, son of the Dagda of the Tuatha Dé Danann.
mobbing	The 'attacking' of a potential predator by small birds, usually in groups. Its function is presumably to confuse the predator. Not only genuine predators are mobbed but also some birds which have similar flight shapes to certain types of raptor, such as the Grey Heron (*Ardea cinerea*) and the Cuckoo (*Cuculus canorus*).
Morrigan	In Irish mythology, a fallen war goddess.
omnivore	An animal which eats both animal and vegetable matter.
Other World	In Celtic mythology, the 'Other World' or *orbis alia* was the dominion of the dead and/or the fairies and gods, and generally a happy place. It was sometimes thought of as a physical place underground or across the western sea or as a sort of invisible parallel universe 'behind the veil' of which we could sometimes get a glimpse.
passerine	A word describing small perching song birds, including the crows.
pelagic	Living in or on open oceans, far from shore.
pigeon's milk	A secretion from the crop of members of the pigeon family (*Columbidae*) used for feeding the young and forming a milky fluid. Its proportion in the diet of the nestlings is reduced as they grow older.
powder down	A powdery substance, into which certain tiny body feathers break down, found in members of the heron family (*Ardeidae*). It may soak up aquatic slime from the plumage and provides some waterproofing. Other types of birds also produce powder from their feathers, for example pigeons (*Columbidae*), 'powder impressions' of which may be left on windows into which they have accidentally flown.
preen gland	(also uropygial gland) A gland found on birds that use oil for preening, found near the base of the tail. Found in many birds, it is well developed in water birds such as ducks.
purring	Description of the song of a Turtle Dove (*Streptopelia turtur*).
quartering	Covering a piece of ground by ranging from side to side while travelling forward, as practised by hunting owls, harriers, kites, buzzards and other bird of prey.
raft	A group of sea birds like auks or sea ducks floating together at sea.
raptor	A bird of prey or any bird that kills with its feet.
reeling	Producing a continuous, monotonous trill, somewhat resembling the sound of a fishing reel, for example the song of the Grasshopper Warbler (*Locustella naevia*). A rather similar sound is churring.

ringtail	A female Hen Harrier (*Circus cyaneus*) or a female Montagu's Harrier (*C. pygargus*).
riparian	Living on the banks of inland rivers and lakes.
roding	The owl-like courtship flight of a Woodcock (*Scolopax rusticola*) in which the bird flies over a roughly regular course giving two types of call, a low croak and a fairly high tick. This performance takes place at dusk.
sharming	The pig-like grunts and squeaks of the Water Rail (*Rallus aquaticus*).
solstice	One of two times a year when the sun is at a point furthest away and closest to the earth and daylight is at its longest and shortest respectively (summer solstice occurs about 22 June, winter solstice occurs about 22 December). The solstices occur at the midpoint between the equinoxes and vice versa.
spring	A small flock of Teal (*Anas crecca*) or similar small dabbling duck, which have a rapid, almost vertical, take-off.
stoop	The spectacular, rapid dive of the hunting Peregrine Falcon (*Falco peregrinus*) or similar raptor.
tremolo	The vibrato-like singing by rapid repetition of a single note or alternation of two notes, similar to a trill, such as the call of a diver.
trilling	The repetitive tremulous call of certain birds such as that of a Mistle Thrush, Skylark, Nightjar or warbler.
trip	A group of Dotterels (*Charadrus morinellus*).
triumph ceremony	A type of display which follows a successful aggressive encounter, usually given by a pair of birds. It is well seen in Whooper Swans (*Cygnus cygnus*) and Bewick's Swans (*C. columbianus*) and consists of raising the neck and wings and calling loudly.
wheeling	The swinging or banking from left to right or the rotational motion of a flock of flying birds, usually waders.
whiffling	Descending rapidly from a height once the decision to land has been made, involving fast side-slipping first one way and then the other. The term is usually applied to geese (*Anatidae*), whose flocks whiffle spectacularly, especially when wishing to avoid a long, slow descent over an area where wildfowling is practised.
winnowing	Rapid wing-beating through a very shallow arc in swift flight. It is characteristic of some falcons (*Falconidae*), notably the Hobby (*Falco subbuteo*) and the Peregrine (*F. peregrinus*), which alternate winnowing with gliding on outstretched wings.
wreck	(or 'seabird wreck') An occurrence where large number of seabirds are found dead, usually at a coastal location and usually after a significant weather event. Often associated with auks but any bird can be involved.

BIBLIOGRAPHY

Aburrow, Yvonne, *Auguries and Omens, The Magical Lore of Birds* (1994)

Achtanna an Oireachtais 1922–2003 (Acts of the Oireachtas 1922–2003)

Ainmneacha Plandaí agus Ainmhithe, An Roinn Oideachais, Rialtas na hÉireann, (Baile Átha Cliath, 1978)

Allen, Darina, *The Complete Book of Irish Country Cooking. Traditional and Wholesome Recipes from Ireland* (USA, 1996)

Armstrong, Edward A., *The Folklore of Birds* (New York, 1970)

Audubon, John James, *Birds of America*, First Octavo Edition (1840)

Audubon, John James, *Ornithological Biography Vol. III* (Edinburgh, 1835)

Barrett-Hamilton, G. E. H., 'The Introduction of the Magpie into Ireland', *Zoologist* 3.15:247 (1891)

Benson, Rev. Charles William, *Our Irish Song Birds* (1886)

Best, R. I., *Prognostications from the Raven and Wren*, Eriu (Dublin, 1916)

Bewick, Thomas, *A History of British Birds* (London, 1821, 1826)

Boate, Gerard, *Irelands Naturall History* (1652, translation 1726)

Braidwood, J., *Local Bird Names in Ulster: a glossary.* Ulster Folk-Life (11, 12) (1965, 1966)

Brewer, Ebenezer Cobham, *The Dictionary of Phrase & Fable*, 1894

Cashen, William, *Manx Folk-Lore* (Douglas, 1912)

Chance, Edgar Percival, *The Truth about the Cuckoo* (New York, 1940)

Conroy, Don & Jim Wilson, *Bird Life in Ireland* (Dublin, 1994)

D'Arcy, Gordon, *Ireland's Lost Birds* (1999)

Danaher, Kevin, *Irish Customs and Beliefs* (2004)

Daniels, Cora Linn, (Ed.) *Encyclopaedia of Superstitions, Folklore and the Occult Sciences of the World* (Honolulu, 1903)

De Bhaldraithe, Tomás, *English–Irish Dictionary* (2006)

Dillon, Terence Patrick, *A Dictionary of Hiberno-English* (2006)

Dinneen, Rev. Patrick Stephen, *Foclóir Gaedhilge agus Béarla* (1927)

Edwards, George, *A discourse on the emigration of British birds; or, This question at last solv'd: whence come the Stork and the turtle, the Crane and the Swallow, when they know and observe the appointed time of their coming?: Containing a curious . . . account of the . . . birds of passage . . . To which are added; reflections on . . . the annual migration of birds.* (London, 1814)

Evans, E. Estyn, *Irish Folkways* (London & New York: first printed in 1957, reprinted in 1988).

Fenton, James, *The Hamely Tongue, A Personal Record of Ulster-Scots in County Antrim* (2006)

Fergusson, Rosalind, *The Penguin Dictionary of Proverbs* (1983, 1995)

Flanagan, Deirdre & Laurence, *Irish Place Names* (1994, 2002)

Flower, Robin, *The Western Isle or the Great Blasket* (Oxford, 1944)

Gibbons, Reid, Chapman, *The New Atlas of Breeding Birds in Britain and Ireland* (1988–1991) (1993)

Gill, F. & M. Wright, *Birds of the World: Recommended English Names* (Princeton, 2006)

Giraldus Cambrensis (Gerald of Wales), *The Historical Works of Giraldus Cambrensis containing, The Topography of Ireland, and the History of the Conquest of Ireland,* translated by Thomas Forester, Bohn (London, 1863)

Giraldus Cambrensis (Gerald of Wales), *Topographia Hiberniae (The History and Topography of Ireland*), twelfth century (translated John J. O'Meara, 1982)

Gmelch, Sharon, *Nan: The Life of an Irish Travelling Woman* (London, 1986)

Goldsmith, Oliver, *A History of the Earth, and Animated Nature,* in six volumes, (London, 1816)

Greenhalgh, Jeff. A, *British Bird Names Explained* (2007)

Greenoak, Francesca, *British Birds, their Folklore, Names and Literature* (1997)

Haggerty, Bridget, *The Traditional Irish Wedding* (1999, 2004)

Hamilton, Barrett, 'Zoologist' (1891)

Hardy, Thomas, *Poems of the Past and Present* (1901)

Hare, C. E., *Bird Lore* (London, 1952)

Henderson, George, *Survivals in Belief Among the Celts,* (Glasgow, 1911)

Holloway, Simon, *The Historical Atlas of Breeding Birds in Britain and Ireland: 1875–1900* (2002)

Hull, Robin, *Scottish Birds, Culture and Tradition* (Edinburgh, 2001)

Joyce, Patrick Weston, *Irish Place Names,* (1984)

Keary, Charles Francis, *Outlines of Primitive Belief Among the Indo-European Races* (London, 1882)

Keats, John, *The Poetical Works of John Keats* (1841)

Keating, Geoffrey, (Seathrún Céitinn), *History of Ireland (Foras Feasa ar Éirinn), Vol III* (1634)

Kennedy, Rutledge & Scroope, *The Birds of Ireland* (Edinburgh, London, 1954)

Kirby, Michael, *Skelligs Calling* (2003)

Knowling, Philip, *A Wisdom of Owls* (1998)

Lack, Peter, *The Atlas of Wintering Birds in Britain and Ireland* (1986)

Lambert, Mike & Alan Pearson, *Éin* (1996)

Le Fanu, William Richard, *Seventy Years of Irish Life, Being Anecdotes and Reminiscences* (London, 1893)

Lloyd, C. S., *The Status of Seabirds in Britain and Ireland* (1991)

Lockwood, W. B., *The Oxford Dictionary of British Bird Names* (Oxford, 1993)

Lysaght, Patricia. *Food-Provision Strategies on the Great Blasket Island: Sea-bird Fowling.* Food from Nature: Attitudes, Strategies and Culinary Practices, Uppsala: Royal Gustavus Adolphus Academy (2000)

Mac Conghail, Muiris, *The Blaskets: People and Literature* (Dublin, 1994)

Mac Culloch, J. A., *The Religion of the Ancient Celts* (Edinburgh, 1948)

MacGillivray, William, *History of British Birds, Indigenous and Migratory, Vol II* (London, 1839)

Magnus, Olaus, *History of the Northern Peoples,* (Magni, Olai, *Historia de Gentibus Septentrionalibus,* Romae, 1555) (Rome, 1658)

Mahoney, Rosemary, *The Singular Pilgrim: Travels on Sacred Ground,* (2004)

McCionnaith, Lambert, *Foclóir Béarla agus Gaedhilge* (1935)

Mead, Chris, *The State of the Nation's Birds* (2000)

Morris, Rev Francis Orpen, *A History of British Birds, Vol II* (London, 1852)

Moryson, Fynes, *An Itinerary,* 1607 (part republished as *History of Ireland From the Year 1599–1603* (Dublin, 1735)).

Ní Lamhna, Éanna, *Straight Talking Wild (More Wildlife on the Radio)* (2006)

Ní Lamhna, Éanna, *Talking Wild (Wildlife on the Radio)* (Dublin, 2002)

Ó Dónaill, Niall, *Foclóir Gaeilge-Béarla* (2005)

O'Farrell, Padraic, *Irish Blessings Toasts & Curses* (Dublin, 2005)

O'Farrell, Padraic, *Irish Folk Cures* (Dublin, 2004)

O'Farrell, Padraic, *Superstitions of the Irish Country People* (Dublin, 2004)

Ó hÓgáin, Dáithí, *The Lore of Ireland: An Encyclopaedia of Myth, Legend and Romance* (2006)

Ó Ruadháin, Micheál, 'Birds in Irish Folklore', *In Acta XI Congressus Internationalis Ornithologici, Basel* (1954)

O'Sullivan, Patrick V., *Irish Superstitions and Legends of Animals and Birds* (Dublin, 1991)

O'Sullivan, Seán, *Folktales of Ireland* (1999)

Opie, Iona and Moira Tatem, *A Dictionary of Superstitions* (1989)

Patterson, Robert Lloyd, *The Birds, Fishes and Cetacea of Belfast Lough* (1881)

Payne, Robert, '*A Brife description of Ireland made in this yeere 1589*' (1589)

Payne-Gallwey, Sir Ralph, *The Fowler in Ireland* (First printed 1882, reprinted 1985)

Periodical: *Birds and all Nature,* Vol. VII, No. 1, January 1900, A. W. Mumford

Periodical: *Birds,* Vol. III, No. 4, April 1898, A. W. Mumford

Periodical: *Birds,* Vol. III, No. 5, May 1898, A. W. Mumford

Periodical: *Irish Shield and Monthly Milesian,* Vol. I (New York 1829)

Pilkington, James, *A View of the Present State of Derbyshire* (1789)

Pliny the Elder (Gaius Plinius Secundus), *Natural History (Historia Naturalis)* (1st century AD)

Porter, Noah, *Webster's Revised Unabridged Dictionary* (1913)

Power, Rev. P. Canon, *The Place-names of Decies* (1952)

Sharrock, J. T. R., *The Atlas of Breeding Birds in Britain and Ireland* (1976)

Smith, Charles, M. D., *The History of the City and County of Cork* (Dublin, 1750)

Stanley, Rev Edward, *Familiar History of Birds* (London, 1835)

Staav, R. and T. Fransson, *EURING list of longevity records for European birds* (http://www.euring.org/data_and_codes/longevity.htm) (2006)

Staford, Frank, 'Ða Engliscan Gesiðas', *The Ornithology of Anglo-Saxon England*

Swainson, Rev. Charles, *The Folk Lore and Provincial Names of British Birds*, Published for the Folk-Lore Society (London, 1886)

Synge, John M., *The Aran Islands*, (Dublin, 1906) Edited with an introduction and notes by Tim Robinson (London, 1992)

Tennyson, Alfred Lord, *Demeter, and Other Poems* (London, 1889)

The Banquet of Dún na nGedh and the Battle of Magh Rath, translated by John O'Donovan, The Irish Archaeological Society (1862)

The Book of Leinster (Lebor Laignech), manuscript (c. 1160)

Thompson, William, *Natural History of Ireland, Vol I* (1849)

Thompson, William, *Natural History of Ireland, Vol. III* (1849, 1851)

Traveller Ways, Traveller Words (Dublin: Pavee Point Publications, 1992)

Ua Maoileoin, Pádraig, *Dúlra Duibhneach* (2000)

Ussher, Richard John., *Birds of Ireland* (London, 1900)

Vol. VIII of the *South Mayo Family Research Journal* (1995)

Waddell, John, Jeffrey W. O'Connell, and Anne Korff, *The Book of Aran.* (Kinvara, County Clare, 1994)

Watters, John J., *The Natural History of the Birds of Ireland*, (Dublin & London, 1852)

Weidensaul, Scott, *Living on the Wind* (New York, 2000)

Weld, Charles Richard, *Vacations in Ireland* (London, 1857)

Wells, Diane, *100 Birds and How They Got Their Names* (North Carolina, 2002)

West, B. and B-X Zhou, 'Did chickens go north? New evidence for domestication', *World's Poultry Science Journal*, 45, 205–218 (1989)

Wilde, Lady Jane Francesca Agnes (Speranza), *Ancient Legends, Mystic Charms and Superstitions of Ireland* (1887)

Williamson, Kenneth, *The Atlantic Islands* (London, 1948)

Wordsworth, William, *The Complete Poetical Works* (London, 1888)

USEFUL WEBSITES

Birds Ireland   **www.birdsireland.com**

BirdLife International   **www.birdlife.org**
BirdLife International is a global partnership of conservation organisations that strives to conserve birds, their habitats and global biodiversity, working with people towards sustainability in the use of natural resources.

BirdWatch Ireland   **www.birdwatchireland.ie**
BirdWatch Ireland is an independent conservation organisation in Ireland that aims to conserve wild birds and their natural habitats.

British Trust for Ornithology   **www.bto.org**
The British Trust for Ornithology is an independent, scientific research trust, investigating the populations, movements and ecology of wild birds in the British Isles.

Colm Ó Caomhánaigh   **www.gofree.indigo.ie/~cocaomh/HomePage.htm**
Colm has collated the Irish names of birds – an invaluable pair of online Irish-English and English-Irish bird-name dictionaries.

European Union for Bird Ringing **www.curing.org**
The European Union for Bird Ringing promotes research needed to inform the conservation and scientific understanding of wild birds.

Habitas   **www.habitas.org.uk**

International Ornithological Congress
                             www.i-o-c.org

Irish Birding   **www.irishbirding.com**

Irish Rare Birds Committee   **www.irbc.ie**
The IRBC is responsible for maintaining a list of the birds recorded in the Republic of Ireland. Its primary function is the assessment of records of certain rare and scarce species. (The NIBA Records Committee (NIBARC) performs a similar role in Northern Ireland and the two committees work together to maintain a comprehensive record of birds found on the island of Ireland.)

Longevity list of birds ringed in Europe
                            www.euring.org/data_and_codes/longevity.htm

Northern Ireland Ornithologists' Club
                            www.nioc.co.uk

Recommended English Bird Names
                            www.worldbirdnames.org

Royal Society for the Protection of Birds (RSPB)
                            www.rspb.org.uk
The RSPB is a UK conservation organisation working to conserve wild birds and the environment. It aims to secure a healthy environment for birds and other wildlife. For Northern Ireland, see www.rspb.org.uk/northernireland

Ulster Wildlife Trust   **www.ulsterwildlifetrust.org**

REFERENCES

1 – HOW TO USE THIS BOOK

[1] Figures taken from the European Union for Bird Ringing. Staav, R. and Fransson, T. EURING list of longevity records for European birds (2006), (http://www.euring.org/data_and_codes/longevity.htm).

2.1 – A BRIEF HISTORY OF BIRDS IN IRELAND

[1] Pliny the Elder (Gaius Plinius Secundus), *Natural History (Historia Naturalis)* (1st century AD)

[2] Turner, William *Avium praecipuarum, quarum apud Plinium et Aristotelem mentio est, brevis et succincta historia* (A short and succinct history of the principal birds noted by Pliny and Aristotle), published in 1544.

[3] Or *Vindiciae Hiberniae Contra Giraldum.*

[4] Moryson, Fynes, *An Itinerary*, 1607 (part republished as *History of Ireland From the Year 1599–1603* (Dublin, 1735).

[5] A phrase common in the middle ages and quoted by Shakespeare. A 'handsaw' is a 'heronshaw' or heron. Hence the phrase was originally a falconer's jibe at a lay person who could not identify a flying bird.

[6] Formed by David Cabot in 1964.

2.2 – BIRDS AS PREDICTORS OF THE FUTURE

[1] From the Athenian playwright Aristophanes 'comedy *The Birds*, fifth century BC.

[2] From the Latin *avis* meaning bird and *specere*, to observe.

[3] Best, R. I., *Prognostications from the Raven and Wren*, Eriu (Dublin, 1916)

2.4 – BIRDS AS FOOD

[1] O'Farrell, Padraic, *Irish Folk Cures* (Dublin, 2004)

[2] Payne-Gallwey, Sir Ralph, *The Fowler in Ireland*, The Field Library, First printed 1882, (reprinted Southampton 1985)

[3] Ibid.

[4] Ibid.

[5] Which replaced the Game Preservation Act and Wild Birds (Protection) Act of 1930.

2.5 – BIRD FOLKLORE THEMES

[1] Believe neither scald-crow nor Raven – don't believe in omens!

[2] Daniels, Cora Linn, (Ed.) *Encyclopaedia of Superstitions, Folklore and the Occult Sciences of the World* (Honolulu, 1903)

[3] O'Sullivan, Patrick V., *Irish Superstitions and Legends of Animals and Birds* (Dublin, 1991)

[4] Opie, Iona and Tatem, Moira, *A Dictionary of Superstitions* (Oxford, 1989)

[5] Ibid.

[6] Ibid.

[7] Ibid.

[8] Danaher, Kevin, *Irish Customs and Beliefs* (Cork, 2004) (Orig. pub. as *Gentle Places and Simple Things*, 1964)

[9] Cobham Brewer, Ebenezer, The Dictionary of Phrase & Fable, 1894

[10] Periodical: Birds, Vol. III, No. 4, April 1898, A. W. Mumford (Chicago, New York)

[11] Danaher, op. cit.

[12] Wells, Diane, *100 Birds and How They Got Their Names* (North Carolina, 2002)

[13] Danaher, op. cit.

[14] Ibid.

[15] Aburrow, Yvonne, *Auguries and Omens, The Magical Lore of Birds* (Chievely, Berkshire, 1994)

[16] Black-browed Albatrosses or Mollymawks (*Diomedea melanophris*) are seen very rarely in Irish waters.

[17] Periodical: *Birds*, Vol. III, No. 4, April 1898, A. W. Mumford (Chicago, New York)

[18] Ní Lamhna, Éanna, *Talking Wild (Wildlife on the Radio)* (Dublin, 2002)

[19] Daniels, op. cit.

[20] O'Sullivan, Patrick, op. cit.

[21] Daniels, op. cit.

[22] Wilde, Lady Jane Francesca Agnes (Speranza), *Ancient Legends, Mystic Charms and Superstitions of Ireland,* (1887)

[23] Wilde, Lady Jane, op. cit.

[24] Ibid.

[25] O'Sullivan, Stephen, Dún Laoghaire, Personal Correspondence (2008)

[26] Periodical: *Birds*, Vol. III, No. 4, April 1898, A. W. Mumford (Chicago, New York)

[27] *Lá Fhéile na gCoinneal* (2 February)

[28] Opie, op. cit.

[29] Danaher, op. cit.

[30] O'Sullivan, Patrick, op. cit.

[31] Ibid.

[32] Wilde, Lady, op. cit.

[33] Periodical: *Birds*, Vol. III, No. 4, April 1898, A. W. Mumford (Chicago, New York)

[34] O'Farrell, Padraic, *Superstitions of the Irish Country People* (Cork, 2004)

[35] Kirby, Michael, *Skelligs Calling* (Dublin, 2003)

[36] O'Farrell, Padraic, op. cit.

[37] O'Sullivan, Patrick, op. cit.

[38] Daniels, op. cit.

[39] Ní Lamhna, Éanna, op. cit.

[40] Le Fanu, William Richard, *Seventy Years of Irish Life, Being Anecdotes and Reminiscences* (London, 1893)

[41] Wilde, Lady, op. cit.

[42] Lá Fhéile Bríde, Lá Feabhra (Imbolg, the feast of the goddess Brigit, 1 February)

[43] O'Sullivan, Patrick, op. cit.

[44] O'Sullivan, Patrick, op. cit.

[45] Danaher, op. cit.

[46] Wilde, Lady, op. cit.

[47] Ó hÓgáin, Dáithí, *The Lore of Ireland* (Cork, 2006)

[48] Danaher, op. cit.

[49] Giraldus Cambrensis (Gerald of Wales), *Topographia Hiberniae* (The History and Topography of Ireland), twelfth century (Dublin, 1982)

[50] Giraldus Cambrensis, op. cit.

[51] Now home to many wintering Barnacle Geese.

[52] Wells, Diane, op. cit.

[53] Daniels, op. cit.

[54] Danaher, op. cit.

[55] Staford, Frank, *Ða Engliscan Gesiðas*, The Ornithology of Anglo-Saxon England, Periodical.

[56] Ní Lamhna, Éanna, op. cit.

[57] Ibid.

[58] O'Farrell, Padraic, op. cit.

[59] O'Sullivan, Patrick, op. cit.

[60] Opie, op. cit.

[61] Ibid.

[62] O'Sullivan, Patrick, op. cit.

[63] Daniels, op. cit.

[64] O'Farrell, Padraic, *Irish Folk Cures* (Dublin, 2004)

[65] O'Sullivan, Patrick, op. cit.

[66] *Lá Fhéile Bríde, Lá Feabhra* (Imbolg, the feast of the goddess Brigit, 1 February)

[67] O'Sullivan, Patrick, op. cit.

[68] Danaher, op. cit.

[69] Payne-Gallwey, Sir Ralph, op. cit.

[70] Danaher, op. cit.

[71] O'Sullivan, Patrick, op. cit.

[72] Danaher, op. cit.

[73] Ibid.

[74] O'Sullivan, Patrick, op. cit.

[75] Payne-Gallwey, Sir Ralph, op. cit.

[76] Or *scairbhín na gcuach* in Kerry.

[77] Wilde, Lady, op. cit.

[78] O'Sullivan, Patrick, op. cit.

[79] Payne-Gallwey, Sir Ralph, op. cit.

[80] O'Sullivan, Patrick, op. cit.

[81] Kirby, Michael, op. cit.

[82] Kirby, Michael, op. cit.

[83] Ní Lamhna, Éanna, op. cit.

[84] O'Sullivan, Patrick, op. cit.

[85] Ní Lamhna, Éanna, op. cit.

[86] Periodical: Irish Shield and Monthly Milesian, Vol. I (New York, 1829)

[87] Edwards, George, *A discourse on the emigration of British birds* (London, 1814)

[88] Armstrong, Edward A., *The Folklore of Birds* (New York, 1970)

[89] Fergusson, Rosalind, *The Penguin Dictionary of Proverbs* (London, 1983)

[90] Ua Maoileoin, Pádraig, *Dúlra Duibhneach* (Baile Átha Cliath, 2000)

[91] Ó Duibhín, Ciarán, Foclóir Oirthear Uladh – Consolidated Glossary of East Ulster, Personal Correspondence

[92] Le Fanu, op. cit.

[93] O'Sullivan, Patrick, op. cit.

[94] O'Farrell, Padraic, *Irish Blessings Toasts & Curses* (Cork, 2005)

[95] O'Farrell, Padraic, *Irish Blessings . . .* op. cit.

[96] Ibid.

[97] Ibid.

[98] O'Sullivan, Patrick, op. cit.

[99] O'Farrell, Padraic, *Irish Blessings . . .* op. cit.

[100] Ibid.

[101] Ibid.

[102] Ibid.

[103] Phosphorosis.

[104] O'Farrell, Padraic, *Irish Blessings . . .* op. cit.

2.6 – BIRD NAMES

[1] Flann O'Brien, *At Swim-Two-Birds* (Longman Green & Co, 1939)

[2] Gill, F. and M. Wright., *Birds of the World: Recommended English Names* (Princeton 2006)

[3] *Ainmneacha Plandaí agus Ainmhithe*, An Roinn Oideachais, Rialtas na hÉireann (Baile Átha Cliath, 1978)

3.1 – LOONS (DIVERS) – LÓMAÍ

[1] Wells, Diane, op. cit.

[2] Ibid.

[3] In addition, White-Billed Divers (Yellow-Billed Loon, Lóma Gobgheal, *Gavia adamsii*) are extremely rare visitors.

[4] Commonly known as the Great Northern Diver.

[5] *Éan dubh na scadán* is a Razorbill.

[6] Commonly known as the Black-throated Diver.

[7] Commonly known as the Red-throated Diver.

[8] Watters, John J., *The Natural History of the Birds of Ireland* (Dublin & London, 1852)

3.2 – GREBES – FOITHIGH

[1] More often called Slavonian Grebes.

[2] Also used for other grebes.

[3] Also a Coot.

3.3 – HERONS & EGRETS – CORRA 'S ÉIGRITÍ

[1] The menu also contained: 400 swans, 2,000 geese, 1,000 capons (roosters), 200 Pheasants, 500 partridges, 400 Woodcocks, 100 Curlew, 400 plovers, 2,000 chickens, 4,000 Mallards and Teals, 400 pigeons and similar numbers of other animals.

[2] Periodical: *Birds and all Nature*, Vol. VII, No. 1, January 1900, A. W. Mumford (Chicago, New York)

[3] Payne-Gallwey, Sir Ralph, op. cit.

[4] Opie, op. cit.

[5] Swainson, Rev. Charles, *The Folk Lore and Provincial Names of British Birds* (London, 1886)

[6] Keating, Geoffrey, *(Seathrún Céitinn)*, History of Ireland *(Foras Feasa ar Éirinn)*, Vol III (1634)

[7] Danaher, op. cit.

[8] Bewick, Thomas, *A History of British Birds* (London, 1821, 1826)

[9] Traditionally there is no 'J' in Irish.

3.4 – DUCKS, GEESE & SWANS – LACHAIN, GÉANNA 'S EALAÍ

[1] Or in some traditions a black cock.

[2] Wilde, Lady, op. cit.

[3] Evans, E. Estyn, *Irish Folkways* (London & New York, first printed in 1957, reprinted in 1988).

[4] Wilde, Lady, op. cit.

[5] O'Sullivan, Patrick, op. cit.

[6] Ibid.

[7] Ibid.

[8] Ibid.

[9] 'The Silver Swan', Orlando Gibbons, 1612

[10] from 'The Wild Swans at Coole', W. B. Yeats, 1919

[11] Daniels, op. cit.

[12] Ó hÓgáin, Dáithí, op. cit.

[13] O'Sullivan, Patrick, op. cit.

[14] Payne, Robert, *A Brife description of Ireland made in this yeere 1589*

[15] Genitive case of Lear.

[16] Armstrong, Edward A., op. cit.

[17] Ibid.

[18] Payne-Gallwey, Sir Ralph, op. cit.

[19] This is an old Irish name for Whooper Swans and should not be confused with today's Whistling Swans of North America.

[20] Standardised name: Brant Goose.

[21] Greenhalgh, Jeff. A, *British Bird Names Explained*, self-published, 2007

[22] Watters, John J., op. cit.

[23] Payne-Gallwey, Sir Ralph, op. cit.

[24] Boate, Gerard, *Irelands Naturall History*, 1652 (translation 1726)

[25] Watters, John J., op. cit.

[26] Giraldus Cambrensis, op. cit.

[27] An Carghas (from Ash Wednesday (*Céadaoin an Luaithrigh*) to Easter (Cáisc)).

[28] Audubon, John James, *Birds of America*, First Octavo Edition (1840)

[29] Payne-Gallwey, Sir Ralph, op. cit.

[30] Also a Bean Goose.

[31] More often a Greylag Goose.

[32] Payne-Gallwey, Sir Ralph, op. cit.

[33] Watters, John J., op. cit.

[34] Also a Merganser.

[35] Payne-Gallwey, Sir Ralph, op. cit.

[36] Watters, John J., op. cit.

[37] A whinyard was a knife or sword resembling a Shoveler's bill.

[38] Payne-Gallwey, Sir Ralph, op. cit.

[39] Watters, John J., op. cit.

[40] Payne-Gallwey, Sir Ralph, op. cit.

[41] Ibid.

[42] Thompson, William, *Natural History of Ireland Vol. III*, Reeve, Benham and Reeve, 1849, 1851

[43] Also a Scoter.

[44] Lockwood, W. B., *The Oxford Dictionary of British Bird Names* (Oxford, 1993)

[45] Payne-Gallwey, Sir Ralph, op. cit.

[46] Ibid.

[47] Watters, John J., op. cit.

[48] Probably the same as 'whinyard' for which see Shoveler (Section 3.4.7).

[49] Giraldus Cambrensis, op. cit.

[50] Payne-Gallwey, Sir Ralph, op. cit.

[51] The American Green-winged Teal may be a separate species *Anas carolinensis.*

[52] Also a Merganser.

[53] Also a Wigeon or Grebe.

[54] Also a Merganser.

[55] Payne-Gallwey, Sir Ralph, op. cit.

[56] Usually Teal.

[57] Payne-Gallwey, Sir Ralph, op. cit.

[58] Watters, John J., op. cit.

[59] More commonly, Common Scoters.

[60] *An Carghas* (from Ash Wednesday to Easter).

[61] Watters, John J., op. cit.

[62] Also a Scaup.

[63] Meaning 'Scandinavian duck'. Also a Muscovy Duck.

[64] Watters, John J., op. cit.

[65] Names standardised as Common Merganser.

[66] Watters, John J., op. cit.

[67] Greenhalgh, Jeff, op. cit.

[68] Ibid.

[69] Also a Shelduck.

[70] Also a Teal.

[71] Also a Shelduck or Quail or Diver.

3.5 – OTHER WATER BIRDS

[1] Danaher, op. cit.

[2] Also an Oystercatcher.

[3] The most likely Shearwater species to be encountered in Irish waters are: the Manx, the Sooty, the Mediterranean (Balearic), the Great, Cory's and the Little.

[4] Porter, Noah, *Webster's Revised Unabridged Dictionary* (Springfield, 1913).

[5] *An Carghas* (from Ash Wednesday to Easter).

[6] Wilson's Petrels may be the most abundant seabirds in the world, breeding in millions in Antarctica. They were named after the Scottish/American naturalist Alexander Wilson (1766–1813) 'the Father of American Ornithology' who wrote *The Natural History of the Birds of North America.*

[7] Weidensaul, Scott, Living on the Wind (New York, 2000)

[8] Note the Giant Fulmars of the Pacific are known as Mother Carey's Geese.

[9] Kirby, Michael, op. cit.

[10] Kirby, Michael, op. cit.

[11] The name mutton-bird has been used for several species of petrel, shearwater and fulmar and is primarily used in the southern hemisphere.

[12] Note Wilson's Petrel is also known as Mother Carey's Chicken.

[13] Thompson, William, op. cit.

[14] Danaher, op. cit.

[15] Could be Fairies' Rock.

[16] Also a Scoter.

[17] Ó hÓgáin, Dáithí, op. cit.

[18] Danaher, op. cit.

[19] O'Sullivan, Patrick, op. cit.

[20] Swainson, Rev. Charles, op. cit.

[21] Ní Lamhna, Éanna, op. cit.

[22] Danaher, op. cit.

[23] Bewick, Thomas, op. cit.

[24] Also a Quail or Corn Bunting.

[25] Also a Raven or Bittern.

[26] Ó Duibhín, Ciarán, op. cit.

[27] Watters, John J., op. cit.

[28] Bewick, Thomas, op. cit.

[29] Payne-Gallwey, Sir Ralph, op. cit.

[30] Also a Little Grebe.

[31] Also a Red Grouse.

[32] Name now standardised as Parasitic Jaeger.

[33] Name now standardised as Long-tailed Jaeger.

3.6 – BIRDS OF PREY – ÉIN CHREICHE

[1] Name now standardised as the Northern Harrier

[2] See the owls in Section 3.12.

[3] Montagu's Harriers were named after the British naturalist Col. George Montagu (1753–1815) who wrote an Ornithological Dictionary in 1802. They were once known as Ash-coloured Harriers in Ireland.

[4] Golden Eagle Re-Introduction Project.

[5] Periodical: Birds, Vol. III, No. 5, May 1898, A. W. Mumford (Chicago, New York)

[6] Now regarded as a separate sub-species *Circus hudsonius.*

[7] William Faulkner. Interview in 'Writers at Work' (First Series, ed. By Malcolm Cowley, 1958).

[8] Golden Eagle Re-Introduction Project.

[9] Standardised name: Roughleg.

[10] Giraldus Cambrensis, op. cit.

[11] Dichloro-Diphenyl-Trichloroethane

[12] Giraldus Cambrensis, op. cit.

[13] Also a swift or martin.

[14] From *The Windhover: To Christ our Lord*, Gerard Manley Hopkins.

[15] Wells, Diane, op. cit.

[16] Wells, Diane, op. cit.

[17] Greenhalgh, Jeff, op. cit.

[18] Or Tassel, Tercel, Terzel.

3.7 – OTHER LARGE LAND BIRDS

[1] Strictly speaking, the name is standardised as 'Willow Ptarmigan'.

[2] Swainson, Rev. Charles, op. cit.

[3] Giraldus Cambrensis, op. cit.

[4] Moryson, Fynes, op. cit.

[5] Now the river Rioni in Georgia.

[6] Moryson, Fynes, op. cit.

[7] Danaher, op. cit.

[8] Also perhaps a Woodcock.

[9] Giraldus Cambrensis, op. cit.

[10] Also a Corncrake or Corn Bunting.

[11] 'Welcome, the sweetest bird on the branch' [Cuckoo], *Fáilte don Éan*, Séamas Dall Mac Cuarta, (1650?–1732)

[12] Very rare birds in Ireland.

[13] Chance, Edgar, *The Truth about the Cuckoo* (Country Life, 1940)

[14] Opie, op. cit.

[15] Conroy, Don & Jim Wilson, *Bird Life in Ireland* (Dublin, 1994)

[16] Wilde, Lady, op. cit.

[17] O'Farrell, Padraic, *Superstitions . . .* op. cit.

[18] Wilde, Lady, op. cit.

[19] Danaher, op. cit.

[20] O'Sullivan, Patrick, op. cit.

[21] Ibid.

[22] Danaher, op. cit.

[23] Wilde, Lady, op. cit.

[24] Periodical: *Irish Shield and Monthly Milesian*, Vol. I (New York, 1829)

[25] Swainson, Rev. Charles, op. cit.

[26] Named after the male bird's 'appendage'.

[27] Or *garbhshíon na gcuach* or *scairbhín na gcuach* in Kerry.

[28] Wilde, Lady, op. cit.

[29] Fenton, James, *The Hamely Tongue, A Personal Record of Ulster-Scots in County Antrim* (Ullans Press, 2006)

[30] Hare, C. E., *Bird Lore* (London 1952)

[31] Morris, Rev Francis Orpen, *A History of British Birds, Vol II* (London, 1852)

[32] Also a Swallow.

3.8 – WADERS (SHORE BIRDS) – LAPAIRÍ

[1] Waders are called 'shore birds' in North America.

[2] Danaher, op. cit.

[3] Aburrow, Yvonne, *Auguries and Omens, The Magical Lore of Birds*, (Chievely, Berkshire, 1994)

[4] Swainson, Rev. Charles, op. cit.

[5] Also a Gannet.

[6] Ó hÓgáin, Dáithí, op. cit.

[7] See Stonechat (*Máire an Trúis*).

[8] Also a Lapwing.

[9] Payne-Gallwey, Sir Ralph, op. cit.

[10] Danaher, op. cit.

[11] Conroy, Don & Jim Wilson, op. cit.

[12] Payne-Gallwey, Sir Ralph, op. cit.

[13] Watters, John J., op. cit.

[14] *Míog* is a specific Irish word describing the cry of a plover or Jacksnipe.

[15] Payne-Gallwey, Sir Ralph, op. cit.

[16] Watters, John J., op. cit.

[17] Greenhalgh, Jeff, op. cit.

[18] Payne-Gallwey, Sir Ralph, op. cit.

[19] Also a tern, in Ulster.

[20] Payne-Gallwey, Sir Ralph, op. cit.

[21] Ibid.

[22] Mead, Chris, *The State of the Nation's Birds* (Suffolk, 2000)

[23] Cashen, William, *Manx Folk-Lore* (Douglas, 1912)

[24] Thompson, William, op. cit.

[25] O'Sullivan, Patrick, op. cit.

[26] Danaher, op. cit.

[27] Scene of the Battle of Curlew Pass between an English force and Red Hugh O'Donnell in 1599.

[28] Also a Kestrel.

[29] Also a Bar-tailed Godwit.

[30] Also a Whimbrel.

[31] O'Farrell, Padraic, *Irish Folk Cures . . .* , op. cit.

[32] Payne-Gallwey, Sir Ralph, op. cit.

[33] Also Dunlin, Rock Pipit.

[34] Perhaps originally 'bird of the sea-inlet'. *Gabhlán* means 'forked' and is also used for martins and swifts.

[35] See Greenshank.

[36] More usually an Oystercatcher.

[37] Could be a Knot, Dunlin or the like.

[38] Payne-Gallwey, Sir Ralph, op. cit.

[39] Danaher, op. cit.

[40] More often a Bittern.

[41] More often a tit.

[42] Payne-Gallwey, Sir Ralph, op. cit.

[43] Previously known as the Grey Phalarope.

[44] Watters, John J., op. cit.

3.9 – GULLS & TERNS – FAOILEÁIN 'S GEABHRÓGA

[1] Scológ, also a hard-working young man.

[2] Also a Dunlin.

[3] Kirby, Michael, op. cit.

[4] Daniels, op. cit.

[5] Payne-Gallwey, Sir Ralph, op. cit.

[6] Named after the Copeland family who settled there in the twelfth century or perhaps from the Norse 'cop' for trading.

[7] Mead, Chris, op. cit.

[8] Watters, John J., op. cit.

[9] One of the Blasket Islands off County Kerry.

[10] Hull, Robin, *Scottish Birds, Culture and Tradition* (Edinburgh, 2001)

[11] Watters, John J., op. cit.

[12] Also a Black Guillemot.

[13] Swainson, Rev. Charles, op. cit.

[14] Watters, John J., op. cit.

[15] Audubon, John James, *Ornithological Biography Vol. III* (1835)

3.10 – AUKS – FALCÓGA

[1] Conroy, Don & Jim Wilson, op. cit.

[2] The name has been standardised as 'Common Murre'.

[3] Watters, John J., op. cit.

[4] Also the young of the Kittiwake.

[5] See Razorbill.

[6] *Éan glas na scadán* is a Great Northern Diver.

[7] Lockwood, W. B., op. cit.

[8] Also a Fulmar or Shearwater.

[9] Also a Razorbill.

[10] Also a Barnacle Goose.

[11] Also a Sandpiper.

[12] Also a Razorbill.

[13] Also Razorbill and Puffin.

3.11 – PIGEONS & DOVES – COLÚIR 'S FEARÁIN

[1] William Shakespeare, *King Henry the Fourth, Part II*

[2] *Colm imirce* – migrating pigeon.

[3] O'Farrell, Padraic, *Superstitions . . .* op. cit.

[4] Ó hÓgáin, Dáithí, op. cit.

[5] From the French *deuil* meaning mourning.

[6] Name now standardised as 'Common Pigeon'.

[7] Robert Burns, *The Complete Works of Robert Burns* (Boston, 1855)

[8] Ibid.

[9] William Wordsworth, *The Complete Poetical Works* (London, 1888)

[10] Sir Walter Scott, 'The Lord of the Isles'

[11] O'Sullivan, Patrick, op. cit.

[12] Ibid.

[13] William Shakespeare, *Romeo & Juliet.*

3.12 – OWLS – ULCHABHÁIN

[1] Anon. c. 1607

[2] See also the Grey Heron (Section 3.3.2)

[3] Watters, John J., op. cit.

[4] Knowling, Philip, *A Wisdom of Owls* (Devon, 1998)

[5] Daniels, op. cit.

3.13 – SWALLOWS, MARTINS & SWIFTS – FÁINLEOGA 'S GABHLÁIN

[1] O'Farrell, Padraic, *Superstitions . . .* op. cit.

[2] Swainson, Rev. Charles, op. cit.

[3] Ibid.

[4] Magnus, Olaus, *History of the Northern Peoples* (Rome, 1658) *Magni, Olai, Historia de Gentibus Septentrionalibus* (Romae, 1555)

[5] Ní Lamhna, Éanna, *Straight Talking Wild (More Wildlife on the Radio)* (Dublin, 2006)

[6] Swainson, Rev. Charles, op. cit.

[7] Ibid.

[8] Ibid.

[9] Also a Swift.

[10] Swainson, Rev. Charles, op. cit.

[11] Opie, op. cit.

[12] Ibid.

[13] Ibid.

[14] Also a Swift.

[15] Staford, Frank, op. cit.

[16] *Gabhlán* can mean fork (as in forked tail)

[17] Also a Swallow.

3.14 – PIPITS – RIABHÓGA

[1] Swainson, Rev. Charles, op. cit.

[2] Also a Twite.

[3] Also a Dunlin or Redshank.

3.15 – WAGTAILS – GLASÓGA

[1] Name now standardised as 'White Wagtail'.

[2] Periodical: *Birds*, Vol. III, No. 4, April 1898, A. W. Mumford, (Chicago, New York)

[3] Wilde, Lady, op. cit.

[4] Ibid.

[5] Also a Willow Warbler.

3.16 – THRUSHES – SMÓLAIGH

[1] Danaher, op. cit.

[2] O'Sullivan, Patrick, op. cit.

[3] *Lá Fhéile na gCoinneal* (2 February).

[4] Opie, op. cit.

[5] From *The Blackbird of Derrycairn*, Austin Clarke.

[6] Fenton, James, op. cit.

[7] Danaher, op. cit.

[8] Or in the 'Temple of the Rock' at Glendalough.

[9] Giraldus Cambrensis, op. cit.

[10] Periodical: *Birds*, Vol. III, No. 5, May 1898, A. W. Mumford (Chicago, New York).

[11] Swainson, Rev. Charles, op. cit.

[12] Ibid.

[13] O'Sullivan, Patrick, op. cit.

[14] Also a Song Thrush.

[15] Periodical: *Birds*, Vol. III, No. 5, May 1898, A. W. Mumford (Chicago, New York)

[16] Also a Bilberry (*Vaccinium myrtillus*).

[17] Philomela = nightingale = darkness lover.

[18] Swainson, Rev. Charles, op. cit.

[19] Periodical: *Birds*, Vol. III, No. 5, May 1898, A. W. Mumford (Chicago, New York).

[20] Pliny, op. cit.

[21] Hardy, Thomas, *Poems of the Past and Present* (1901).

[22] Tennyson, Alfred Lord, *Demeter, and Other Poems* (London, 1889).

[23] MacGillivray, William, *History of British Birds, Indigenous and Migratory, Vol II* (London, 1839).

[24] Also a female Blackbird.

[25] Benson, Rev. Charles William, *Our Irish Song Birds* (Dublin, 1886).

[26] Ussher, Richard John & Robert Warren, *Birds of Ireland* (London, 1900).

[27] Mistletoe is not native to Ireland.

[28] Periodical: *Birds*, Vol. III, No. 5, May 1898, A. W. Mumford (Chicago, New York).

[29] Holm is another word for Holly or Ilex (*Ilex aquifolium*).

[30] Also a Snow Bunting.

[31] See also Starling.

3.17 – WARBLERS – CEOLAIRÍ

[1] Mead, Chris, op. cit.

[2] Swainson, Rev. Charles, op. cit.

[3] More often a Whitethroat.

[4] Also a Yellowhammer.

[5] A. A. Milne.

[6] Aka Sallow or Pussy Willow.

[7] Greenhalgh, Jeff, op. cit.

[8] Garden Warblers, rare summer visitors to Ireland were known as Greater Pettychaps.

[9] Specifically Bulrushes.

[10] Periodical: *Birds*, Vol. III, No. 4, April 1898, A. W. Mumford (Chicago, New York).

[11] More usually, a Willow Warbler.

[12] Also a Siskin.

[13] There is some evidence that Robins were also referred to as Irish Nightingales.

[14] See also Stonechat for which there is some confusion in the Irish language.

[15] Swainson, Rev. Charles, op. cit.

3.18 TITS – MEANTÁIN

[1] William Wordsworth.

[2] Swainson, Rev. Charles, op. cit.

[3] Carotenoid pigments are naturally occurring pigments responsible for the red, yellow and orange coloration in some animals and carrots!

[4] Swainson, Rev. Charles, op. cit.

[5] Name now standardised as 'Long-tailed Bushtit'.

3.19 – PRÉACHÁIN, CARÓGA

[1] O'Sullivan, Seán, *Folktales of Ireland* (Chicago, 1999).

[2] Wilde, Lady, op. cit.

[3] Opie, op. cit.

[4] Danaher, op. cit.

[5] Watters, John J., op. cit.

[6] Also a Raven.

[7] Both *Feannóg* and *Caróg Liath* are acceptable standard names.

[8] This could be a Kite or Hen Harrier.

[9] Periodical: *Birds*, Vol. III, No. 4, April 1898, A. W. Mumford (Chicago, New York).

[10] O'Farrell, Padraic, *Irish Blessings* ... op. cit.

[11] More often an Osprey but also a Kingfisher.

[12] Also a Kite.

[13] Also a Raven.

[14] Genesis 8:6–7.

[15] Mac Culloch, J. A., *The Religion of the ancient Celts* (Edinburgh, 1948).

[16] Wilde, Lady, op. cit.

[17] Ibid.

[18] Periodical: *Birds*, Vol. III, No. 4, April 1898, A. W. Mumford (Chicago, New York).

[19] Wilde, Lady, op. cit.

[20] Ibid.

[21] Giraldus Cambrensis, op. cit.

[22] Armstrong, Edward A., op. cit.

[23] O'Farrell, Padraic, *Irish Folk Cures* . . ., op. cit.

[24] Belfast County Borough.

[25] Also a Rook.

[26] Also a Bittern.

[27] Periodical: *Birds*, Vol. III, No. 4, April 1898, A. W. Mumford (Chicago, New York).

[28] Opie, op. cit.

[29] Also a Chough or Jay.

[30] Also a Crossbill.

[31] Payne-Gallwey, Sir Ralph, op. cit.

[32] Cobham Brewer, op. cit.

[33] Also a Jackdaw or Jay.

[34] Also a Hooded Crow.

[35] Giraldus Cambrensis, op. cit.

[36] Moryson, Fynes, op. cit.

[37] Smith, Charles, M. D., *The History of the City and County of Cork* (Dublin, 1750).

[38] Barrett-Hamilton, G.E.H. *The Introduction of the Magpie into Ireland*, Zoologist 3.15:247 (1891).

[39] Periodical: *Birds*, Vol. III, No. 4, April 1898, A. W. Mumford, (Chicago, New York).

[40] Keary, Charles Francis, *Outlines of Primitive Belief Among the Indo-European Races* (London, 1882).

[41] *Traveller Ways, Traveller Words* (Dublin: Pavee Point Publications, 1992).

[42] Le Fanu, op. cit.

[43] Keary, op. cit.

[44] Wilde, Lady, op. cit.

[45] Higgins, Mary, Mayo, Personal Correspondence.

[46] Ó hÓgáin, Dáithí, op. cit.

[47] Danaher, op. cit.

[48] O'Farrell, Padraic, *Irish Blessings* . . . op. cit.

[49] May be an Anglicisation of an Irish word for Magpie, *Pioghaid*.

[50] William Shakespeare, from *The Taming of the Shrew*.

[51] Mead, Chris, op. it.

[52] Also a Chough or Jackdaw.

3.20 – FINCHES – GLASÁIN

[1] Bewick, Thomas, op. cit.

[2] Also a Yellowhammer.

[3] Wells, Diane, op. cit.

[4] Keats, John, The Poetical Works of John Keats (1884).

[5] Also a Yellowhammer.

[6] Also a Yellowhammer.

[7] Muire can also refer to St Brigid (Mary of the Gael – Muire na nGael).

[8] Also a Chaffinch.

[9] Fenton, James, op. cit.

[10] Swainson, Rev. Charles, op. cit.

[11] Ibid.

[12] Also a Sedge Warbler.

[13] From 'The Lake Isle of Inisfree', W. B. Yeats.

[14] Periodical: *Birds*, Vol. III, No. 4, April 1898, A. W. Mumford (Chicago, New York).

[15] See also Whinchat.

[16] Also a Meadow Pipit.

3.21 – BUNTINGS – GEALÓGA

[1] Periodical: *Birds*, Vol. III, No. 4, April 1898, A. W. Mumford (Chicago, New York).

[2] Greenoak, Francesca, *British Birds, their Folklore, Names and Literature* (London, 1997).

[3] Braidwood, J., *Local bird names in Ulster: a glossary*. Ulster Folk-Life (11, 12) (1965, 1966).

[4] O'Sullivan, Patrick, op. cit.

[5] Bewick, Thomas, op. cit.

[6] More usually a Goldfinch.

[7] Also a Goldfinch.

[8] Also a Goldcrest.

[9] More usually a Mistle Thrush. See also *Truisc*, a Moorhen.

[10] More usually the Sedge Warbler.

[11] See Blackcap, Ringed Plover, Stonechat.

[12] Also a Stonechat.

3.22 – OTHER SMALL LAND BIRDS – ÉANLAITH BEAGA EILE

[1] from *Farewell to Poesy: The Kingfisher*, William Henry Davies (1910).

[2] Giraldus Cambrensis, op. cit.

[3] Roman Poet (BC 43–17 AD)

[4] O'Sullivan, Patrick, op. cit.

[5] Opie, op. cit.

[6] Giraldus Cambrensis, op. cit.

[7] Might also mean 'bird of the reeds or marshy-place'.

[8] Also a Sea Eagle.

[9] Also the Dipper.

[10] More often, an Osprey.

[11] Shelley, Percy Bysshe, *Prometheus Unbound. A Lyrical Drama in Four Acts, With Other Poems* (London, 1820).

[12] Wilde, Lady, op. cit.

[13] Lá Fhéile Bríde, Lá Feabhra (Imbolg, the feast of the goddess Brigit, 1 February).

[14] O'Sullivan, Patrick, op. cit.

[15] Ó hÓgáin, Dáithí, op. cit.

[16] Shelley, Percy Bysshe, *Prometheus Unbound. A Lyrical Drama in Four Acts, With Other Poems* (London, 1820).

[17] Original name was *Lár Choille*, the centre of the wood.

[18] Also a Pipit.

[19] Periodical: *Birds*, Vol. III, No. 4, April 1898, A. W. Mumford (Chicago, New York).

[20] Also a Meadow Pipit.

[21] Can't see the Cuckoo's eggs.

[22] Also a pipit.

[23] William Blake, from *Auguries of Innocence* (1803, pub. 1863).

[24] Wilde, Lady, op. cit.

[25] Le Fanu, op. cit.

[26] Ní Lamhna, Éanna, *Straight Talking Wild . . .*, op. cit.

[27] Wilde, Lady, op. cit.

[28] Ó hÓgáin, Dáithí, op. cit.

[29] Ní Lamhna, Éanna, *Straight Talking Wild . . .*, op. cit.

[30] Swainson, Rev. Charles, op. cit.

[31] From which we get the Feast of Bel or Bealtaine (1 May).

[32] Hare, C. E., op. cit.

[33] O'Farrell, Padraic, *Irish Folk Cures . . .*, op. cit.

[34] Swainson, Rev. Charles, op. cit.

[35] Was *Saxicola torquata rubicola*.

[36] Swainson, Rev. Charles, op. cit.

[37] Also a Hedge Sparrow.

[38] Also a Wheatear.

[39] Also a Wheatear.

[40] Also a Reed Bunting.

[41] Also a Linnet.

[42] Swainson, Rev. Charles, op. cit.

[43] Hull, Robin, op. cit.

[44] Also a Stonechat.

[45] The cunning little old man under a stone.

[46] Also a Stonechat.

[47] Swainson, Rev. Charles, op. cit.

[48] Giraldus Cambrensis, op. cit.

[49] Periodical: *Birds*, Vol. III, No. 5, May 1898, A. W. Mumford (Chicago, New York).

[50] Greenhalgh, Jeff, op. cit.

[51] Conroy, Don & Jim Wilson, op. cit.

[52] Swainson, Rev. Charles, op. cit.

[53] Ibid.

[54] Ó hÓgáin, Dáithí, op. cit.

[55] Swainson, Rev. Charles, op. cit.

[56] Ibid.

[57] Similar to the 'Swallow Boys' of Rhodes and the 'Crow-boys' of Greece.

[58] The opposite is also reported: The Wren being buried outside the house that gave the most money.

[59] Swainson, Rev. Charles, op. cit.

[60] There are numerous variations.

[61] Swainson, Rev. Charles, op. cit.

[62] Ibid.

[63] Ibid.

[64] Pliny, op. cit.

[65] May refer to a warbler or Goldcrest. *Trochilus* was a small Egyptian bird said by ancient writers to pick the teeth of crocodiles.

[66] Swainson, Rev. Charles, op. cit.

[67] Hare, C. E., op. cit.

[68] Perhaps a Willow Warbler (Willow Wren).

[69] Periodical: *Birds*, Vol. III, No. 4, April 1898, A. W. Mumford (Chicago, New York)

[70] Ibid.

[71] Pliny, op. cit.

[72] Mead, Chris, op. it.

[73] Or perhaps Doves or Martlets!

[74] Periodical: *Birds*, Vol. III, No. 4, April 1898, A. W. Mumford (Chicago, New York)

[75] Samuel Pepys Library, Magdalen College Cambridge.

[76] From Samuel Pepys ' ballad, *A Battell of Birds, Most Strangely Fought in Ireland . . .* (1621), from, The Pepys Library, Magdalene College, Cambridge.

[77] Micheál Ó'Ruadháin, 'Birds in Irish Folklore', ACTA XI Congressus Internationalis Ornithologici (Basel, 1954).

[78] Swainson, Rev. Charles, op. cit.

[79] From a belief that the bird foretold the falling of snow.

[80] See also Fieldfare.

[81] Danaher, op. cit.

[82] Also a Jackdaw.

[83] Psalm 102:7.

[84] *Binne* might be the genitive case of *beann* which has a number of meanings including 'gable' or 'branch'.

[85] Daniels, op. cit.

[86] Swainson, Rev. Charles, op. cit.

[87] O'Sullivan, Patrick, op. cit.

[88] Lios na nGealbhán or Lios Mhic Ghiolláin (Mac Giollán's fort).

4 – POULTRY & DOMESTICATED BIRDS – ÉANLAITH CHLÓIS, ÉIN TÍ

[1] West, B. and Zhou, B-X., *Did chickens go north? New evidence for domestication*, World's Poultry Science Journal, 45, 205–218 (1989)

[2] Meaning 'Scandinavian duck'. Also an Eider.

[3] Fenton, James, op. cit.

[4] Figures compiled from several sources.

[5] Payne-Gallwey, Sir Ralph, op. cit.

[6] Pliny, op. cit.

[7] Payne-Gallwey, Sir Ralph, op. cit.

[8] Opie, op. cit.

[9] O'Farrell, Padraic, *Irish Folk Cures . . .*, op. cit.

[10] Ibid.

[11] All species of tansy are toxic!

[12] O'Farrell, Padraic, *Irish Folk Cures . . .*, op. cit.

[13] O'Farrell, Padraic, *Irish Blessings . . .*, op. cit.

[14] Wilde, Lady, op. cit.

[15] O'Farrell, Padraic, *Irish Blessings . . .*, op. cit.

[16] Armstrong, Edward A., *op. cit.*

[17] Payne-Gallwey, Sir Ralph, op. cit.

[18] Eating the gander.

[19] *Fleadh Dúin na nGéadh* (The banquet of goose fort).

[20] *Cath Maige Rath.*

[21] *The Banquet of Dún na nGedh and the Battle of Magh Rath*, translated by John O'Donovan, The Irish Archaeological Society, 1862.

[22] 'L'Allegro', John Milton.

[23] See Nightjar.

[24] Gmelch, Sharon, Nan: *The Life of an Irish Travelling Woman* (London, 1986).

[25] O'Sullivan, Patrick, op. cit.

[26] Wilde, Lady, op. cit.

[27] Ibid.

[28] O'Sullivan, Patrick, op. cit.

[29] O'Farrell, Padraic, *Superstitions . . .*, op. cit.

[30] Giraldus Cambrensis, op. cit.

[31] Fenton, James, op. cit.

[32] O'Farrell, Padraic, *Irish Folk Cures . . .*, op. cit.

[33] Daniels, op. cit.

[34] O'Sullivan, Patrick, op. cit.

[35] Wilde, Lady, op. cit.

[36] Ibid.

[37] Ibid.

[38] Ibid.

[39] *An Carghas* (from Ash Wednesday to Easter).

[40] *Máirt na hInide.*

[41] *Aoine an Chéasta.*

[42] *Domhnach Cásca*

[43] O'Sullivan, Patrick, op. cit.

[44] Wilde, Lady, op. cit.

[45] Daniels, op. cit.

[46] Opie, op. cit.

[47] O'Sullivan, Patrick, op. cit.

[48] Opie, op. cit.

[49] Fenton, James, op. cit.

[50] Could be Woodcock.

[51] Having a spotted marking resembling an eye.

[52] G. K. Chesterton on Christmas.

[53] Fenton, James, op. cit.

[54] This could be a reference to the 'Turkey-Cock', an old word for the guineafowl.

[55] 'Lord of Ireland' 1509–1541, King of Ireland 1542–1547.

[56] King of UK 1901–1910.

[57] Dillon, Terence Patrick, *A Dictionary of Hiberno-English* (Dublin, 2006)

[58] A third species *Afropavo congensis*, the Congo Peafowl, is rarely seen in captivity.

5 – BIRDS FROM OUR PAST

[1] The likes of us will never be again. (Old Irish saying.)

[2] Bewick, Thomas, op. cit.

[3] Goldsmith, Oliver, *A History of the Earth, and Animated Nature, in six volumes* (London, 1816)

[4] Mead, Chris, op. it.

[5] *Birds*, Vol. III, No. 4, April 1898, A. W. Mumford (Chicago, New York)

[6] Goldsmith, Oliver, op. cit.

[7] Ibid.

[8] Also a Tern or Starling.

[9] Also a Raven.

[10] Wells, Diane, op. cit.

[11] Giraldus Cambrensis, op. cit.

[12] Giraldus Cambrensis, op. cit.

[13] O'Sullivan, Patrick, op. cit.

[14] Giraldus Cambrensis, op. cit.

[15] *The Book of Leinster* (Lebor Laignech), manuscript, c. 1160.

[16] Aka St Bean, St Beoc, St Dabeoc.

[17] Giraldus Cambrensis, op. cit.

[18] D'Arcy, Gordon, *Ireland's Lost Birds* (Dublin, 1999).

[19] Giraldus Cambrensis, op. cit.

[20] D'Arcy, Gordon, op. cit.

[21] More often a Bittern.

[22] Probably Broad Beans (*Vicia faba*).

[23] Also a White-fronted Goose.

[24] Watters, John J., op. cit.

[25] Also a Hen Harrier and Kite.

[26] Alfred Lord Tennyson, 'The Eagle'.

[27] Mead, Chris, op. it.

[28] GET has also initiated projects to reintroduce White-tailed Eagles in Kerry and Red Kites in Wicklow.

[29] Giraldus Cambrensis, op. cit.

[30] Ibid.

[31] Ó hÓgáin, Dáithí, op. cit.

[32] Payne-Gallwey, Sir Ralph, op. cit.

[33] Swainson, Rev. Charles, op. cit.

[34] Mentioned in Peig by Peig Sayers as her birthplace.

[35] William Blake, *The Marriage of Heaven and Hell*, 1790–1793.

[36] Staford, Frank, op. cit.

[37] Possibly an Osprey or Kite.

[38] Also Osprey.

[39] Tonsured, meaning 'shaven-headed' as a monk.

[40] Payne-Gallwey, Sir Ralph, op. cit.

[41] Giraldus Cambrensis, op. cit.

[42] Wells, Diane, op. cit.

[43] Periodical: *Birds*, Vol. III, No. 5, May 1898, A. W. Mumford (Chicago, New York).

[44] Possibly a Kite or Eagle.

[45] Also Sea Eagle.

[46] Thompson, William, op. cit.

[47] Daniels, op. cit.

[48] Possibly an Osprey or Eagle.

[49] Scottish birds were re-introduced from Sweden in the eighteenth century.

[50] D'Arcy, Gordon, op. cit.

[51] Giraldus Cambrensis, op. cit.

[52] D'Arcy, Gordon, op. cit.

[53] Also Pheasant and Woodcock.

[54] D'Arcy, Gordon, op. cit.

[55] Watters, John J., op. cit.

[56] *An Carghas* (from Ash Wednesday to Easter).

[57] *Miliaria calandra* is also correct.

[58] Ussher, op. cit.

[59] Also a Quail or Corncrake.

6 – BIRD CONSERVATION IN IRELAND

[1] Royal Society for the Protection of Birds, Northern Ireland.

ENGLISH AND GENERAL INDEX

Page numbers in bold indicate the main entry.

IRISH INDEX

SCIENTIFIC INDEX